TWENTIETH-CENTURY TEXAS

A Social and Cultural History

edited by
John W. Storey
and Mary L. Kelley

University of North Texas Press
Denton, Texas

Permissions:
University of North Texas Press
P.O. Box 311336
Denton, TX 76203-1336

The paper used in this book meets the minimum requirements of the
American National Standard for Permanence of Paper for Printed
Library Materials, z39.48.1984. Binding materials have been chosen for
durability.

Library of Congress Cataloging-in-Publication Data

Twentieth-century Texas : a social and cultural history /
edited by John W. Storey and Mary L. Kelley.
p. cm.
Includes bibliographical references and index.
ISBN 978-1-57441-245-1 (cloth : alk. paper) —
ISBN 978-1-57441-246-8 (pbk. : alk. paper)
1. Texas—History—20th century. 2. Texas—Social conditions—
20th century. 3. Texas—Intellectual life—20th century. I. Storey, John
W. (John Woodrow), 1939– II. Kelley, Mary L., 1949–
F386.T965 2008
976.4'063—dc22
2007043791

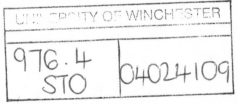

Contents

★

Acknowledgments..v

Introduction 1

1. Manifestations of the Lone Star:
    The Search for Indian Sovereignty
    by Gerald Betty 9

2. The Quest for Identity and Citizenship:
    Mexican Americans in Twentieth-Century Texas
    by Anthony Quiroz 41

3. The Struggle for Dignity:
    African Americans in Twentieth-Century Texas
    by Cary D. Wintz 69

4. From Farm to Future:
    Women's Journey through Twentieth-Century Texas
    by Angela Boswell 105

5. Pagodas amid the Steeples:
    The Changing Religious Landscape
    by John W. Storey..135

6. Over Here:
    Texans on the Home Front
    by Ralph A. Wooster..164

7. From Yellow Roses to Dixie Chicks:
    Women and Gender in Texas Music History
    by Gary Hartman ....

8. Goodbye Ol' Paint, Hello Rapid Tr
    Texas Literature in the Twentie
    by Mark Busby ....

9. Lone Star Cinema:
    A Century of Texas in the Movies
    by Don Graham...245

10. "Wider Than the Limits of Our State":
    Texas Art in the Twentieth Century
    by Michael R. Grauer...267

11. The Games Texans Play
    by Bill O'Neal 300

12. Private Wealth, Public Good:
    Texans and Philanthropy
    by Mary L. Kelley..324

13. Public Schools Come of Age
    By Gene B. Preuss 358

14. Lone Star Landscape:
    Texans and Their Environment
    by Tai Kreidler...387

15. The Second Texas Revolution:
    From Cotton to Genetics and the Information Age
    by Kenneth E   kson
    and C 417

                                   443

                                   196
                                   220

Acknowledgments

An edited volume such as this one is a collaboration among many individuals. We would therefore like to acknowledge those who helped make possible *Twentieth-Century Texas: A Social and Cultural History*. We are particularly indebted to each of the contributors, all of whom are on tight schedules, for lending their expertise to this project and to the University of North Texas Press, especially Ron Chrisman for his support and patience during every stage of the publication process. A special thanks goes to Patty Renfro, administrative associate to the history department at Lamar University, who cheerfully gave her valuable time and capable assistance to help with editing, compiling, and completing the manuscript. Also, we extend our thanks to Professor Carol Atmar, who read and offered insightful advice on many of the essays.

Mary would particularly like to acknowledge Dr. Ben Procter, professor emeritus at Texas Christian University, who has served as a trusted friend, lifelong mentor, and demanding editor who "comforted me when I was afflicted and afflicted me when I was comfortable." During the formative stage of my career as a historian he taught me the value of constructive criticism, and whatever skills I brought as editor are in large measure due to his influence.

The editors dedicate this book to the next generation of Texans—Chris and Shor Kelley, Sara McKnight, and Bailey Katherine Payne.

Introduction

LITERATURE ON TEXAS ABOUNDS. Historians, folklorists, and novelists have seemingly explored the Lone Star State from every imaginable perspective, from the Great Plains to the Alamo to Spindletop, from ranchers and cowboys to wildcatters and oil field roughnecks to timber barons and lumberjacks, from Catholic missionaries to Protestant evangelists to Buddhist monks. Until recently much of this scholarship tended to concentrate on the nineteenth century, the founding period of Texas. For those authors, the state's identity, uniqueness, and relevance to modern life were embedded in the frontier experience and Anglo culture.

Given such a large body of scholarship, another study of Texas seems hardly necessary. What, then, do the authors of this anthology have to offer that has not already been investigated? In terms of political and economic history, very little, if anything! Those topics have been covered quite thoroughly, most recently by Randolph Campbell's outstanding work, *Gone to Texas* (2003), which will likely remain a standard for some years. In terms of social and cultural history, however, they have quite a lot to say, inasmuch as that side of the state's development is often given short shrift, especially the twentieth century. Illustrative here is *Gone to Texas*, which virtually ignores social and cultural matters altogether, and in that respect it is typical of much of the literature about the state. A notable exception is William Ransom Hogan's *The Texas Republic: A Social and Economic History* (1946), a first-rate account that presented a more balanced treatment of the state's past, albeit with

1

a nineteenth-century bias. In the sixty years since its publication, however, Texas has undergone remarkable change, particularly with regard to race, ethnicity, gender, religion, and the environment.

Most of these topics, to be sure, have been examined to some degree by previous anthologies. *Texas: A Sesquicentennial Celebration* (1984), edited by Donald W. Whisenhunt, as well as *The Texas Heritage* (2003) by Ben Procter and Archie P. McDonald, readily come to mind. Although both are quite good and devote additional attention to the twentieth century, they include politics and economics along with society and culture. Another, *Texas Vistas* (2006), edited by Ralph A. Wooster, Robert A. Calvert, and Adrian Anderson, has just been released in its third edition. It consists of eighteen essays taken from the *Southwestern Historical Quarterly*, fifteen of which were written over the last two decades. While the editors included much new scholarship, modern Texas garnered only five articles. In addition, there are several specialized anthologies, such as those edited by Char Miller and Heywood T. Sanders, *Urban Texas, Politics and Development* (1990), Fane Downs and Nancy Baker Jones, *Women and Texas History, Selected Essays* (1993), Roy R. Barkley *et al.*, *The Handbook of Texas Music* (2003), and Donald Willet and Stephen Curley, *Invisible Texans: Women and Minorities in Texas History* (2005). These studies, however, have a narrow focus and do not treat—in one volume—all the significant social and cultural developments of twentieth-century Texas.

Along with anthology editors, individual authors have also moved in new historiographical directions. They have pursued new research trends that address multiple perspectives, social issues, and cultural diversity within a modern, more complex society. Examples include Arnoldo De León, *Ethnicity in the Sunbelt: A History of Mexican Americans in Houston* (1989), Elizabeth Enstam, *Women and the Creation of Urban Life* (1998), Merline Pitre, *In Struggle Against Jim Crow: Lulu B. White and the NAACP, 1900-1957* (1999), Ty Cashion, *Pigskin Pulpit, A Social History of Texas High*

School Football Coaches (1999), Keith L. Bryant, Jr., *Culture in the American Southwest* (2001), Guadalupe San Miguel, Jr., *Tejano Proud: Tex-Mex Music in the Twentieth Century* (2002), and Carlos K. Blanton, *The Strange Career of Bilingual Education in Texas* (2004).

Although *Twentieth-Century Texas: A Social and Cultural History* traverses some of the same terrain as these earlier studies, it focuses solely on the past century, bringing the story up-to-date. Each contributor is an expert in their respective field and has researched and/or published on their topic. Collectively, the fifteen essays herein elaborate on and update themes of major importance in modern Texas, such as immigration, industrialization, urbanization, ethnicity, class, race, gender, cultural identity, and religious pluralism. A list of suggested further readings concludes each essay.

Texas changed enormously from 1900 to 2000—from a rural to an increasingly urban society characterized by sprawling metropolitan areas such as Houston, Dallas, and San Antonio, from a predominantly agricultural and ranching economy to a highly sophisticated industrialized and communications giant, from an Anglo-dominated populace to a racial and ethnic kaleidoscope, from a Protestant bastion of Methodists and Baptists to Catholic ascendancy and religious pluralism, from a male-controlled state to one where women stand much closer in equality, from primitive frontier medical practices to a major center of world-class medical institutions dedicated to cutting-edge technology and research. The social and cultural impact of such changes has been dramatic, and that is the subject of this anthology.

As several contributors have pointed out, the early decades of the twentieth century still resembled in many ways the latter nineteenth century. In 1900 Texans remained largely rural, agricultural, and Anglo. Nevertheless, broad currents of change were underway, especially the movement from the farm to the city, so that by 1940 more Texans officially lived in urban areas. But urbanization and modernization also brought social problems, namely inadequate schools, poor health-care facilities, and environmental concerns.

Several authors address the effects of this accelerated demographic change. Gene B. Preuss, in "Public Schools Come of Age," focuses on the evolution of the state school system from its rudimentary, rural one-room school house to a basic restructuring of Texas education emphasizing "equity, efficiency, liberty, and excellence." Educational reform then became the hallmark of continued growth and prosperity in the state. Spurred by the state's petroleum industry, major medical, technological, and scientific research centers located in the burgeoning Texas cities. In "The Second Texas Revolution: From Cotton to Genetics and the Information Age," Kenneth E. Hendrickson and Glenn M. Sanford document the growth of important institutions, such as M. D. Anderson in Houston, the electronics giant Texas Instruments, and NASA, the Cold War-era space agency. These advances ranked Texas "second to none" among the other states. However, modernization and urbanization severely affected the environment. As Tai Kreidler points out in "Lone Star Landscape: Texans and Their Environment," the seemingly limitless Texas frontier of the nineteenth century was transformed by increasing pressure on its finite resources. Unfettered capitalism, with its attendant exploitation of the natural habitat, had reduced the availability of the public domain, pure air, abundant wildlife, and clean water, resulting in a growing awareness of the need for conservation, regulation, and environmental protection.

Several of the essays call attention to the impact of immigration. Multitudes of Mexicans migrated northward in the wake of the 1910 revolution, and sizeable numbers of Asians settled in Texas after changes in the nation's immigration laws in the mid-1960s. The effects are everywhere, from ethnic restaurants and Spanish-language programming to Vietnamese enclaves and Islamic centers. In

"Pagodas amid the Steeples: The Changing Religious Landscape," John W. Storey describes how Catholics finally overtook Baptists to become the state's largest religious body. In turn, these denominations have had to make room for Muslims, Hindus, Buddhists, and others. Mexican Americans, soon to be the dominant ethnic group in Texas by 2030, also became more numerous and more assertive. Anthony Quiroz, in "The Quest for Identity and Citizenship: Mexican Americans in Twentieth-Century Texas," chronicles not only their pursuit for acceptance and equal treatment, but also an emerging sense of Americanism, especially after World War II. The influence of immigration is also seen in music and other forms of cultural expression as various ethnic groups expressed their unique history and folk culture. Gary Hartman, for example, in "From Yellow Roses to Dixie Chicks: Women and Gender in Texas Music History," explains how *corridos* recall the epic tales of heroic Mexican Americans, frequently emphasizing Anglo-Mexican tensions. That immigration has made Texas considerably more diverse is undeniable.

Social change rarely comes easily, and individuals and groups that agitate for more equitable treatment and prod society to become more inclusive frequently face everything from mild ridicule and scorn to physical harassment and deadly violence. For proof of this one has only to scan the history of Native Americans, African Americans, Mexican Americans, and women. As for the Indians, the twentieth century represented both a continuation of and a departure from basic themes of conflict and assimilation associated with tribal history. Gerald Betty, in "Manifestations of the Lone Star: The Search for Indian Sovereignty," focuses on the three remaining official tribes in Texas—the Alabama-Coushatta, the Tigua, and the Kickapoo—as well as the recent phenomenon of "urban Indians." Despite numerous threats to tribal integrity and autonomy, Betty argues that modern Texas Indians have not only maintained their cultural identity but have also flourished.

For the other aforementioned groups, early twentieth-century Texas was about as rigidly segregated as other parts of the Old South, and deeply felt racial and gender attitudes made discrimination against them an accepted way of life. Cary D. Wintz, in "The Struggle for Dignity: African Americans in Twentieth-Century Texas," shows how blacks suffered from negative prejudicial images in the aftermath of the Galveston storm of 1900. While organization, protests, and legal pressure gradually eroded many of the obstacles to racial equality, episodes of racism and violence against African Americans were frequent, as seen in the savage murder of the young African American Jesse Washington at the hands of a frenzied mob in Waco in 1916. Although the discrimination and segregation that Mexican Americans also experienced was less virulent, it still relegated them to a position of second-class citizenship. Even their enlistment and service in World War II did not combat racism at home. For example, Anthony Quiroz, in "The Quest for Identity and Citizenship," relates the treatment of Private Felix Longoria, a war hero who in 1949 was refused burial by a Three Rivers funeral home due to his Hispanic status. At the same time, World War II was pivotal for women, who in the absence of the fighting men proved they could handle "men's work" as well as any Texas male. But even with the political, economic, and legal gains of the past century, Angela Boswell, in "From Farm to Future: Women's Journey through Twentieth-Century Texas," contends that women continue to face difficulties in balancing their traditional duties with the new roles and opportunities they achieved. One third of the essays herein explore all these matters in some depth.

Industrialization, another key marker of modern Texas, was noticeable by the turn of the century, particularly in the cities, but in rural areas as well. During the twentieth century Texas was transformed from a state with a rural, colonial economy to one with a world-class scientific, medical, and research infrastructure. World War II in particular had a major impact as military camps and defense plants located in Texas, a Sun Belt state. Ralph A. Wooster, in "Over Here: Texans on the Home Front," describes the growth of that expansion as thousands of Texans were employed in war-related industries. In turn, the rise of key industries such as petrochemicals, medical, and electronics also produced great wealth for a few Texans. In "Private Wealth, Public Good: Texans and Philanthropy," Mary L. Kelley shows how a new millionaire class used wealth for positive social and cultural change. In some cases the new industries influenced even the shaping of the state's image. Don Graham, in "Lone Star Cinema: A Century of Texas in the Movies," contrasts the classic portrayal of Texans as ranching and oil barons in *Giant* with *Hud,* the 1963 film that juxtaposed a fading pastoral way of life to an emerging industrialized economy characterized by crass materialism and cynicism.

Cultural expression through literature, art, and music has kept pace with the economic growth of the state. While much of it tended to reflect the state's heroic and romantic past, new currents moved beyond the staid stereotypes of the pioneering generation to an emphasis on the state's more ethnically diverse, urban population. In "Goodbye Ol' Paint, Hello Rapid Transit: Texas Literature in the Twentieth Century," Mark Busby chronicles not only the contributions of the "Texas Triumvirate"—Dobie, Bedichek, and Webb—but also newer literary currents that recognize the reality of an urban Texas and ethnic diversity. In a society that denied them legal, political, or economic equality, Texas women found in music a public voice to express their beliefs, values, and concerns. Gary Hartman's essay exposes the gendered nature of Texas music from the famous ballad of "The Yellow Rose of Texas," concerning Emily West's relationship with the Mexican General Antonio Lopez de Santa Anna, to the political criticism of George W. Bush by the Dixie Chicks, which to many breached the boundaries of "proper" womanhood. Although Texans have not always appreciated them, Michael R. Grauer, in "'Wider Than the Limits of Our State': Texas

Art in the Twentieth Century," shows that Texas has always had
painters and sculptors whose reputations transcended the state's
boundaries.

That Texans love sports, particularly football on Friday nights,
is legendary. In "The Games Texans Play," Bill O'Neal delves into
the varied athletic activities and the heroes and heroines who have
achieved sporting immortality. Such physical competitions, he argues, stem from the state's frontier roots that emphasized both individual effort and teamwork in a competitive environment.

By the outset of the twenty-first century Texas had essentially
shed its frontier heritage, but Hollywood films, local rodeos, state
fairs, urban cowboys, dance halls, and museum exhibits still provide
nostalgic snapshots into its storied past. Even so, the image of a
rural, male-dominated, homogeneous society no longer rings true
with the reality of an urban, diverse, heterogeneous state. The social
and cultural changes of the twentieth century—ethnic, racial, and
religious diversity, changing gender roles, environmental concerns,
urban sprawl, high-tech industries, expanding educational and philanthropic opportunities, and cultural and artistic expression—have
transformed the state, making it more like other cosmopolitan parts
of the nation. For the near future these trends will likely continue as
Texans of all stripes and backgrounds put their stamp on the Lone
Star State.

Manifestations of the Lone Star

The Search for Indian Sovereignty

Gerald Betty

IN MANY WAYS THE history of American Indians in the twentieth century is a departure from the narrative chronicling frontier
trade relations, official government relations, physical competition
for resources, military conquest, and enforced assimilation. Yet the
history of American Indians during the twentieth century is also
a continuation of the various themes that have always characterized their intense interaction with Euro-Americans. Tribes continue
to have an economic relationship with outsiders and tribal sovereignty has been preserved, serving as the basis of self-government
and tribal decisions. Although tribal peoples no longer face military
conquest, numerous conflicts flare up from time-to-time with national and state governments, as well as with non-Indians living in
their midst. Likewise, enforced assimilation ceased to be an official
policy of the government over the course of the century. Nevertheless, assimilation has characterized American Indian history from
the beginning and continues unabated to this day. This essay—
focusing on the history of the three official Texas reservation tribes
of the Alabama-Coushatta in the Big Thicket of Polk County, the
Tiguas of Ysleta in El Paso, and the Kickapoo Traditional Tribe
near Eagle Pass, as well as the so-called "urban Indians" from met-

ropolitan areas throughout the state—shows how the experience of Indians in Texas during the twentieth century is at the same time a departure from and a continuation of the basic themes associated with American Indian history in general.

The dynamic course of Texas Indian history should be seen as a process of persistence and preservation rather than one of destructive change. Consider the case of the Alabama-Coushattas. Historians have noted the perseverance of these people in the face of processes that tend to erode the cohesiveness of tribal consanguinity. Today roughly 500 Alabama-Coushattas live on a reservation just to the east of Livingston in a wooded wilderness known as the Big Thicket. Another 500 or so live off the reservation. The isolated nature of the east Texas woods attracted the Alabama Indians and their Coushatta kinsmen from the Southeast sometime prior to 1805. The tribes are essentially branches of Creek Indians who speak a mutually intelligible Muskhogean dialect.[1]

The Alabama-Coushattas were not the first Indians to have lived in the region that became Texas. The Tiwa-speaking Tigua Pueblo Indians of El Paso preceded the Alabama-Coushattas by over a hundred years. The Pueblo Indian ancestors of the 1,300 Tigua Indians presently living in El Paso originally lived near modern-day Albuquerque. After the outbreak of the Pueblo Indian Revolt in 1680, they joined fleeing Spanish refugees and settled at present-day Ysleta, Texas, named for their ancestral settlement of Isleta, New Mexico. Like the meanderings of the Rio Grande, the twentieth-century history of the Tiguas is characterized by many twists and turns, taking the tribe from the brink of extinction to an energetic expression of tribal sovereignty.[2]

Many contemporary Texans have assumed that the Alabama-Coushattas and the Tiguas were the only Indians in Texas, but another tribe existed in the state by the turn of the twenty-first century. The least familiar of the state's three officially recognized tribes is the Kickapoo Traditional Tribe of Texas. The name "Kickapoo" is derived from the Algonquian *ki-wika-pa-wa*, meaning "he moves about, standing now here, now there." Kickapoos never stayed in one place too long. Since the 1600s various tribal factions made their way from the upper Great Lakes region to Kansas, Oklahoma, Mexico, and ultimately into Texas. Moving about is as much an expression of their ancestral tradition as their Algonquian language, and twentieth-century Kickapoos continue the search for sanctuary and sovereignty that began with the arrival of Europeans.[3]

Numerous individuals representing tribes other than Alabama-Coushattas, Tiguas, and Kickapoos also began living in various metropolitan areas of Texas during the twentieth century. These "urban Indians" claimed official membership in various tribes from across the United States, and they appeared in Texas after World War II as a result of a federal program to move Indians from reservations to designated cities across the country. The Dallas-Fort Worth metroplex attracted many of them because of its designation as an official relocation site. By the end of the century, however, individuals of American Indian descent could be found living in almost all Texas cities. By founding intertribal organizations and holding powwow festivities across the state, these urban Indians gave rise to a new expression of American Indian identity in Texas.

All Indians have made some accommodation with the dominant culture. The Alabama-Coushattas, for instance, converted to Presbyterianism during the 1880s due to the tribe's increased interaction and intermarriage with local whites in southeast Texas and the efforts of Presbyterian missionaries, who founded a mission church and school among the tribe. By the turn of the century, all tribal members had embraced the Protestant religious and educational practices of southeast Texas.[4]

The Tiguas experienced a similar transformation by the 1880s. Their pueblo of Ysleta had been incorporated as a town in 1880, and the tribe had intermarried with the local population. Although the Tiguas maintained their traditional tribal and clan structure,

Missionary teacher, Emma Chambers and students outside Presbyterian Church on Alabama-Coushatta Indian Reservation near Livingston, Texas, October 1925. From UTSA's Institute of Texan Cultures, No. 072-1734, courtesy Mrs. E. S. (Dorothy) Shills.

they had long ago abandoned their ancestral faith in favor of the Roman Catholicism of the early Spanish colonists of New Mexico. In 1895 the tribe adopted a constitution that preserved its Catholic traditions and tribal form of self-government. The Tiguas had become intimately integrated into the greater El Paso community by 1900, but they continued to express a traditional concern with various issues regarding their tribal sovereignty in relation to municipal organization.[5]

The twentieth century began sorrowfully for the Tiguas when their ancient Spanish-mission church burned down in May 1907. By July 1908 a beautiful new church with a hand-carved altar had been built at the old location. The following year the El Paso *Herald* reported that the Indians conducted the tribe's annual Saint Anthony's Day celebration on June 13 with processions, tribal dances, "fire water," and war whoops. Tribal festivities resumed that autumn as the Indians held their annual celebration of the harvest. The Tiguas also participated in another series of elaborate tribal celebrations around Christmas time, and they held other dances associated with national holidays such as Independence Day. Despite the destruction of their church, the Tiguas persevered, determined to remain loyal to their ancestral traditions. This demonstrated the ongoing vibrancy of the tribe.[6]

For the Alabama-Coushattas, school attendance and missionary activity introduced non-Indian behavior and activities that became closely associated with Alabama-Coushatta tradition. Basketball, for instance, became a favorite sport, Anglo-style clothing became common, the boys and men cut their hair short, and European surnames either acquired through intermarriage or based on the names of employers became widely accepted. As the early twentieth century progressed, the homes built on the reservation increasingly departed from the traditional log design in favor of frame houses. This all underscored not only the assimilation of the Alabama-Coushattas, but also the emergence of European-American practices as defining aspects of the tribe's subsequent culture.[7]

The continued existence of the Alabama-Coushattas' tribal organization and reservation homeland owed a great deal to the efforts of community leaders in east Texas. James C. Feagin, a Livingston attorney, who feared that the tribe was in danger of extinction, campaigned tirelessly at the local, state, and national levels on behalf of the Alabama-Coushattas from 1896 until 1927. Feagin ultimately persuaded Congressman Samuel Bronson Cooper to sponsor bills in the U.S. House of Representatives granting the Indians 25,000 acres of land in east Texas, and he influenced the Commissioner of Indian Affairs to conduct a study exploring the status of the Indians. While the initial efforts of Feagin and Cooper failed in their immediate goal of providing the tribes with federal assistance, they nevertheless brought significant local, state, and national attention to the plight of the Alabama-Coushattas.[8]

The campaign to secure official recognition and assistance from state and national governments finally succeeded after another Livingston attorney, Clem Fain, Jr., took up the cause. In 1927 Fain headed to Austin in search of direct aid and support for the Indians. The legislature created the new position of state Indian agent and appointed Fain to the post. He teamed up with the Texas Federation of Women's Clubs and conducted a statewide consciousness-raising campaign that culminated in an appearance by tribal representatives before the U.S. Congress. The delegation made a passionate appeal to the "Great White Chiefs" and the "Great White Father" to relieve their poverty and undernourishment. The Assistant Commissioner of Indian Affairs reported that it was his "opinion that if the American government owes anything to any Indians it is to the Alabama-Coushatti [*sic*] of Texas." Before returning to Texas the delegation had brief meetings with President Calvin Coolidge and other government officials, who all expressed sympathy for the Indians' case.[9]

Based on the tribal testimony, Congress authorized a $102,000 appropriation for the Alabamas and Coushattas. Among other things, the money was to be used to purchase land and livestock, fund educational facilities, and supply medical aid. The bill also stipulated that the State of Texas assist in providing relief to the Indians. Thus, the state legislature earmarked an extra $40,000 for the tribe, providing funds for the building of homes, dental and medical services, and fencing material. The following year the state appropriated an additional $47,000 for the construction of a gymnasium, a hospital, a home for the tribe's agent, and the building of more modern homes for tribe members. By these measures the national and state governments effectively created a reservation of 4,315 acres for the Indians in Polk County and established an official trusteeship with both governments.[10]

The Indian Reorganization Act of 1934 restructured the Alabamas and Coushattas. This "Indian New Deal" transformed U.S.

Indian policy and restored tribal sovereignty by permitting tribes to draft constitutions and bylaws, which made the tribes self-governing municipalities able to negotiate with local, state, and national governments. Essentially the act allowed the Alabama-Coushattas to establish a tribal constitution and thereby incorporate under a federal charter. The constitution limited tribe membership to individuals born of two Alabama-Coushatta parents, established a seven-member tribal council elected at large by tribe members, and preserved the traditional elected offices of principal chief and a second chief.[11]

Although the state and federal governments did not extend the same official recognition to the Tiguas, the El Paso Indians sought to preserve their tribal status and autonomy as it related to the local and county governments. In 1934 the El Paso county attorney recommended that the Indians be allowed to vote without having to pay the poll tax, and individual Tiguas freely participated in that year's state primary election. But four years later a district court reversed this decision, concluding that the Indians were in fact subject to the poll taxes. The tribe ceremoniously expressed its autonomy in official fashion in June 1936 during "El Paso Day" at the Texas Centennial celebration in Dallas. On this occasion Tigua Chief Damasio Clomenero presented President Franklin Roosevelt with a traditional Tigua headdress and conferred the titles of "Honorary Cacique of the Tiguas" upon him and "Honorary Squaw" upon First Lady Eleanor Roosevelt. Expressing his gratitude, the president affixed the traditional headwear over his fedora.[12]

The greatest threat to tribal sovereignty came in 1955 with the annexation of Ysleta by the city of El Paso. This development meant that individual tribal members would be subject to greater taxation. Since Spanish colonial times, the Ysleta Indians had been hostile towards outside taxes, claiming that a grant conferred by the Spanish king in 1751 exempted them from such collections. Nevertheless, Tigua families now not only owed city taxes, but also faced fore-

(l. to r.) Aniceto Granillo, Damaso Colmenero, Sebastion Duran (hold-ing drum called Juanchiro or "one that speaks with great thunder"), and Cleofas Calleros (whom the Tiguas named an honorary *adelantado* in 1932). Photographed in Ysleta, Texas, between 1930 and 1936. From UTSA's Institute of Texan Cultures, No. 071-0362, courtesy Cleofas Cal-leros Estate.

closure on their property because of inability to pay. Despite this erosion of Tigua sovereignty at the local level, the Indians main-tained their tribal organization and independent operation under their tribal constitution.[13]

The Alabama-Coushatta tribe exercised its autonomy during this time by working towards the establishment of a tribal educa-tion system. The tribe organized a school district in 1932 and re-ceived $15,000 in appropriations for educational purposes. Tribal leaders served as the district school board, and they developed a curriculum that focused on English language skills, proficiency in elementary mathematics, vocational training for boys, and home economics for the girls. By 1940 the school offered nine grades of instruction, after which students could transfer to either Livingston High School or Indian schools in Oklahoma. During World War II, however, favorable economic conditions associated with wartime mobilization prompted many Indians to leave school for employment in the lumber and other local industries. Consequently, after the war the tribe merged its reservation school with the Big Sandy school district, a move that offered Indian students greater opportunities. Tribal enthusiasm for the Big Sandy school remained high throughout the late 1940s, as represented by the 94 percent attendance rate among Indians from 1945 to 1949. After 1950 more Alabama-Coushatta students began to attend schools in Livingston and Woodville to take advantage of a wider variety of courses and programs.[14]

World War II had considerable impact on Indians all across the country. Military service helped many Texas Indians develop greater proficiency in English and become more acculturated to American society in general. The Alabama-Coushattas had demonstrated their loyalty before, during the Texas Revolution, the Civil War, and World War I, when half the male population of the tribe volunteered for duty. The United States did not accept reservation Indians for military service during World War I, but actively encouraged their enlistment during World War II. Many Alabama-Coushattas responded to the call, and 47 tribe members ultimately served in the armed forces with distinction in every theater of battle around the world. Other Alabama-Coushatta men left the reservation to search for war-related work in the surrounding communities, or in Houston and Dallas. And yet others contributed to the effort by buying war bonds in excess of the average American citizen.[15]

The wartime experience profoundly affected many Alabama-Coushattas. Many returning veterans now found life on the reservation routine, dull, and unfulfilling. As a result, many Indian men sought opportunities elsewhere, either moving to the city, making a career of the military, or attending college. Unfortunately, there was also a negative aspect to the postwar era. Families broke apart as individuals left the reservation, and alcoholism and substance abuse became more widespread among tribe members.[16]

During the mid-1940s developments in northern Mexico contributed to the diversity of American Indians and tribes living in Texas. Since the 1830s many Kickapoo Indians had sought refuge from persecution and enforced assimilation in Texas and the United States by relocating to a site called Nacimiento in the northern Mexican state of Coahuila. Over the course of the nineteenth century Nacimiento became a sanctuary for Kickapoos and other American Indians seeking the isolation necessary to preserve ancestral ways. The Mexican government welcomed these Indians, seeing them as a frontier defense against marauding Comanches, Kiowas, and Apaches. The tribes living in seclusion at Nacimiento preserved their old ways associated with the cultivation of corn and hunting until the early twentieth century. Serious drought conditions during the 1940s caused crops to fail, livestock to die, and deer to disappear. Together with the construction of a nearby reservoir, mechanized agriculture, and the fencing of surrounding ranches, these developments all seriously disrupted the tribe's ability to maintain its livelihood. Beginning in 1944 several desperate Mexican Kickapoos sought farm-labor work across the northern border near Eagle Pass. They settled at the site of a traditional hunting campground on the north bank of the Rio Grande under the International Bridge. In time more Kickapoos joined the farm-labor workforce at Eagle Pass and eventually entered into the migrant-labor stream that extended from south Texas to faraway locations in California, Montana, and New York. By 1960 U.S. immigration and naturalization laws allowed Kickapoos to freely cross the international border. Almost all Mexican Kickapoos left Nacimiento that year for the migrant-farm working season, which lasted from April to November.[17]

Greater changes came to the Alabama-Coushatta reservation with the onset of the national government's program to terminate federal trust responsibilities and obligations to the Indian tribes across the country. Compared to other Indian reservations, the administration of the Alabama-Coushatta reservation by combined state and federal authorities was unusual. This unique relationship reflected the historical peculiarities of the Alabama-Coushattas' migration to Texas, the tribe's association with the Texas Republic, and the post-Civil War assumption of federal responsibility for Indians in general. The process to terminate federal responsibilities in Texas began in 1951 when Governor Allan Shivers suggested the development of a forest conservation project on the reservation that allowed the commercial cutting of timber. Approximately 75 percent of the proceeds would be used for the purchase of more lands for the tribe's usage. The tribe agreed to this plan, and the Department of the Interior's Bureau of Indian Affairs (BIA) took the steps necessary to allow the State of Texas to assume the exclusive responsibility of managing the forest resources within the borders of the reservation. Shortly thereafter the state legislature approved a resolution accepting trust responsibilities for the Alabama-Coushattas if the U.S. government terminated its trust relationship with the tribe. In 1953 the tribe requested that all trust responsibility be transferred to Texas and placed under the supervision of the Texas State Hospital Board. Consequently, in the summer of 1955 the Department of the Interior announced the suspension of federal supervision of the tribe.[18]

Federal termination had little immediate impact on the Alabama-Coushatta tribe and its reservation. Since 1928 Texas had traditionally provided the lion's share of funding for all tribal concerns. Federal responsibility had initially been significant, but had diminished over the years, limited primarily to the funding of education. Some tribal members feared the transfer of authority would result in a loss of benefits, but this was not the case. The state continued to fund the tribe as it had since 1938 and ultimately assumed responsibility for tribal health care. The federal government, responding to requests made by the tribal council, agreed to continue allowing Alabama-Coushattas access to government hospitals and Indian trade schools located outside of Texas, and to never dispose of the reservation without approval of the majority of the tribe. Despite these concessions, the ultimate objective of termination was the cessation of all trust responsibilities for the tribe, and in 1959 the state auditor avowed that "the state will be able to relinquish its trusteeship of [the Indians] sooner than was once believed." By the 1960s Alabama-Coushatta culture increasingly resembled the surrounding community, and it appeared that termination and complete assimilation were underway. More individuals lived off the reservation, and others married either non-Indians or Indians from different tribes. Alabama-Coushatta children went to school in surrounding communities and became exceedingly proficient in English. Protestantism became more widespread as nearby Baptist and Assembly of God denominations attracted tribe members.[19]

The Bureau of Indian Affairs' program to terminate reservation Indians included a corollary program aimed at relocating them to urban areas across the country. Lawmakers and bureaucrats saw relocation as a placement program allowing Indians from overcrowded and destitute reservations access to better educational opportunities, vocational training, and economic development. Placement programs had been initially instituted among the Navajos and Hopis of Arizona in the late 1940s, providing tribe members with seasonal employment through local employment agencies. By 1954 the BIA made its placement activities a permanent program with relocation offices located in major cities, beginning with Chicago and Los Angeles. The economic opportunities associated with World War II attracted an increasing number of out-of-state reservation Indians to the Dallas-Fort Worth area. Beginning in 1952 the Bureau began helping Navajos find jobs in the metroplex. In 1957 the BIA established an official Field Employment Assistance Office in Dallas. According to the 1960 census, 1,032 Indians lived in

Dallas and Tarrant counties. The majority of the Indians relocated to the DFW area hailed from Oklahoma, but a significant number considered Arizona and New Mexico their home state. By the time the relocation program was terminated in 1973, the field office had helped over 10,000 Indians find employment and housing and adapt to the city environment.[20]

Despite the general undermining of tribal sovereignty on the local, state, and national levels, the Tigua tribe continued to operate independently under its tribal constitution. When tribal chief Colmenero died in June 1941, an El Paso reporter was astonished that the number of "fullblooded" Tiguas had seriously diminished due to death and intermarriage with local Mexicans. In 1962 another Texas newspaperman announced that only thirty-five "fullblood" Tiguas remained. Despite gloomy depictions of the tribe's condition, the Tiguas continued to exercise tribal autonomy and to celebrate their ancestral heritage. In 1961 the tribe elected a new cacique and celebrated Saint Anthony's Day that June with customary processions, prayers, drumming, and shotgun blasts. Although tribal population and sovereignty appeared to be eroding by the early 1960s, the Tigua tribe endured. Boldly defiant, the tribe openly expressed its ancient ancestral legacy of cultural survival in the face of daunting social conditions.[21]

Developments that took place during the last four decades of the century, however, reversed the process of termination and contributed to a revitalization of tribalism among Indians across the state. By the mid-1950s a debate emerged between the Alabama-Coushatta tribal council and the state Indian agent over the management of the reservation economy. The tribe criticized the agent's agriculture-oriented plans and petitioned the state legislature for greater tribal sovereignty as it related to economic management of the reservation. The newly appointed state Indian agent introduced an innovative economic plan that stressed greater autonomy featuring a tribe-managed tourism program. The suggestion that

Alabama-Coushattas attract tourists to their reservation with traditional Indian dances, crafts, and other activities initially stirred
controversy among the staunchly Christian tribe members, and the
Presbyterian pastor of the reservation led a battle against the rein-
troduction of Indian traditions among the tribe.[22]

Nevertheless, in 1962 the Tribal Enterprise Tourist Project
was launched, and the next year the state legislature appropriated
$40,000 for the construction of a museum, a restaurant, and an arts
and crafts shop. Later, with the help of state and federal economic
development grants, the tribe constructed a dance arena, a council
house, a dam creating a twenty-six acre lake, and a campground
with a nature trail. The tribe's comprehensive approach to tourism
during the 1960s and 1970s mostly focused on attracting visitors to
the reservation with traditional dance performances and powwow
ceremonies. Since traditional dancing among the Alabama-Coushattas had fallen out of practice by the 1960s, the tribe hired a Taos
Indian to teach them native dances. Tribe members created a traditional dance troupe that performed exhibitions for tourists and in
1969 organized a powwow committee to administer the meetings
held on the reservation. The tribal tourist initiative proved to be
successful. In 1962 the state provided the Alabama-Coushatta tribe
with its total budget of $72,039. By 1972 the budget had grown
to $344,014, with proceeds from tourism accounting for the vast
majority of the increase.[23]

The Alabama-Coushattas' tourist program furthered the renewal
of Indian identity and the expansion of pan-Indianism among tribe
members. In a reversal of earlier twentieth-century developments,
individual Alabama-Coushattas began to embrace their Indian heritage and intensified their identification and interaction with members of other tribes throughout the United States. Intertribal powwows, the resumption of ancestral customs such as long-leaf pine
needle basket weaving and beadwork, and the establishment of an
Indian club to preserve general Indian traditions helped Alabama-

Coushattas firmly embrace American Indian identity after World War II.[24]

Similar initiatives aimed at increasing the Tiguas' tribal sovereignty developed around the same time. The annexation of Ysleta into El Paso imposed serious hardships on the tribe, but the Indians had important and influential friends in the city of El Paso. Because of the difficulty paying city taxes, Mayor Ralph Seitsinger sought assistance for the tribe from the Bureau of Indian Affairs. The mayor argued that the Tiguas of his city deserved the same rights, privileges, and protections the federal government accorded other Indians throughout the country. Officials at the BIA responded coolly, stating they no longer accepted responsibility for any Indians in Texas. As the city tried to resolve the legal status of the Ysleta Indians as it related to taxation, local attorney Tom Diamond volunteered to investigate the confusing matter and ultimately began acting as the tribe's legal representative. It was disheartening to Diamond to learn that for the Tiguas to receive any federal protections he had to substantiate the tribe's legal claim to its land, cultural integrity, and legitimacy. This realization set Diamond and the Ysleta Tiguas on a twenty-plus year odyssey seeking federal recognition for the tribe.[25]

Early in 1966 supporters launched a media campaign to draw attention to the plight of the Tiguas. An El Paso headline blared that the "Tigua Indian Tribe of Ysleta [was] in Danger of Becoming Extinct." Frank X. Tolbert announced later in the *Dallas Morning News* that "the government ignores the Texas Tigua Indians." The sense of urgency in these headlines brought support to the Tiguas and led to a drawn-out process that culminated in federal recognition in 1987. With the assistance of an anthropologist studying the cultural persistence and social organization of the tribe, Diamond initially presented his case for official recognition of the Indians to the Texas State Historical Survey Committee (TSHSC). The TSHSC agreed that the Tiguas had maintained their cultural integrity and issued a resolution that the tribe was entitled to recognition, protection, and preservation. The Isleta Pueblo Indians of New Mexico also offered their support to their Texas cousins. Diamond now took the case to the state attorney general who sympathized with the Tiguas but claimed that the state's hands were tied until the federal government officially recognized the tribe. So Diamond began working both ends, seeking legislative action from both the state and national governments.[26]

Diamond's position as El Paso County Democratic Party chairman allowed him access to important Texas legislators in Austin and Washington, D.C. The Tiguas received general support in the Texas legislature when it agreed to establish a reservation and to assume trust responsibilities for the Indians once the federal government recognized the tribe. In August 1966 the U.S. House Committee on Indian Affairs took steps toward recognition of the Tiguas. But getting Senate approval demanded some old-fashioned politicking, inasmuch as Senator Clinton Anderson of New Mexico stalled the bill on behalf of his Pueblo Indian constituents, who were still bitter over Tigua support of the Spanish in the Pueblo Revolt of 1680. Texas Senator Ralph Yarborough, who had lived and worked in El Paso in the late 1920s as a young lawyer and was sympathetic to the Tiguas, finally convinced the New Mexican senator to remove his opposition. The bill officially recognizing the "Tiwa Indians of Ysleta, Texas" was passed by Congress and signed into law by President Lyndon B. Johnson on April 13, 1968.[27]

Recognition of the Tiguas allowed only for the establishment of a state trusteeship for the Indians. Nevertheless, the tribe filed suit with the U.S. Indian Claims Commission in May 1969. They staked a $48 million claim to the lands of west Texas, including the city of El Paso, as well as fishing and water rights in the Rio Grande, hunting rights in the Franklin, Hueco, Quitman, and Organ mountains, and the salt deposits at the base of the Guadalupe Mountains. State trusteeship allowed for state administered health care, education, and economic development programs, and the Tiguas' standard of living improved as Texas provided for the construction of modern homes with electricity and plumbing. The Texas Indian Commission also helped the tribe open a restaurant, a visitor center, and a museum. These facilities, along with the tribe's acquisition of lands from the state at the Hueco Tanks east of El Paso pointed towards economic self-sufficiency. Tours of historical sites, sales of traditional arts and crafts, and public performances of traditional tribal dances contributed to the tribe's improvement[28]

Indians from outside Texas continued to move to the state's metropolitan areas throughout the 1960s and 1970s. Although Dallas-Fort Worth continued to be the primary destination, many Indians settled in cities throughout the state. For example, the Indian population of the Houston area grew enormously, increasing from 391 in 1960 to 8,282 in 1970. Area Indians established an American Indian Center (AIC) in Dallas in 1969, helping create a sense of "Indianness" and community through social support, job programs, counseling and substance abuse services, and powwows for the tribal peoples of the metroplex. The Dallas Inter-Tribal Center, established in 1971, complemented the AIC, but also offered health services through its non-profit clinic. These organizations received their funding from agencies like the national Office for Economic Opportunity, the Community Services Administration, the Indian Health Service, and the National Health Service Corps, while the Texas Educational Agency supported other assistance programs. Houston-area Indians founded the Intertribal Council of Houston in 1978, which not only promoted Indian culture and community, but also established a referral service that offered support in the areas of health, education, and housing. Such activities and support services became the framework for a vibrant community of urban Indians.[29]

This growing identification of Texas Indians with their ancient heritage and traditions intensified during the late twentieth cen-

tury, culminating in the official reinstatement of the federal trust
relationship in the 1980s. This process began in 1965 when Texas
created the Texas Commission on Indian Affairs to take charge of
overseeing the administration of the Alabama-Coushatta tribe. The
state and federal assistance received by the tribes throughout the
1970s and into the 1980s funded the tourist program, the building of modern brick homes, a multipurpose community center, an
adult education program, a library, a youth activities center, counseling offices, a vocational training program, and other recreational
activities. Even so, some tribe members were disgruntled by state
administration. The tribe's ongoing expansion necessitated additional state funding precisely at a time when the state's economy
waned dramatically due to the precipitous decline of the oil market.
This resulted in a strained relationship that came to a breaking point
when the tribe and the state disputed hunting licensing jurisdiction.
In 1983 the state attorney general declared that the Alabama-Coushatta reservation and the tribe itself no longer existed, and that the
tribe should be considered an "unincorporated association of persons." This opinion essentially terminated the Alabama-Coushatta
tribe in the eyes of the state. As a result, the state imposed taxes on
tribe members for the first time and ceased appropriating funds for
the operation and administration of the reservation. The tribe challenged the attorney general's decision in federal court.[30]

Earlier in 1977 the Texas legislature recognized the Kickapoos
living in Texas along the Rio Grande as an official Indian tribe.
The Mexican Kickapoos had maintained federal recognition status
since the nineteenth century because they remained on the Kickapoo tribal rolls in Oklahoma. As such, they received indirect federal
support through their Oklahoma-based kinsmen. In 1981 several
persons working on behalf of the Mexican Kickapoos in Texas introduced a bill in the House of Representatives aimed at clarifying
the status of the Indians in relation to the U.S. government. President Ronald Reagan later signed a 1983 law giving the Kickapoos

in Texas the authority to buy land for a reservation and obligated the federal government to provide the tribe with the same services accorded all recognized tribes. The tribe received U.S. citizenship and became officially known as the Kickapoo Traditional Tribe of Texas. The Indians purchased land for a reservation and moved from under the Eagle Pass International Bridge to their new home-site south of town by the end of the 1980s.[31]

In response to their growing dispute with Texas, and following the lead of the Kickapoos, the Alabama-Coushattas began negotiating in 1982 with the Bureau of Indian Affairs to restore the federal trust relationship that had been terminated earlier in the 1950s. In August 1987 the Alabama-Coushatta tribe once again became a trustee of the federal government, and in 1989 the state dismantled the Texas Indian Commission. Federal authorities acted quickly, providing expanded social, health, and economic programs and constructing a multipurpose tribal cultural center in 1994.[32]

By 1982 the Tiguas' enthusiasm for state trusteeship also began to sour, especially after the attorney general's ruling revoking the state's special treatment of recognized Indian tribes. Like the Alabama-Coushattas, the Tiguas sought federal trusteeship in order to establish a more independent relationship with Texas. Again, Tom Diamond led the way. He wanted to link the Tigua bid for federal recognition to that of the Alabama-Coushattas, thinking this would enhance the chances for the Tiguas. The BIA, however, objected because the Tiguas had never enjoyed federal trustee status. But the BIA ultimately relented because of the 1968 act that had offered the Tiguas federal recognition in order to become a trustee of the state—with one catch. For the first time in its history the BIA imposed a "blood quantum" at one-eighth degree of descendancy as a condition on the Tiguas in exchange for recognition. The BIA also insisted that the Tiguas agree to a ban on gambling on their reservation.[33]

The Alabama-Coushattas sought to further expand their tribal sovereignty under federal trusteeship during the last decade of the twentieth century. At the beginning of the 1992–1993 school year the Big Sandy High School barred several Alabama-Coushatta boys from registering because the length of their hair violated the school's dress code. The students, regular performers at tribal pow-wows, protested the school's dress policy, insisting that they intended to keep the length of their hair in spite of the policy. When several other Alabama-Coushatta students were prevented from registering in the school system, the tribe organized an effort to get the school district to make an exception for the boys. The school board rejected the request, but the tribe ultimately won its case in a 1994 appeals court decision.[34]

Another controversial matter concerned the establishment of casino-style gambling on Indian reservations. In the late 1970s and early 1980s the Seminole tribe in Florida and the Barona Group of the Capitan Grande Band of Mission Indians in California successfully challenged in lower federal courts their respective states' ability to regulate tribal bingo operations. As the Indian gaming industry expanded in the 1980s, states like California continued to impose gambling regulations on the tribes. The Cabazon and Morongo Bands of Mission Indians responded by disputing California's jurisdiction over their reservations in federal court. These challenges culminated in the landmark 1987 Supreme Court decision in *California v. Cabazon Band of Mission Indians*, ruling that California tribes had the right to conduct gaming on their reservations free from state regulation. The following year Congress passed the Indian Gaming Regulatory Act of 1988, which required tribes to negotiate gaming compacts with their home states if any form of gaming was permitted, including for the benefit of charities. Texas already allowed gaming for charitable causes and pari-mutuel betting at the time the Tiguas came under federal trusteeship. The tribe's attorney, Tom Diamond, alleged in 1994 that the state's acceptance of these forms of gaming, together with the recently instituted lottery, "opened the door" to casino-style gaming on their reservation. The Tiguas operated a high stakes bingo hall, but figured that a greater variety of high stakes gaming, such as slot machines and table games, could bring them more revenue. The state strongly opposed such plans and the tribe sued. Although the Tiguas initially won their case against the state, the ruling was overturned based on the attorney general's 1994 decision that casino-style gaming was unconstitutional in Texas. The ruling shocked the tribe, which had anticipated a favorable result. Defiantly, the tribe nevertheless established Speaking Rock Casino on their reservation.[35]

The Alabama-Coushatta tribe also considered the idea of gaming in 1994, and a vote was held on the issue. It was soundly defeated because of the tribe's longstanding and strong Protestant moral traditions. Nevertheless, in 1999 the tribe reversed its opposition and voted in favor of casino-style gambling. The defiance of the Tiguas and the success of their Coushatta cousins' tribal casino in Louisiana convinced the Alabama-Coushatta tribe of Texas that it could benefit from a similar operation. The tribe's vote in favor of gambling contributed to the vociferous political debate throughout the state. In due course, plans to establish casino gambling on their reservation foundered when a 1999 federal court ruling blocked the establishment of an Alabama-Coushatta casino. Ironically, the Coushatta tribe of Louisiana played an important role in blocking Alabama-Coushatta casino operations in Texas, hiring powerful lobbyists to work for their interests in Austin and Washington, D.C., at the expense of their Texas cousins.[36]

The operation of slot machines and table games on the Tigua reservation not only brought the wrath of the state down on the tribe, but it also contributed to the development of some serious divisions among tribal members. Despite grand plans for the anticipated gambling largess, the tribe divided over issues concerning legitimate authority, accusations relating to the misappropriation of tribal funds, and arguments over the legitimacy of individuals' tribal ancestry. The intra-tribal conflict turned especially spiteful in 1998,

resulting in the seizure of the tribe's sacred drum and the banish-
ment from the community of those accused of not being sufficiently
Tigua. The disobedience that gripped the tribe in the mid-1990s
also spurred defiance in the face of the Texas government. When
Governor George W. Bush claimed that the Tiguas had violated
state law with their casino, the tribe unsuccessfully sued him for
slander. In 1999 the state aggressively pursued its case against the
Tiguas. By the turn of the century several major issues surrounding
the Tiguas' vast land claims and the legal status of their casino business remained unresolved. Ultimately Texas defeated the casino in
2002, but the land claims remain unsettled.[37]

Besides these political problems, the Tiguas recognized a barrier to their ability to physically persist as a tribe. Intermarriage and
acculturation with the local Hispanic population had long been a
Tigua tradition, and by the conditions of Tigua "blood quantum"
under U.S. law, the tribe realized that intermarriage would lead to
its extinction in three or four generations. Because the Ysleta del
Sur Pueblo and the Alabama and Coushatta Indian Tribes of Texas
Restoration Act of 1987 set the conditions for recognizing individuals as tribe members, only the U.S. Congress could change those
rules. Thus, the tribe began lobbying Congress to amend the 1987
act in order to allow persons having at least one Tigua great-great-
grandparent to be classified as official tribe members with trustee
status. Congress discussed the issue in September 2000, despite the
objections of the BIA, which opposed the "creation" of new Indians over which the Bureau would bear responsibility. Like the
Tigua gambling issue and tribal land claims, passage of the blood-
quantum issue remained in doubt at the end of the century.[38]

The Kickapoos also saw casino gambling as a means of increasing the tribe's treasury and bringing development to their reservation. Besides providing for housing, a community center, and a day-
care center, the tribe also used funds from the federal government
to help build a high-stakes bingo hall. The Kickapoos benefited

from the difficulties of the Tiguas with Texas over gambling on their El Paso reservation. Because the Kickapoos' federal trustee status was through their relationship with the Oklahoma branch of their tribe, their status with the state was of a more independent nature. As the government shut down the Tigua casino, the Kickapoos expanded their operations and built the Lucky Eagle Casino to accommodate 1,000 slot machines. By the turn of the century it looked like the Kickapoos would be the only tribe operating a casino within the state. Ultimately, the casino operations contributed to serious divisions within the tribe as members fought over control of the proceeds. But the tribe suffered from other problems during the 1990s as well. Inhalant and alcohol abuse, in addition to teen delinquency, illiteracy, and the lack of adequate treatment programs and job training, all confronted the Kickapoo tribe by the year 2000.[39]

In 1994 the Alabama-Coushattas staked a historical claim for monetary damages and the return of 10 million acres in the Big Thicket area of southeast Texas. A U.S. claims court ultimately ruled in favor of the tribe, which received monetary compensation for its land claims in 1999. The tribe also sought in 2000 to establish its own legal jurisdiction on the reservation to resolve civil disputes between tribal members. Major crimes, including murder, would fall under federal jurisdiction in such a tribal jurisdictional arrangement. Reversing a longstanding and exclusive emphasis on the English language, the Alabama-Coushatta tribe also sought to restore their customary heritage by instituting courses in 2000 to instruct their children in their tribal language.[40]

Like the reservation Indians, Texas urban Indians have experienced a renewal of ethnic and cultural identity. Intertribal organizations and services have mushroomed as the state's Indian population increased during the last three decades of the twentieth century. By 2000, about 20,000 Indians lived in the Dallas-Fort Worth area, followed by approximately 12,000 Indians in the

Houston area. But urban Indians could be found in all Texas cities; 3,000 lived in San Antonio, while almost 2,000 lived in Austin, Amarillo, and Corpus Christi. Each of these cities has intertribal organizations that organize powwows and other cultural events, as well as provide a variety of social services. Powwows are held year round across the state at numerous venues, and a regular circuit has emerged with dancers performing in Odessa, Lubbock, Dallas-Fort Worth, Austin, San Antonio, Houston, Corpus Christi, and the Rio Grande Valley. American Indian chambers of commerce have been established in Dallas and Houston, and urban Indians have received legal services and advice from the American Indian Law Project of Legal Services of North Texas and the Texas Indian Bar Association. Urban Indian activists have launched campaigns aimed at the elimination of Indian-themed school mascots, and the application of the Native American Graves Protection Act of 1990 at archeological sites. These movements have had mixed success, as many Texas schools still identify with the state's Indian heritage, and as state law favors private land owners over tribes in disputes about archeological artifacts and remains.[41]

With the removal of nearly all Indians from Texas by the 1880s, the Alabama-Coushattas remained the most recognizable tribe in the state. Since then, Texans have identified the tribe as an important symbol of their state's historical heritage. The advocacy of concerned citizens in the early part of the century, along with the Alabama-Coushattas' ongoing recognition of their traditional tribal bonds, established an important precedent that other tribes like the Tigua and the Kickapoo followed. All three tribes faced serious threats to their tribal integrity at various times due to reduction of trusteeship responsibilities, assimilation, migration, and a variety of social ills. Despite the challenges to their tribal integrity the recognized tribes of Texas have not only maintained their existence, but they have flourished. The reestablishment of federal trusteeship among the Alabama-Coushattas, Tiguas, and Kickapoos in the latter part of the century preserved their tribalism and allowed for the expression of tribal sovereignty. Although the practice of tribal autonomy in Texas has not been without controversy, it represents a striking departure from the state's historical undermining of American Indian independence. Indians living in cities have also benefited from this twentieth-century development. Initially, it was believed that World War II hastened the disappearance of tribalism. However, non-reservation Indians compensated their loss of tribalism with intertribal organizations, rituals, and festivals. Thus, intertribalism provided urban Indians with a means to articulate tribal and ethnic pride, as well as endowed them with a distinctive form of autonomy. The history of Texas Indians in the twentieth century then is mainly a departure from the past and attempts to destroy tribalism. Over the course of the last century, Texas Indians have remarkably sustained their devotion to a traditional existence—one that is innately independent and dynamic. These are traits that Texans tend to admire.

Selected Bibliography

Barlett, Donald L. "George Bush vs. the Tigua." *Time* 160, no. 26 (December 23, 2002): 63.

Fixico, Donald L. *The Urban Indian Experience in America*. Albuquerque: University of New Mexico Press, 2000.

Folsom-Dickerson, W. E. S. *The White Path*. San Antonio: Naylor, 1965.

Gerald, Rex E. *Aboriginal Use and Occupation by Tigua, Manso, and Suma Indians*. New York: Garland, 1974.

Govenar, Alan. "Almost Invisible: The Uncertain Fate of American Indians in Dallas." *Texas Observer* (October 9, 1981): 1, 10–13.

Guinn, Jeff. *Our Land Before We Die: The Proud Story of the Seminole Negro*. New York: Tarcher/Putnam, 2002.

Hook, Jonathan B. *The Alabama-Coushatta Indians*. College Station: Texas A&M University Press, 1997.

Latorre, Felipe A., and Dolores L. Latorre. *The Mexican Kickapoo Indians*. Austin: University of Texas Press, 1976.

La Vere David, *The Texas Indians.* College Station: Texas A&M University Press, 2004.

Reid, Jan. "The Forgotten People," *Texas Monthly* 25, no. 2 (February 1997): 74–81.

Schulze, Jeffery M. "The Rediscovery of the Tiguas: Federal Recognition and Indiannessin the Twentieth Century." *Southwestern Historical Quarterly* 105, no. 1 (July 2001): 15–39.

Wright, Bill. *The Tiguas: Pueblo Indians of Texas.* El Paso: Texas Western Press, 1993.

Wright, Bill, and E. John Gesick, Jr. *The Texas Kickapoo: Keepers of Tradition.* El Paso: Texas Western Press, 1996.

Endnotes

1. Jonathan B. Hook, *The Alabama-Coushatta Indians* (College Station: Texas A&M University Press, 1997), 3, 15–17, 22, 30, 107; David La Vere, *The Texas Indians* (College Station: Texas A&M University Press, 2004), 232; *Handbook of Texas Online*, s.v. "Alabama-Coushatta Indians," http://www.tsha.utexas.edu/handbook/online/articles/AA/bma19.html.

2. La Vere, *Texas Indians*, 93; *Handbook of Texas Online*, s.v. "Ysleta, Texas," http://www.tsha.utexas.edu/handbook/online/articles/YY/hny6.html; *Handbook of Texas Online*, s.v. "El Paso del Norte," http://www.tsha.utexas.edu/handbook/online/articles/EE/hdelu.html; *Handbook of Texas Online*, s.v. "Tigua Indians," http://www.tsha.utexas.edu/handbook/online/articles/TT/bmt45.html.

3. Jan Reid, "The Forgotten People," *Texas Monthly* 25, no. 2 (February 1997): 74; La Vere, *Texas Indians*, 236–37; Bill Wright and E. John Gesick, Jr., *The Texas Kickapoo: Keepers of Tradition* (El Paso: Texas Western Press, 1996), 3, 5.

4. Hook, *Alabama-Coushatta Indians*, 44–49; Prairie View Malone, *Sam Houston's Indians: The Alabama-Coushatti* (San Antonio: Naylor, 1960), 39–42; *Handbook of Texas Online*, s.v. "Alabama-Coushatta Indians"; *Handbook of Texas Online*, s.v. "Samuel Fisher Tenney," http://www.tsha.utexas.edu/handbook/online/articles/TT/fte42.html.

5. Rex E. Gerald, *Aboriginal Use and Occupation by Tigua, Manso, and Suma Indians* (New York: Garland, 1974), 42–44, 179–84; Bill Wright, *The Tiguas: Pueblo Indians of Texas* (El Paso: Texas Western Press, 1993), 18.

6. Gerald, *Aboriginal Use and Occupation,* 187–89. For various dances and celebrations held up to 1969, see pages 190–200; Wright, *Tiguas,* 20; Stan Steiner, *The Tiguas: The Lost Tribe of City Indians* (New York: Crowell-Collier, 1972), 58.

7. Hook, *Alabama-Coushatta Indians,* 52–58; *Handbook of Texas Online,* s.v. "John Scott," http://www.tsha.utexas.edu/handbook/online/articles/SS/fsc70.html.

8. Malone, *Sam Houston's Indians,* 34; *Handbook of Texas Online,* s.v. "Alabama-Coushatta Indians"; *Handbook of Texas Online,* s.v. "Samuel Bronson Cooper," http://www.tsha.utexas.edu/handbook/online/articles/CC/fco61.html.

9. Malone, *Sam Houston's Indians,* 47–48; *Handbook of Texas Online,* s.v. "Alabama-Coushatta Indians"; *Handbook of Texas Online,* s.v. "Charles Martin Thompson," http://www.tsha.utexas.edu/handbook/online/articles/TT/fth67.html; *Handbook of Texas Online,* s.v. "Earle Bradford Mayfield," http://www.tsha.utexas.edu/handbook/online/articles/MM/fma91.html; *Handbook of Texas Online,* s.v. "Eugene Black," http://www.tsha.utexas.edu/handbook/online/articles/BB/fbl62.html; *Handbook of Texas Online,* s.v. "Thomas Lindsay Blanton," http://www.tsha.utexas.edu/handbook/online/articles/BB/fbl17.html.

10. Malone, *Sam Houston's Indians,* 51–53; "Briggs Indian Bill Blocked in House," *Dallas Morning News,* May 13, 1928, sec. 1, p. 4; *Handbook of Texas Online,* s.v. "Alabama-Coushatta Indians"; *Handbook of Texas Online,* s.v. "Board of Control," http://www.tsha.utexas.edu/handbook/online/articles/BB/mdb2.html; *Handbook of Texas Online,* s.v. "Thomas Terry Connally," http://www.tsha.utexas.edu/handbook/online/articles/CC/fco36.html; *Handbook of Texas Online,* s.v. "Clay Stone Briggs," http://www.tsha.utexas.edu/handbook/online/articles/BB/fbr46.html.

11. Hook, *Alabama-Coushatta Indians,* 60, 64–65, 124 n. 23; La Vere, *Texas Indians,* 233; Jake Page, *In the Hands of the Great Spirit: The 20,000 Year History of American Indians* (New York: Free Press, 2003), 359–60; *Handbook of Texas Online,* s.v. "Alabama-Coushatta Indians"; Alabama-Coushatta Tribe of Texas, "The Legend of the Twin Manifestations," http://www.alabama-coushatta.com/History/TheLegendofTheTwinManifestations/tabid/63/Default.aspx; Alabama-Coushatta Tribe of Texas, "Tribal Leadership," http://www.alabama-coushatta.com/Departments/TribalLeadership/tabid/70/Default.aspx. Tribal membership is usually described in terms of "blood quantum," a term that is actually a metaphor for birth. According to the initial Alabama-Coushatta constitution, tribal membership was defined by the standard of 100 percent Indian blood quantum, which refers to someone whose parents are both Alabama-Coushatta. Of course, each parent would have to be descended from two Alabama-Coushatta parents to be considered tribe members.

12. Gerald, *Aboriginal Use and Occupation,* 190–91; Wright, *Tiguas,* 21; Steiner, *Tiguas,* 12; "Exposition Lists Initial Programs For Folk Festival," *Dallas Morning News,* May 31, 1963, sec. 2, p. 4; "Roosevelt Will Be Made Chief of Oldest Texans Here June 12," *Dallas Morning News,* June 7, 1936, sec. 1, p. 1; "President's Visit," *Dallas Morning News,* June 12, 1936, sec. 1, p. 1; "El Paso Citizens Bring Indians, Orchestra to Fair," *Dallas Morning News,* sec. 1, p. 5; "Many Delegations," *Dallas Morning News,* sec. 2, p. 1; "Fair Attracts Great Throngs During Sunday," *Dallas Morning News,* sec. 1, p. 1; "Folk Festival at Centennial Not Erudite but Genuine Fun," *Dallas Morning News,* sec. 1, p. 6; "Centennial Sidelights," *The Dallas Morning News,* sec. 1, p. 7; *Handbook of Texas Online,* s.v. "Cleofas Calleros," http://www.tsha.utexas.edu/handbook/online/articles/

CC/fcadb.htm ; *Handbook of Texas Online*, s.v. "Texas Centennial," http://www.tsha.utexas.edu/handbook/online/articles/TT/lkt1.html.

13. Gerald, *Aboriginal Use and Occupation*, 192–94; Wright, *Tiguas*, 21; Steiner, *Tiguas*, 12; Thomas A. Green, "Folk History and Cultural Reorganization: A Tigua Example," *Journal of American Folklore* 89, no. 353 (July-September 1976): 311; Jeffery M. Schulze, "The Rediscovery of the Tiguas: Federal Recognition and Indianness in the Twentieth Century," *Southwestern Historical Quarterly* 105, no. 1 (July 2001): 17–18.

14. Hook, *Alabama-Coushatta Indians*, 66–67; Darryl Lynn Morris, "Alabama Coushatta Education: A Public School Perspective," (Ph.D. diss., Texas A&M University, 1993), 5–6.

15. Hook, *Alabama-Coushatta Indians*, 67; Malone, *Sam Houston's Indians*, 46, 53–54; *Handbook of Texas Online*, s.v. "Alabama-Coushatta Indians."

16. Hook, *Alabama-Coushatta Indians*, 69.

17. Felipe A. Latorre and Dolores L. Latorre, *The Mexican Kickapoo Indians* (Austin: University of Texas Press, 1976), 25; La Vere, *Texas Indians*, 236; Wright and Gesick, Jr., *Texas Kickapoo*, 20, 24; Reid, "Forgotten People."

18. Hook, *Alabama-Coushatta Indians*, 73–76; Page, *In the Hands*, 368.

19. Hook, *Alabama-Coushatta Indians*, 76–83; La Vere, *Texas Indians*, 233; "State Appropriations For Indian Tribe Held Legal," *Houston Post*, March 7, 1957, in Malone, *Sam Houston's Indians*, 55; "Fadeout of Texas' Only Indian Reserve Is Seen," *Houston Post*, March 31, 1959, in Malone, *Sam Houston's Indians*, 56.

20. Francis Paul Prucha, *The Great Father: The United States Government and the American Indians* (Lincoln: University of Nebraska Press, 1984), 2:1079–81; Alan Govenar, "Almost Invisible: The Uncertain Fate of American Indians in Dallas," *Texas Observer* (October 9, 1981): 1, 10; Robert M. Schacht, "A Needs Assessment of American Indians With Disabilities in the Dallas-Fort Worth Metroplex, Final Report: Phase I, Revised" (Flagstaff: Northern Arizona University, American Indian Rehabilitation Research and Training Center, 1993), 2.

21. Gerald, *Aboriginal Use and Occupation*, 192–95; Frank X. Tolbert, "Tolbert's Texas: There are Only 35 Tiguas Left," *Dallas Morning News*, February 13, 1962, sec. 4, p. 2.

22. Hook, *Alabama-Coushatta Indians*, 89–91.

23. Hook, *Alabama-Coushatta Indians*, 91–92; *Handbook of Texas Online*, s.v. "Alabama-Coushatta Indians"; C. K. Chamberlain, "East Texas," *East Texas Historical Journal* 7, no. 1 (1969): 115; Tommie Pinkard, "Weaving Ways," *Texas Highways* 25, no. 11 (November 1978): 10–13; W. E. S. Folsom-Dickerson, *The White Path* (San Antonio: Naylor, 1965), 29–34; John H. Bounds, "The Alabama-Coushatta Indians of Texas," *Journal of Geography* 70, no. 3 (March 1971): 182.

24. Hook, *Alabama-Coushatta Indians*, 92–93; Herman Kelly, "Pow-Wow," *Texas Highways* 21, no. 5 (May 1974): 8; Pinkard, "Weaving Ways," 10–13; Tommie Pinkard, "A Stitch From Time," *Texas Highways* 27, no. 6 (June 1980): 28–29; Frank X. Tolbert, "Tolbert's Texas: On 'Delicious Calm' Of Indian Reserve," *Dallas Morning News*, April 2, 1974, sec. A, p. 21; Frank X. Tolbert, "Tolbert's Texas:

Indian Chief Battise Enters Chili Cookoff," *Dallas Morning News*, November 1, 1970, sec. A, p. 31; "Wick Fowler Wins World's Chili Contest," *Dallas Morning News*, November 8, 1970, sec. A, p. 4; "Chili Royalty," *Dallas Morning News*, November 9, 1970, sec. A, p. 19; Frank X. Tolbert, "Tolbert's Texas: Indians' Big Chief is Barbecue Artist, too," *Dallas Morning News*, September 2, 1971, sec. A, p. 23; Tommie Pinkard, "Feast for a Chief," *Texas Highways* 25, no. 11 (November 1978): 14–15; Tommie Pinkard, "Fulton Battise, Mikko Choba," *Texas Highways* 33, no. 6 (June 1986): 40–41.

25. Gerald, *Aboriginal Use and Occupation*, 195–96; Schulze, "Rediscovery of the Tiguas," 18.

26. Gerald, *Aboriginal Use and Occupation*, 196–97; Schulze, "Rediscovery of the Tiguas," 25–26; Frank X. Tolbert, "Tolbert's Texas: Government Ignores Texas Tigua Indians," *Dallas Morning News*, March 16, 1966, sec. D, p. 1.

27. Gerald, *Aboriginal Use and Occupation*, 168–201; Schulze, "Rediscovery of the Tiguas," 23, 27–28; Steiner, *Tiguas*, 17, 61–63; Wright, *Tiguas*, 24–25; La Vere, *Texas Indians*, 235; Pamela Colloff, "The Blood of the Tigua," *Texas Monthly* 27, no. 8 (August 1999): 112–23; Frank X. Tolbert, "Tiguas Required to Prove That They're Really Indians," *Dallas Morning News*, April 14, 1967, sec. D, p. 3; "House OK's Tigua Bill," *Dallas Morning News*, April 29, 1967, sec. D, p. 3; "Tiguas Give Connally Honorary Chief Title," *Dallas Morning News*, May 24, 1967, sec. A, p. 5; "Senate Passes Bill to Provide Reservation for Tigua Indians," *Dallas Morning News*, May 5, 1967, sec. A, p. 4; "Tigua Indian Legislation," *Dallas Morning News*, August 22, 1967, sec. A, p. 6; "House Approves," *Dallas Morning News*, August 22, 1967, sec. A, p. 6; "Tigua Tribe Adopts Lawmakers," *Dallas Morning News*, August 2, 1967, sec. A, p. 4; "Tigua Indian Legislation," *Dallas Morning News*, August 22, 1967, sec. A, p. 6; "Senate Near Action on Tigua Tribe," *Dallas Morning News*, March 28, 1968, sec. A, p. 6; "Senate Passes Indian Measure," *Dallas Morning News*, April 5, 1968, sec. AA, p. 8.

28. Wright, *Tiguas*, 26; Schulze, "Rediscovery of the Tiguas," 29–30; "Indians File Suits for Land Of $48 Million,*" Dallas Morning News*," May 22, 1969, sec. A, p. 26; Frank X. Tolbert, "Tolbert's Texas: 'Federals' Admit Tiguas Own Part of El Paso," *Dallas Morning News*, May 10, 1970, sec. A, p. 31; Frank X. Tolbert, "Tolbert's Texas: 'Cotton-Picking Indian Chief' Could Own El Paso," *Dallas Morning News*, January 23, 1971, sec. A, p. 17; Frank X. Tolbert, "Tolbert's Texas: Tiguas Friendly to La Cucaracha," *Dallas Morning News*, May 13, 1971, sec. A, p. 27; "Texas Indians Make $100,000 in Profits," *Dallas Morning News*, November 29, 1972, sec. C, p. 8; Frank X. Tolbert, "Tolbert's Texas: Hueco Tanks Were Tigua Summer Home," *Dallas Morning News*, September 30, 1975, sec. D, p. 3; Frank X. Tolbert, "Tolbert's Texas: Why Tigua Indians Fire Shotguns at Terlingua," *Dallas Morning News*, November 9, 1971, sec. A, p. 23; Frank X. Tolbert," Tolbert's Texas: Tiguas Friendly With Cockroaches," *Dallas Morning News*, October 9, 1975, sec. D, p. 3; "Schedule Announced for Puebloan Center," *Dallas Morning News*, July 25, 1976, sec. G, p. 10.

29. Donald L. Fixico, *The Urban Indian Experience in America* (Albuquer-

que: University of New Mexico Press, 2000), 136; Robert M. Schacht, "A Needs Assessment of American Indians With Disabilities in the Houston Metropolitan Area and Adjacent Rural Counties, Final Report, Phase I" (Flagstaff: Northern Arizona University, American Indian Rehabilitation Research and Training Center, 1993), 6; Govenar, "Almost Invisible," 10; Robert Finklea, "Dallas Indian Center Praised by Indian Association Official," *Dallas Morning News*, April 2, 1971, sec. D, p. 3; Pat Svacina, "Funding to Assist Indians in Dallas," *Dallas Morning News*, December 22, 1971, sec. A, p. 16; Pat Svacina, "Pow-wow Draws Tribes of Dallas," *Dallas Morning News*, January 16, 1972, sec. A, p. 15; Terry Kliewer, "Indian Center Seeking Funds," *Dallas Morning News*, May 20, 1972, sec. A, p. 8; Mitch Lobrovich, "Program Assists Alcoholic Indians," *Dallas Morning News*, November 20, 1972, sec. A, p. 12; "Indians Awarded Grant of $15,000 for Center," *Dallas Morning News*, May 29, 1973, sec. A, p. 10; Norma Adams Wade, "DIC to Open Center Serving Area Indians, *Dallas Morning News*, January 12, 1975, sec. A, p. 14; "Low-Income Housing Project Approved for Urban Indians," *Dallas Morning News*, December 1, 1976, sec. A, p. 11; Dianna Hunt, "Native Texans; Urban Indians Come Out of the Shadows; Groups Seeking Identity, Opportunity," *Houston Chronicle*, July 3, 1994, Sunday, 2 star ed., sec. A, p. 1.

    30. Hook, *Alabama-Coushatta Indians*, 93; La Vere, *Texas Indians*, 234; "First Alabama-Coushatta Lawyer," *Dallas Morning News*," May 16, 1973; Ann Atterberry, "He's Red and Proud of Indian Contributions," *Dallas Morning News*, July 9, 1976; *Handbook of Texas Online*, s.v. "Oil and Gas Industry," http://www.tsha.utexas.edu/handbook/online/articles/OO/doogz.html; Morris, "Alabama Coushatta Education," 8–9.

    31. Wright and Gesick, Jr., *Texas Kickapoo*, 25, 187 n. 70; La Vere, *Texas Indians*, 236–37.

    32. Hook, *Alabama-Coushatta Indians*, 94; La Vere, *Texas Indians*, 234; *Handbook of Texas Online*, s.v. "Alabama-Coushatta Indians"; Morris, "Alabama Coushatta Education," 9; Alabama-Coushatta Tribe of Texas, "Chief Kina Health Clinic," http://www.alabama-coushatta.com/Services/ChiefKinaHealthClinic/tabid/65/Default.aspx.

    33. Schulze, "Rediscovery of the Tiguas," 34–35.

    34. Hook, *Alabama-Coushatta Indians*, 95–96; Suzanne Gamboa, "Native Americans' Suit Part of Growing Trend," *Austin American-Statesman*," January 2, 1994, Sunday; Suzanne Gamboa, "Battle Over Hair Length Sent Back to Court," *Austin American-Statesman*, April 5, 1994, sec. city/state.

    35. Steven Andrew Light and Kathryn R. L. Rand, *Indian Gaming and Tribal Sovereignty: The Casino Compromise* (Lawrence: University Press of Kansas, 2005), 39–44; Dianna Hunt, "'Texas Has Opened the Door' for Casino, Indians Tell Court," *Houston Chronicle*, April 7, 1994, sec. A, p. 29; "Tiguas Must Go to Court Again to Argue for Casino," *Houston Chronicle*, May 20, 1994, sec. A, p. 32; Dianna Hunt, "The Native Lands of Texas; Taking Control After 300 Years; Tiguas Bank on Gambling as a Way to be Successful," *Houston Chronicle*, June 26, 1994, sec. state, p. 1; R. G. Ratcliffe, "Politicians Winning Big Over Casinos;

Gambling Firms Seek to Win Over Officials," *Houston Chronicle*, August 8, 1994, 2 star ed., sec. A, p. 1; Ross Ramsey and Dianna Hunt, "Casinos Get a Bad Hand From Appeals Court; Tigua Ruling Lengthens Odds on More Gambling," *Houston Chronicle*, October 26, 1994, 2 star ed., sec. A, p. 1.

36. Dianna Hunt, "Indians Defeat Plan for Casino On Reservation," *Houston Chronicle*, June 16, 1994; Cindy Horswell, "East Texas Tribe OKs Gambling; State Vows to Fight Any Casino Plans," *Houston Chronicle*, October 23, 1999; "Indian Tribe Approves Gambling at Site Outside of Houston," *Austin American-Statesman*, October 24, 1999; Associated Press state and local wire, "Proposed Indian Casino Lights Political Fire," November 13, 1999; James Kimberly, "Tribal Council Ready to Roll the Dice; Alabama-Coushattas Look to Gambling to Ease Reservation Poverty, Joblessness," *Houston Chronicle*, April 23, 2000; Suzanne Gamboa, "Texas Tribe Names Abramoff, Reed in Suit," *Washington Post*, July 12, 2006.

37. La Vere, *Texas Indians*, 235–236; Colloff, "Blood of the Tigua," 112–23; Donald L. Barlett, "George Bush vs. the Tigua," *Time* 160, no. 26 (December 23, 2002): 63; Dianna Hunt, "Native Texans; Tribal Lawsuits Stake Claim to Most of Texas; Indians Seem Certain to Win Some Land," *Houston Chronicle*, June 26, 1994, sec. A, p. 11; "Artifact Theft Charges Set," *Houston Chronicle*, April 9, 1998, sec. A, p. 26; "Casino In Cross Hairs," *Houston Chronicle*, May 21, 1998, Thursday 3 star ed., sec. A., p. 38; "Tribe Sues Governor," *Houston Chronicle*, May 27, 1998, Wednesday 3 star ed., sec. A, p. 18; Clay Robison, "Wheel Still Spinning on Reservation Casino," *Houston Chronicle*, June 14, 1998, Saturday 2 star ed., sec. Outlook, p. 2; "Removed From Tribal Rolls," *Houston Chronicle*, June 16, 1998, Tuesday 3 star ed., sec. A, p. 14; "Tribe Dealt Casino Setback," *Houston Chronicle*, August 28, 1998, Tuesday 3 star ed., sec. A, p. 14; "Tribal Checkpoints," *Houston Chronicle*, December 31, 1998, Thursday 3 star ed., sec. A, p. 33; "Casino Probe to Begin," *Houston Chronicle*, July 29, 1999, Thursday 3 star ed., sec. A, p. 30; "State Sues Tribe on Casino," *Houston Chronicle*, September 28, 1999, Tuesday 3 star ed., sec. A, p. 16; "State Will Go to Court to Shut Down Casino," *Houston Chronicle*, February 7, 2001, Wednesday 2 star ed., sec. A, p. 24.

38. Wright, *Tiguas*, 27; Schulze, "Rediscovery of the Tiguas," 37; House Committee on Resources, *Amending the Ysleta del Sur Pueblo and Alabama and Coushatta Indian Tribes of Texas Restoration Act*, 106th Cong., 2d sess., 2000, H. Rep. 106-830; Senate Committee on Indian Affairs, Amending the Ysleta del Sur Pueblo and Alabama and Coushatta Indian Tribes of Texas Restoration Act to Decrease the Requisite Blood Quantum Required for Membership in the Ysleta del Sur Pueblo Tribe, 106th Cong., 2d sess., 2000, S. Rep. 106-464.

39. Reid, "Forgotten People," 74; Rich Burk, "Gaming on Indian Lands in Sight," Racing Notebook, *Houston Chronicle*, November 22, 1992, sec. Sports 2, p. 33; Dianna Hunt, "The Native Lands of Texas; A Better Life on Reservation; Kickapoos Upbeat About Future Despite Poverty," *Houston Chronicle*, June 26, 1994, Sunday 2 star ed., sec. state, p. 1; John W. Gonzales, "Use of Tribal Funds Questioned; Leaders' Status in Limbo as 'Golden Goose' Casino Sits Idle," *Houston Chronicle*, November 24, 2002, Sunday 4 star ed., sec. A, p. 37.

40. Dianna Hunt, "Native Texans; Tribal Lawsuits Stake Claims to Most of Texas; Indians Seem Certain to Win Some Land," *Houston Chronicle*, June 26, 1994; James Kimberly, "Court Ruling May Mean 'Millions' to Alabama-Coushatta," *Houston Chronicle*, July 7, 2000; Mary Lee Grant, "Indian Tribe Could Receive Millions in Land Dispute," Associated Press state and local wire, July 7, 2000; Mary Lee Grant, "East Texas Indian Tribe Votes On Setting Up Their Own Legal System," Associated Press state and local wire, June 29, 2000; Mary Lee Grant, "Alabama-Coushatta Work to Preserve Culture," Associated Press state and local wire, July 25, 2000.

41. Dianna Hunt, "Native Texans; Urban Indians Come Out of the Shadows; Groups Seeking Identity, Opportunity," *Houston Chronicle*, July 3, 1994, Sunday 2 star ed., sec. A, p. 1; Patty Reinert, "Of Artifact and Fiction," *Houston Chronicle*, May 30, 1999, Sunday 2 star ed., sec. state, p. 1; Associated Press state and local wire, "In Show of Sensitivity, Area School Dropping Indian Mascots," May 24, 1999, Monday, PM cycle; Associated Press state and local wire, "Illegal Collecting of American Indian Artifacts More Common, Law Officers Say," November 8, 1999, Monday, PM cycle; Ruth Sorelle, "Native Americans Weigh Need for Clinic; Council Sponsors Health Screening," *Houston Chronicle*, March 28, 1992, Saturday 2 star ed., sec. A, p. 27; Kevin Moran, "Indian Group Lodges Subdivision Protest; Claims Galveston Graves Desecrated," *Houston Chronicle*, March 11, 1992, Wednesday 2 star ed., sec. A, p. 20; "Federal Clinic Sought for American Indians," *Houston Chronicle*, October 29, 1993, Friday 2 star ed., sec. A, p. 36; Marty Racine, "Not Enough Warriors; Lawrence Simpson Fought for the U.S.; Now He Fights For His People," *Houston Chronicle*, April 28, 1998, Tuesday 2 star ed., sec. Houston, p. 1; Salatheia Bryant, "Group Attacks Use of Indian-Related Mascots in Schools," *Houston Chronicle*, October 3, 1999, Sunday 4 star ed., sec. A, p. 37; Salatheia Bryant, "Indian Leader Says HISD Retreats on Mascot Issue," *Houston Chronicle*, October 5, 1999, Tuesday 3 star ed., sec. A, p. 24; Angus Durocher, "The Spirit of Tradition American Indian Heritage," *Austin American-Statesman*, November 3, 1994, sec. XL Entertainment; "Intertribal Council Plans Powwow," *Houston Chronicle*, May 22, 1992, Friday 2 star ed., sec. Weekend Preview, p. 2; "Weekend Powwow," *Houston Chronicle*, May 30, 1993, Sunday 3 star ed., sec. B, p. 19; "American Indian Artists Show Off Their Works," *Houston Chronicle*, February 26, 1993, Friday 2 star ed., sec. Weekend Preview, p. 1;"American Indians Plan Gathering," *Houston Chronicle*, May 27, 1994, Friday 2 star ed., sec. Weekend Preview, p. 1; "Tribal Reflections Festival is Born," *Houston Chronicle*, November 11, 1994, Friday 2 star ed., sec. Weekend Preview, p. 1; "Texas A&M Plans Native American Week," *Houston Chronicle*, February 4, 1995, Saturday 2 star ed., sec. Houston, p. 3; Edward Hegstrom, "American Indian Leaders Gather in Bid to Organize Politically, Celebrate Culture," *Houston Chronicle*, July 16, 1999, Friday 3 star ed., sec. A, p. 32; Rebecca Mowbray, "Houston Livestock Show and Rodeo; Cowboys and Indians; Native Americans Finally Welcomed to Join Rodeo Festivities," *Houston Chronicle*, February 22, 2000, Tuesday 3 star ed., sec. A, p. 16.

The Quest for Identity and Citizenship

Mexican Americans in Twentieth-Century Texas

Anthony Quiroz

THE TWENTIETH CENTURY WAS one of challenge, failure, triumph, and change for the Mexican-American population of Texas.
During this one-hundred-year period, Mexican Americans engaged
in an armed revolt that led to a vicious official reaction and served
in every major U.S. war and international conflict. Through it all,
Mexican Americans created an identity for themselves as first-class
American citizens, an identity that then shaped their struggles for
civil rights. Despite the persistence of problems such as poverty,
limited opportunity, and racism, Mexican Americans in the 1900s
became better educated and developed a vibrant professional class
that is gaining increasing levels of national influence. This progress
was made possible by the efforts of various individual leaders and
organizations that challenged the status quo and ultimately created
a more equitable society for all citizens.

Given the complexity of Mexican-American history in the
twentieth century, it is helpful to divide the story into four periods, in order to analyze the discrete conditions people faced at a
given point in time. These four periods are 1900–1930, the immigrant generation; 1930–1960, the Mexican-American generation;

1960–1980, the Chicano generation; and 1980–present, the Hispanic generation. To be sure, people's actions did not fit neatly into these packages; there was overlap. But, generally speaking, these clusters identify the essential historical trajectory of Texas' Mexican Americans. Each of these periods presented Mexican Americans with specific challenges, led to different responses, and engendered a unique identity. Emerging from this study are several themes that further illuminate the Mexican-American experience. One crucial theme for understanding Mexican-American history is what theorists refer to as "alterity," or "otherness," which means having one's status defined as standing outside the dominant society. Such groups or individuals are seen as unassimilable, as well as undesirable, and are the victims of discrimination and oppression. At the start of the century the Anglo population generally viewed Mexican Americans as "other," as different, and as foreigners. *Tejanos* experienced this treatment even though they claimed Indian and Spanish roots dating back to the eighteenth century. Because of the political and social upheavals of the nineteenth century that separated Texas from Mexico, Mexicans living in Texas after 1836 (or those living in the American Southwest after 1848) became "indigenous immigrants." As immigrants in their own territory, Tejanos were ascribed second-class citizenship and experienced rampant discrimination and marginalization. [1]

The pressures of this second-class status gave rise to two other key themes: identity and citizenship. Throughout the twentieth century Tejanos struggled for recognition as citizens, the equals of Anglos. Voting, suing to end discriminatory practices, organizing communities and workers, and pursuing ever-increasing levels of educational attainment, Tejanos sought their place in Texas society as first-class citizens. The battle for citizenship was driven by the issue of identity. As Tejanos developed a self-image as American citizens, they then sought inclusion as equal citizens. As the social environment around them changed and as the nature of their own American identity also shifted throughout the century, so too did their goals and methods of resistance. In the first half of the century, for example, Tejano identity formed within the context of a society that conceived of itself as white and Protestant and whose bloodlines and intellectual and cultural traditions were traceable to northern and western Europe. People from other parts of the world with different histories, features, traditions, and religions were all viewed with suspicion and considered as potentially unworthy of the appellation "citizen." Understanding this, Mexican-American activists argued for acceptance as members of the white race. In the 1960s and 1970s, however, many activists redefined themselves as Chicanos who were distinct from whites. These individuals emphasized the indigenous portion of their roots, shunning the Spanish, European oppressor in their genetic past. More recently, Mexican-American identity has metamorphosed into a new manifestation: Hispanic.[2]

One final theme is immigration. Unlike European immigrants who stand separated from their roots and culture by time and an ocean, Mexican immigrants have family members and other ties to a neighboring nation. Three waves of immigration have had a profound demographic impact on the nation and the state. One occurred during and after World War II, and the final one began toward the end of the century and still continues. But the first massive wave of immigration from Mexico commenced with the onset of the Mexican Revolution of 1910. Pushed out by the turbulence of that revolution and pulled northward by the hope of jobs, safety, and security, over 600,000 Mexicans moved into the United States from 1910 to 1930, thus giving rise to the appellation "immigrant generation." A good number of these revolutionary refugees wound up in Texas. The Mexican-born population of the state grew from 71,000 in 1900 to over 266,000 in 1930. The Mexican population of San Antonio grew from 13,000 to over 82,000 during this same period. This wave of immigration had a direct impact on local communities. [3]

The majority of immigrants were peasant workers who took jobs on farms and ranches. These individuals supplied rural employers with an inexpensive, easily exploitable workforce upon which many south Texas agricultural fortunes were built. Wealthier immigrants enjoyed a measure of independence because they brought their expertise and resources with them. Ignacio E. Lozano, for instance, came to San Antonio from Mexico in 1908. In 1913 he founded *La Prensa*, thereby adding significantly to an already strong Spanish-language press in the state. *La Prensa*, along with similar publications in cities like Laredo and El Paso, focused on events in Mexico and instances of mistreatment of Mexican Americans. To a large degree, the presence of this press contributed to the continuation of a Mexican culture and identity even as other sociological processes were creating a more Americanized self-image.[4]

In the midst of the turmoil caused by the Mexican Revolution and the ensuing emigration north to the United States sprang a stunning, but little known, revolutionary plot. In 1915 a Mexican named Basilio Ramos was arrested in San Diego, Texas. Authorities discovered among his personal possessions a document entitled "el plan de San Diego," which called for an uprising of the Mexican, black, and Native American populations in the American Southwest. And, in fact, there were some instances of violence against Anglos in south Texas until the Texas Rangers arrived and carried out a bloody crackdown, brutally killing several thousand Tejanos and Mexican immigrants. Although the uprising was crushed, it contributed to a nascent sense of identity, as Tejanos began to think of themselves as American citizens deserving not only the protection of the law, but protection from it as well.[5]

The 1920s gave rise to nativism as expressed by the growth of the Ku Klux Klan and a strong anti-foreigner sentiment. Immigrants had been flooding into the country, not only from Mexico, but also primarily from southern and eastern Europe since the late nineteenth century. The first two decades of the twentieth century, however, were by far the busiest in terms of such immigration. As a result, Congress passed two major anti-immigration bills in the 1920s: the Emergency Immigration Act of 1921, which limited the number of immigrants from any one country to the number represented by 3 percent of that nationality's 1910 presence in the U.S., and the Johnson-Reed Act of 1924, which tightened those restrictions to 2 percent of a given population in 1890, a time when there were even fewer members of "undesirable" groups such as Greeks, Slavs, and Italians. Mexicans, however, found themselves largely exempted from this legislation thanks to the needs of southwestern farmers. As David Montejano has shown, a substantial portion of south Texas landowners switched from ranching to commercial farming in the early decades of the twentieth century. This economic shift created the need for more low-wage workers than ever before. Thus, the "push" effect of the Mexican Revolution was complemented by the "pull" of a growing labor market north of the Rio Grande. [6]

Meanwhile, long-term residents, some of whom claimed Texan lineage back to the days of early Spanish settlement, were undergoing a change in their own personal identity. Much like the newcomers from Mexico, these old-timers had traditionally seen themselves as Mexicans who happened to live in the United States. Their language, culture, and political loyalties remained staunchly Mexican. Indeed, the resistance movements of the nineteenth century, as manifested by Juan Cortina and Gregorio Cortez, were celebrated, not because they led to instant equality or significant social change. Rather, the memories of these men and others like them were revered because they stood for resistance to Anglo domination of American society. But with the slow growth of a Mexican-American middle class and the experience of World War I, Tejanos increasingly came to see themselves as Americans who happened to be of Mexican origin. Certainly, not all Tejanos saw themselves in this light, but the trend was in that direction by the 1920s. Gradually, with increasing levels of educational and business success, combined with military service during World War I, a war "to make the world safe for democracy," these individuals and their families developed a strong sense of themselves as American citizens and believed they had license to assert this identity in their quest for citizenship.

But this new identity was complicated. To say that these citizens saw themselves now as Americans did not mean that they gave up their language, culture, religion, food, or traditions. Rather, it meant that they had come to understand that their future lay on the northern side of the Rio Grande. They developed a belief in the American system of government and its political system. This outlook defined the general worldview of the Mexican-American generation that dates from about 1930 to 1960. Indeed, one of the earliest public expressions of this new American identity came from a new organization created in Corpus Christi in 1929: the League of United Latin American Citizens (LULAC).[7]

LULAC arose from the merging of numerous other civil rights organizations that had sprung up in the post-World War I years, such as the Order of Sons of America (OSA) and the Sons of America (SOA). Driven by a budding middle class of businessmen and professionals, LULAC was conceived as a bicultural civic organization to promote equality for Mexican Americans by endorsing patriotism, an acceptance of American values, practices, traits, and beliefs, and usage of the English language, but retaining fealty to the Spanish language and Mexican cultural traditions.[8]

If LULAC exemplified the desires of the middle class, then mutual aid societies and labor unions represented the concerns of workers. Much like other immigrant groups, Mexicans formed mutual aid societies, or *mutualistas,* in the nineteenth and twentieth centuries. They were designed to help members cope with the economic hardships of poverty by acting as a type of insurance agency. They also offered the security of numbers and acted as public advocates for social justice. The earliest such organization in Texas was the *Sociedad Benito Juárez*, formed in Corpus Christi in 1879. Similar groups soon sprang up in Brownsville and other parts of the state with heavy Mexican and Tejano populations. Beyond insurance-type benefits and a public voice, *mutualistas* often provided members fraternity and socialization opportunities through fundraisers and benefits. In so doing they softened the harsh realities of life for Tejanos, as did labor unions. Because of racism among American unions, however, Tejanos sometimes turned for protection to Mexican unions or created their own. Hence, Tejanos in El Paso and other places occasionally organized themselves and went on strike for higher wages, fairer treatment, and better working conditions. [9]

Throughout the first three decades of the century, Mexican Americans actively sought social change through either working-class organizations, the newly created LULAC, or other similar groups. Unfortunately, the creation of LULAC, which was a key marker of the onset of the Mexican-American generation, came just before the October 1929 stock market crash, which plunged the economy into a tailspin. With the onset of the Great Depression, Mexican Americans turned their focus from citizenship to survival.

The Great Depression caused Americans to rethink their assumptions about poverty as a sign of individual weakness. Suddenly, educated or skilled workers found themselves unemployed. Mounting unemployment taxed local charitable agencies beyond their limits. Institutions designed to help a small number of needy people for brief periods of time were quickly overextended as they were unable to handle massive unemployment and underemployment that were fated to last until the onset of World War II. Tejanos reacted in various ways to the effects of the Great Depression. Some were fortunate enough to get work through various New Deal programs, such as the Civilian Conservation Corps and the Public Works Administration. Additionally, Tejano labor organization increased during the depression. In one particularly celebrated instance, Mexican-American women organized themselves and struck against the pecan shelling industry.[10]

On January 31, 1938, pecan shellers, who were predominantly Mexican-American women on San Antonio's West Side, went on strike under the banner of the United Cannery, Agricultural, Packing and Allied Workers of America (UCAPAWA), a union that belonged to the newly formed Congress of Industrial Organizations (CIO). Led by Emma Tenayuca, the striking workers embarked on a three-month-long ordeal. They were protesting a recent cut in wages, a move employers justified on the curiously racist argument that if the workers received more pay they would leave work early and fritter away their money on tequila and other inconsequential items. Such charges were of course false, as these were poor women trying to support their families. During the strike Police Chief Owen Kilday's force used strong-arm tactics and harassment against the strikers and their supporters. Governor James Allred ordered an investigation by the Texas Industrial Commission (TIC), which found that the police had violated strikers' civil rights and had unfairly prohibited the legal, peaceful assembly of the picketers. At best, this was merely a pyrrhic victory, for company owners soon replaced the strikers with machines.[11]

During this time of crisis a new negative stereotype of the Mexican emerged: that of a threat to economic stability. Prior to the Great Depression, Mexicans had been reviled as an inferior race, as practitioners of the corrupt Catholic faith, and as generally dirty, lazy, promiscuous, and untrustworthy. Now they came to be seen by Anglo Texans as a burden to an already debilitated job market. In response to this perceived threat, some states and the federal government engaged in a massive repatriation effort, forcing many Mexicans from states like Texas and California to return to Mexico, which was also in the grips of the global depression. From 1929 through 1939 approximately 250,000 "Mexicans" were sent back to Mexico from Texas, even though some of the repatriates were

American citizens. This was a period when the dominant Anglo society made no distinction between foreign-born Mexicans and American-born Mexicans. The latter's American citizenship made no difference in the way they were treated. Indeed, it was exactly this attitude that organizations such as LULAC were resisting. Meanwhile, as the depression dragged on, war clouds were gathering over Europe and Asia.[12]

Fascism had been on the rise since the early 1930s. The aggressive behavior of Italy, Germany, and Japan, the Axis powers, prompted the U.S., even before the Japanese bombing of Pearl Harbor on December 7, 1941, to enact the selective service. The first draft number drawn by President Franklin D. Roosevelt in the fall of 1941 was that of Pedro Aguilar of Los Angeles, California. Although not a Texan, the selection of a Mexican American as the first person called for the military draft was symbolically significant. Since early in the century an American identity had been percolating and growing within the Mexican-American community, and the World War II experience strengthened this self-perception of Mexican Americans as Americans of Mexican extraction. But that tendency was about to be challenged seriously once Mexicans were invited back into the United States to work during the war.

Conscription and voluntary enlistment in large numbers resulted in a massive labor shortage at the very time that unprecedented levels of industrial and agricultural production were required. To fill the industrial labor gap, women and minorities, including Mexican Americans, flocked to cities with a large military presence or industrial base in search of jobs. The result was a tremendous agricultural labor shortage that left farmers throughout the nation, particularly the Southwest, deprived of adequate numbers of workers. Thus, on August 4, 1942, the federal government entered into an agreement with Mexico to secure Mexican labor through the *bracero* program. According to the arrangement, Mexican workers were to be paid "prevailing wages" and could not be used as strikebreakers. As events turned out, however, the concept of a "prevailing wage" was ambiguous at best, and *braceros* found themselves, in some cases, used to break strikes. The accord involved other stipulations as well but, lacking an enforcement agency to oversee the program, conditions frequently devolved into a degraded state for imported workers that had been unimagined by either American or Mexican officials. Even so, the arrangement proved lucrative for agribusiness.

Starting in 1943 the Mexican government refused to send workers into Texas because the state had built such a negative image in the minds of Mexican officials. Instead, Mexico developed a blacklist of all Texas counties. Only after convincing the Mexican government that its citizens would be treated fairly could a county be removed from the list. In order to remedy this situation, the Texas legislature passed the Caucasian Race Resolution in 1943. This bill made it illegal to discriminate against any member of the white race, while declaring people of Mexican descent to be white. The implications of this ruling were profound. For the first time in Texas history the state government posited categorically that Mexicans were white. This "other white" status opened the door to litigation that ended school segregation and other forms of discrimination. At the same time the federal Office for Inter-American Affairs, charged by President Roosevelt with strengthening relationships with Latin America, funded a state-level Good Neighbor Commission (GNC) staffed by six men appointed by Governor Coke Stevenson. The purpose of the GNC was to smooth over tensions between Mexicans and Mexican Americans on the one hand, and Anglo Americans on the other. The GNC was replicated at the county level, but some locations took their responsibility less seriously than others. The main weakness of the GNC was its lack of enforcement power. Thus, apart from a request to cease engaging in discriminatory behavior, the agency had no weapons. Despite the fact that exploitation of workers continued and many counties remained formally blacklisted, Mexico lifted the ban on Texas counties in 1947.

The *bracero* episode is important because of what it signified and because of the fact that it marked the second major twentieth-century wave of immigration from Mexico to the United States. Originally designed to help American farmers ride out the wartime labor shortage, the program lasted until 1964, by which time around five million Mexicans had immigrated to the United States. These immigrants, in combination with the resident Mexican-American population, provided the labor for agriculture, mining, railroad operations, and other fundamental industries. But some Mexican Americans criticized the program. After the war's end the American GI Forum (AGIF) and LULAC argued that the project led to human rights abuses and took jobs away from Mexican Americans. Beyond this, the continued influx of Mexican immigrants reinforced negative stereotypes that members of LULAC and the AGIF were attempting to overcome.[13]

At the same time, Mexican-American men were drafted or enlisted in the military. A developing sense of Americanism, along with the resultant patriotism, fueled their participation in military service. Men who were not drafted volunteered willingly to join the fray. Fighting in integrated units, in contrast to black troops, these men interacted with people from all over the United States. Mexican-American servicemen were surprised to learn that men from Pennsylvania, Indiana, New York, and other places did not harbor the anti-Mexican attitudes of their Texas compatriots. Indeed, once in uniform and firing at the enemy overseas, all GIs were regarded by Europeans and Asians as "Americans."

Further, many Tejano servicemen received job training and other skills, resulting in the creation of a group of individuals who felt newly competent and empowered. These men and their families entered the post-war era steeled by their wartime experiences to engage another old enemy at home: continued discrimination. They were spurred on by two factors. First, they believed that, as a group, they had earned equal American citizenship by virtue of their bravery and contributions during the war. They had made those sacrifices in a war against fascist totalitarian societies that had been established on the principles of hierarchy and social inequality, racism, and genocide. Second, this generation built upon the spirit of Americanism that had been growing since the 1920s. Tejanos embraced widely held American ideals and pursued material success by seeking education and economic mobility. They accepted the extant political structure and encouraged voting and political activism. For these reasons Mexican Americans began to demand equality from the society for which they had fought and died.

Two post-war episodes involving GIs represent this new attitude. The first concerned Macario García, who was born in 1920 in Villa de Castaño, Mexico. In 1923 his family of twelve moved to the United States and settled near Sugar Land, where García worked until drafted into the army in November 1942. García served overseas with distinction, earning several awards, including the Medal of Honor for single-handedly, and while severely wounded, eliminating two German machine-gun nests. Upon returning to Texas after the war, García was refused service at a diner in Richmond, Texas. Despite the pleadings of two Anglo sailors who pointed out García's medals, the owner was unmoved. A fight ensued. Law enforcement officials arrived and promptly arrested García. By this time, however, García's name was already well-known around the state because of his bravery. The media backlash was swift and harsh. But the most significant aspect of this incident was the way in which it represented the willingness of Mexican Americans to continue fighting for equality at home.[14]

The second event involving GIs in the immediate post-war period centered on the burial of a soldier from south Texas. Private Felix Longoria of Three Rivers, a small town about eighty miles from Corpus Christi, died in combat in the Philippines in 1945. In January 1949 his remains were found and shipped home. His widow, Beatriz Longoria, sought to hold Longoria's wake at the

Rice Funeral Home, the only one in town. Owner Tom Kennedy refused her request, explaining that local Anglos "would not like it" if he served a Mexican family. The local, segregated cemetery underscored his point. Beatriz' sister, Sara Moreno, then contacted Dr. Hector P. García, president of the fledgling American GI Forum. García called Kennedy and tried to reason with him. When that failed, García contacted public officials, including the newly elected U.S. Senator from Texas, Lyndon B. Johnson. Johnson informed García that no existing law applied to the situation. As senator, however, Johnson could arrange for Longoria to be interred at a military cemetery in San Antonio, or in Washington, D.C., at Arlington National Cemetery. Meanwhile, the Corpus Christi *Caller-Times* had been covering the unfolding events, and the story quickly assumed national proportions. In an attempt to save face, the mayor of Three Rivers, J. K. Montgomery, argued that the entire affair was the result of a misunderstanding. The Three Rivers newspaper, the *Three Rivers News*, editorialized in defense of the city in an effort to salvage the city's tarnished image. But it was too late. The story was out and the damage was done. The Longoria family opted to have Private Longoria buried in Arlington National Cemetery. In this instance, Longoria was doubly the hero. Having given his life to protect the country he loved, his death and burial contributed to an up-and-coming Mexican-American civil rights movement. Meanwhile, actions were being taken to combat racism on other fronts.[15]

Education was central to the ideology of the ascendant Mexican-American leadership, as represented by LULAC and the AGIF. To Mexican Americans of all economic backgrounds, education seemed to hold the key to a better future. So when veterans returned from the war and found their children still relegated to separate, inferior schools, they turned to the courts for relief. Mexican Americans had been placed in educational facilities separated from both Anglo and African-American students since early in the twentieth century. Thus, after the war, groups such as LULAC and the AGIF began cooperating with attorneys to bring suit against districts that engaged in such discrimination.

In Texas, the first significant school segregation suit took place in Bastrop in 1948 when LULAC and AGIF joined forces to fund a team of attorneys led by Gus C. García, who demonstrated clearly to federal judge Ben Rice that wholesale separation of Mexican children on the basis of race was unconstitutional according to guarantees of equal protection under the Fourteenth Amendment. Persuaded by the plaintiff's arguments, Rice ruled that children could be separated only through the first grade, and only after students were tested individually for language deficiencies. Otherwise, students were to be placed in integrated schools. Despite this landmark ruling, segregation continued around the state, forcing LULAC, AGIF, and a cadre of attorneys, such as García, Carlos Cadena, Ed Idar, James DeAnda, John J. Herrera, and others to challenge the institutionalized racism in the Driscoll, Kingsville, Cuero, Kyle, and other districts. The problem was not only that students were being sent to separate schools from Anglos, but also the inferior quality of the so-called "Mexican schools." [16]

In Texas, Anglo schools were better furnished and supplied. Teachers at Anglo schools received higher pay and often held stronger credentials. Play areas at Mexican schools lacked equipment, and in some cases even grass. In Mathis, the outhouse at the Mexican school was so filthy and putrid that students had to "do their business" outside the building. But as troubling as any of these problems was the fact that the Mexican-school curriculum was designed to teach basic English and math skills to prepare pupils for life as laborers, not to give them the intellectual tools necessary to succeed in college and the professions.

Ultimately, separate Mexican schools were shut down one at a time throughout the state. What emerged instead was a system of de facto segregation through segregated neighborhood schools.

Mexican Ward School. Courtesy Dr. Hector P. Garcia Papers, Special Collections & Archives, Mary and Jeff Bell Library, Texas A&M University-Corpus Christi.

Modern Mathis High School. Courtesy Dr. Hector P. Garcia Papers, Special Collections & Archives, Mary and Jeff Bell Library, Texas A&M University-Corpus Christi.

Even with this development, however, more and more Mexican-American children began attending and completing elementary and secondary school as well as enrolling in college. Indeed, it was the children of this activist generation who began attending school in unprecedented numbers. This in turn gave rise to the youth movement in the Chicano uprising of the 1960s and early 1970s.

Mexican Americans employed the courts to challenge more than just educational discrimination. In 1950 Pete Hernandez had been charged, tried, convicted, and sentenced to death for the murder of Joe Espinosa of Edna, Texas. Four years later Gus C. García and Carlos Cadena took his case on appeal. It was the all-Anglo composition of the Jackson County jury that eventually won Hernandez a retrial. In arguments before the U.S. Supreme Court in January 1954, García showed that no Mexican American had served as a juror in Jackson County in the past twenty-five years even though Mexican Americans accounted for 14 percent of the county's population. Further bolstering Hernandez's case was the fact that even the public restrooms at the Jackson County courthouse, where the Hernandez trial had been held, were segregated. The Court found the case compelling and ruled that Hernandez had not received a fair jury trial of his peers. The high court concluded that historical practices in Jackson County relegated Mexican Americans, though members of the white race, to a second-class status. As such, they endured the same discrimination as non-whites. Hence, Hernandez was retried, and once again found guilty and sentenced to prison, but this time the jury was drawn from a pool that included Mexican Americans.[17]

Also bringing about positive change by the Mexican-American generation was a belief in the American political ideology and the two-party system. Thus, Mexican Americans also turned to political activity in the years following World War II. LULAC, the AGIF, and numerous other local Mexican-American organizations encouraged individuals to pay their poll taxes and vote. Before the

Twenty-fourth Amendment ended the practice in federal elections, poll taxes were a common method used by states to prevent minorities and poor whites from voting. Although relatively inexpensive, the poll tax was prohibitive to a family on a shoestring budget. Beyond the price of the tax, however, was the intimidation that accompanied a visit to the county clerk's office to register. Public servants in the American Southwest were not always welcoming of "undesirables" such as African and Mexican Americans. And compounding the problem for Mexican Americans was the insecurity engendered by a relative lack of education. To entice voters to register and pay the tax, organizations often held "pay your poll tax" and "get out the vote" drives, or held dances or other functions in which the price of admission was a poll tax receipt. Local organizations also held forums through which local voters could listen to and interact with candidates running for office. Their activities resulted in greater Mexican-American political participation, but the high point for large-scale electoral activism came with John F. Kennedy's campaign for the presidency in 1960.[18]

During the Kennedy campaign Mexican Americans in Texas and around the country created "Viva Kennedy" clubs. To Mexican-American voters, JFK represented a new day in American politics. Catholic, liberal, Democratic, interested in civil rights, Kennedy made a much more appealing candidate to Mexican Americans than his Republican opponent, Richard M. Nixon. And when Kennedy chose Senator Lyndon B. Johnson as his running mate, the Democratic ticket was irresistible to Mexican Americans, who remembered Johnson's assistance with the burial of Private Felix Longoria.

The Kennedy-Johnson ticket turned out to be a mixed blessing for Mexican-American activists. Adhering to a traditional black/white racial paradigm, Kennedy not only focused primarily on African-American concerns, but also moved cautiously on civil rights so as not to alienate conservative southern Dixiecrats. After Kennedy's assassination in November 1963, Johnson proved more willing to act. Pushing through Great Society initiatives like the Civil Rights Act of 1964 and the Voting Rights Act of 1965, Johnson led the fight on Capitol Hill for minorities, women, and the poor. Unfortunately, while Johnson understood the plight of Mexican Americans in Texas and elsewhere, most of the bureaucrats under him did not. They neither fully grasped nor adequately responded to Mexican-American concerns, and efforts aimed at solving black/white issues did not always apply directly to Mexican Americans.[19]

Meanwhile, Mexican-American activists in Texas and around the Southwest were waging war on other fronts and using different tactics. In southern California in 1962 César Chávez and Dolores Huerta organized Filipino and Mexican workers into the United Farm Workers of America (UFWA). Made up primarily of Mexicans and Mexican Americans, this new union engaged the public's support in a five-year grape strike that led to union recognition and somewhat improved wages and working conditions. The UFWA came to Texas in 1966 under the name United Farm Workers (UFW). In subsequent years the UFW engaged in strikes and boycotts to improve the lives of agricultural workers. One high point of the civil rights era in Texas was *la marcha,* a minimum-wage demonstration, from the Rio Grande Valley to Austin. Supported by numerous organizations, including the AGIF and LULAC, south Texas farm workers made the trek to draw attention to their plight. Governor John Connally refused to meet with the marchers in Austin, instead seeing them briefly in New Braunfels, where he rejected their calls for a special session of the legislature to address their concerns. The appearance of predominantly Mexican-American unions and attendant strikes marked a new era in the Mexican-American struggle for civil rights. Whereas activists during the Mexican-American generation employed the vote and the courts for improving conditions, organizers of the 1960s and 1970s resorted more directly to confrontational tactics and embraced an ideology more in keeping with the identity shift from Mexican American to Chicano.[20]

Whereas Mexican Americans had heretofore adopted a white identity, as Chicanos they now stressed their uniqueness as the descendents of Aztecs who had swept into central Mexico from their mythical homeland in the American Southwest, a territory known to activists as Aztlán. This new identity embraced the Spanish language and Mexican customs. Chicanos felt no need to appear acceptable to whites. Indeed, Chicanismo was marked by a strong sense of cultural nationalism and separatism. In contrast to the ideology of the Mexican-American generation, which Chicanos reviled as overly accommodationist, the Chicano worldview embraced a stinging critique of capitalism, the political structure, and what the new generation of activists criticized as half-hearted measures toward educational and social equality. Nationally, the Chicano movement manifested its ideology and objectives in four ways: the organization of farm workers, the land reclamation project led by Reies Lopez Tijerina in New Mexico, the youth movement, and the Raza Unida party. While Tijerina's land reclamation initiative never extended beyond New Mexico, Texas was an integral part of the youth and political movements.[21]

In Texas the most vivid expression of youth activism was the Mexican American Youth Organization (MAYO). Created in San Antonio by José Angel Gutiérrez, William ("Willie") Velásquez, Mario Compean, Ignacio Pérez, and Juan Patlán, MAYO organized school walkouts, also known as "blowouts," across the state in places like Edcouch, Elsa, Weslaco, Crystal City, Corpus Christi, and other locations. In 1969 Gutiérrez returned to his hometown of Crystal City, a community in which Mexican Americans constituted a majority but whose political structures were dominated by local Anglo businessmen. Eager for change, Mexicans had swept the city council elections and the mayoral race in 1963, but they retained control for only one term, inasmuch as the Anglo opposition engaged in a campaign of slander and resistance that undercut the slate's ability to sustain its momentum. Local Texas Ranger A. Y.

Allee even refused to hand over the keys to city hall offices after the group won the election. Six years later, when Gutiérrez returned, local Chicano high school students were embroiled in a controversy over the cheerleader selection process, which limited the number of Mexicans who could cheer. Gutiérrez immediately organized the students and their parents and led an electoral takeover of the school board and city council. After successfully organizing voters in Crystal City in 1969, MAYO turned its attention to creating a national third party—the Raza Unida Party (RUP)—to serve Chicano interests. This political movement is the fourth manifestation of the Chicano movement.[22]

Holding its first national convention in El Paso in 1972, the new party chose Gutiérrez as national chairman after a long, divisive struggle against Rodolfo "Corky" Gonzales of Denver. The convention also nominated Ramsey Muñiz, a young attorney from Corpus Christi, as the party's candidate for governor in that year's race. Clearly, Muñiz' chances of success were virtually non-existent, yet he and his supporters ran a vigorous campaign and took 6 percent (over 214,000 votes) of the total popular vote in the November general election. To be sure, this was hardly a competitive figure, but it made the contest between the Democrats and the Republicans much tighter than usual. By 1972 the Republican Party had been making slow but steady electoral gains around the state. Normally, the Democratic candidate for governor won easily, but this year the race was unusually close and Muñiz' 6 percent came from the Democratic ranks. Although Democrat Dolph Briscoe won anyway, he did so with a mere plurality, not a solid majority as in years past. Muñiz and the RUP presented a potential problem to the Democratic Party. Muñiz ran again in 1974, this time garnering only 190,000 votes. Meanwhile, RUP candidates were running for local offices in a handful of counties around south Texas, winning in Zavala County (Crystal City) and a few other locations, such as Kyle and Lockhart.[22]

But the RUP represented a very tenuous coalition that survived by carefully balancing the conflicting interests of its various constituencies, such as businessmen and students, urban interests and rural needs. When the Corpus Christi *Caller-Times* announced in the summer of 1975 that Ramsey Muñiz was wanted by federal officials on drug smuggling charges, the party began to fall apart. Not wanting to be tarred with a broad brush, more conservative elements began to drop out. In the 1978 gubernatorial election the party's candidate, Mario Compean, received only 15,000 votes. Thereafter the party effectively crumbled and the Chicano era faded. Even so, the movement left a lasting legacy. First, post-World War II activism in the form of political action and lawsuits, combined with the labor organization and comparative radicalism of the Chicano era, made clear that Mexican Americans would no longer be satisfied with second-class citizenship. Second, new groups, such as the Mexican American Legal Defense and Education Fund (MALDEF) and the Southwest Voter Registration and Education Project (SWVREP), which was created by MAYO co-founder Willie Velásquez arose from the ferment of the Chicano movement. Simultaneously, a new identity took shape. By the early 1980s forces outside the Mexican-American community, such as political developments, mass media hype, and business' discovery of a growing demographic, melded Mexican Americans with Puerto Ricans, Cubans, and other Spanish-speaking ethnic groups into a new kind of person: the Hispanic.[23]

In 1981 Henry Cisneros was elected mayor of San Antonio, becoming the first Mexican-American mayor of a major American city. He went on to serve as secretary of Housing and Urban Development during President Bill Clinton's second term. Cisneros' successful political trajectory paralleled the rise of other Spanish-surnamed politicians, such as Bob Martinez (Cuban) of Florida and Federico Peña (Mexican) of Denver. Cisneros' victory marked the beginning of a new wave of electoral victories for Mexican-American political candidates around the state. Two major factors explain this phenomenon. First, the rising education level of Mexican Americans now paid dividends in terms of a visible, viable, professional class of individuals who were educated, financed, and confident enough to run potentially successful campaigns. Second, MALDEF instigated a series of lawsuits around the state challenging at-large voting practices on the grounds they were inherently unfair to minorities. This effort prompted many cities and counties to replace the at-large system with a new system of single member districts, which enhanced the electoral chances of minority candidates. With increased public visibility, Mexican-American professionals and politicians have come to occupy high-ranking offices. In Texas Hispanics have become state attorney general (Dan Morales), viable candidates for governor (Tony Sanchez), as well as fire chiefs, police chiefs, judges, state representatives and senators, and national representatives. [24]

The 1980s and 1990s also witnessed a boom in the expansion of Mexican-American culture in Texas. The Tejano music industry grew by leaps and bounds as audience demands created a new market for cumbias, polkas, waltzes, rancheras, and others. In the early 1990s one of the biggest talents on the Tejano scene was Selena Quintanilla Perez. Born and raised in Corpus Christi and part of a musical family, Selena performed with her family and was a rising star. She was on the verge of crossing over into the English-language market when her life was cut tragically short by Yolanda Saldivar, a 32-year-old woman who had founded Selena's fan club and managed the young star's San Antonio boutique. On March 31, 1995, Saldivar shot Selena at a Corpus Christi motel after being confronted with evidence that she had been embezzling money from the boutique. In October a Corpus Christi jury found Saldivar guilty of murder and sentenced her to life in prison. Tejano music fans from around the state and nation mourned the loss not only of such a talented young singer who was only 23, but also of the seemingly limitless possibility that she represented. Despite her death, the Tejano music scene continued to flourish unabated. Fitting with the theme of "Hispanicization," it was apropos that Jennifer Lopez, a Puerto Rican singer/actress from New York, played the lead role in the film *Selena*.

As is usually true of historical progression, people living at a specific moment—in this case, several generations of Mexican Americans—are not consciously aware of behaving in a certain way because of the calendar year. They simply respond to contemporary events and conditions in ways that make sense to them. Each subsequent generation builds upon the one that came before it, either embracing or rejecting earlier ideologies. Only in retrospect can one identify common traits that cut across each period and, presumably, carry over into the future. That is certainly the case with the generations discussed herein. First, Tejanos of any era have maintained some measure of loyalty to their language, history, and traditions. Second, Mexican Americans have utilized political activism to bring about change, either through voting, suing, demonstrating, running for office, or organizing an alternative political party. Mexican-American activists have always looked to politics as an important weapon against an oppressive society. Finally, educational advancement has had the most durable impact on Mexican-American history. A comparison of any city directory from ten, twenty, or forty years ago to the most current one will reveal a dramatic increase in Hispanic-surnamed accountants, judges, attorneys, dentists, MDs, teachers, business owners, and college professors.

That things have generally improved for Mexican Americans is undeniable, yet ongoing vigilance is required to protect gains made since the 1960s. In 1995, for instance, the state Fifth Circuit Court of Appeals ruled in *Hopwood v. Texas* that the University of Texas Law School could use neither race nor ethnicity in making admissions decisions. More recently, as immigration reform has taken center stage nationally, a group of private citizens from Arizona calling themselves the "Minutemen" have begun patrolling

the U.S.-Mexican border to report sightings of illegal aliens crossing into the United States. That movement has spread to California and now Texas. Minutemen activists argue that they are simply
trying to help an overburdened Border Patrol secure the border.
To date, however, Minutemen actions and rhetoric have clearly focused on Hispanic immigrants coming from the south rather than
other immigrants coming in from the north, and their actions have
been criticized as vigilantism. Recent large-scale demonstrations in
support of immigrant rights have met with a backlash of anti-immigrant sentiment across the state and nation. Too frequently the
term "immigrant" has become code for "Hispanic."

Part of the reason for this image of illegal immigrants as Hispanic is due to the fact that since the 1970s the number of immigrants
to the United States from third-world nations in Latin America, the
Caribbean, and Asia has grown dramatically. As Mexicans, Guate-
malans, Salvadorans, and the like continue to move northward and
cluster in their own ethnic enclaves, as have all immigrant groups
before them, their presence has become more noticeable. One difference between this recent wave of immigration and the two previous instances (during the Mexican Revolution, and the later *bracero*
program) is that while the majority of immigrants still come from
Mexico, this time the immigrants are also coming in larger numbers than before from Central and South America. Together these
immigrants are moving to more non-traditional areas, such as the
Deep South and the small towns of the Midwest and Northeast.
The 2000 census shows that over half of the foreign-born population came from Latin America. In Texas, for instance, there were
approximately 2.9 million foreign-born residents in 2000, of whom
2.17 million came from Latin America. It is too early to tell the future impact of this latest round of immigration, but some outlines
can be identified with careful qualifications.[25]

First, the diversity of the Spanish-speaking immigrant community will have important sociological effects. Obviously, it will

help reinforce society's tendency to homogenize immigrants into a singular Hispanic identity. Second, tensions may emerge between various groups such as Mexicans, Puerto Ricans, and Cubans, not to mention potential friction as African Americans come to see their visibility eclipsed by the growing number of Hispanics. Further, the economic mobility of this large group of people will bode well or poorly for society depending on whether or not the middle and upper classes continue to flourish. At the same time, the needs of the poor must be addressed through jobs and education programs. The anti-immigrant lobby posits that Hispanic immigrants refuse to assimilate and that their presence will undermine American culture. Yet studies show that for Mexican immigrants, as with other immigrant groups in our nation's history, English becomes the dominant language by the third generation. While many Mexican Americans continue to retain their Spanish skills, others do not. English acquisition aside, Mexican and Hispanic cultures will to some degree continue to shape and inform the future of Texan popular culture. Already easily visible are billboards in Spanish. Numerous Spanish-language television systems (Azteca America, Univision, Telemundo) broadcast to large audiences. Salsa has become the nation's predominant condiment; Mexican food has infiltrated all levels of restaurants from fast food (Taco Bell) to more traditional restaurants such as the Taqueria Acapulco chain in Corpus Christi.

Texas stands today at a crossroads. More than ever its future is intertwined with that of its Hispanic residents, the majority of whom are Mexican Americans. How Texans react to this reality will shape the social, political, and economic future of the state. Indeed, Texas, along with other states such as California, New Mexico, and New York where demographics are also changing rapidly, may well serve as a barometer of sorts for the future socio-cultural makeup of the nation as a whole.

Selected Bibliography

Blanton, Carlos. *The Strange Career of Bilingual Education in Texas, 1836–1981.*
     College Station: Texas A&M University Press, 2004.
Foley, Neil. *The White Scourge: Mexicans, Blacks, and Poor Whites in Texas Cotton
     Culture.* Berkeley: University of California Press, 1997.
García, Ignacio, *Hector P. García: In Relentless Pursuit of Justice.* Houston: Arte
     Público Press, 2002.
García, Mario T. *Desert Immigrants: The Mexicans of El Paso, 1880-1920.* New
     Haven: Yale University Press, 1981.
García, Richard A. *Rise of the Mexican American Middle Class: San Antonio,
     1929–1941.* College Station: Texas A&M University Press, 1991.
Gutiérrez, José Angel. *The Making of a Chicano Militant: Lessons from Cristal.*
     Madison: University of Wisconsin Press, 1998.
Kreneck, Tom. *Mexican American Odyssey: Felix Tijerina, Entrepreneur and Civic
     Leader, 19051965.* College Station: Texas A&M University Press, 2001.
Montejano, David. *Anglos and Mexicans in the Making of Texas, 1836–1986.* Aus-
     tin: University of Texas Press, 1987.
Peña, Manuel. *Musica Tejana.* College Station: Texas A&M University Press,
     1999.
Richardson, Chad. *Batos, Bolillos, Pochos, and Pelados: Class and Culture on the
     South Texas Border.* Austin: University of Texas Press, 1999.

Endnotes

1. Mario T. García outlines a generational model for understanding Mexican-American history in *Mexican Americans: Politics, Leadership, Ideology, 1930-1960* (Princeton: Yale University Press, 1989), 14–21. Ignacio García and others have identified the "Chicano Generation" as having occurred in the 1960s and 1970s. Further, García has identified the period from 1980 onward as the "Hispanic Generation" in *Chicanismo: The Forging of a Militant Ethos among Mexican Americans* (Tucson: University of Arizona Press, 1997). This essay will follow that general temporal outline. In this essay, *Mexicans* refers to Mexican citizens, and *Mexican Americans* describes people of Mexican descent living in Texas specifically or in the United States generally. *Tejanos* will be used to identify Mexican Americans specifically in Texas. Anthony Quiroz, *Claiming Citizenship: Class and Consensus in a Mexican American Community* (Ph.D. dissertation, University of Iowa, 1998), 2.

2. In this chapter, *Anglos* will refer to the segments of the white population allowed access to power (primarily those who could trace their roots to northern and western Europe) and their culture. *White* will refer to the racial construction around which citizenship was defined. Thus, while Tejanos may have struggled to be considered "white" for legal purposes, they did not always seek to be culturally "Anglo." Arnoldo De León, in *They Called Them Greasers: Anglo Attitudes toward*

Mexicans, 1821–1900 (Austin: University of Texas Press, 1983), explains Anglo/Mexican tensions in the nineteenth century and details the roots and expressions of anti-Mexican bigotry. Further, I will use the terms *Tejano* and *Mexican American* interchangeably, while *Chicano* will refer to a specific subset of 1960s and '70s activists within the Mexican-American population.

3. R. Reynolds McKay, "Texas Mexican Repatriation during the Great Depression" (Ph.D. dissertation, University of Oklahoma, 1982), 66. See also Arnoldo De León, *Mexican Americans in Texas: A Brief History*, 2nd ed. (Wheeling, Ill.: Harlan Davidson, 1999), 68, 70.

4. Robert C. Overfelt, "Mexican Americans," in *Handbook of Texas Online*, *http://www.tsha.utexas.edu/handbook/online/articles/MM/pqmhe.html* (accessed March 16, 2006).

5. The single best source on *el plan de San Diego* is Benjamin Heber Johnson's *Revolution in Texas: How a Forgotten Rebellion and Its Bloody Suppression Turned Mexicans into Americans* (New Haven: Yale University Press, 2003).

6. Rodolfo Acuña, *Occupied America: A History of Chicanos*, 5th ed. (New York: Pearson/Longman, 2004), 198–201.

7. For a detailed analysis of LULAC's history, see Benjamin Márquez, *LULAC: The Evolution of a Mexican American Political Organization* (Austin: University of Texas Press, 1993) and Craig A. Kaplowitz, *LULAC: Mexican Americans and National Policy* (College Station: Texas A&M University Press, 2005).

8. For a discussion of Mexican-American attitudes and behaviors during and after the war, see Carole Christian, "Joining the American Mainstream: Texas's Mexican Americans during World War I," *Southwestern Historical Quarterly* 92 (April 1990).

9. José Amaro Hernández, *Mutual Aid for Survival: The Case of the Mexican American* (Malabar, Fla.: Robert E. Krieger, 1983), 64-65; Acuña, *Occupied America*, 158-9. For more information on organized labor among Tejanos, see also Emilio Zamora, *The World of the Mexican Worker in Texas* (College Station: Texas A&M University Press, 1993).

10. Acuña, *Occupied America*, 210–11 on repatriation; 220–22 on labor organization.

11. Richard Croxdale, "Pecan Sheller's Strike," in *Handbook of Texas Online*, http://www.tsha.utexas.edu/handbook/online/articles/PP/oep1.html (accessed March 17, 2006). Consult also Croxdale's bibliography.

12. Arnoldo De León, *Mexican Americans in Texas*, 68.

13. For a more in-depth look at Mexican-American reactions to the *bracero* program, see Carl Allsup, *The American GI Forum: Origins and Evolution* (Austin: Center for Mexican American Studies, University of Texas Press, 1982), especially chapters 8 and 9; Henry A. J. Ramos, *The American GI Forum: In Pursuit of the Dream, 1948–1983* (Houston: Arte Público Press, 1998), 68–74; Kaplowitz, *LULAC*, 40–43.

14. Acuña, *Occupied America*, 245, and Arnoldo De León, *Mexican Americans in Texas*, 108.

15. Patrick J. Carroll provides the definitive explanation of the Longoria incident in *Felix Longoria's Wake: Bereavement, Racism, and the Rise of Mexican American Activism* (Austin: Texas A&M University Press, 2004), 10–11. See also Allsup, *American GI Forum,* 39–49, and Ramos, *American GI Forum,* 9–17.

16. Guadalupe San Miguel, *"Let All of them Take Heed': Mexican Americans and the Campaign for Educational Equality in Texas, 1910–1981,* 2nd ed. (College Station: Texas A&M University Press, 2001), 123–28.

17. Acuña, *Occupied America,* 291; Julie Leininger Pycior, *LBJ and Mexican Americans: The Paradox of Power* (Austin: University of Texas Press, 1997), 93–95.

18. Quiroz, *Claiming Citizenship,* 123–4.

19. Kaplowitz, *LULAC,* 98–104, 117–20.

20. Arnoldo De León, *Mexican Americans in Texas,* 126–7.

21. Acuña, *Occupied America,* 312–14, 321–27, 341–44.

22. The fullest treatment of the Raza Unida party is Ignacio García's *United We Win: The Rise and Fall of La Raza Unida Party* (Tucson: University of Arizona Press, 1989). For specific treatment of Muñiz' gubernatorial races, see especially 180–93.

23. For a detailed explanation of this process of homogenization, see Arlene Davila, *Latinos Inc.: The Marketing and Making of a People* (Berkeley: University of California Press, 2001).

24. Meantime in the 1980s and 1990s a wave of Spanish-surnamed entertainers such as George Lopez (Mexican), Jennifer Lopez (Puerto Rican), Ricky Martin (Puerto Rican), Antonio Banderas (Spanish) and Gloria Estefan (Cuban) began changing the face of American popular culture.

25. Texas State Data Center and Office of the Demographer Table DP-1. Profile of General Demographic Characteristics: 2000, http://txsdc.utsa.edu/data/census/2000/dp2_4/pdf/04048.pdf (accessed June 10, 2006).

The Struggle for Dignity

African Americans in Twentieth-Century Texas

Cary D. Wintz

AS TEXAS ENTERED THE twenty-first century, the state's African Americans were, by most measures, more prosperous and secure in their rights than at any time in their history. By no means had prejudice, discrimination, and racial violence disappeared, and African Americans continued to lag behind the white majority in most social and economic measures. Even so, the twentieth century had witnessed a radical change in the role and the status of blacks in the Lone Star State, though falling short perhaps of expectations. African Americans in Texas and across the nation had greeted the arrival of the twentieth century with great hope. There was talk of a "New Negro" for the new century, a concept that Booker T. Washington celebrated in a book by that title and W. E. B. Du Bois made the theme of his classic work, *The Souls of Black Folk*. Unfortunately, the reality of race relations at the dawn of the century did not justify such hope. Racial violence was on the increase as lynching and race riots became far too common in Texas and other parts of the country. The new century also brought renewed efforts to impose segregation on most aspects of public and private life, while political "reforms" denied blacks any meaningful political power. For African Americans in Texas, the twentieth century would be the era of their struggle for dignity against racism, oppression, and Jim Crow.[1]

Over 620,000 African Americans lived in Texas at the beginning of the twentieth century. As in the previous century, the overwhelming majority resided in the eastern third of the state, from the Red River south, along and a bit west of what is now the I-35 corridor to the San Antonio area, then east to the Gulf of Mexico. Only about 10 percent of the black population lived outside these boundaries. Almost 80 percent lived on farms or in rural areas. Some were ranchers or cowboys, but the vast majority farmed cotton. Approximately 25 percent of black farmers owned their own land. The rest were tenants, mostly sharecroppers, and usually very poor. Even those who owned their own farms struggled to break even as expenses frequently surpassed income. The average value of a black farmer's holdings in 1910 was approximately one-fifth that of a white farmer.

Some 20 percent of black Texans lived in cities and towns at the beginning of the twentieth century. While Houston contained the largest number of blacks, Austin, Dallas, Waco, and Galveston also contained substantial black populations. Urban blacks accounted for about 25 percent of the non-farm workforce at the turn of the century. Most held jobs as laborers, domestic workers, or personal servants. Together, these occupations accounted for 80 percent of black urban workers. Fewer than 5 percent entered the professions, mostly as teachers or preachers. However, Texas had 136 black physicians, more than any other state. While the number of professionals compared favorably with other southern states, the percentage of African Americans who were skilled craftsmen was smaller in Texas than in other states.

Blacks in the workforce suffered from discrimination. Their wages were low, averaging about $2 daily. Although black and white workers who performed the same jobs generally were paid at the same rate, discrimination occurred in the assignment of jobs.

Black women received substantially lower wages than black men even when they performed the same jobs. Labor unions also discriminated. In the lumber, railroad, and shipping industries there were large numbers of black workers, and many were involved in the organization of unions. However, most unions either refused to admit blacks or, more commonly, discriminated against them in pay or denied them access to higher-paying jobs. Management, in turn, frequently used black workers as strikebreakers. Only on the docks of Houston and Galveston did African Americans approach equity in the work place. Black longshoremen, organized in their own unions, shared equally in the available work.

African Americans also owned and operated businesses, though generally these enterprises were few in number and quite small. Often they were family-operated service businesses such as grocery stores, restaurants, taverns, or blacksmith shops, and they usually, but not always, served only the black community. There were several black insurance companies, most connected with black fraternal groups, and there were at least eight black banks in business in early twentieth-century Texas.

Black education suffered from inadequate funding and, under the terms of the Texas Constitution of 1876, schools were segregated. Even so, black illiteracy declined during the last quarter of the nineteenth century from over 75 to less than 40 percent in 1900. Texas ranked fifth among southern states in the enrollment and daily attendance of black students and third in the number of black teachers. In spite of these gains at the turn of the century, education lacked adequate funding, facilities, and faculty. Secondary education suffered most of all. As late as 1900 there were only nineteen high schools in the state that served African Americans, forcing students who wanted a high school education to move to one of the towns or cities where such a high school existed. The typical black student seeking an education in Texas at this time could attain little more than basic literacy.

All in all, the situation of black Texans at the turn of the century suggests a mixture of regression and progress. Economically, they were at a disadvantage when compared with their white neighbors. Poverty was common among white Texans, but black people were even poorer. Education for blacks was not equal to that offered whites, and black access to political power declined in the 1890s and would decline further early in the twentieth century. Mortality rates for blacks were much higher than those for whites, probably the result of inadequate diet and limited access to medical care. Most troubling of all was the reality that both segregation and racial violence were intensifying as the nineteenth century came to an end.

In the first two decades of the twentieth century, African Americans in Texas again experienced both advances and setbacks. Institutions like the church matured, black newspapers became common in the larger communities, and blacks organized to improve their situation both within the segregated system and by challenging the system itself. On the other hand, segregation became institutionalized, blacks were excluded from political participation, and racial violence was widespread. The most significant positive developments in the early twentieth century were the emergence of black leadership and the creation of the institutions that would take the lead in pushing for social and economic advancement and ultimately equal rights. Accomplishments in these areas built on the foundations laid during Reconstruction and the post-Reconstruction eras. In terms of leadership, black Texans continued the traditions established by nineteenth-century leaders such as George T. Ruby, Matthew Gaines, John B. Raynor, and Norris Wright Cuney.

In the new century some black leaders gained national prominence. For example, Emmett J. Scott, a Houston newspaper publisher, became Booker T. Washington's private secretary, then held positions at Howard University and in the War Department. In 1903 Alice Dunn Logan served as a member of the executive committee of the National Afro-American Council, the only organization to bring together all elements of national black leadership. Other black leaders based their activities in Texas. The latter group included newspaper editors like C. N. Love of the *Texas Freeman*, Clifford F. Richardson of the Houston *Informer*, W. E. King of the Dallas *Express*, and W. L. Davis of the *Western Star*, who along with business leaders, ministers, and educators not only established successful institutions in the black community, but also often took the lead in criticizing racial stereotypes and pressing for equality.

The principal difference between black leaders in the nineteenth century and those of the early twentieth century was that the former were generally based in political organizations—most notably the Republican Party—while early in the twentieth century politics as an avenue to power was not available to African Americans in Texas. However, new institutions had emerged to voice the interests of the black community, most notably the press. Building on the dramatic increase in black literacy, African-American newspapers appeared in the state late in the nineteenth century, and by World War I they served most major communities. As these newspapers achieved a degree of economic stability, outspoken editors made the black press a significant force in the black community. In addition, African Americans also had access to periodicals with a national circulation, such as various black church publications, the Chicago *Defender*, and *The Crisis*, published by the National Association for the Advancement of Colored People (NAACP) under the editorship of W. E. B. Du Bois.

Black Texans also created literally dozens, possibly hundreds, of black organizations of all types. Some were religious; some were social and fraternal; and others were political. These groups differed in their objectives, in their targeted membership, in their leadership and organizational structure, and in their relationships with both the black and the white communities. It is important to remember that as segregation and political disfranchisement cut blacks off from traditional means of asserting their interests, the churches, fraternal and business organizations, and women's clubs assumed increased importance in the African-American community. They took the place of political parties and became the vehicles through which black Texans would assert themselves in the struggle for dignity.

The most pervasive black organization was the church. Even the smallest African- American community had a church, and most had at least two—a Baptist church and one of the several African-American branches of the Methodist Church (African Methodist Episcopal, Colored Methodist Episcopal, or African Methodist Episcopal Zion church). Larger communities also had a number of evangelical churches, such as the Church of God in Christ, and in some areas there were Catholic churches that served African Americans. Generally, Baptists outnumbered Methodists more than two to one, while other denominations were even smaller. Throughout the first two decades of the century church membership grew, and there was a proliferation of evangelical churches, especially in the state's urban areas. The black church went far beyond addressing the spiritual needs of its members. It was a social and cultural center for its members. It set up educational institutions—especially for higher education. It was a place where members could express their beliefs and their frustrations, and it was a training ground for black leaders. Some pursued leadership positions within the church, such as Lacey Kirk Williams of Dallas, who became the president of the National Baptist Convention in 1922. Others became community leaders and spokespersons for civil rights and equality.[2]

Joining the churches was a large variety of fraternal organizations. Black branches of fraternal organizations such as the Masons, the Odd Fellows, and the Knights of Pythias established branches in Texas during the nineteenth century. They were very popular among middle-class blacks and served as social clubs, provided networking opportunities, and often offered insurance policies and burial benefits. Many also addressed the political and economic needs of the community, including lobbying for improved social and municipal services and for civil rights. The state conventions of these fraternal orders were well-attended, and many Texans also traveled to the national conventions. In the early twentieth century African Americans established college fraternities and sororities. These organizations formed alumni chapters in several Texas cities and became important institutions in the black community. The sororities were particularly active in addressing the needs of children and the poor.

Women also founded a number of clubs that were especially popular among middle- and upper-class black women and college graduates. Excluded from white women's clubs, the black club-women in 1905 formed the Texas Federation of Colored Women's Clubs under the leadership of Mrs. M. E. Y. Moore of Fort Worth, who called on black women to "improve the home, moral and social life in Texas communities." By the next year there were active affiliates in Houston, San Antonio, and Austin; two years later Josephine E. Holmes was elected recording secretary of the National Association of Colored Women. Women's clubs in Texas stressed cultural activities (many had their roots as literary societies), as well as charitable and social service work. Some established nursery schools, promoted high moral standards among women, pursued charitable activities, and advocated political and racial causes. They promoted public health issues, established facilities for orphans, supported education and libraries, challenged racial stereotypes, defended interracial marriage, and lobbied the state legislature for the creation of a training school for delinquent black girls. Later, in the 1910s Christia Adair and others joined the campaign for women's suffrage, even though most white suffragettes opposed their efforts.[3]

While the advances made in the black community during the first two decades of the twentieth century were impressive, few blacks took much satisfaction. Segregation, the loss of political rights, and an upsurge in racial violence clouded the future and undermined many of the accomplishments achieved since emancipation. Furthermore, in addition to the overt examples of prejudice and discrimination, blacks faced a deep-seated ideology of racism that colored the way most white Texans viewed and reacted to them. Such racism was so endemic to life in Texas that few whites consciously analyzed it. Yet it influenced both thought and action, as vividly seen in the treatment and depiction of blacks in the aftermath of the great storm that devastated Galveston on September 8, 1900. The magnitude of the storm and the destruction it brought almost defied description. No completely accurate count of the fatalities was ever made, but estimates of 6,000 were commonly heard, and many placed the figure much higher. When the waters receded, the city was in ruins, with thousands of people left homeless.

In the chaos that followed, Galveston's African Americans were singled out in news reports of looting and especially for scavenging items of value from the bodies of the dead. Some of the descriptions were particularly gory. Black "ghouls" were reported to have cut fingers and ears off victims for their rings and earrings. Blacks even were said to have been apprehended with these fingers in their pockets. Furthermore, the local and national press reported that a number of blacks (the number ranged from 45 to 75) were shot for looting. In addition, Galveston's *Daily News* claimed that blacks would not work in the cleanup efforts unless forced at the point of a bayonet. Prejudicial images of black Galvestonians dominated local and national coverage of the tragedy. Pen and ink illustrations depicted black figures "skulking" around the scenes of death and destruction. Blacks were either portrayed as villainous looters and ghouls, as lazy slackers who refused to join in the cleanup efforts, or as weak and childlike in the face of the destruction. These images intensified prevailing stereotypes of African Americans throughout Texas.[4]

The truth was quite different. Police accounts list only six executions for stealing from the dead and only eight arrests for loot-

This African-American child sits on a pile of rubble in the wake of the 1900 Galveston Hurricane. The local and national press used the storm to spread images of blacks as cowards or grave robbers. The truth, as this picture illustrates, is that blacks (like whites) were both victims and survivors of this great catastrophe. Courtesy Library of Congress.

ing—no racial breakdown was provided. The all-black Cotton Jammers' Association, a union of dockworkers, volunteered for cleanup duty, and in the first call for volunteers to clean up the downtown area, 14 of the 25 recruits were black. But the truth did not matter. Whites accepted uncritically the negative images spread through the press, literature, art, and popular culture. In early twentieth-century Texas racism was intensifying as politicians and the press used the race issue to justify the legal and social subjugation of African

Americans. Texas was not unique in this. Prejudice, discrimination, and racial violence were the norm across the South and, indeed, across the country as Jim Crow became public policy. [5]

Segregation began in nineteenth-century Texas as conservative Democrats dismantled the racial reforms of Reconstruction. The Texas Constitution of 1876 ordered the segregation of the state's nascent public school system, even though this apparently violated provisions of the Fourteenth Amendment and the federal civil rights acts of 1866 and 1875. In 1891 the state legislature mandated segregation on railroad cars. In 1896 the Supreme Court in *Plessy v Ferguson* upheld the constitutionality of a Louisiana law requiring separate railroad cars for whites and blacks. While this case applied only to railroad segregation, the Court's use of the principle of "separate but equal" opened the door to the widespread segregation of public facilities, and Texas responded.

Segregation in Texas was achieved through legislation at the state and local levels, as well as by custom, policy, and practices such as zoning and deed restrictions. The overwhelming majority of white Texans supported the practice to the point that the religious-minded believed it was ordained by God, while the secularists defended it as the natural order. Nevertheless, segregation and its boundaries were never totally clear, and a series of court challenges and a patchwork of laws, ordinances, and legal decisions provided the structure of the practice in the state. Furthermore, beyond the legal implementation of segregation lay its true nature—extra-legal custom and practice, and the frequent use or threat of violence to impose the often-unwritten code.

The Texas legislature enacted several laws establishing segregation on the state's railroad system. In addition to the 1891 measure, in 1909 the lawmakers required separate waiting rooms in railway stations and in 1911 separate employee compartments. Two decades later, when Houston was constructing its imposing Grand Central Station, initial plans for the mammoth building had to be altered to prevent black and white passengers from using the same entrance ramp to board the trains. The state also either provided segregated state facilities, including "insane asylums, juvenile rehabilitation schools, and deaf, dumb, and blind schools," or ignored altogether the needs of blacks. There was no state facility for African-American orphans until 1929, and no facility other than the women's prison for delinquent black girls until 1945. State law established separate prisons for blacks and whites in 1909 and continued the use of whipping for black prisoners long after it had been abolished for whites. Higher education was segregated. The only state-supported facility for blacks prior to 1947, Prairie View A&M, was established in 1879. However, it was not authorized to offer college-level arts and sciences courses until 1901, and did not begin to offer a full range of bachelor degrees in the arts and sciences until 1919.[6]

Local government also segregated facilities. Houston and Galveston each opened libraries for blacks in the first decade of the century; the state legislature authorized each county to provide a separate library for African-American residents. Most city buildings and their facilities were segregated. Separate restrooms and drinking fountains were common. Health-care facilities were also segregated. In most communities hospitals provided separate wards for black patients, usually with only a handful of beds. In most cases black physicians were prohibited from practicing in white hospitals. By the mid-1920s Houston opened the Houston Negro Hospital, a public facility with a white director, but where black doctors could treat their patients. Medical education was limited in Texas. There was no medical school until one operated briefly under the direction of the Texas State College for Negroes in the late 1940s. The first nursing school for blacks opened in Dallas in 1912, followed by nursing programs at Prairie View in 1920 and in Galveston in 1921. In 1927 the Houston Independent School District established Houston Colored Junior College, a tax-supported institution of higher education. It was expanded in 1935 to a four-year college, Houston College for Negroes.

In 1907 the Texas legislature enacted a law allowing local communities to segregate or prohibit African Americans from theaters and amusement parks. Most cities segregated these facilities, allowing blacks to sit in separate sections of the theater, usually the balcony, or setting aside separate days or times for black patrons. Amusement parks often admitted blacks one day per week, or on special occasions, like Juneteenth. Restaurants and hotels were segregated by practice rather than by law. Some restaurants allowed blacks to eat in the kitchen or pick up take-out meals at the back door or window. Hotel accommodations were usually not available; black travelers typically found housing in private homes. Department stores and other retail facilities happily sold to blacks, but generally required them to wait until all white patrons had been served and did not allow black customers to try on clothing, hats, or shoes.

As if segregation in separate and unequal facilities were not enough, Texas stripped its African-American citizens of their political rights early in the twentieth century. This process took several forms. First, blacks were excluded from juries, usually by the action of court officials. The results were predictable. Blacks generally received harsher sentences than whites, especially for assaults committed on a member of the other race. Restrictions on black voting began under the guise of voter reform. Citing widespread voter fraud in the political contests of the 1890s, the state enacted a series of measures restricting suffrage. These included a constitutional amendment approved by voters in 1902 imposing a poll tax on voters and two election laws—the Terrell Election Laws of 1903 and 1905. The 1903 law strengthened voter residency requirements and the voter registration process, while the 1905 act required that primary elections be held for any political party that received at least 100,000 votes in the previous election and permitted county executive committees to exclude blacks from voting in the primary elections. Early in the twentieth century only the Democratic Party had enough voters to be affected. In 1923 these restrictions were tightened when state law expressly prohibited blacks from voting in any Democratic Party primary election.[7]

The impact of these election "reforms" was dramatic. Residency requirements, the registration process, and the poll tax impacted lower income voters, a disproportionate number of whom were blacks. The white primary, in a one-party state like Texas, effectively eliminated African-American political power, since the winner of the Democratic Party primary invariably won the general election. Voter intimidation, especially in counties where blacks were a majority, also added to the decline in black political participation. In 1897 Robert L. Smith, the last of over 40 black legislators who had served following the Civil War, made his final speech; 70 years would pass before blacks returned to the statehouse. In 1906 only about 5,000 African Americans voted in Texas, down from about 100,000 in the 1890s.[8]

Racial violence was a natural byproduct of racism, discrimination, and the elimination of African-American political power. Late in the nineteenth century lynching had reached epidemic proportions in Texas. From 1883 through 1903 an estimated 199 blacks were lynched in the state; from 1904 to 1930 another 171 lost their lives at the hands of lynch mobs. During the first decade of the century over 100 blacks were lynched, 24 in 1908 alone. Contemporary explanations for the lynchings do not ring true. It is a myth that lynch mobs generally responded to the rape of a white woman by a black— only a small minority of lynchings had any connection to rape, and the victims of lynching included black women and children. Moreover, with a white-dominated criminal justice system and with blacks excluded from juries, lynching was not necessary to prevent black criminals from escaping justice. Yet a number of the victims were seized from police custody. In 1916 Jesse Washington was dragged from the courtroom in Waco following his conviction for murder, taken downstairs where he was beaten, burned, and hanged, then dragged around town as citizens grabbed pieces of his charred body for souvenirs. All this was captured on film by the town photographer, as several thousand well-dressed citizens, some accompanied by their wives and children, crowded into the town square in the middle of the day to witness the spectacle. Violence of this magnitude can be explained only as pure racial hatred inflicted by a frenzy-driven crowd to terrorize the African-American population.[9]

As lynching began its slow decline following the widely publicized horror at Waco, another form of racial violence continued. Race riots, characterized by armed white mobs attacking black communities, did not always have a clear cause. Sometimes they were a response either to an imagined crime or grievance or to teach blacks "a lesson"; other times the goal was to drive African Americans out of the community. The worst riots in Texas occurred in Longview in 1919 and Beaumont in 1943, but there were a dozen or more clashes between whites and blacks in the first half of the century, including incidents in Beaumont in 1902 and again in 1908, San Angelo in 1909, and Port Arthur in 1919. In 1910 eighteen blacks in Anderson County lost their lives in a series of raids by whites.

The presence of African-American troops in Texas communities also triggered racial violence. In these cases much of the violence was committed by black soldiers, either in retaliation for white violence, or in response to discrimination and other racial incidents. A case that achieved national publicity occurred in Brownsville in August of 1906 when a clash between African-American troops and civilians led to the death of one civilian and the wounding of a policeman. President Theodore Roosevelt responded by ordering the summary discharge "without honor" (and without a hearing) of three black infantry companies, totaling 167 soldiers. Black leaders claimed that the soldiers were innocent of any wrongdoing, but the president and Congress refused to launch a thorough investigation. Over the next ten years there were additional problems between black troops and the communities in which they were stationed. Racial tensions surfaced in El Paso in 1906–1907 and San Antonio in 1911, and racial violence or threats of violence occurred in Del Rio in 1916, Waco in 1917, and El Paso in 1943. By far the worst incident involving black troops took place in Houston on the night of August 23, 1917, when African-American troops mutinied at Camp Logan west of the city. They broke into the armory, seized rifles and ammunition, and marched on the city, shooting white civilians—especially police officers. Nineteen people died in the violence, including four soldiers. In the aftermath 19 black soldiers were executed and 91 were sentenced to prison. [10]

Racism and racial violence became institutionalized in the twentieth-century version of the Ku Klux Klan. The new Klan was founded in Georgia in November 1915 as a direct outgrowth of D. W. Griffith's extremely popular and remarkably racist film, *The Birth of a Nation*. This new Klan was active in Texas by the early 1920s. Its membership ranged from approximately 100,000 in 1922, when it scored a number of successes at the polls, to an estimated 150,000 at its peak in 1923. While it is easy to dismiss the Klan as an organization of uneducated bigots, the Texas Klan was a well-organized political machine that exercised significant political power in a number of Texas cities, including Dallas, San Antonio, and Houston. In 1922 it elected its candidate, Earle Mayfield, to the U.S. Senate. The Klan was ardently and violently anti-black, as well as anti-immigrant, anti-Catholic, and anti-Semitic. Its racial violence was well-publicized. Victims included a black bellhop in Dallas whom the Klan "branded" with acid, and another African-American man who was castrated for his relationships with white women. The Klan also targeted black newspapers. After receiving death threats from the Klan, Clifford F. Richardson, editor of the Houston *Informer*, continued his outspoken criticism of segregation and discrimination, but proudly brandished a pistol he carried for protection. The Dallas *Express* received similar threats.[11]

The Klan's political power and its influence declined rapidly after 1923. Several factors contributed to its demise. First, blacks like Richardson and others refused to back down. Second, the Klan made political enemies, most notably ex-Governor Jim Ferguson, who directed his wife's 1924 gubernatorial campaign largely by ridiculing her opponent, an ardent Klansman. A young reform-minded district attorney from Williamson County, Dan Moody, achieved fame through his vigorous prosecution of Klan members' violent crimes. Texas voters rewarded him with the office of attorney general in 1924 and governor in 1926. Happily, the tolerance of Texans for racial violence declined in the mid-1920s. There is no evidence that racism was receding, but many Texans seemed more concerned with attracting business and investment to the state rather than brutalizing blacks. In the 1920s and 1930s an occasional Texas public figure would speak out against lynching or even question the morality of discrimination without alienating his constituents. The last lynching in Texas occurred in 1935.[12]

Table 1
African-American Population in Texas
1900–2000

Year	African-American Population	% African American
1900	620,722	20.4
1910	690,049	17.7
1920	741,694	15.9
1930	854,964	14.7
1940	924,391	14.4
1950	977,458	12.7
1960	1,187,125	12.4
1970	1,399,005	12.5
1980	1,710,175	12.0
1990	2,021,632	11.9
2000	2,421,653	11.6

Source: *U.S. Census Bureau*

Black Texas changed dramatically during the second quarter of the century, demographically being the most obvious. The African-American population increased by 15.5 percent, from 741,694 in 1920 to 924,391 two decades later. On the other hand, the percentage of African Americans in the total population continued to decline, slipping from over 20 percent in 1900 to less than 15 percent in 1930; this trend continued through the rest of the century. Also, black Texans became more urbanized as the number living in urban areas increased by over 106,000 to more than one out of every three in 1930, and over 45 percent in 1940. This demographic shift was the Texas phase of the Great Migration, which saw hundreds of thousands of African Americans relocate from the rural South to industrial cities in the North. Blacks in Texas were not immune to the appeals of the black migration. Poverty, prejudice, the lack of opportunity, and racial violence motivated them to leave the state. However, these factors were relative. Between 1900 and 1930, the peak of the out-migration, almost as many blacks moved into Texas from other states as left. The difference between in-migration and out-migration during this decade was only 11,877, or 1.4 percent of the black population of the state. By contrast, Georgia lost more than 334,070, or 23.8 percent to migration during the 1920s. Although some of Texas' migrating blacks moved north, they were far more likely to settle in Oklahoma or California than Chicago or Harlem.[13]

As the African-American population grew and became increasingly urbanized, a more sophisticated and more self-confident black culture emerged. In the 1920s and 1930s, Texas blacks participated in the cultural and literary blossoming known as the Jazz Age, or the Harlem Renaissance. National developments in literature and music stimulated a similar outpouring in Texas. Houston's Third, Fourth, and Fifth Wards and Dallas' Deep Ellum became "little Harlems" with jazz clubs and speakeasies that attracted racially mixed audiences looking for an evening of good music, dancing, drinking, and the excitement of crossing (though briefly) the racial barriers. Black poets of the Harlem Renaissance, like Langston Hughes, held readings and sold their books on Texas' black campuses, while artist Aaron Douglas provided a mural for the Hall of Negro Life at the Texas Centennial Exposition in Dallas. Writers, artists, and musicians also emerged during this period. Professor Melvin B. Tolson of Wiley College in Marshall achieved a national reputation as a Harlem Renaissance poet. In other communities writers like El Paso poet Bernice Love Wiggins received local acclaim for their literary efforts. But most important to black Texans was music. National headliners like Bessie Smith and Duke Ellington played for Texas audiences, black and white. But Texas also produced its own musical talent. Beginning with ragtime great Scott Joplin, a series of black Texas musicians—including Blind Lemon Jefferson, T-Bone Walker, Leadbelly, and Lightnin' Hopkins—achieved fame through music—ragtime, jazz, but especially the blues.[14]

In spite of demographic and cultural changes, basic living and working conditions remained pretty much the same. Discrimination, disfranchisement, segregation, and racial violence continued to inflict a heavy toll, especially during the first half of the twentieth century. But blacks did not surrender to oppression. African-American history in Texas was a constant struggle to survive, to construct and protect family, community, and culture, and to overcome racial injustice. Central to this struggle was the creation of organizations or institutions that could mobilize and focus black energy and resources. However, blacks did not always agree, even among themselves, about the most effective means of combating inequality. Nor did they agree on the institutions or individuals to direct this endeavor.

During the early decades of the twentieth century, several organizations addressed African-American issues. The National Negro Business League, founded by Booker T. Washington in 1900, had both members and chapters in Texas. Though formed primarily to promote black economic development, it also addressed social and political concerns. Marcus Garvey's Universal Negro Improvement Association, founded during World War I, was a short-lived black nationalist movement that briefly attracted a large membership and had adherents in several Texas cities. However, much of the early leadership in the struggle for dignity fell on the shoulders of individuals—ministers, labor leaders, and especially newspaper editors. For example, Charles N. Love began publishing the *Texas Freeman* in 1893. Early in the twentieth century he used the newspaper to attack segregation laws and to demand equal pay for black teachers. From 1919 to 1931 Clifford Richardson published the Houston *Informer,* through which he exposed racial injustice, police brutality, and especially the activities of the Ku Klux Klan. In 1931 Houston attorney Carter Wesley took over the *Informer* and merged it with the *Texas Freeman* to create the *Houston Informer and Texas Freeman.* He then expanded this base into an *Informer* newspaper empire that published editions of the *Informer* across the state and in Louisiana and Alabama. At its peak the newspaper chain employed 1,500 people and published separate editions in Houston, Galveston, Dallas, Beaumont, and Austin (as well as New Orleans and Mobile), and put out a statewide edition that circulated in small towns across the state. Wesley used this forum to promote his political ideas and attack those he opposed. He helped publicize the struggle against the white primary and for black political participation, and he pushed for equal funding of black education and teachers' salaries. In the 1940s he advocated the creation of a full-service black branch of the University of Texas in Houston, a position that put him in conflict with those pushing for the desegregation of higher education.[15]

Ultimately, the most influential civil rights organization in Texas was the National Association for the Advancement of Colored People. The NAACP was founded as an interracial civil rights organization in New York in 1910. While an attempt may have been made in 1912 to establish a branch in Houston, the first sustained NAACP chapter appeared in El Paso in 1915, where in the early 1920s it launched a legal struggle against the white primary. Other chapters were created across the state during World War I, and at the end of the war, with 31 branches and over 7,000 members, Texas led all states in membership. Except for the El Paso branch, most of these early efforts failed in the 1920s. A combination of official state opposition, white racism and intimidation evidenced by the 1919 Longview race riot and the rise of the Klan, and poor and divided local leadership reduced the Texas NAACP to only five active chapters by 1923. Through the 1920s local branches enjoyed brief sporadic revivals before sinking again into inactivity, and the organization would not be a major force across the state until the late 1930s and the 1940s. In 1936 a civil rights leader from Dallas, Antonio Maceo Smith, established the "Texas State Conferences of Branches, NAACP" in an effort to revitalize the organization in the state. Joined by two successful branch leaders, Lulu White of Houston and Juanita Craft of Dallas, local branches were reestablished across the state and membership soared. By the end of the 1930s, the Texas NAACP was positioned to take the lead in the attack on Jim Crow.

In the second quarter of the century, the civil rights struggle in Texas focused on two issues—voting rights and equal education. Black Texans never acquiesced in the restrictions on suffrage. The white primary generally prevented them from voting in primary elections, but many city elections were non-partisan and black participation continued. Black property owners could also legally vote in bond and school board elections. Even when voting was restricted, blacks united to lobby for municipal improvements. In the 1920s, for example, Dallas blacks established an Independent Voters League in an effort to improve their schools and get better city services in their neighborhoods, while in Houston blacks threatened to vote against school bonds unless a share of funds was allocated to improve black schools.

As the struggle against segregation intensified in the 1940s, NAACP members took the lead in demanding equal access to education in Texas. This 1947 demonstration in Houston occurred at the time of Heman Sweatt's lawsuit seeking admission to the University of Texas law school. The author wishes to thank the National Association for the Advancement of Colored People for authorizing the use of this work.

More significantly, blacks challenged the white primary laws, first by attempting to register and vote, then by filing suit against the laws in federal court. As long as the imposition of the white primary was left to the discretion of local Democratic election officials, blacks had some success evading it. In Waco, when a local nonpartisan primary tried to exclude blacks, a district court overturned the exclusion. However, when the legislature in 1923 prohibited black participation in the Democratic primary, the situation became more serious. An El Paso physician, Dr. Lawrence Nixon, with the support of the NAACP, challenged the law. The battle appeared to be won in 1927 when the U.S. Supreme Court ruled in *Nixon v. Herndon* that the legislature could not, by state law, establish a white primary. The legislature, however, quickly adopted legislation permitting, rather than requiring, parties to maintain white primaries, and most areas of the state continued the practice. Nixon again took the issue to federal court, and in 1932 the Supreme Court again ruled in his favor, and again the Texas legislature adjusted the law. In 1936 political activists in Houston and Dallas, including Maceo Smith, Clifford Richardson, and Richard Grovey, launched an unsuccessful challenge to the law. Ultimately, the new Legal Defense Fund of the NAACP assigned lawyers William Hastie and young Thurgood Marshall to the case, and a new lawsuit was filed when Houston dentist Dr. Lonnie Smith was denied the right to vote in the 1942 Democratic primary. In the resulting decision, *Smith v. Allwright* (1944), the Supreme Court found the white primary unconstitutional. While much of the white political leadership vowed to resist the decision or abolish the primary system altogether, the fact was that by 1946 most of these hardliners courted black voters. There was some sporadic resistance, especially in east Texas, but 75,000 blacks voted in the 1946 Democratic primary. The truth is that by 1950 blacks in the state's population had declined to only 12.7 percent, a factor that made their suffrage easier for white Texans to accept.[16]

Education was the second major concern of black Texans. Reforms in school financing during the Thomas Campbell administration early in first decade of the century, and subsequent reforms at the state and local level in the 1920s, neglected the educational needs of the state's African-American children. With the pattern of segregation as rigid as ever, black schools, already far behind those for white students, failed to share equally in the educational gains. Salaries for black teachers and per-pupil funding for black students were set at lower levels than for whites, and blacks still suffered from a lack of access to high schools. On the positive side, by 1930 the illiteracy rate for African Americans had declined to 13.4 percent, and the 1924 comprehensive survey of public education in Texas reported that mental testing conducted on black school-age children determined that they possessed the mental ability to profit from increased educational opportunity.[17]

Through the 1930s the strategy of black leaders was to fight for equal facilities within the separate but equal educational system. In Houston black leaders in the 1920s used school bond elections to pressure local officials to set aside funds for black educational needs. These efforts bore some fruit. Blacks gained new facilities, including two new high schools. In 1941 the Colored Teachers State Association established the Texas Commission for Democracy in Education to push for equality within the segregated public education system. The organization supported a lawsuit filed against the Dallas school board to equalize the pay of black and white teachers. When the court ordered the Dallas school board to implement a plan to end the dual pay scale, the Houston school board agreed to a similar plan, as did most other school districts by the 1945–1946 school year.[18]

Black Texans also raised issues concerning the status of higher education in the state. In 1930 Prairie View A&M began hosting an annual conference on the subject, and at the 1937 conference delegates focused on accessibility to higher education, concluding that the unfulfilled nineteenth-century promise to create a black University of Texas in Austin was the ultimate solution. As an interim measure, they proposed that the state award scholarships to black students who normally enrolled in out-of-state institutions because they could not pursue their chosen curriculum, especially in professional or graduate studies. The application of blacks to several professional programs at the University of Texas prompted the legislature to provide limited funding for this program. However, NAACP officials in Dallas and Houston were not satisfied. In 1947 they teamed again with Thurgood Marshall and the national NAACP to launch a carefully planned assault on segregation in higher education. Under their direction Heman Marion Sweatt applied for admission to the law school at the University of Texas. When, as expected, his application was denied, the NAACP filed suit.[19]

In an effort to defeat the suit, the state legislature in 1947 authorized the creation of the long-promised black University of Texas—Texas State University for Negroes in Houston. The NAACP continued its suit, determined to desegregate higher education rather than create another "separate but equal" institution. The ensuing struggle divided the black community. Some supported the creation of the black university, administrated and staffed by blacks, rather than admitting a few African-American students to the University of Texas. In 1950 the Supreme Court ruled in *Sweatt v. Painter* that "separate but equal" was inherently unequal, at least in professional education, and it directed the University of Texas to admit Sweatt to its law school. The black university, renamed Texas Southern University, continued to exist, but it never achieved the funding or the range of programs promised by the 1947 legislation.[20]

By 1954 the state's African Americans had achieved two major victories that placed them well ahead of the states of the Deep South. They had defeated the white primary and regained the right to vote in all elections, and they had begun the desegregation of graduate and professional education. For black Texans the civil rights movement would involve the consolidation and organization of their newly gained political power, the completion of their efforts to desegregate education, and the dismantling of Jim Crow in all public accommodations and wherever else it still existed. Substantial progress was achieved in all of these areas, but racism, far more resistant, continued.

Following the 1944 decision in *Smith* v. *Allwright*, political barriers fell fairly quickly. Some resistance by white citizens lingered, but as the number of black voters increased in the late 1940s, the impact began to be felt. The first significant electoral victory came in 1956 when Hattie Mae White won her race for a position on the Houston school board. By 1958 more than one-third of the potential black voters in the state had registered, and in some areas the figure was as high as 70 percent.[21]

In the 1960s additional changes impacted black voting. The 1965 Voting Rights Act and the 1966 U.S. Supreme Court decision declaring the poll tax unconstitutional greatly reduced most remaining impediments. By 1968 over 80 percent of eligible blacks had registered to vote. Other political changes made it easier for blacks to gain elected office. Federal court rulings forced significant redistricting in 1960 and 1970, providing greater representation for the state's urban areas where black voters were increasingly concentrated. Court decisions, as well as pressure from the Justice Department under the Voting Rights Act, ended the practice of at-large voting districts in the legislature and local political bodies, including city and county government and school boards. Single-member districts allowed concentrated minority voting blocs to elect their candidates.

School desegregation was not so easy to accomplish. The NAACP Legal Defense Fund and Thurgood Marshall continued their assault on school segregation, resulting in the landmark 1954 decision in *Brown v. Board of Education of Topeka*. The Court concluded "that in the field of public education the doctrine of separate but equal has no place." Instead of ordering immediate desegregation, the Court directed the lower federal courts to implement the ruling "with all deliberate speed," setting up a process that dragged on for decades. Reaction to the *Brown* decision divided Texans along racial lines. Polls reflected four-to-one opposition in the white community and two-to-one support in the black community. Tensions began to build. Though Governor Allan Shivers left little doubt of his opposition to the decision, his stand, on the whole, was not as militant as that of some southern leaders. He did not shut down the public school system or stand in the schoolhouse door. However, he did use race baiting, accusing his opponent in the 1956 Democratic primary of advocating complete integration, and in the fall of 1956 he intervened to block the efforts of black students under a federal court order to attend the local high school in Mansfield near Fort Worth. Shivers used threats of mob violence to send in the Texas Rangers to ensure order. No violence occurred, but the black students were not allowed to enroll. Most white voters supported the governor. When they went to the polls for the July 1956 Democratic primary, they found three segregation issues on the ballot: a measure favoring stronger laws against racial intermarriage, a law exempting white students from attending integrated schools, and a law authorizing state action to block federally mandated desegregation of local schools. Voters approved all three measures. In spite of the clash at Mansfield, integration proceeded peacefully in some other districts, with more than 120 enrolling some black students in previously all-white schools by the 1957 school term.[22]

Opposition to school desegregation did not disappear. In response to the July 1956 referendum supporting segregation, the legislature passed a law in 1957 making mandatory the assent of the voters in school districts before the races could be mixed. The penalty for noncompliance was the withdrawal of all state aid for the district. In reaction to the desegregation crisis at Little Rock, the legislature approved another law that closed any public school at which troops were stationed. But legislation against integration had little effect. Governor Price Daniel, elected in 1956, made no effort to interpose state authority against the federal agencies charged with carrying out the judicial decrees, and the legislative acts were quickly declared unconstitutional. Ultimately, federal judges ordered each local school district to file plans for desegregation.

The desegregation of colleges and universities generated much less opposition. Del Mar Junior College in Corpus Christi deseg-

regated in 1952, followed by the University of Texas and Southern
Methodist University in 1955. A mob of outsiders sought to prevent blacks from entering Lamar State College of Technology in
Beaumont in 1956, but without success, though a similar mob had
succeeded in its efforts the previous year at Texarkana Junior College. By 1958 approximately two-thirds of the colleges and universities of Texas had integrated their classes. In 1964 and 1965 Rice
University and the University of Texas integrated their faculties,
and in 1965 the University of Texas desegregated its dorms and the
Southwest Conference integrated its athletic programs.[23]

While the effort to desegregate the public schools inched along
through the 1960s and into the 1970s, the civil rights movement
shifted its focus to the desegregation of public facilities. Stimulated
by the February 1960 student sit-ins in Greensboro, North Carolina, on March 4, 1960, Texas Southern University students launched
their own sit-in movement in Houston, targeting the lunch counter
at the Weingarten's supermarket near their campus. In the months
that followed, nonviolent protests spread to other lunch counters,
the city hall cafeteria, and the dining facilities at the railroad and
bus stations; movie theaters, hotels, and restaurants were the next
targets. The demonstrations in Houston remained peaceful in large
part due to the efforts of white leaders who wanted to maintain the
city's image as a good place to do business and the cooperation of
black leaders. Houston's efforts to secure a major league baseball
team required the desegregation of the stadium and led to the removal of racial barriers at the city's hotels and restaurants. By the
end of May 1963 the battle in Houston was won.[24]

In Dallas, Austin, San Antonio, Lubbock, Denton, and other Texas cities black and white students challenged the Jim Crow
system with similar results. Though the movement was undoubtedly influenced by similar events occurring across the South, the
leadership in Texas was local—students, black community leaders,
and white business leaders guided events with little or no support

from national civil rights organizations. By the time the 1964 Civil Rights Act passed Congress, public facilities in most Texas cities already had been peacefully desegregated.

In the late 1960s the civil rights movement gave way to "Black Power," and organizations like the Student Nonviolent Coordinating Committee (SNCC) and the Congress of Racial Equality (CORE), led by Texan James Farmer, replaced the more moderate NAACP. This changed the nature of the civil rights struggle. "Black Power" replaced desegregation. Nonviolence gave way as ghettos burned in Watts, Detroit, and a score of other northern cities. In 1968 Martin Luther King, Jr., fell to an assassin's bullet, and the Black Panther Party, with its advocacy of armed self-defense, seemed to symbolize the new direction of the struggle for "black liberation."

Although Texas avoided the ghetto riots experienced in other parts of the country, it did not escape racial violence. A major issue throughout the twentieth century was the strained and hostile relationship between police and minority groups. African Americans had long claimed that they were victims of police harassment and brutality. The rise of civil rights activism, especially the militancy that appeared in the late 1960s, increased the potential for conflict, and a number of confrontations occurred. On the campus of Texas Southern University in May 1967 rumors of trouble and a gathering crowd of black students led to violence involving the students and the Houston police. Rocks and bottles were thrown, shots were fired, and a state of siege existed for several hours around one of the dormitories. Before order could be restored, a policeman was killed, apparently by a stray police bullet, and the police rampaged through the dorm, destroying student property, but finding no weapons. Three years later, in the summer of 1970, a shootout between the Houston police and People's Party II, a militant black group affiliated with the Black Panthers, left the leader of that organization dead.

Violent confrontations also occurred in Midland in 1968, in Lubbock in 1971, as well as in other cities. Frequently, African-American community activists charged that the police resorted to undue force in making arrests and were too quick in the use of their guns. In an effort to add minorities to the police force and thereby lessen the tensions, a number of police departments adopted special programs to recruit minority officers in the early 1970s, but problems persisted. Between 1975 and 1978 there were more than thirty official charges of police brutality. These incidents diminished across the state in the 1980s and 1990s as Houston and other Texas cities hired black police chiefs, but the issue did not totally disappear. Between 1984 and 1990 Texas led the nation in the number of civil rights complaints linked to police action.[25]

A different type of racial violence shocked Texans on June 7, 1998. In Jasper an African-American man, James Byrd, was brutally tortured and killed for no apparent reason by three white men who dragged him behind their speeding pickup until his body was dismembered. His assailants had connections with white-supremacist groups. The brutality of the crime and the obvious racial overtones attracted national attention. In contrast to such incidents at the beginning of the century, the perpetrators of this "lynching" were quickly arrested, tried, and convicted. Two of the three men involved received the death sentence.

Turning to a more positive matter, music dominated the arts scene in the black community during the second half of the twentieth century. Building on the base of jazz and the blues, which had emerged in the first half of the century, late twentieth-century black music encompassed rhythm and blues, gospel, zydeco, and hip-hop. Houston was the hub of much of this musical creativity. From its roots in Louisiana and black Creole music, zydeco was a new musical form that originated in the Bayou City and southeast Texas in the last quarter of the century. Clifton Chenier and other zydeco pioneers headquartered in Houston, especially its Fifth

Ward neighborhood of Frenchtown. At the end of the century, Houston's Fifth Ward nurtured a distinctive hip-hop genre, beginning with the Geto Boys in the early 1990s and flowering in the first decade of the twenty-first century. By 2005, according to *The New Yorker*, Houston hip-hop enjoyed "musical hegemony." Adding to Houston's luster as a major center of African-American music was the presence of the internationally acclaimed female rhythm and blues pop group, Destiny's Child, and the emergence of Beyoncé Knowles as a superstar solo performer.[26]

As the twentieth century entered its last decades, the civil rights movement had faded, and Black Power was almost forgotten. Black leadership was still found in the churches, especially the new megachurches, but the black press had declined in importance, as black faces appeared with regularity on local and national television news shows. Politics had become the principal vehicle for blacks to achieve power and leadership.

In 1967, seventy years after Robert L. Smith made his last speech in the legislature—an impassioned plea to end lynching—blacks returned to the statehouse. The previous November Texas voters had elected Barbara Jordan of Houston to the state senate, while Curtis Graves of Houston and Joseph E. Lockridge of Dallas were elected to the Texas House. Jordan served in the Texas Senate from 1967 to 1973; then in 1973 she became the first black ever to represent Texas in the U.S. Congress. Meanwhile, with the support of a number of organizations on both the state and the local levels, African-American candidates entered more contests, and the number of African- American officeholders in the legislature and in local governments steadily increased. In 2003 the Texas House of Representatives included 14 African Americans, while two served in the Texas Senate. Two African Americans represented Texas in the U.S. Congress. In the 2002 election the Democratic Party nominated an African American for the U.S. Senate. Black politicians on the local level also enjoyed unprecedented success. By the end of the century most major Texas cities had elected a black mayor, and in most Texas cities blacks served on city councils, in county government, and on local school boards. In 2001 Roderick Paige, who earlier had served as dean of education at Texas Southern University and superintendent of the Houston Independent School District, became the first Texan and the first African American to serve as secretary of education.

As the twentieth century came to an end many questions remained about the status of blacks in Texas and their future in the state. Compared to 1900 there had been great improvement; however, many problems remained. For the most part, segregation had come and gone. African Americans dine in restaurants, attend theaters, patronize hotels, and enroll in colleges and universities with few problems, but a great many blacks still live in neighborhoods that are largely black, and most black children attend schools that remain essentially segregated. Furthermore, schools with large black enrollments almost always are characterized by a high percentage of ill-prepared teachers and poorly performing students. Many blacks go to college and attend professional schools, but they remain underrepresented in most professions and at the highest levels of corporate and professional leadership. Poverty is more prevalent among blacks than whites. Young black men are far more likely to be found in prison than are whites. Few Texans advocate a return to segregation or disfranchising African Americans, but efforts to "level the playing field," or compensate blacks for past injustice through affirmative action, are opposed by a great many white Texans. The issue of reparations is opposed by a majority. In other words, the vestiges of racism and discrimination have not vanished, and the post-civil rights demands of some black leaders remain very controversial.

In the aftermath of the civil rights revolution, the economic and social status of many blacks improved substantially. New opportunities for African Americans opened as many blacks, once almost automatically relegated to low-paying, unskilled-labor jobs, assumed responsible and influential posts in industry, business, the professions, and government. However, as another new century begins, equality for African Americans remains a goal, not a reality. Too many blacks still remain in low-paying, low-status jobs. In addition, challenges to methods of increasing opportunity for African Americans, such as affirmative action, have been successfully waged in the courts. As a result, there is increasing concern within the African-American community about whether the gains made during the last quarter century will endure and expand, or whether a new era of discrimination will arise. Most Texans are committed to equality, but continued progress in this area will be a challenge.

Figure 1

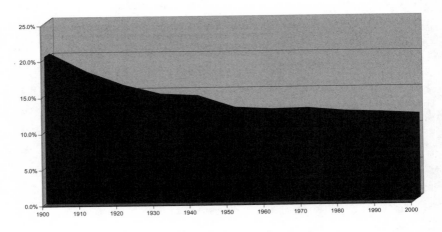

Percent African Americans
in Texas Population
1900-2000

Source: *U.S. Census Bureau*

Table 2

Projected African-American Population
2000–2040

Year	African-American Population	% African American
2000	2,421,653	11.6
2010	2,863,397	11.1
2020	3,309,068	10.2
2030	3,694,283	9.1
2040	3,995,349	7.9

Source: Murdock, Steve H., Steve White, Md. Nazrul Hogue, Beverly Pecotte, Xuihong You, and Jennifer Balkin. *The New Texas Challenge: Population Change and the Future of Texas.* College Station: Texas A&M University Press, 2003, 24-27. Note: the projections are based on the 1.0 migration scenario, which assumes that migration trends of the 1990s will continue.

Demographic changes in Texas will continue to impact race relations, as well as the economic and social position of African Americans in the state. For the most part demographic trends remained fairly constant throughout the twentieth century. The black population grew steadily in absolute numbers, while it declined steadily as a percentage of the population. As Figure I illustrates, African Americans constitute an increasingly smaller proportion of the Texas population. Furthermore, as Table 2 illustrates, population projections indicate that this trend will continue at least through the first four decades of the new century. History consists of the analysis and understanding of the past, not the future, but without question the changing demographics of the state will influence the role that African Americans play and the problems they will face in the twenty-first century.

Selected Bibliography

Barr, Alwyn. *Black Texans: A History of African Americans in Texas, 1528–1995.* 2nd ed. Norman: University of Oklahoma Press, 1996.

Beeth, Howard O., and Cary D. Wintz, eds. *Black Dixie: Afro-Texan History and Culture in Houston.* College Station: Texas A&M University Press, 1992.

Bryson, Conrey. *Dr. Lawrence A. Nixon and the White Primary.* Rev. ed. El Paso: Texas Western Press, 1992.

Christian, Garna L. *Black Soldiers in Jim Crow Texas, 1899–1917.* College Station: Texas A&M University Press, 1995.

Cole, Thomas R. *No Color Is My Kind: The Life of Eldrewey Stearns and the Integration of Houston.* Austin: The University of Texas Press, 1997.

Foley, Neil. *The White Scourge: Mexican, Blacks, and Poor Whites in Texas Cotton Culture.* Berkeley: University of California Press, 1997.

Murdock, Steve H., Steve White, Md. Nazrul Hogue, Beverly Pecotte, Xuihong You, and Jennifer Balkin. *The New Texas Challenge: Population Change and the Future of Texas.* College Station: Texas A&M University Press, 2003.

Obadele-Starks, Ernest. *Black Unionism in the Industrial South.* College Station: Texas A&M University Press, 2000.

Phillips, Michael. *White Metropolis: Race, Ethnicity, and Religion in Dallas, 1841–2001.* Austin: University of Texas Press, 2006.

Pitre, Merline. *In Struggle against Jim Crow: Lulu B. White and the NAACP, 1900–1957.* College Station: Texas A&M Press, 1999.

Shabazz, Amilcar. *Advancing Democracy: African Americans and the Struggle for Access and Equity in Higher Education in Texas.* Chapel Hill: University of North Carolina Press, 2004.

Winegarten, Ruthe. *Black Texas Women: 150 Years of Trial and Triumph.* Austin: University of Texas Press, 1995.

Endnotes

1. W. E. B. Du Bois, *The Souls of Black Folk* (Chicago: McClurg, 1903); Booker T. Washington, *A New Negro for a New Century: An Accurate and Up-to-Date Record of the Upward Struggles of the Negro Race* (Chicago: American Publishing House, 1900).

2. Alwyn Barr, *Black Texans: A History of African Americans in Texas, 1528–1995,* 2nd ed. (Norman: University of Oklahoma Press, 1996), 165–67.

3. Ruthe Winegarten, *Black Texas Women: 150 Years of Trial and Triumph* (Austin: University of Texas Press, 1995), 190–95.

4. Patricia Bellis Bixel and Elizabeth Hayes Turner, *Galveston and the 1900 Storm* (Austin: University of Texas Press, 2000), 78–79.

5. Ibid.

6. David G. McComb, *Houston: The Bayou City* (Austin: University of Texas

Press, 1969), 158; Barr, *Black Texans*, 140–41.

7. Barr, *Black Texans*, 140–41.

8. Ibid., 80.

9. See Patricia Bernstein, *The First Waco Horror: The Lynching of Jesse Washington and the Rise of the NAACP* (College Station: Texas A&M University Press, 2005).

10. For further information on the Brownsville episode, see John D. Weaver, *The Brownsville Raid* (College Station: Texas A&M University Press, 1970; reprint, 1992) and Garna L. Christian, *Black Soldiers in Jim Crow Texas, 1899–1917* (College Station: Texas A&M University Press, 1995), 61–91. The publication of Weaver's book in 1970 prompted the U.S. Army to reopen the investigation so the Brownsville incident. In 1972 the Army found the Brownsville soldiers innocent of wrongdoing, and President Nixon reversed their dishonorable discharges. Christian's book also contains a discussion of the Houston mutiny. See also Robert V. Haynes, *A Night of Violence: The Houston Riot of 1917* (Baton Rouge: Louisiana State University Press, 1976).

11. Barr, *Black Texans*, 139.

12. The murder of James Byrd in Jasper, Texas, in 1996 was a lynching in the opinion of many Texans.

13. U.S. Department of Commerce, Bureau of the Census, *Negroes in the United States, 1920–32* (Washington, D.C.: U. S. Government Printing Office, 1935), 41–46.

14. For a discussion of the Harlem Renaissance in Texas, see Bruce A. Glasrud, "Harlem Renaissance in the United States: 8—Texas and the Southwest," in *Encyclopedia of the Harlem Renaissance*, eds. Cary D. Wintz and Paul Finkelman (New York: Routledge, 2004), 521–25. For an overview of black music, see Roger Wood, *Down in Houston: Bayou City Blues* (Austin: University of Texas Press, 2003), 23–70.

15. Merline Pitre, *In Struggle against Jim Crow: Lulu B. White and the NAACP, 1900–1957* (College Station: Texas A&M Press, 1999), 90–94.

16. Barr, *Black Texans*, 174–75.

17. Amilcar Shabazz, *Advancing Democracy: African Americans and the Struggle for Access and Equity in Higher Education in Texas* (Chapel Hill: University of North Carolina Press, 2004), 119–20.

18. Barr, *Black Texans*, 204–6.

19. Shabazz, *Advancing Democracy*, 22–23.

20. Coordinating Board, Texas College and University System, "Legislation Establishing Texas State University for Negroes," in *Compilation of Constitutional and Statutory Laws Affecting Public Colleges and Universities* (Austin: Coordinating Board, November 1967): 305; *Sweatt v. Painter*, 339 U.S. 629 (April 4, 1950).

21. Barr, *Black Texans*, 177.

22. Ibid., 207

23. Shabazz, 142–97.

24. For a detailed discussion of the sit-in movement in Houston, see Thomas R. Cole, *No Color Is My Kind: The Life of Eldrewey Stearns and the Integration of Houston* (Austin: University of Texas Press, 1997).

25. Rupert N. Richardson, Adrian Anderson, Cary D. Wintz, and Ernest Wallace, *Texas: The Lone Star State*, 9th ed. (Upper Saddle River, N.J.: Pearson Prentice Hall, 2005), 409; Barr, *Black Texans*, 234.

26. For a detailed discussion of zydeco, see Roger Wood, *Texas Zydeco* (Austin: University of Texas Press, 2006); and Sasha Frere-Jones, "A Place in the Sun: Houston Hip-Hop Takes Over," *New Yorker* (July 22, 2007), http://www.newyorker.com/archive /2005/11/14/051114 crmu_music (accessed July 20, 2007).

From Farm to Future

Women's Journey through Twentieth-Century Texas

Angela Boswell

ALTHOUGH THE TWENTIETH CENTURY would bring dramatic changes in the lives and roles of women in Texas, in 1900 most women could not see the slightest glimmer of what was to come. At the dawn of the twentieth century, 83 percent of Texans still lived in rural areas where women spent their lives much like their nineteenth-century mothers and grandmothers. Some of these rural women were practically pioneers in remote places of west Texas, but by 1900 most rural families were producing for the market not just subsistence. Whether growing citrus in the Rio Grande Valley, ranching in west or south Texas, or growing cotton in the eastern and central areas of the state, women were crucial not only to the physical well-being of the family but also to its financial stability.

Most rural women lived in families tied to the struggling cotton agriculture that dominated the Texas and southern economy in the late nineteenth and early twentieth centuries. Many African-American women had grandmothers who had worked in the cotton fields as slaves, but twentieth-century blacks faced a labor system that exploited women's labor in a different way. Although some African-American families owned land, most black families in rural eastern and central Texas were sharecroppers or tenant farmers. Most land in these cotton-growing regions was still owned by white families, but the percentage of white families had decreased significantly since the Civil War. Whereas perhaps two-thirds or more of the white families had owned and worked their own land before the Civil War, by 1900 three-quarters of the farms were worked by sharecroppers. Falling cotton prices along with the crop-lien system had caused many farmers to lose their land to debt and made it nearly impossible for sharecroppers to save enough money to buy their own land.[1]

Whether landowners, sharecroppers, tenant farmers, or wage laborers, women's labor within a family played an important role in paying the debts, feeding the family, and holding onto the family property. Women of sharecropping and tenant families often found themselves helping with field work, and women of families working for wages—especially migrant workers who primarily worked during cotton-picking season—could not avoid it. While often directly contributing labor to the main support of the family, women's principal work remained housework and household production, an exclusively female domain.[2]

A woman bore the responsibility for making sure her family was clothed. Women often obtained cloth from peddlers either by trading eggs, butter, and the other produce from their gardens or paying for the cloth with money made from selling such goods. Because general stores were still male domains and women's work in the household did not allow much time for travel, wives often sent instructions with their husbands concerning the type, color, and quantity of fabric to purchase. Additional sources of cloth were feed sacks and flour sacks. In fact, in the 1920s flour companies began printing their sacks with designs to capitalize on this widespread use.[3]

Once they had acquired the cloth, women made clothing for their large and constantly growing families—rural Texas families still averaged one to three more members than urban families. Women also sewed and stuffed their own mattresses and pillows, as well as made the sheets and curtains for doors and windows. For winter, women made quilts and other bedding. The economic contribution of homemade clothing and bedding was so immense that it often made sense even for sharecropping families to purchase a sewing machine. Those without machines borrowed or shared them with others. Treadle machines were a great improvement over hand stitching even though almost no rural women had electric sewing machines until mid-century. Only those closest to urban areas had electricity before the 1930s.[4]

Clothing had to be constantly mended, and clothes that were completely worn out could be made into something else. Clothing had to be washed, one of the largest and most difficult chores of all—and the first household chore to be hired out to poorer women if a family could afford to do so. Making the lye soap required saving wood ashes, mixing them with water and allowing them to settle to make lye, and then cooking the lye with lard in an iron pot over a fire. The wealthiest families could buy soap, but store-bought soap was usually a luxury reserved for washing bodies, not clothing. The next and most difficult ingredient was water for washday. The few families lucky enough to live close to creeks or other clear surface water would carry the laundry and soap to the water. Other families had to haul water from cisterns or wells. Many families had no wells or cisterns of their own and actually had to haul water from other farms, a major chore since in order to do a family's wash for the week, a woman usually needed about 50 gallons of water. Very few rural families had indoor plumbing until the 1930s, and even by 1940 less than a quarter of the rural families had such. Of course, once the water was hauled to the house, the washing began, usually involving boiling water, washing, rinsing, and hanging the clothes to dry. Only a few rural women had the help of washing machines even after World War I when they became more readily available.[5]

Friederike Recknagel, photographer, and daughter, Louise Recknagel, scrubbing clothes on washboards in metal washtubs, Round Top, Texas, ca. 1905. From UTSA's Institute of Texan Cultures, No. 085-0372, courtesy Mr. and Mrs. E. W. Ahlrich.

Women on cotton farms could save their families money by making their clothing, keeping it clean, mending and re-using the clothing, and making their own soap, although these tasks were arduous and time-consuming. The fewer clothes the family bought on credit, the more likelihood that when the cotton crop was sold the family would owe less than they did the year before. For tenant farmers and sharecroppers this could mean the possibility of moving to better land and better homes. For landowners, this meant that they could continue to own their land.

In addition to taking care of family clothing needs, women made many other contributions to the family economy. While men initially procured the three main staples of farm life—pork, corn-meal, and syrup—women daily turned these staples into meals that nourished the workers in their families. At hog-killing time, women stayed busy inside scraping and cleaning intestines, as well as grinding and seasoning pork to make sausage that would last the year. They also salted pork to be cured in smokehouses and rendered lard for use throughout the year. These tasks were similar in most rural households that had access to hogs either by raising their own or through the generosity of neighbors. However, Mexican-American women had additional ways of cooking and preserving pork, cutting it into chunks and frying it as well as making tamales out of the hogs' heads.[6]

Corn was preserved by having it ground into meal, usually by the men at commercial mills, but women also preserved the corn by drying it and later by canning. The lack of refrigeration and electricity usually made long-term storage one of the more significant challenges. The dried corn was later made edible through a painstaking process of boiling with lye before cooking it to make hominy. White and black women turned the cornmeal into fried patties or cornbread in skillets over hot stoves, a particularly miserable job in the summer months. Mexican-American women used the ground corn to make tortillas. Although the three staples served as the basis for most meals, this food alone could not provide enough vitamins for families, so women raised extra food through gardens, poultry, and milk cows. The produce of the gardens then had to be dried or otherwise preserved. In spite of the hard work that went into just feeding and clothing the family, women also worked hard to keep their homes clean and attractive. [7]

Women on the cattle ranches of western and southern Texas contributed to their families' well-being through similar hard work: raising gardens and chickens, preserving food, preparing meals, making and caring for clothing, milking cows. Of course, on cattle ranches, beef replaced pork as the main meat for the family. Much of the work with the actual cattle was considered more appropriate to men, but like farmwomen, who worked in the fields when necessary, ranching women did what was best for their families despite gendered expectations. Hallie Crawford Stillwell, for instance, learned how to ride on her father's ranch chasing off bandits and fixing fences. After marriage, she assisted her own family in finding scattered cattle over miles and miles of rough terrain, in gathering them into the pen, and in throwing and tying them down for branding. Women on ranches also arranged provisions for and often accompanied the men of their family on overnight campouts when trying to round up the cattle. Women with sons could expect to work less as the boys matured and took over the duties. In addition to women in families that owned ranches, there were also the wives and daughters of the hired ranch hands. These women often worked for wages, usually washing laundry or assisting with food preparation.[8]

Like the women of the ranching regions, many rural women throughout the state lived in families that neither owned land nor had the fortune of sharecropping. These women either depended solely upon the wages of a husband and older children, or, more commonly, also had to work in someone else's fields. According to census reports, before the 1930s the largest occupation for women was that of agricultural laborer. Women who had to work fulltime in the fields contributed substantially to their families' well-being, but this work decreased the amount of time they could spend caring for their families, procuring and preparing foods, and otherwise saving the family expenses. Most women working as agricultural laborers were black women in the cotton-growing regions of the state. They usually moved only once a year at the most. Many Mexican-American women, however, participated in a more migratory pattern of labor. Whole families would follow the crops, harvesting spinach in the Rio Grande Valley from November through April, tending onions April through May, and then moving to central Texas in the fall to provide extra labor during the cotton-picking season. This migratory pattern made housing uncertain at best, and smokehouses, shacks, and overcrowded tents provided most of the lodging. In such conditions one hot meal a day was the most women could provide for their families. They used rocks and hot coals to make the necessary tortillas and open fires to cook whatever meat could be acquired. [9]

Between the day-to-day struggle for survival, the amount of work needed to contribute to the household economy, and long-observed social customs, women rarely left the farm, and even then almost always in the company of husband and family. Religion remained an important part of women's lives, but even church attendance took a secondary place to the work that needed to be done. Even a wife who gathered eggs or made butter for sale at the local store usually sent these items with her husband. When time allowed, families would visit other families, whether they were friendly neighbors or extended family members. But even then women depended on their husbands for transportation—socially, both horses and, later, cars in the earliest years were seen as male responsibilities, and so women were usually unfamiliar or uncomfortable with their use. Such isolation discouraged women from associating with and relating to other women as women. Identifying primarily with their families' interests, women were unlikely to challenge the family structure that placed the male at the head.[10]

Although the majority of women remained isolated in rural areas, urbanization—the trend that transformed the state after World War II—was slowly emerging even at the beginning of the twentieth century. The number of women living in urban areas increased gradually but steadily throughout the first half of the century. Urban living did not yet differ drastically from rural living: water, gas, electricity, and sewer lines were expensive and scarce even in larger cities like Dallas. Urban women performed most of the same chores familiar to rural women, such as sewing, laundering, preparing meals from scratch, and even tending gardens, raising poultry, and milking cows on their urban lots to provide much of their families' meals. Rural ways prevailed with women producing up to 80 percent of the household food, but the availability of markets did lead to a decline in other types of household production. Expectations of cleanliness rose, however, forcing women to spend more time on such chores as sweeping and mopping rather than productive work.[11]

Urban areas spawned the rise of a middle class, where men earned enough to support their families and enough to ease their wives' burdens by hiring domestic help. This, in turn, created more jobs for domestic work in the cities and towns. By 1920, 25 percent of women earning wages outside the home were doing domestic work. The vast majority of these domestic servants were black or Hispanic. In Dallas, for example, 90 percent of domestic workers were black in 1900. These domestic jobs for women helped spur the growth of the towns and cities, providing incentive particularly for black migration during the first three decades of the century when the percentage of black Texans living in urban areas increased from 19 to 39 percent. Although opportunities for professional or skilled jobs for black women barely rose during this period, urban growth brought new opportunities for other types of employment for white women. Teaching and nursing attracted the bulk of women working outside the home, as these occupations were increasingly seen as related to women's traditional roles of nurturing and caring for others. Other common jobs traditionally related to women's work inside the home included hairdressing, millinery and dressmaking, and running boardinghouses or lodges. Other positions, however, opened for women in sales and clerical occupations, predominantly as secretaries and telephone operators. In addition to the traditional jobs, some newly flourishing industries in the cities employed women. A few women began earning their wages in non-traditional ways, but often this was because urban areas were more likely to allow widows to carry on the businesses, from publishing companies to foundries, of their deceased husbands. [12]

The greater leisure of the urban areas, the sufficient congregation of women in proximity to one another, and the fervent desire for educational opportunities led to the popularity of women's clubs. Initially, these were mainly literary and cultural clubs, which served a vital purpose for middle- and upper-class women, who had more leisure and education, but very restricted opportunities for advanced education or professional careers. Nationwide, only 2.8 percent of young women attended college in 1900. Many adult women in Texas had been denied opportunities for high school educations, and a college education, though available to women at many places in Texas, was only a dream for most before 1912. The elite women who did achieve an education or who had professional careers were drawn to the clubs as a place to meet with women of similar interests. [13]

Minority women were even less likely to have an opportunity for higher education. Yet a small but growing middle class of black women felt similar yearnings for social interaction, as well as literary and cultural self-edification. Excluded from the white clubs by racism and Jim Crow, the process of segregation in the South, black women formed their own clubs. Hispanic women were not invited to join white clubs either, but early in the century Mexican-American women made up only a small portion of the Texas population (less than 8 percent) and the expectations of their traditional cultures dictated that women stay home. As a result, Mexican-American women in Texas did not organize in clubs until after the Great Depression.[14]

In 1892, 495 white women's clubs joined together to create the General Federation of Women's Clubs with 100,000 members nationwide. The state affiliate, the Texas Federation of Women's Clubs, was founded five years later. Like the local clubs, these two organizations were for whites only, but black women's clubs successfully formed their own national and state alliances, the National and the Texas Association of Colored Women's Clubs. These alliances introduced Texas women, white and black, to a national progressive agenda. Information funneled to the local clubs from the national and state federations urged women not only to study literature, but also to acquaint themselves with the social issues of the day, such as the environment, illiteracy, conditions of working women, and child labor. Many clubwomen moved from self-education to reform on issues such as health, sanitation, and child welfare. Active clubwomen began new organizations, such as the Texas Congress of Mothers (later the Parent-Teacher Association), the Young Women's Christian Association, and even home extension clubs. Black women's clubs, exercising considerably less political clout, focused on educational, philanthropic, and welfare projects to help their own community since most political institutions and white women's clubs ignored them.[15]

Clubwomen's interest in reforming society led them into politics and attempts to influence political decisions, such as passage of child labor acts, stricter enforcement of pure food ordinances, and public support for home economics programs. When entering the political arena, Texas women had to face pervasive stereotypes that women did not belong in this public male domain. Social mores held that women were weaker, intellectually inferior, and more morally pure. Men thus supposedly protected women's nature by performing the difficult job of governing, as well as shielding themselves from the "poor" decisions women would make. Southerners resisted political activism by women and saw the woman suffrage campaign of the nineteenth century as a peculiarly northern agitation. Some women's suffrage groups in Texas had worked for the right to vote near the end of the nineteenth century, and some large women's groups such as the Women's Christian Temperance Union had endorsed suffrage. But these efforts failed to convince Texans either that women were individuals with equal rights to men or that they needed the vote to protect their rights. The clubwomen of the early twentieth century had greater political success for several reasons. First, they embraced the ideology that women were different from men. Indeed, they argued that women were purer and less self-interested than men, and for that reason women must have influence over governments. Second, the clubwomen were effective because of the influence they held with upper- and middle-class husbands who actually sat on the boards, city councils, and the state legislature.[16]

The women's clubs created the circumstances that would lead to a new Texas campaign for women's suffrage. Bonding together to work for common political goals, women learned organizing techniques. Running for office in the local, state, and national women's clubs taught them the basics of the political process and politicking. Reform issues were articulated in a weekly column of the *Dallas Morning News* by a progressive clubwoman, Isadore Miner Callaway, writing as Pauline Periwinkle. Periwinkle prodded the women to greater efforts and brought attention to the work that women were doing throughout the state. She also highlighted the work they could not do because of male political intransigence. The frustration of working for legislative agendas without being able to vote and thereby pressure elected officials also brought about a new call

for women's suffrage. Finally, progressivism articulated a new justification for women's right to political participation that appealed to
more traditional-minded Texans: women needed the right to vote
because they were different from men, not because they were like
them. Women with power would clean up government in a way
that men could not, much like women were able to clean house,
what historians have called "municipal housekeeping."[17]

In 1912 Texas women, with the assistance of the National
American Woman Suffrage Association, revived defunct local suffrage societies and formed the Texas Woman Suffrage Association,
later renamed the Texas Equal Suffrage Association (TESA), recruiting nearly 10,000 members statewide by 1916. While two earlier state suffrage associations had failed to win the vote or to attract
enough members to sustain growth, this group was eventually successful on both counts. Local branches concentrated on cultivating
positive sentiment for suffrage in their communities by advocating
that women's right to vote was necessary for progressive reforms,
the protection of children, and the "cleaning up" of politics.[18]

Under the leadership of the state president, Minnie Fisher Cunningham, TESA pressured the Texas legislature both in 1915 and
1917 to consider an amendment to the state constitution granting
women the vote. Legislative committees reported favorably both
times, but the amendment failed to receive the necessary number
of votes. Opponents spoke of "protecting" women from the vote
that would "rob her of those modest charms so dear to us Southern
men." But two other concerns were also prominent in the minds of
legislators: black women and prohibition. Critics of women's suffrage often argued that the means by which black men were kept
from the polls would not work with women and that a constitutional amendment would open up the question of black suffrage
generally. Recognizing the potency of the racial issue, the all-white
TESA was not inclined to accept black members. When a black
women's club in El Paso asked for admission to the organization, it

was first suggested that the black group withdraw its application to avoid embarrassing the suffrage campaign. A vote on the application was subsequently postponed until after suffrage had been won. The connection between women and the attempts to outlaw alcohol was so strong that liquor associations across the nation fought women's suffrage, sure that women would vote for prohibition. Women suspected that their inability to get a suffrage amendment passed by the Texas legislature was due to Governor Jim Ferguson's strong ties to the liquor lobby. When Ferguson was impeached, women brought pressure to bear on the incoming governor, William Hobby, who saw benefits to courting the women's vote. In 1918 the Texas legislature passed a law enabling women to vote in primary elections. After women's patriotic participation in World War I, a national constitutional amendment was sent to the states, where TESA's organizing led to Texas' ratification. In August 1920 the nineteenth amendment to the U.S. Constitution finally granted woman suffrage (although black women were not really able to exercise this right until the civil rights movement decades later due to white-only primaries and other subterfuges to keep African Americans from exercising political power).[19]

Their right to vote secured, many women took full advantage of it. The Texas League of Women Voters replaced the TESA and joined with several other statewide women's groups to form the Joint Legislative Council. This group lobbied successfully for improved funding for public education and health, prison reform, enforcement of prohibition, and new labor laws. In the very first election in which Texas women cast ballots, Annie Webb Blanton won the Democratic nomination and went on to become the first woman elected to a statewide office. Blanton, the first female president of the Texas State Teachers Association, was highly qualified for the position of the state's superintendent of public instruction. While Blanton clearly benefited from TESA support, her campaign for office also advanced the suffrage movement by increasing female voter turnout in this first test of their political power in Texas.[20]

TESA Treasurer Jessie Daniel Ames turned her organizing abilities gained from work in the suffrage movement to leadership of the Association of Southern Women for the Prevention of Lynching. TESA President Minnie Fisher Cunningham went on to become active in both Democratic Party politics and the newly formed League of Women Voters. In an ironic twist, Miriam Ferguson, wife of impeached Governor Jim Ferguson, a foe of women's suffrage, became the first female governor in 1924. Although seen as merely a "stand-in" for her husband, she was insulated by her gender against the appearance of corruption that had so stained her husband's reputation. Her race divided many women, inasmuch as some could not forgive her husband's opposition to women's suffrage. Others worked for her election because of her anti-Ku Klux Klan stance. And other women voted for her because the campaign convinced them that they could vote for a woman and still uphold traditional womanhood.[21]

While obtaining the vote seemed to offer limitless possibilities, it also stalled the women's political movement in some ways. Many women throughout the state remained active in politics, but they lacked the cohesion that the single issue of suffrage had provided. Once the vote was won, the TESA metamorphosed into the League of Women Voters. But numerous local suffrage leagues disbanded and women turned to other, or more local, concerns. After her success as superintendent of public instruction, Blanton mounted a campaign for U.S. Congress in 1922. The TESA was not there this time to support her candidacy, however, and her opponents specifically appealed to some women's groups, successfully splitting the women's vote. While Blanton had convinced voters that it was appropriate for a woman to hold the position of overseeing children's education, voters were less convinced that women were qualified for general legislative positions. A similar fate awaited Minnie Fisher

Cunningham when she unsuccessfully ran for the U.S. Senate in 1928. Even many former suffragists had doubts about the suitability of women running for such high offices. And in this campaign Cunningham lost the support of rural women, illustrating that her primary appeal was among the women in towns and cities, the places where women's clubs and suffrage societies had flourished.[22]

Despite the differences between urban and rural, nearly all women suffered during the Great Depression of the 1930s. As the price of cotton, vegetables, and cattle dropped, women in land-owning families had to stretch their resources even farther than before by mending clothing that was practically threadbare, cooking more meals without meat, and raising more foods in their gardens. For ranch hands and migratory laborers, the work practically disappeared. Tenant farmers and sharecroppers were also hit hard. It was almost impossible for them to make enough money on cotton to break even, and then New Deal policies geared toward decreasing cotton production prompted landowners to turn the sharecroppers off the land. Black agricultural families were even worse off because they were the least likely to own land and, because of prevalent racism, were the first to be evicted from sharecropping land and the last to be hired on farms for wages.[23]

By 1932 some 400,000 people in Texas were out of work. While some men left home in search of jobs, others, shamed by their inability to provide, abandoned their families, leaving more women with the economic responsibility of caring for themselves and the children. Despite the hard times, however, most families stayed together, relying upon each other and extended families.[24]

In rural areas families scrounged to make ends meet, but increasingly they chose to move. The number of farm tenants dropped by nearly half in some central Texas counties. By 1930 urban and rural populations were almost equal, and by 1940 more Texans lived in urban than rural areas. Although many agricultural families relocated to other rural areas, most young single people, especially women, were attracted to towns and cities, which seemed to offer greater promise for the future.[25]

Urban areas fared little better than rural areas during the Depression, however, for jobs were no more available for men in the cities than in the countryside. On the other hand, "women's work," along with the lower wages, was more available. Women often took up the slack by taking jobs or otherwise bringing in cash by taking in boarders or washing. Statewide, 75 percent of the women remained in the home, contributing to the household economy in traditional ways and stretching home resources as far as they would go. In the urban areas, however, women were much more likely to take jobs for wages: 25 percent of Anglo women, 25 percent of Mexican-American women, and 55 percent of African-American women worked for wages. Depression-era employers freely discriminated in hiring. Many positions were reserved for men only, while in some professions, including teaching, men were given preference. Married women were banned by many employers, and the Federal Economy Act of 1932 barred the federal government from employing both husband and wife, effectively preventing wives of government employees from working since men with higher paying jobs would be the ones who continued employment. Jobs reserved for women were usually deemed appropriate for women because of their connection to the household: jobs in domestic work, laundries, or the garment industry.[26]

Discrimination based upon race and ethnicity also shaped the types of jobs available to women. Industrial jobs went to Mexican-American or Anglo women. The increase of Mexican-American women in cities contributed to the development of certain industries such as pecan shelling, garment production, and cigar making. Jobs in these industries were better than domestic work, but potential workers exceeded the number of jobs, resulting in miserably low wages. Attempts to organize unions by the AFL and CIO, as well as by a very determined activist named Emma Tenayuca who led pecan shellers on a strike in San Antonio in 1938, had only limited success at increasing wages in these industries. Shortage of work, lack of language skills (immigrant women were less likely to be educated and learn English than immigrant men), and Mexican cultural traditions that dictated women should stay home decreased the number of Mexican-American women who worked despite the desperate need.[27]

Black women faced no such language barrier or traditional taboo against working for wages. However, industries deemed black women unsuitable employees. Black women were concentrated in domestic work, both commercial and private. Three-quarters of all employed African-American women worked as domestic servants. They worked in the private homes of affluent families that could still afford to hire help, and black women made up one-third of all hotel and restaurant female workers and one-fourth of all laundry workers. Black women also suffered more during the Depression because both private and government relief efforts discriminated against them. Even when New Deal policies tried to address the suffering caused by low wages and dislocations, minimum wage laws and other standards were not applied to domestic work performed predominantly by black women. Furthermore, wages for domestic work were driven downward by the dearth of jobs, due to the poor economy and to increased competition from Anglo and Mexican-American women.[28]

While many white women, desperate for jobs, would take whatever position was available, including domestic work, most white women were less likely to be so desperate for a wage because white men were more likely to hold onto their jobs. Moreover, many other jobs were open to white women. Shops hired them as sales clerks, and businesses and government offices employed them for clerical work. Women found work in hotels and cafes, beauty parlors, variety stores, and as telephone operators. Although New Deal programs were more likely to assist white women with training, these programs treated women only as extra or temporary workers. As a result, the training rarely prepared them for professional positions.[29]

The Depression also affected middle- to upper-class women, forcing them to cut back, make do, and stretch resources. Even so, their privileged positions and experience with club work led them to attempt to relieve the suffering of others through charitable organizations. Given the extent of the problems, these organizations were inadequate to the task; and given the prevalence of racism, what assistance they did offer was restricted primarily to helping their own race and class.[30]

Entry into World War II abruptly ended the Great Depression and opened new possibilities for women. Texans did their share to support the war, and Texas men and women were generous to-

Four unidentified women working on Army Air Force aircraft engine at Brayton Flying Service, Cuero, Texas, 1943. From UTSA's Institute of Texan Cultures, No. 099-0880, courtesy Rollie Brantley.

ward women who helped the war effort. One Texan, Oveta Culp Hobby, organized the Women Army Auxiliary Corps. Women Air Force Service Pilots trained at Ellington Army Base in Houston, then at Avenger Field near Sweetwater, Texas. Texans welcomed the women, recognizing both the sacrifices they were making for their country and the government dollars that were being funneled into the Texas economy as a result of the women being based there. In addition to the air corps, many Texas women served in the Army and Navy Nurse Corps, the Women Accepted for Voluntary Emergency Service, the Women's Reserve of the Coast Guard, and the Marine Corps Women's Reserves.[31]

Of course, not all Texas women entered the military. Most stayed at home and continued to conserve and stretch their resources, but this time for patriotic as well as financial reasons. Life on farms became easier for women during, and increasingly after, the war as better roads and better vehicles allowed them greater mobility and opportunities to leave their rural areas. Electrification projects begun in the 1930s were completed and, following the war, money to buy time-saving conveniences, such as refrigerators, washing machines, and gas stoves, greatly eased the toil of many farm women.

The federal government pumped money into the Texas economy for military bases and war materiel, but the state also benefited from the demand for oil and oil-based products. Because necessity during the Depression had already removed the stigma of women working for wages, because of the rapid demand for workers of all kinds, and because of the reduction of available men as they joined the military, women in Texas went to work in record numbers in World War II, and many of them did so in non-traditional jobs in war industries. The availability of higher paying "male" jobs led to a decline in women working in traditional female positions during the war. For the first time ever, the number of black women in domestic-service positions declined, as they took higher paying jobs.

Most of the new jobs for black women remained unskilled or semi-skilled, but black women also made their first real advancement in industrial positions as well.[32]

Not only were more women entering the workforce, but also they were doing so increasingly in urban areas. Farm mechanization, the rural-to-urban trend begun during the Depression, and the attractiveness of employment in wartime industries drew to the cities half a million rural Texans, as well as thousands of migrants from other states. The massive shift toward the cities, which continued in the postwar years, would have long-term effects on women's political, social, and economic status. While work attracted people to the cities in general, accessible and affordable automobiles, low-interest home loans for returning soldiers, and improved roads and highways encouraged many families to move to the suburbs. Nationally, the population of suburbs doubled in the 1950s, and in Texas that trend continued for the remainder of the twentieth century. The population of Houston's central city, for instance, increased 31.2 percent between 1960 and 1970, while the population of the surrounding area grew by 57 percent. There was a similar pattern for the same period in Dallas, whose central city increased by 24.2 percent, its suburbs by 61.8 percent.[33]

The move to the suburbs was celebrated in the press and the media as the answer to postwar adjustment. Women would leave their high-paying wartime jobs to raise children in suburban nuclear families, thereby opening jobs for returning soldiers who would then use the money to support families, buy homes, and, above all, consume. But educated women, deemed unpatriotic if they chose to pursue careers or occupations of their own, nevertheless sought outlets for their talents beyond the home, and they found socially acceptable avenues in civic, community, and other volunteer organizations. They joined such groups in huge numbers and in some cases wielded considerable power through them. A case in point was the Minute Women, a militant anti-communistic organization made up mostly of physicians' and businessmen's wives in the River Oaks area of Houston.[34]

Although the "ideal" postwar family had one male breadwinner and a stay-at-home mother, in reality women worked in record numbers. To be sure, postwar cutbacks in Texas, as in the rest of the nation, practically eliminated women from the high-paying, heavy industrial jobs, but even so the workforce had been irrevocably altered. A study by historian Fane Downs, for instance, noted that between 1920 and 1950 the percentage of jobs held by Texas women in several occupations had dramatically increased. From only 18 percent in 1920, women became 41 percent of the authors, editors, and reporters by 1950. While certain existing occupations became more feminized, new ones arose that particularly drew women. In 1920 social workers, dietitians, file clerks, and bank tellers were mostly men, but by 1950, respectively, 67 percent, 94 percent, 86 percent, and 43 percent of these positions were held by women. Gains made in industrial jobs during the war, however, did not become permanent. Only very small advancements were seen in most craft and manufacturing occupations, except the textile and apparel industries. Having turned to them during the Depression and World War II, these two industries continued to employ large numbers of women, increasing from 31 percent in 1920 to 72 percent by 1950.[35]

Increased urbanization during the war years also brought a critical mass of African Americans to the cities of Texas, where they faced new and different types of discrimination. Sixty-three percent of Texas blacks lived in urban areas by 1950, compared to 18 percent in 1900. African-American men and women who made sacrifices to help the United States win a war against fascism abroad became more vocal about their discontent with discrimination at home. The collective fight against segregation and discrimination relied upon women as much as men. Houston NAACP chapter officer Lulu B. White waged a determined struggle against segregation, leading her chapter in legal battles to overturn the white Democratic primary, to integrate the University of Texas, to elect more blacks to office, and to open more economic opportunities for black men and women. Meanwhile, on the local levels, women such as Juanita Craft in Dallas led fights to desegregate cities.[36]

Mexican Americans also carried out a postwar fight for equal rights and an end to segregation and discrimination. *Tejanas* used the American G.I. Forum Women's Auxiliary and LULAC to support legal battles to overturn school segregation. A grassroots campaign headed by women defended the right of a Mexican-American soldier's remains to be treated with dignity. Women also played significant roles in protests, strikes, and attempts to organize agricultural workers.[37]

As it happened throughout the nation, civil rights movements against the oppression of racial minorities paved the way for a recognition of and protest against women's oppression. In the 1960s it was still common practice for job advertisements to be divided by gender, just one of the clearest indications of discrimination against women in hiring. Once employed, women's wages were considerably less than men's, even when performing the same work, justified by the belief that men were required to support families but women were not. A married woman, although she might be one of the growing women professionals in the postwar era, was still considered legally subsumed under her husband's identity. Since the early nineteenth century a married Texas woman could own separate property and even had legal title to half of all the property accrued during marriage. However, she had no legal control over that property except to will it away at her death. All money, bank accounts, and property owned before marriage came under the husband's control at marriage, and he could direct a bank to not allow his wife access to her own money. She could not have credit without her husband's signature, which made opening her own business difficult. Married men, on the other hand, had complete control of their own property and needed no permission from their wives to borrow, lend, or sell. Until the mid-1950s women were not allowed to serve on juries, and thereafter they were granted easier exemptions than men.[38]

In the 1960s and 1970s thousands of brave women worked to end such discrimination. Texas women formed groups to address the problems they faced: job discrimination, rape, violence against women, sexism in the media, access to abortion, health care, and unequal treatment of women under the law. In 1972 women achieved a tremendous victory when they successfully lobbied for and campaigned to pass a state constitutional amendment guaranteeing that "equality under the law shall not be denied or abridged because of sex." Texas was also one of the 35 states to ratify the Equal Rights Amendment to the U.S. Constitution, which eventually fell three states shy of the 38 necessary for ratification.[39]

Despite the state's southern conservative roots, Texas and Texas women played a prominent national role in the women's rights movement. Sarah T. Hughes was one of the first women to be nominated for vice president of a major political party as early as 1952. Although she withdrew her name immediately by previous agreement, the gesture was intended to encourage more women to aspire to high offices. As the first female federal judge from Texas, Hughes is also the only woman to have presided over a presidential inauguration when she administered the oath of office to Lyndon B. Johnson on Air Force One after the assassination of President John F. Kennedy in Dallas. Texan Sarah Weddington, the youngest lawyer to ever win a case before the Supreme Court, argued *Roe v. Wade* (1973), which established a woman's right to an abortion. Also in 1973, Barbara Jordan became the first black woman from a southern state to serve in Congress and the first woman to give the keynote address at the Democratic National Convention in 1976. Texas women hosted the National Women's Conference for International Women's Year, the first such conference of its kind, in Houston in November 1977. Many Texas women, such as Ann Richards, were prominent among the founders of the National Women's Political Caucus in 1971, and Houston hosted the first national convention of that organization in 1973.[40]

The association's state affiliate, the Texas Women's Political Caucus, formed in 1972, went on to champion many women's rights, effectively focusing on educating, training, and supporting women to run for public office. And by the 1980s women had firmly established themselves in the Texas political process. Carole Keeton Rylander of Austin and Kathy Whitmire of Houston became mayors of major cities before 1981, and nearly every major city has had a woman mayor since that time. When the caucus began in 1972 there were only two women in the Texas legislature; by end of the century there were thirty-three. And, of course, women made great achievements at the statewide level. In 1982 Ann Richards became the first woman to win a statewide race since the 1920s. Just eight years later Richards won a tight race to become governor, and two women, Kay Bailey Hutchinson and Nikki van Hightower, vied for the state treasurer's position. This 1990 election epitomized the last decade of the twentieth century for women. A progressive Democratic woman won the top office in the state, while a Republican woman won another important statewide office. By 1993 the Republican Hutchinson had gone on to become the first woman U.S. Senator from Texas. Clearly, by the end of the century women were far from united in their political and social views, but whether liberal or conservative, the question of women's right to political participation had been settled.[41]

Along with women's advancements in politics went additional changes in the workforce. Male barriers still existed, but since the 1960s some women managed to start their own businesses. Mary Kay Ash not only engineered a beauty empire for herself, but also empowered many other women to become millionaires working with her products. Bette Nesmith Graham became an entrepreneur after marketing her new product, later known as Liquid Paper, to her fellow secretaries in a Dallas office. By 1997 there were 1.5 million women-owned businesses in Texas and California, accounting for 27.2 percent of all such businesses in the United States. Women's presence in professional positions continued to grow, and by the 1990s Texas women had even broken into the ranks of upper-level executive positions in prominent businesses, ranging from Texas Instruments to the Harris County Hospital District. Such success notwithstanding, Texas women in the late twentieth century continued to hit a "glass ceiling" that prevented many of them from moving beyond middle-management levels.[42]

Not all women, of course, were vying for the top positions in multi-national corporations. Texas women continued to fill predominantly "pink-collar" jobs, such as secretaries and assistants, to work in a variety of minimum wage positions, and to make up the vast majority of public school teachers, holding 80 percent of elementary and secondary school positions in 1990. One of the larger shifts in the Texas workforce at the end of the century occurred with the increased number of Hispanic, Asian, and African-American women, as the general population of these groups increased significantly. Between 1980 and 1990 the Hispanic population in Texas increased by 45 percent and the African-American population by 17 percent. In the next decade these groups had increased again by 54 percent and 19 percent, respectively, with the Asian population increasing 76 percent. The impact of these new women workers on the Texas economy has yet to be fully investigated or appreciated.[43]

Even with the political, economic, and legal gains of the last three decades of the twentieth century, Texas women faced difficulties in balancing traditional women's duties with the new roles and opportunities they had achieved. As thousands of new jobs, careers, and political offices opened to women, they struggled with home and career, with working for wages and paying for childcare, with making the best decisions for themselves and their families. One of the many stories epitomizing this conflict is that of Texas Representative Libby Linebarger. Elected in 1988, she earned a reputation within both parties as a hardworking, intelligent, and fair legislator with the "potential to become the first female speaker of the House." After three terms in which she was highly successful at advancing her legislative agenda and solving some of the state's stickiest issues, such as school finance reform, Linebarger chose not to run for office again after missing her daughter's tenth birthday because of her work at the Capitol: "When you miss significant events in your children's lives that you can never relive, maybe it's time to rethink your priorities."[44]

At the beginning of the century a woman's role was well-defined as a contributor to a family household with very little expectation of a different life for herself or her daughter. Even so, as urbanization provided the circumstances, women took the initiative to develop different roles for their future. Through self-education clubs, they came to understand that women could and should contribute in a greater capacity to the welfare of Texas. Pushing for and winning suffrage for themselves and their daughters, they claimed a political role for women that expanded throughout the century. Whereas the Great Depression forced women to take on new and greater roles of household production and wage earning, World War II offered more favorable incentives, such as patriotism, higher-paying jobs, and greater social acceptance. After the war, even though they were fired from the highest-paying industrial jobs, women continued to work in increasing numbers, timesaving conveniences eased household maintenance, and urbanization increased social and economic opportunities. Women organized for civil rights and then for women's rights once again, challenging racial and gender discrimination in employment, facilities, and society at large. By the 1980s women emerged full-scale into economic and political positions of power, but still felt the tug of traditional responsibilities to the family and the household. By the end of the twentieth century, though, unlimited opportunities lay ahead for women and their daughters.

Selected Bibliography

Acosta, Teresa Palomo, and Ruthe Winegarten, *Las Tejanas: 300 Years of History.* Austin: University of Texas Press, 2003.

Blackwelder, Julia Kirk. *Women of the Depression: Caste and Culture in San Antonio, 1929–1939.* College Station: Texas A&M University Press, 1984.

Cottrell, Debbie Mauldin. *Pioneer Woman Educator: The Progressive Spirit of Annie Webb Blanton.* College Station: Texas A&M University Press, 1993.

Jones, Nancy Baker, and Ruthe Winegarten. *Capitol Women: Texas Female Legislators, 1923–1999.* Austin: University of Texas Press, 2000.

McArthur, Judith N. *Creating the New Woman: The Rise of Southern Women's Progressive Culture in Texas, 1893–1918.* Urbana: University of Illinois Press, 1998.

McArthur, Judith N., and Harold L. Smith. *Minnie Fisher Cunningham: A Suffragist's Life in Politics.* New York: Oxford University Press, 2003.

Pitre, Merline. *In Struggle against Jim Crow: Lulu B. White and the NAACP, 1900–1957.* College Station: Texas A&M University Press, 1999.

Sharpless, Rebecca. *Fertile Ground, Narrow Choices: Women on Texas Cotton Farms, 1900–1940.* Chapel Hill: University of North Carolina Press, 1999.

Taylor, Elizabeth A. *Citizens at Last: The Woman Suffrage Movement in Texas.* Austin: Temple, 1987.

Turner, Elizabeth Hayes. *Women, Culture, and Community: Religion and Reform in Galveston, 1880–1920.* New York: Oxford University Press, 1997.

Weigand, Cindy. *Texas Women in World War II.* Lanham: Republic of Texas Press, 2003.

Winegarten, Ruthe. *Black Texas Women: 150 Years of Trial and Triumph.* Austin: University of Texas Press, 1995.

Endnotes

1. Rebecca Sharpless, *Fertile Ground, Narrow Choices: Women on Texas Cotton Farms, 1900–1940* (Chapel Hill: University of North Carolina Press, 1999), 7–12.

2. Sharpless, *Fertile Ground*, 70.

3. Sharpless, *Fertile Ground*, 96–99; Elizabeth York Enstam, *Women and the Creation of Urban Life*, Dallas, Texas, 1843–1920 (College Station: Texas A&M University Press, 1998), 91–92. See also LuAnn Jones, *Mama Learned Us to Work: Farm Women in the New South* (Chapel Hill: University of North Carolina Press, 2002), 171–83.

4. Sharpless, *Fertile Ground*, 80–81, 88–89, 96–101.

5. Sharpless, *Fertile Ground*, 90–95, 102–6; Enstam, *Women and the Creation of Urban Life*, 93.

6. Sharpless, *Fertile Ground*, 112–19.

7. Sharpless, *Fertile Ground*, 87–89, 113–16, 121; Teresa Palomo Acosta and Ruthe Winegarten, *Las Tejanas: 300 Years of History* (Austin: University of Texas Press, 2003), 95–96.

8. Elizabeth Maret, *Women of the Range: Women's Roles in the Texas Beef Cattle Industry* (College Station: Texas A&M University Press, 1993), 27–31; Acosta and Winegarten, *Las Tejanas*, 97.

9. Acosta and Winegarten, *Las Tejanas*, 97–99; Sharpless, *Fertile Ground*, 76–77, 88, 155; David Montejano, *Anglos and Mexicans in the Making of Texas, 1836–1986* (Austin: University of Texas Press, 1987), 175–77.

10. Sharpless, *Fertile Ground*, 222–23.

11. Enstam, *Women and the Creation of Urban Life*, 90–92.

12. Enstam, *Women and the Creation of Urban Life*, 75–84, 91; Fane Downs, "Texas Women at Work," in Donald W. Whisenhunt, ed., *Texas: A Sesquicentennial Celebration* (Austin: Eakin, 1984), 319–22; Ruthe Winegarten, *Black Texas Women: 150 Years of Trial and Triumph* (Austin: University of Texas Press, 1995), 156; Elizabeth Hayes Turner, *Women, Culture, and Community: Religion and Reform in Galveston, 1880–1920* (New York: Oxford University Press, 1997), 22–24; Jacquelyn Dowd Hall, *Revolt against Chivalry: Jessie Daniel Ames and the Women's Campaign Against Lynching* (New York: Columbia University Press, 1993), 29.

13. Turner, *Women, Culture, and Community*, 151–53.

14. Winegarten, *Black Texas Women*, 189; Judith N. McArthur, *Creating the New Woman: The Rise of Southern Women's Progressive Culture in Texas, 1893–1918* (Urbana: University of Illinois Press, 1998), 5–6; Arnoldo De León, *Mexican Americans in Texas: A Brief History* (Wheeling, Ill.: Harlan Davidson, 1999), 62; Acosta and Winegarten, *Las Tejanas*, 124–25.

15. McArthur, *Creating the New Woman*, 14; Turner, *Women, Culture, and Community*, 153; Winegarten, *Black Texas Women*, 189.

16. Turner, *Women, Culture, and Community*, 187–227.

17. McArthur, *Creating the New Woman*, 25; Jacquelyn Masur McElhaney, *Pauline Periwinkle and Progressive Reform in Dallas* (College Station: Texas A&M University Press, 1998).

18. Elizabeth A. Taylor, *Citizens at Last: The Woman Suffrage Movement in Texas* (Austin: Temple, 1987), 24–28, 30–34; McArthur, *Creating the New Woman*, 97–100; Turner, *Women, Culture, and Community*, 265–70.

19. Representative W. T. Bagby, *House Journal*, Reg. sess., 1915, p. 617, quoted in Taylor, *Citizens at Last*, 36; Taylor, *Citizens at Last*, 13–48; Judith N. McArthur and Harold L. Smith, *Minnie Fisher Cunningham: A Suffragist's Life in Politics* (New York: Oxford University Press, 2003), 44–67; Hall, *Revolt against Chivalry*, 42–43.

20. Cary D. Wintz, "Women in Texas," in *The Texas Heritage*, eds. Ben Procter and Archie P. McDonald (Wheeling, Ill.: Harlan Davidson, 1998), 202; Debbie Mauldin Cottrell, *Pioneer Woman Educator: The Progressive Spirit of Annie Webb Blanton* (College Station: Texas A&M University Press, 1993), 42–63.

21. Hall, *Revolt against Chivalry*; McArthur and Smith, *Minnie Fisher Cun-*

ningham; Shelley Sallee, "'The Woman of It': Governor Miriam Ferguson's 1924 Election," *Southwestern Historical Quarterly* 100 (July 1996): 1–16.

22. Cottrell, *Pioneer Woman Educator*, 74; McArthur, *Minnie Fisher Cunningham*, 145.

23. Winegarten, *Black Texas Women*, 177; Sharpless, *Fertile Ground*, 231–34

24. Sharpless, "Women and Work during the Great Depression in Texas," in Donald Williett and Stephen Curley, eds., *Invisible Texans: Women and Minorities in Texas History* (Boston: McGraw Hill, 2005): 19–20.

25. Winegarten, *Black Texas Women*, 177; Sharpless, *Fertile Ground*, 231–34; Sharpless, "Women and Work," 148–49.

26. Sharpless, "Women and Work," 148–52.

27. Winegarten, *Black Texas Women*, 156; Julia Kirk Blackwelder, *Women of the Depression: Caste and Culture in San Antonio, 1929–1939* (College Station: Texas A&M University Press, 1984), 10, 91, 151; Acosta and Winegarten, *Las Tejanas*, 142–44; Zaragosa Vargas, "Tejana Radical: Emma Tenayuca and the San Antonio Labor Movement during the Great Depression," *Pacific Historical Review* 66 (November 1997): 553–80; Sharpless, "Women and Work," 152.

28. Winegarten, *Black Texas Women*, 178–79; Blackwelder, *Women of the Depression*, 7, 42, 128–29.

29. Winegarten, *Black Texas Women*, 178–9; Blackwelder, *Women of the Depression*, 128–29.

30. Blackwelder, *Women of the Depression*, 59.

31. Dora Dougherty Strother, "Women of the WASP: An Introduction," in Anne Noggle, *For God, Country, and the Thrill of It: Women Airforce Service Pilots in World War II* (College Station: Texas A&M University Press, 1990), 3–8; Clarice F. Pollard, "WAACs in Texas during the Second World War," *Southwestern Historical Quarterly* (1989): 60–74; Cindy Weigand, *Texas Women in World War II* (Lanham: Republic of Texas Press, 2003).

32. Rose M. Brewer, "Black Women Workers: Yesterday and Today," in *Women in the Texas Workforce: Yesterday and Today*, eds. Richard Croxdale and Melissa Hield (Austin: People's History in Texas, 1979), 42.

33. Edward F. Haas, "The Southern Metropolis, 1940–1976," in Blaine A. Brownell and David R. Goldfield, *The City in Southern History: The Growth of Urban Civilization in the South* (Port Washington, N.Y.: Kennikat Press, 1977), 177.

34. Ruth Rosen, *The World Split Open: How the Modern Women's Movement Changed America* (New York: Penguin, 2000), 8–27; Don E. Carlton, "McCarthyism in Houston: The George Ebey Affair," *Southwestern Historical Quarterly* 80 (October 1976): 168.

35. Downs, "Texas Women at Work," 320–23.

36. Bernadette Pruitt, "'For the Advancement of the Race': The Great Migrations to Houston, Texas, 1914–1941, *Journal of Urban History* 31 (May 2005): 464; Merline Pitre, *In Struggle against Jim Crow: Lulu B. White and the NAACP, 1900–1957* (College Station: Texas A&M University Press, 1999); Stephanie Decker, "Women in the Civil Rights Movement: Juanita Craft Versus the Dallas Elite," *East Texas Historical Journal* 39 (Spring 2001): 33–42.

37. Acosta and Winegarten, *Las Tejanas*, 223–33.

38. Louise Ballerstedt Raggio, *Texas Tornado: The Life of a Crusader for Women's Rights and Family Justice* (New York: Citadel, 2003), 174–76.

39. Wintz, "Women in Texas," 205–7; Rodric B. Schoen, "The Texas ERA after the First Decade: Judicial Developments, 1978–1982," *Houston Law Review* 20 (October 1983): 1321.

40. Moira Davison Reynolds, *Women Advocates of Reproductive Rights: Eleven Who Led the Struggle in the United States and Great Britain* (Jefferson, N.C.: McFarland, 1994); Mary Beth Rogers, *Barbara Jordan: American Hero* (New York: Bantam, 1998); Darwin Payne, *Indomitable Sarah: The Life of Judge Sarah T. Hughes* (Dallas: Southern Methodist University Press, 2004); Ellen Pratt Fout, "'A miracle occurred!': The Houston Committee of International Women's Year, Houston, 1977," *The Houston Review* 1 (Fall 2003): 4–11.

41. Wintz, "Women in Texas," 206–7; Nancy Baker Jones and Ruthe Winegarten, *Capitol Women: Texas Female Legislators, 1923–1999* (Austin: University of Texas Press, 2000), 279–80.

42. Alan Farnham, "Mary Kay's Lessons in Leadership," *Fortune* 128 (September 20, 1993): 68; Paul Rosenfield, "The Beautiful Make-Up of Mary Kay," *Saturday Evening Post* (October 1981): 58–63, 106–7; Anne Dingus, "Texas Myth #92," *Texas Monthly* 35 (March 2007): 1; and U.S. Small Business Administration Office of Advocacy, *Women in Business, 2001* (Washington, D.C., 2001), 18–19; "Women in Healthcare," *Modern Healthcare* 18 (March 25, 1988): 22–25; Kristi Coale, "Women Making Gains in IS Sphere," *InfoWorld* 14 (March 9, 1992): 53, 56; Alison Eyring and Bette Ann Stead, "Shattering the Glass Ceiling: Some Successful Corporate Practices," *Journal of Business Ethics* 17 (February 1998): 245–51.

43. U.S. Bureau of the Census, *1990 Census of Population: Social and Economic Characteristics, Texas*, Section 1 (Washington, D.C.: U.S. Government Printing Office, [1992]); U.S. Bureau of the Census, *Texas: 2000, Summary Population and Housing Characteristics* (Washington, D.C.: U.S. Government Printing Office, 2002); *Handbook of Texas Online*, s.v. "Census and Census Records," http://www.tsha.utexas.edu/handbook/online/articles/CC/ulc1.html (accessed July 29, 2007).

44. *Austin American Statesman*, September 11, 1993, quoted in Jones and Winegarten, *Capitol Women*, 240. *Texas Monthly*, as late as 1989 published an article entitled "The Mommy War," highlighting women's differences of opinions on whether women should have careers and families. Jan Jarboe, "The Mommy War," *Texas Monthly* 17 (July 1989): 78.

Pagodas amid the Steeples

The Changing Religious Landscape

John W. Storey

DRAMATIC CHANGE CHARACTERIZED TWENTIETH-CENTURY Texas, no less so in religion than in any other aspect of the state's culture. In 1906 Protestants, mainly Baptists, representing 33 percent of the churchgoing public, and Methodists, 27 percent, along with the Disciples at 7 percent, Presbyterians, 5 percent, and Lutherans, Episcopalians, and others constituting another 3 percent, dominated the landscape. Catholics, while a sizeable 25 percent, were nonetheless an island in a Protestant ocean. By century's end Catholics had overtaken Southern Baptists to become the state's largest religious group, and members of several non-Christian faiths—Muslims, Hindus, Buddhists, and others—had established themselves in major urban centers. Church steeples, admittedly still dominant, now shared the urban skyline with pagodas, mosques, mandirs, gurdwaras, and synagogues. Texas had become pluralistic, and Texans in general had become decidedly more religious in tone if not in practice. Matching the religiosity of the American populace in general, polls since the 1980s showed that while only about 44 percent of Texans claimed to attend worship services weekly, 70 percent regarded religion as very important, 54 percent reportedly had had a "born again" experience, and 82 percent would applaud a child entering the clergy. And Texans acknowledging formal religious affiliation had risen steadily from about 40 percent in 1916 to 56.2 percent in 1970, remaining fairly constant thereafter for the remainder of the century. [1]

Immigration and changing demographics account for much that happened in twentieth-century religion. Texas experienced astounding population growth from 1900 to 2000, increasing from 3,000,000 to almost 21,000,000. And, significantly, as the percentage of African Americans steadily declined, that of Hispanics, primarily Mexicans, steadily rose. From 30 percent in 1860, African Americans constituted only 11.6 percent in 2000, and projections for the early twenty-first century pointed toward less than 10 percent. Simultaneously, the percentage of Mexicans rose sharply, from a little less than 6 percent in 1910 to 32 percent in 2000, making Mexican Americans the largest minority in the state. Whereas early in the century most Mexican Americans resided in south Texas along the Rio Grande, with San Antonio the principal center, by 1980 they could be found in every county in the state, with heavy concentrations in San Antonio, Dallas, Fort Worth, and Houston—especially Houston, which by the early twenty-first century had eclipsed San Antonio as the most Hispanic city in Texas. By 2005 a combination of Mexican Americans and other minorities made Texas, along with California, New Mexico, and Hawaii, a state in which minorities had become the majority. It was estimated that by 2030 Hispanics alone would be the majority.[2]

Considering that Mexican Americans were as likely to be Roman Catholics as African Americans Baptists, the religious impact of this population shift was enormous, as attested to by the current status of Catholicism. Certain statistics point toward unparalleled advancement for Catholicism in twentieth-century Texas. From approximately 150,000 members in 1880, the church numbered some 750,000 by 1930. Most of these newcomers were Mexicans displaced by the violence and anticlericalism of the Mexican Revolution of 1910. By 1960 the Catholic population was some 1,800,000, and by 1990 it totaled 3,575,728, making Catholics the most numerous group in the state. In 2000 there were 4,368,969 Catholics, 849,510 more than the nearest rival, Southern Baptists.[3]

Such growth compelled major diocesan restructuring. Until 1926, when the Diocese of San Antonio became the state's first archdiocese, the five dioceses of Texas belonged either to the Archdiocese of Santa Fe, New Mexico, or the Archdiocese of New Orleans. The Diocese of El Paso remained in the province of Santa Fe for some years to come, but the others—Galveston, Corpus Christi, and Dallas, as well as the newly fashioned Diocese of Amarillo—became part of the new province of San Antonio. Other dioceses followed—Austin, 1947; Galveston-Houston, 1959; Brownsville and Beaumont, 1965; Fort Worth, 1969; Victoria, 1982; Lubbock, 1983, and Tyler, 1987. In late 2005 the Diocese of Galveston-

St. Mary's Cathedral in Galveston, built in 1847, is Texas' oldest cathedral. Courtesy Carol Atmar.

Houston was elevated to an archdiocese, making Texas one of only two states to have two archdioceses. With fifteen dioceses, the Texas province was the largest in the world by 2004, and this was definitely a factor in the elevation of Archbishop Daniel DiNardo of the Archdiocese of Galveston-Houston to cardinal in November 2007. He became the first cardinal from not only Texas, but also the southern United States.[4]

These impressive figures give a false coloring to the total picture, however, for all was not well with Texas Catholics. Paralleling numerical growth was a shortage of priests and a serious decline in sisters and brothers. While the Catholic population more than doubled from 1960 to 2000, the number of priests remained about the same, wavering between 1,900 and 2,100. Meanwhile, the ranks of sisters fell from 4,950 in 1968 to 3,270 in 1993, and the brothers plummeted from 440 in 1967 to 240 in 1972, remaining fairly constant for the remainder of the century. This forced the church to close many of its schools, contributed to a decline in the percentage of Catholic children receiving formal religious teaching, and prompted some to wonder if the time had come for women priests and a married priesthood.[5]

There were also sharp internal divisions within the church itself throughout most of the century over matters of race, ethnicity, and class, as exemplified by the burgeoning Mexican population. Many church leaders early in the twentieth century, disclosing a bias toward Anglo and European Catholics of German, French, Czech, and Polish ancestry, viewed Mexicans, many of whom were wretchedly poor, as "social pariahs" with "few redeeming traits." Even the genuineness of their Catholicism was suspect, inasmuch as they often married outside the church, attended services sporadically, ignored certain sacraments, and established home altars, a tradition unsanctioned by the church. Until the 1930s most church officials made little or no distinction between immigrants and American-born Mexicans, considering "both groups . . . downtrodden foreigners . . . in dire need of spiritual and material uplift." But instead of integrating them into the main body of Catholicism, church leaders, citing the language barrier, usually provided separate churches for Anglo and Mexican worshippers.[6]

This resulted in Mexican Americans becoming something of a church unto themselves, a church within a church that attended their specific needs. Many refugee nuns and priests who themselves had fled revolutionary Mexico conducted worship services for them and expanded parochial schools in south Texas. An exiled group of Ursuline Sisters in Corpus Christi opened two schools for Mexican children in 1915, and an order composed entirely of Mexican-American women, the Missionary Catechists of Divine Providence, was organized in 1930 to minister to Houston's growing Mexican populace. Giving some cohesion to Mexican-American Catholicism was the Shrine of Our Lady of San Juan del Valle, constructed in the lower Rio Grande Valley in 1954 to honor the Virgin of San Juan, for whom Mexican Catholics had a strong commitment. The shrine has since become the most frequented Catholic pilgrimage site in the U.S.[7]

Given the sheer weight of numbers, Texas' Mexican community could not be ignored. By the 1920s the Chicago-based Catholic Church Extension Society and the American Board of Catholic Missions, a committee of the National Catholic Welfare Council, increased their funding of "Mexican work," an initiative soon handicapped by the Great Depression. In 1945 Archbishop Robert E. Lucey of San Antonio was instrumental in founding the Bishops' Committee for the Spanish Speaking, which focused on the religious, medical, and educational needs of Mexican Americans. Accordingly, it organized religious instruction classes for children and child-care programs for mothers, conducted voter-registration drives, and supported equal pay for Mexican workers, the rights of migratory farm laborers, and unionization of Corpus Christi bus drivers, 70 percent of whom were Hispanic.[8]

The quest for social justice initiated by the Bishop's Committee hastened in the 1960s as Mexican Americans themselves demanded greater social responsibility from the church. Individual priests and nuns readily joined the effort, as in the case of Father Antonio Gonzales of Houston's Immaculate Heart of Mary parish. Although a protest march of striking farm workers in the summer of 1966 from the Rio Grande to Austin failed in its primary objective, Gonzales nevertheless successfully used *la marcha* to raise the political and ethnic awareness of Mexican Americans. Three years later Father Patricio Flores of the Diocese of Galveston-Houston launched *Padres Asociados para Derechos Religiosos, Educativos y Sociales*, a militant priests' organization that prodded the church by preaching, marching, and picketing to become more attentive to Mexican Americans. Coincidentally, Flores became the Catholic Church's first Mexican-American bishop in 1970.[9]

Not to be left out, two activist nuns, Gregoria Ortego and Gloria Gallardo, created *Las Hermanas* in Houston in April 1971. Through rallies and boycotts this group aggressively advanced feminist issues, as well as a range of other social inequities affecting Mexican Americans in general. And the church responded. In 1969 it established the Campaign for Human Development (CHD), which addressed the causes of poverty. The CHD's most successful program was Communities Organized for Public Service, started in San Antonio in 1973. The Mexican American Legal Defense and Education Fund also received critical funding from the CHD in 1977. Since the 1970s church leaders, particularly Bishop Flores, who retired in 2005, have sympathized with the plight of undocumented immigrants flooding into Texas and the Southwest, assisting them through the Sanctuary Movement.[10]

That Mexican Americans had made significant strides in the twentieth century within the church and society at large was undeniable. Yet hints of ethnic fissures remained. As seen in the Archdiocese of Galveston-Houston, where in 2005 Hispanics outnumbered Anglos 40 percent to 30 percent, African Americans (19 percent), Asians (7 percent), and others (4 percent) making up the balance, cultural differences still separated many worshippers. At St. Cecilia Catholic Church in Houston's Memorial neighborhood, for instance, 37 percent of the parishioners were Hispanic, the vast majority recently arrived from Mexico. Of the church's six Sunday Masses, two were in Spanish. According to one observer, "the white and Latino communities at St. Cecilia remain fairly distinct, separated by language and culture." Only a few whites participated, for example, in the uniquely Mexican feast of Our Lady of Guadalupe. Even so, one Mexican member saw signs of progress, of a blending of cultures, noting that at the Oktoberfest tamales, gorditas, and roasted corn were as popular as standard German fare. Perhaps there is more than one way to achieve unity and brotherhood. [11]

Just as large-scale Catholic immigration from Mexico made it apparent that Texas would not be the special preserve of Protestantism, so too Asian immigration made it plain that Catholics and Protestants would have to share the territory with a host of non-Christian traditions. Passage of the Immigration and Nationality Act in 1965 made it easier for Asians to enter the United States, and the impact on Texas was soon evident. By 2000 Asians, representing 3.3 percent of the total, constituted the fastest-growing component of the state's population, and with almost 800,000 Asian residents in 2006, Texas was surpassed only by California and New York. The Asian community in Harris County alone, about a third of which was Vietnamese, almost doubled from about 110,000 in 1990 to approximately 217,000 in 2004. An even more dramatic increase occurred over the same period in adjacent Fort Bend County, as its Asian community swelled from about 14,000 to around 67,000, mostly Vietnamese and Chinese. According to some projections, about 7.3 percent of all Texans would be Asians by 2030.[12]

With these newcomers came a host of "strange" religious faiths that stood in glaring contrast to the traditional evangelical backdrop of Texas. And their appearance was swift. In Harris County, for instance, Muslims and Hindus numbered less than 1,000 each in 1970. Within a decade each group claimed about 10,000 adherents. Buddhists, virtually nonexistent in Harris County in 1970, had about 5,000 followers by 1980. Since other major urban areas had similar experiences, Texas had become home to an array of Muslims, Buddhists, Baha'is, Hindus, Sikhs, Jains, Zoroastrians, and Taoists by 2000. Obtaining reliable figures for many of these groups is difficult, and estimates vary wildly. Are there 2,000,000 or 8,000,000 Muslims in the United States, for instance, and are there about 115,000 or almost 400,000 in Texas? The former figure is probably the more accurate for Texas, indicating that the number of Muslims and Jews is roughly equivalent. In any event, Muslims came to Texas in substantial numbers in the latter twentieth century, and their preferred cities were Houston and Dallas. Smaller Muslim communities could be found in Fort Worth, Arlington, Austin, San Antonio, El Paso, Bryan-College Station, Corpus Christi, Kingsville, and Beaumont. Texas had at least ninety-one Islamic centers and mosques by 2000, the majority in Houston and Dallas. Evidence of the Muslim presence could be seen in such organizations as the Muslim Students Association, the Islamic Society of North America, the Muslim Arab Youth Association, the Islamic Circle of North America, and the Al Quaran-Was-Sunnah Society.[13]

The terrorist attack of 9/11 notwithstanding, some native Texans were drawn to the Islamic faith. A 2004 British documentary, *Turning Muslim in Texas*, featured a young white man who had planned to become a Southern Baptist preacher, but who converted to Islam while a student at the University of North Texas. Said he: "Islam is everything I wanted Christianity to be." According to a spokesperson, nine other white Texans converted to Islam at the Dallas Central Mosque in 2005. The Baha'i faith, a nineteenth century offshoot of Iranian Shi'a Islam, also had a notable presence in Texas, with seventy worship centers and almost 11,000 believers in 2000.[14]

Three strands of Buddhism have been planted in the state, with the Mahayana and Theravada forms the most prominent. In urban areas across the state, especially Houston and Dallas, Buddhist rituals conducted by monks or nuns attract a kaleidoscope of Chinese, Korean, Burmese, Cambodian, Thai, and Vietnamese seekers. Ironically, though, most services in the state's eighty-eight Buddhist centers are probably in English, indicative not only of the extent to which Buddhism has been Americanized, but also its appeal to the broader non-Asian community. Indeed, the oldest group in Texas, Nichiren Shoshu of America, which arrived in the early 1960s and claimed about 15,000 followers by 1985, attracted primarily local Texans in El Paso, Houston, and, especially, Dallas. The same was also true of two other Buddhist groups, one devoted to Tibetan Buddhism, the other to Zen Buddhism, which established major centers in Austin in 1974 and Dallas-Fort Worth in 1983, respectively. The Houston Zen Center opened in 2003, attracting locals who found its meditative practices a calming balm to urban stress.[15]

Temples ministering to the needs of specific immigrant groups, particularly the Vietnamese, increasingly appeared in the 1980s, as seen in the Khuon-Viet Buddhist Monastery of America in Grand Prairie, the Vietnamese Buddhist Pagoda Phat-Quang in Houston, and the Buu Mon Buddhist Temple in the coastal city of Port Arthur. The Buu Mon Temple's annual Lotus Garden Tour, begun in 1999, now draws visitors from across the state and nation. This temple also attracted widespread attention in October 2007 with the ordination of a former Catholic Franciscan monk as a senior monk in the Vietnamese Buddhist tradition, thought to be the first white American so honored. When the Texas Cambodian Buddhist Society was founded in Houston in 1982, Theravada, the principal form of Buddhism in Thailand, Burma, Sri Lanka, and Laos, gained a toehold in the Lone Star State.[16]

Hinduism is as varied as Buddhism, and Hindus of different persuasions have found the Texas climate receptive. Officially launched in 1978 to meet the needs of the Houston area's 10,000 Indian families, the Sri Meenakshi Temple was formally consecrated in July 1982. It was the largest *mandir*, or temple, in the nation, and messages of support came from the White House, Texas Governor William Clements, Jr., and Congressman Mickey Leland of Houston. In June 2005 a 500-year old sect, Vallabh Priti Seva Samaj, opened in southwest Houston the largest temple of its faith in the southwestern United States. Over 1,500 people, some from India, celebrated in colorful traditional garb the unveiling of a statue of Lord Krishna. Two months later thousands of Hindus gathered at Houston's Brown Convention Center to celebrate the birth of Krishna, considered an incarnation of Vishnu, a protector-God of Hinduism. To preside over temple services Hindus prefer priests of Brahmin background trained in India, but not all of the thirty-four worship centers in Texas could boast of such a priesthood in

The Buu Mon Buddhist Temple in Port Arthur is indicative of the growing Buddhist presence in Texas. Courtesy Gail Storey.

2000. Closely associated with and sometimes absorbed by Hinduism, Jainism, an ancient faith that promotes vegetarianism and nonviolence and stresses reincarnation and the multifaceted nature of truth, had six temples by 2000.[17]

Many Indian immigrants coming from the Punjab region since 1965 have been Sikhs, and they have formed *gurdwara*s, or temples, in Austin, Dallas, and Houston. By 2000 they had thirteen temples from which a message of religious harmony and the unity of God was proclaimed. Even so, following 9/11 many bearded, turban-wearing Sikh men were mistaken for Muslims and accosted by angry Americans. This prompted the Singa Sabha Gurdwara in Austin to conduct seminars on Sikhism and to sponsor public showings of the documentary *Mistaken Identity*. Rounding out the Asian religious pattern in Texas by 2000, Zoroastrians had three temples, Taoists, one.[18]

There has been a Jewish presence in Texas since the early 1800s, but it was minuscule then, and still negligible in 2000. From approximately 15,000 in 1900, Jews increased to some 30,000 in 1920, about 50,000 in 1945, around 92,000 in 1988, and 128,000 in 2000, or approximately 0.6 percent of the Lone Star State's population. In 1992 the elderly Rabbi Jacob Rader Marcus, an authority on American Jewish history, dismissed Texas as an uninviting outpost for rabbis of real ability. Neither the best nor the brightest, he asserted, would go there. One has to question the rabbi's judgment, considering that Texas rabbis distinguished themselves in confronting the racial bigotry of the Ku Klux Klan, striving for interfaith harmony, chiding Texas lawmakers for considering passage of an antievolution law, objecting to Bible reading in public schools, supporting the civil rights of African Americans, championing the cause of laboring people, and participating actively in the civic and cultural life of the communities in which they resided. All in all, Texas rabbis, as well as the Texas Jewish population in general, exercised influence far out of proportion to their numbers.

Such was certainly the case of Henry Cohen, rabbi of Galveston's
B'nai Israel congregation from 1888 to 1949; Samuel Rosinger,
Beaumont's rabbi from 1910 to 1965; Hyman Judah Schachtel,
rabbi to the oldest, wealthiest, and perhaps most prestigious syn-
agogue in Texas, Temple Beth Israel of Houston, from 1943 to
1975; and Levi Olan, rabbi to the second-largest Jewish congregation in the state, Temple Emanu-El of Dallas, from 1949 to 1970.
And since the 1930s Houston Hillel, The Foundation for Jewish
Campus Life, has afforded Jewish students in Houston-area schools
of higher learning, particularly Rice University and the University
of Houston, a center for sharing and embracing their heritage. Indeed, Houston Hillel is the only institution in Houston that provides rabbinical support to Jewish college students. [19]

With the seizure of power in Germany by Adolf Hitler and the
Nazis, no issue aroused deeper emotions among American Jews in
the 1930s and 1940s than Zionism. But sharp divisions existed over
the nature of Zionism. Was it *national*, pointing toward a Jewish
state in Palestine? Or, was it *cultural*, expressive of a universal pattern of ethics for all humanity rather than a parochial religion identified with a specific ethnic group? Hitler made national Zionists
of most American Jews, but in Texas there was no more powerful
voice for cultural Zionism anywhere than that of Rabbi Schachtel.
Indeed, it was Schachtel's outspoken opposition to a Jewish state
that had attracted Houston's prestigious Beth Israel congregation.
Many of its members, prominent in the commercial world and as-
similated to life in Texas, considered America their Zion. A state in
Palestine would only kindle suspicions of dual loyalty, making Jews
comparable to Roman Catholics, whose Protestant neighbors often
suspected them of placing allegiance to the Vatican ahead of that to
America. With Schachtel as its rabbi, there would be no doubt of
Temple Beth Israel's devotion to the U.S.[20]

Houston's Jews were as accustomed to feuding as Baptists, and
most of the city's seven synagogues by 1943, from Reform to Con-

servative to Orthodox, had resulted from bitter splits. So controversy was nothing new, but the one that erupted soon after Schachtel's arrival in late 1943 drew national attention. Ardent Zionist Robert I. Kahn, an assistant rabbi at Beth Israel who was away serving as a chaplain in the U.S. Army, was disappointed when the congregation bypassed him for Schachtel; he was subsequently dismayed by the strong anti-Zionist position taken by the congregation and its new rabbi. Consequently, in March 1944 Kahn resigned from Beth Israel and in July 1944 agreed to become the rabbi at war's end to some 142 families that had withdrawn from Beth Israel in protest over the Zionist issue to form Temple Emanu El, another Reform congregation, but a fervently Zionist one. Schachtel meanwhile saw clearly the course of events, especially after more revelations of the Holocaust, and by November 1948 he backed away from his previous position on Jewish nationhood and sought thereafter to make peace with his former Zionist opponents. By 2000 Texas had ninety-two synagogues or centers, up considerably from the five in 1888, or the thirty-six in 1950.[21]

To this mixture add other bodies either nonexistent or negligible in 1900—a handful of Amish, Mennonites, and Friends, 50,000 or so Nazarenes, about 155,000 Mormons, and at least 300,000 Pentecostals of different types—and it becomes readily apparent that Texas had become pluralistic by 2000, home to a diverse community of Christian and non-Christian traditions. This speaks well of the ability of Texas, a southern state heretofore dominated by Christian evangelicals of one kind or another, to accommodate a multiplicity of faiths. Illustrative of this religious openness was the evolution of the Interfaith Ministries of Greater Houston. Begun in 1955 as the Church Welfare Bureau, it coordinated Protestant ministries for the needy. With the inclusion of the Jewish community, the Bureau became Protestant Charities in 1964, then Houston Metropolitan Ministries in 1969. And by 1992, when the agency adopted its current name, it had become a microcosm of the state's emerging pluralism, uniting Christians, Jews, Buddhists, Hindus, Muslims, Sikhs, and others in a common humanitarian cause.[22]

That pluralism entails diversity is obvious, but diversity goes beyond a multiplicity of competing Christian and non-Christian faiths. It also involves internal differences within specific religious traditions. As previously observed, for instance, there is a certain amount of pluralism within Texas Catholicism itself, as seen in a Mexican-American service featuring a Mariachi Mass, guitars, and a Spanish-speaking priest. The Baptist General Convention of Texas reflects similar internal diversity. After Baptists surpassed Methodists in 1906, they remained the state's largest denomination until 1990, at which point Roman Catholics claimed 21 percent and Baptists 19.2 percent of the total population. A decade later Baptists had slipped to 16.9 percent, while Catholics held at 21 percent. It may appear so to outsiders, but Baptists have never been monolithic. To be sure, the Baptist General Convention of Texas (BGCT) domi-nated Baptist life throughout the twentieth century, but there were always rival groups. Indeed, there were at least sixteen competi-tors to the BGCT in 2000, from Free Will Baptists, the Missionary Baptist Association, and Landmark Baptists to Primitive Baptists, Two-Seed in the Spirit Baptists, and Southern Baptists of Texas (SBT).[23]

The appearance of this last body, SBT, demonstrates a tension that has long existed within the Baptist fellowship. A fervent com-mitment by practically all Baptists to biblical authority, evangelism, and foreign missions has generally obscured internal divisions over matters of inerrancy, the priesthood of the believer, and social re-sponsibility. But from time to time these differences have surfaced in bitter feuds as Baptists of a fundamentalist bent, those who sub-scribed to biblical literalism and disdained anything that detracted from individual soul winning, accused their more moderate breth-ren of infidelity. J. Frank Norris, for instance, pastor from 1920 to 1952 of the First Baptist Church, Fort Worth, and a fundamentalist of national prominence, embroiled the BGCT in bitter controversy during the 1920s, until moderates closed ranks and evicted him from local and statewide assemblies.[24]

By the 1950s two Baptists of national standing reflected the dichotomy within the state convention—T. B. Maston, professor of Christian ethics at Southwestern Baptist Theological Seminary in Fort Worth from 1922 to 1963, and W. A. Criswell, pastor from 1944 to 1995 of the prestigious First Baptist Church of Dallas. Janus-like, these men disclosed the opposing faces of the BGCT. Whereas Maston stressed the social dimension of faith, insisting that an exclusive emphasis on evangelism was to proclaim only a "partial gospel," Criswell fervently believed evangelism the answer to all ills, personal and social. And whereas Maston took a more nuanced, interpretive approach to the scriptures, Criswell was a biblical literalist who insisted, for example, that the days of creation in Genesis were 24-hour solar days. Baptists of Maston's persuasion forged the Christian Life Commission (CLC) in 1950 and through it called attention to social ethics. Racial matters were a major concern in the 1950s and 1960s. Baptists of Criswell's persuasion launched an offensive in 1979 to purge the Southern Baptist Convention of "liberals" and turn it toward a more "rightward," evangelistic course. Predictably, Maston and Criswell saw the battle for control of the SBC quite differently. The seminarian believed it had more to do with "political power . . . than . . . the Bible," while the preacher reduced it to liberal skunks versus Bible-believing conservatives. Criswell's side won. By 1990 fundamentalists controlled the national convention, and in the opinion of one observer the Dallas pastor had been "the prime mover of the return of fundamentalism."[25]

But the victory was incomplete, according to Criswell, because the state conventions, such as the BGCT, were still "very much liberal." Although fundamentalists were unsuccessful in attempts to control the state body, the fundamentalist threat nevertheless

was serious enough to prompt Baylor University, the denomination's educational flagship, to assert its independence in September
of 1990, lest ultra-conservatives did gain control of the BGCT. In
1998, unable to have their way, a group of fundamentalists pulled
out of the BGCT and organized the SBT. While not a major threat,
this new body attracted some 1,300 congregations, including many
of the megachurches. This resulted in reduced contributions to the
BGCT, forcing it to make cutbacks in staff positions in 2003. So, as
the spiritual heirs of Maston and Criswell, devoted Baptists all, continue to disagree over the best way to fulfill the gospel, the strain
within the Baptist fellowship will likely endure. [26]

Overwhelmingly Anglo at the beginning of the century, the
BGCT has become somewhat more ethnically and racially diverse
as a result of efforts to evangelize the expanding Mexican population and, later, to integrate African Americans. Along with Methodists and Presbyterians, Texas Baptists made overtures early in the
century toward the Mexican population in south Texas. In 1910
the Mexican Baptist Convention of Texas was organized in San Antonio upon recommendation of a BGCT committee. The need for
publicity soon led to publication of *El Bautista Mexicano*, funded
by the SBC, and the need for education prompted local Baptists in
Harlingen and San Antonio, respectively, to open in the late 1940s
the Valley Baptist Academy and the Hispanic Baptist Theological
Seminary (originally the Mexican Bible Institute). Both institutions
later came under the control of BGCT. One of the state convention's more successful initiatives was the Rio Grande River Ministry. Begun in the 1960s to evangelize, build churches, and provide
medical and social services to residents on both sides of the roughly
800-mile river border between Mexico and Texas, the ministry was
credited by 1996 with founding 639 churches, sixty-seven medi-
cal/dental clinics that treated on average 25,000 patients annually,
six children's homes, and six theological-training centers on the
Mexican side of the river.[27]

While it was never intended that the Mexican Baptist Convention should be separate and independent of the BGCT, it nevertheless evolved in that direction because of language and cultural differences. Moreover, there was always a certain tension between Anglo and Mexican Baptists. Though always cordial, some Mexican Americans sensed and resented an air of paternalism on the part of the Anglos, who tended to treat all Mexicans as "foreign newcomers," overlooking the fact that the ancestors of some Mexican Americans had been in Texas long before the Anglos arrived. For their part, Mexican Americans themselves were ambivalent. They wanted to be an integral part of the BGCT, to move into the mainstream, yet preserve their cultural identity, their uniqueness.[28]

Since the 1960s Anglo and Mexican-American Baptists seem to have come to a better understanding of one another. And well they should, for Hispanics have increasingly become an important part of Texas Baptist life. Numerically, progress has been slow but steady. There were about 6,000 Mexican Baptists in 1927, some 30,000 in 1963, and approximately 130,000 in 2002. And in recent years Hispanic congregations in far greater numbers than any other non-Anglo group have been affiliating with the BGCT. In 1997, for example, the convention added 115 Hispanic congregations and only forty-five African-American; in 2000 it was 175 to twenty-two. By 2006 almost 1,300 of the convention's 5,700 congregations, or nearly 23 percent, were Hispanic, and in the near future Hispanics were expected to comprise 50 percent of the Baptist churches in Houston and San Antonio. This partially explains the election of Albert Reyes, whose Texas-Baptist roots extend to the 1880s, as the first Mexican-American president of the BGCT in 2004. But cultural differences between Anglo and Mexican-American Baptists still exist, according to Gus Reyes, a recently appointed ethnic consultant to the BGCT. If Anglos want to continue making progress in the Hispanic community, said Gus Reyes, they must understand one thing—"R-E-S-P-E-C-T" for Hispanic values and customs.[29]

Despite inroads made by Baptists, Methodists, and Presbyterians over the past century, as well as those more recently of Mormons, Jehovah's Witnesses, and Pentecostals, the vast majority of Hispanics in Texas remains Roman Catholic. By the same token, African Americans by comparable margins continue to be Baptists. In 1890, for instance, African-American Baptists statewide totaled 111,138, while Methodists claimed only 42,214. Almost 72 percent of all African-American church members were Baptists in 1916, slipping to almost 67 percent in 1926, but still far ahead of the Methodists at 25 percent. These percentages remained about the same for the rest of the century. Catholics, Presbyterians, and others claimed only a few African Americans.[30]

Although African Americans were Baptists, they were not Southern Baptists affiliated with the BGCT. Texas was a rigidly segregated state in the first half of the twentieth century, and with only a few exceptions most white Baptists preferred it that way. So African Americans forged their own denominational structures. There were several state conventions, such as the American Baptist Convention of Texas (1882) and the General Baptist State Convention (1893). The first national convention to succeed came in 1895. That year African Americans gathered in Atlanta and created the National Baptist Convention of the United States of American (NBC, USA). This body's most successful venture in the early years was the National Baptist Publishing Board, begun in 1897 and headed by Texan Richard Henry Boyd, a former slave of considerable talent who believed African Americans should produce their own educational and religious literature. A dispute over the publishing board led to the formation of the National Baptist Convention of America in 1915, and a split from this group brought about the Progressive National Baptist Convention in 1961. Most African-American congregations in Texas were affiliated with the NBC, USA, which claimed about 250,000 members in the state in 2001.[31]

Things began to change as the civil rights movement gained momentum in the 1950s. White Baptists such as Maston and his colleagues at the CLC prodded fellow church members to open their doors to African Americans, and African Americans themselves became more assertive. In 1954 two black churches in Austin, the 19th Street Baptist Church and the Ebenezer Baptist Church, broke the BGCT's color barrier by applying for admission to the Austin Baptist Association. There was opposition, but it was overcome in 1955. Since then white Baptist churches and educational institutions, though not always gracefully, have accepted blacks, and the BGCT has steadily expanded its work among African Americans. As a result, of the state convention's 5,650 congregations in 2005, about 750, or 13 percent, were African American. Moreover, in 2005 the BGCT elected its first African-American president, Michael Bell, the 54-year old pastor of Fort Worth's Greater St. Stephen First Baptist Church. Known to his Fort Worth neighbors as the bullhorn-toting preacher who in the mid-1990s picketed the predominantly white Tanglewood Elementary School in protest of the district's inequitable distribution of resources, Bell was an aggressive proponent of social justice. Fifty years ago he would have been spurned by the denomination's white establishment, but now, according to Charles Wade, the convention's executive director, Bell's "passion" was exactly what was needed to meet human needs. Further indicative of changing attitudes, Wade also noted that proposals were under consideration to restructure the convention's executive board so that 30 percent of its ninety members would have to be non-Anglo. With African-American and Hispanic congregations combined making up about one-third of the total, such a change would seem warranted.[32]

Three other mainline denominations whose growth stagnated in the latter twentieth century and whose membership actually declined as a percentage of the state's population were Presbyterians, Episcopalians, and Methodists, bodies that made no appreciable headway in the Hispanic and African-American communities. In the last three decades of the century the Presbyterian Church, USA, gained only 33,121 new adherents, increasing from 147,194 in 1970 to 180,315 in 2000, but the church's percentage of the population dipped from 1.3 to 0.9. Likewise, the number of Episcopalians held firm at about 176,000 from 1970 to 2000, but the percentage ebbed from 1.6 to 0.9. The United Methodists fared little better. Although the denomination expanded from 855,733 adherents in 1970 to 1,022,342 in 2000, its percentage of the population fell from 7.6 to 4.9. Typical of the church's condition was the sprawling Houston-based conference that stretches from Galveston to Texarkana. From 1996 to 2006 it established only fifteen new congregations, but closed twenty-nine over the same decade. Painfully aware of the situation, the conference bishop, Janice Riggle Huie, challenged her flock to found 100 new churches by 2016, strongly implying that many of them should be in non-Anglo communities. "It is no longer acceptable that the Texas Annual Conference is 80 percent Anglo," she declared, "when almost half of our population is from a different racial-ethnic group." Overwhelmingly white Presbyterians and Episcopalians face a similar challenge.[33]

Other aspects of Texas religion that in 1900 were either unanticipated or blossomed beyond expectation were televangelism, the proliferation of megachurches, the enormous popularity of apocalyptic visions, the emerging presence of ordained women pastors, and the "culture wars." Religious television, whose base was broadened considerably by satellite broadcasting in the early 1980s, has been essentially a southern phenomenon. The names Billy Graham, Oral Roberts, Jerry Falwell, Pat Robertson, Jim Bakker, and Jimmy Swaggart readily come to mind. While the audience size of the electronic church is debatable (Falwell claimed fifty-million viewers for his *Old-Time Gospel Hour*, for example, but Arbitron and Nielsen put the figure closer to two million), it is generally agreed that most of the viewers (45 to 55 percent) come disproportionately from the South. And Texans contribute to that following, as exemplified by the popular ministries of James Robison, John Hagee, Kenneth Copeland, T. D. Jakes, and Joel Osteen.[34]

Today's megachurches, praised by some observers, excoriated by others, are an extension of trends evident in late nineteenth-century Protestantism. One finds the seeds of the modern mega-church's video-game rooms, bowling lanes, preschools, counseling programs, and food courts in the institutional church and social gospel movement of the 1880s. Especially in the larger urban areas, church as entertainment increasingly became the norm in the latter nineteenth century. Contemporary megachurches have merely refined the trend with twentieth-century technology, especially sophisticated sound systems and big-screen television, and they afford the same respite from life's routine that many Americans derive from going to shopping malls, sporting arenas, and movie theaters.[35]

By definition, a megachurch is one that has a weekly attendance of at least 2,000, and the number of such congregations nationwide grew rapidly in the latter twentieth century. Only six churches, excluding Catholic ones, would have qualified in the early twentieth century, for instance, and only sixteen in 1960. The proliferation began in the 1970s, as many churches increasingly turned to "modern growth strategies" from the fields of marketing, psychology, and communications. By 2005 there were at least 1,210 megachurches nationwide, with Texas at 157 leading the way, along with California. Although most in Texas were Southern Baptist, megachurches usually downplayed their denominational connection, stressing instead a more ecumenical nature with names like Willowbrook Community Church or Riverside Community Fellowship. Although most megachurches fall within the 2,000 to 4,000 average weekly attendance range, the largest in the nation is Houston's nondenominational Lakewood Church, where Pastor Joel Osteen soothes a weekly audience of about 38,000 with an upbeat message of good health and material prosperity. Another of the state's nondenomi-

national megachurches also known for its "prosperity gospel" is
The Potter's House in Dallas, a predominantly African-American
congregation, although whites, Hispanics, and others regularly attend. Begun in 1996 by Bishop T. D. Jakes, a West Virginian of
Pentecostal roots, the church claims 30,000 members and offers an
impressive assortment of programs. Much more political than Osteen, Jakes addressed the Congressional Black Caucus in 2000, was
invited to the White House by Presidents Bill Clinton and George
W. Bush, and was openly supportive of President Bush.[36]

Apocalyptic scenarios built on millennial projections have
long fascinated some Christians, especially evangelicals. Consider
the remarkable success of *The Late Great Planet Earth* (1970) by
Houston native Hal Lindsey, which reportedly sold twenty million copies in fifty-two languages worldwide, and more recently
the *Left Behind* (1995-2006) thrillers, which had sold sixty-two
million copies by 2004. But long before Lindsey and company,
the soil had been prepared by Cyrus I. Scofield, who took the
helm of Dallas's small First Congregational Church in 1882. His
widely read annotated version of the King James Bible, the *Scofield Reference Bible* (1909), which reflected the influence of John
Nelson Darby's dispensational premillennialism, pieced together
an exciting tale about the Rapture, Tribulation, Antichrist, the
Second Coming, Armageddon, and the Day of Judgment. Scofield died in 1921, but three years later his closest disciple, Lewis
S. Chafer, founded Dallas Theological Seminary, dubbed by some
"the Yale of conservative Christianity." Graduates of this school
lead many of today's top Bible institutes, and thousands more
pastor prominent churches. And like Darby and Scofield before
them, they search current events for evidence of biblical prophecy,
for signs that the end is near. It is hard to imagine the remarkable
success of Tim LaHaye and Jerry B. Jenkins without the ground-
work of this Dallas institution, which also upholds tradition regarding men and women in the ministry.[37]

To be an ordained Christian minister and to stand in the pulpit has generally been considered the exclusive preserve of men, especially in the South where evangelicals have held sway. There have been many women preachers, to be sure, but for the most part women were expected to play less prominent roles, such as raising funds for domestic and foreign missions, directing charitable efforts, holding prayer meetings, serving as nurses, teachers, and missionaries, and leading various women's auxiliaries. Even Pentecostals, known for many women preachers, tended to conform to southern culture. The pattern changed dramatically in the latter twentieth century, as most denominations sanctioned the ordination of women, sometimes in the face of strong opposition, and opened their pulpits to them—somewhat. The United Methodists faced the issue in 1956, with Reform and Conservative Jews, Episcopalians, Presbyterians, Disciples of Christ, Evangelical Lutherans, and others following suit in the 1970s and 1980s. The fundamentalist-controlled Southern Baptist Convention bucked the trend in 2001, unequivocally opposing the ordination of women, but the BGCT pointedly rejected the position of the national convention.[38]

Since the 1950s thousands of women have been ordained. Some of them have become senior pastors, as in the cases of Rabbi Barbara Metzinger of Beaumont's Reform Temple Emanuel and Rev. Julie Pennington-Russell of Waco's Calvary Baptist Church, who left Texas for Decatur, Georgia, in June of 2007. Some have become bishops, as in the cases of Bishop Janice Riggle Huie of the Texas Annual Conference and Bishop Dena Harrison of the Episcopal Diocese of Texas. But most ordained women, including those in Texas, have had to settle for secondary positions as assistant pastors, seminary teachers, counselors, directors of various church programs, and so on. Despite the BGCT's stated support of women, for instance, only four of the convention's 5,700 congregations had a female senior pastor in 2006. Perhaps state Baptist leaders were willing, but the flock clearly was not following. As for

Episcopal women, despite the elevation of Dena Harrison of Houston in October 2006, even obtaining ordination could be difficult, since three of the state's five bishops have refused to ordain women priests. By contrast, the state's Methodists and Presbyterians have probably been the most receptive, with women making up about 25 to 30 percent of each group's senior pastors.[39]

Since the 1970s the status of women has, of course, been a factor in the ongoing "culture wars," an extension in many respects of the clash earlier in the century over "modernism." In contemporary debates over prayer in the classroom, the teaching of intelligent design alongside evolution, and the presumed Christian basis of American civilization one hears an echo of the 1920s and glimpses the ghost of J. Frank Norris. Adding to the acrimony of the present discourse, however, are the issues of homosexuality and gay rights. All the major religious bodies, from Catholic, Baptist, Methodist, and Presbyterian, have been perplexed by sexual matters, none more so than the Episcopal Church. Episcopalians have quietly tolerated gay priests since the 1970s, and some bishops have even ordained openly gay priests and deacons since the late 1980s. Even so, conservatives have never approved of this liberal thrust, and so when the triennial General Convention, meeting in Minneapolis in August of 2003, sanctioned not only the ordination of an openly gay bishop in New Hampshire but also same-sex unions, holy war immediately erupted and Texas Episcopalians were at the epicenter.

Leading the assault was the staunchly conservative and fervently evangelistic pastor and founder of Christ Church in Plano, the Rev. Canon David H. Roseberry, whose 4,400-member congregation boasted the largest weekly attendance of any Episcopal church in the nation. All five of Texas' bishops had cast dissenting votes at the triennial gathering. Bishop Jack Leo Iker of Fort Worth angrily announced that he was "shocked and offended" by the decisions. Consequently, when Roseberry and his congregation organized a protest meeting for October 2003, some 2,800 attended, including forty bishops. A subsequent meeting in January 2004 gave birth to the Network of Anglican Communion Dioceses and Parishes, a group that vowed to resist the ordination of gays, refused to take communion with church leaders who favored the practice, and threatened schism. For conservative Episcopalians in Texas, as well as others around the country who agreed with them, the Network became something of an alternative church. Only a few congregations have actually withdrawn from the Episcopal Church, and thus far a schism has been averted. Still, the ordination of gay bishops and approval of same-sex marriages remain explosive topics not only for Episcopalians but other Christians as well.[40]

This all underscores the religious pluralism and the diversity of modern Texas. Yet, a certain uniformity still exists and will likely continue for years to come. Consider that in 2000 Catholics alone comprised 21 percent of the total population, Southern Baptists, 16.9 percent. Together they constituted 68.3 percent of the state's churchgoing public. Add to this the next four largest groups—Assemblies of God (1.1 percent), combined Evangelical and Missouri Synod Lutherans (1.4 percent), Churches of Christ (1.8 percent), and United Methodists (4.9 percent)—and *six* traditional denominations make up 84.3 percent of today's churchgoers. The landscape has certainly changed, marked by pagodas and the temples of other faiths, but the basic skyline is still recognizably Christian, with Catholic, Baptist, and Methodist steeples most prominent.[41]

Selected Bibliography

Bronder, Saul E. *Social Justice and Church Authority, The Public Life of Archbishop Robert E. Lucey*. Philadelphia: Temple University Press, 1982.

Driskill, Frank A., and Grisham, Noel. *Historic Churches of Texas, The Land and the People*. Rev. ed. Austin: Eakin, 1994.

Eckstein, Stephen D. *History of the Churches of Christ in Texas, 1824–1950*. Austin: Firm Foundation, 1963.

Gonzales, Robert O. and LaVelle, Michael J. *The Hispanic Catholics in the United States*. New York: Northeast Catholic Pastoral Center for Hispanics, 1985.

McBeth, Harry Leon. *Texas Baptists, A Sesquicentennial History*. Dallas: Baptistway, 1998.

McQueen, Clyde. *Black Churches in Texas, A Guide to Historic Congregations*. College Station: Texas A&M University Press, 2000.

Moore, James Talmadge. *Acts of Faith, The Catholic Church in Texas, 1900–1950*. College Station: Texas A&M University Press, 2002.

Storey, John W. *Texas Baptist Leadership and Social Christianity, 1900–1980*. College Station: Texas A&M University Press, 1986.

Twitchell, James B. *Branded Nation, The Marketing of Megachurch, College Inc., and Museumworld*. New York: Simon and Schuster Paperbacks, 2004.

Vernon, Walter N. et al. *The Methodist Excitement in Texas*. Dallas: Texas United Methodist Historical Society, 1984.

Weiner, Hollace Ava. *Jewish Stars in Texas, Rabbis and Their Work*. College Station: Texas A&M University Press, 1999.

Endnotes

1. Rupert Richardson et al., *Texas: The Lone Star State*, 9th ed. (Upper Saddle River, N.J.: Prentice Hall, 2005), 431–32; John W. Storey, "Religion," in *New Handbook of Texas*, 6 vols., ed. Ron Tyler et al. (Austin: Texas State Historical Association, 1996), 5: 526–28; Douglas W. Johnson et al., *Churches and Church Membership in the United States, 1971* (Washington, D.C.: Glenmary Research Center, 1974), 191; Bernard Quinn et al., *Churches and Church Membership in the United States, 1980* (Atlanta, Ga.: Glenmary Research Center, 1982), 25; Dale E. Jones et al., *Religious Congregations and Membership in the United States, 2000* (Nashville: Glenmary Research Center, 2002), 1, 38.

2. Richardson, *Texas*, 320, 438–43; *Houston Chronicle*, August 11, 2005, pp. B1, 7.

3. James Talmadge Moore, *Acts of Faith, The Catholic Church in Texas, 1900–1950* (College Station: Texas A&M University Press, 2002), 34, 38, 81; Martin B. Bradley et al., *Churches and Church Membership in the United States, 1990* (Atlanta, Ga.: Glenmary Research Center, 1992), pp. 32–33; Jones, *Religious Congregations*, 38; and Robert E. Wright, "Catholic Church," in *New Handbook*, 1: 1027.

4. Moore, *Acts of Faith*, 98, 109, 123, 207; Wright, "Catholic Church," 1: 1027; *Houston Chronicle*, June 26, 2005, p. A10, and October 18, 2007, pp. A1, 17; and The Archdiocese of Galveston-Houston/History, http: //www.diogh.org/about_history.htm (accessed May 25, 2006).

5. Wright, "Catholic Church," 1: 1027–28.

6. *Ibid*. See also Moore, *Acts of Faith*, 100–101.

7. Moore, *Acts of Faith*, 81–83, 149; Robert R. Trevizo, "Mexican Americans

and Religion," in *New Handbook*, 4:674–75; and Marie Friedmann Marquardt, "Latino Religion," in *Religion*, ed. Samuel S. Hill (Chapel Hill: University of North Carolina Press, 2006), 86–87.

8. Moore, *Acts of Faith*, 82–84; Saul E. Bronder, *Social Justice and Church Authority, The Public Life of Archbishop Robert E. Lucey* (Philadelphia: Temple University Press, 1982), 74–76

9. Trevizo, "Mexican Americans and Religion," 4:674–75.

10. *Ibid*. See also *Houston Chronicle*, December 31, 2005, p. F2.

11. *Houston Chronicle*, June 26, 2005, p. A 10.

12. *Ibid*., May 21, 2006, p. B3; Richardson, *Texas*, 439.

13. Jones, *Religious Congregations*, 38; *Houston Chronicle*, October 30, 1982, sec. 6, p.1; Azhar S. Rauf and Ayman Hajjaar, "Muslims," in *New Handbook*, 4:911.

14. Sam Hodges, "Texans Turning Muslim," *Dallas Morning News*, May 20, 2006, http://www.dallasnews.com/sharedcontent/dws/dn/religion/stories/0; Jones, *Religious Congregations*, 38.

15. *Houston Chronicle*, January 21, 2006, pp. F1, 2; James Breckenridge, "Buddhism," in *New Handbook*, 1:809; Texas Buddhist Directory Tables, BC Categories of Temples, htttp://www2.cs.uh.edu/~tihuang/tbc/tables.htm (accessed May 28, 2006).

16. Jones, *Religious Congregations*, 38; Breckenridge, "Buddhism," 1:809; Texas Buddhist Directory Tables; *Beaumont Enterprise*, June 2, 2006, pp. D1, 3; October 27, 2007, p. B1; *Houston Chronicle*, October 26, 2007, pp. B1, 6.

17. *Houston Chronicle*, June 26, 2005, p. B7, August 27, 2005, pp. F1, 5; Jones, *Religious Congregations*, 38; *Hinduism Today*, "Inaugural Ceremonies Held for Sri Meenaksi Temple in Houston, Texas," August 1982, http://www.hinduismtoday.com/archives/1982/08/1982-08-06.shtml (accessed May 28, 2006).

18. Sam Britt, "Asian Religions," in *Religion*, 34; Jones, *Religious Congregations*, 38.

19. Jones, *Religious Congregations*, 38; James L. Kessler, "Jews," in *New Handbook*, 3:938–39; Hollace Ava Weiner, *Jewish Stars in Texas, Rabbis and Their Work* (College Station: Texas A&M University Press, 1999), xix, 36, 39–61, 68, 73–75, 83–84, 93–94, 96–97, 101, 146, 157–58, 161–62, 167–68, 176, 219–33; Houston Hillel, "About Houston Hillel," http://www.houstonhillel.org/about/index.htm (accessed November 13, 2006).

20. Weiner, *Jewish Stars*, 187–95.

21. *Ibid*., 79, 197–200. See also Jones, *Religious Congregations*, 38.

22. Jones, *Religious Congregations*, 38; Interfaith Ministries for Greater Houston, "The Strength of Shared Beliefs," (accessed May 28, 2006).

23. Bradley, *Churches and Church Membership, 1990*, 32–33; Jones, *Religious Congregations*, 38.

24. John W. Storey, *Texas Baptist Leadership and Social Christianity, 1900–1980* (College Station: Texas A&M University Press, 1986), 39–66. See also Barry Hankins, *God's Rascal, J. Frank Norris and the Beginnings of Southern*

Fundamentalism (Lexington: University Press of Kentucky, 1996), the best work currently available on Norris.

25. W. A. Criswell, interview by author, Dallas, tape recording, November 18, 1988; Dick J. Reavis, "The Politics of Armageddon," *Texas Monthly*, October 1984, 164; *Dallas Morning News*, October 2, 1994, sec. J, p. 11.

26. Criswell interview; Joseph E. Early, Jr., *A Texas Baptist Power Struggle, The Haden Controversy* (Denton: University of North Texas Press, 2005), ix–x.

27. *Encyclopedia of Southern Baptists* (Nashville: Broadman, 1958), 2:854–55, 3:1833–34; Baptist General Convention of Texas, *Proceedings*, 1997, 31–32. (Cited hereafter as BGCT, *Proceedings*); Harry Leon McBeth, *Texas Baptists, A Sesquicentennial History* (Dallas: Baptistway, 1998), 298–370.

28. Trevizo, "Mexican Americans and Religion," 4:675–76; *Encyclopedia of Southern Baptists*, 2:854–55.

29. *Encyclopedia of Southern Baptists*, 2:855; BGCT, *Proceedings*, 1963, 212; 1997, 188; 2000, 190; *Baptist Standard*, July 1, 2002, 2; January 20, 2003, 6; February 24, 2003, 7; February 20, 2006, 9; *Texas Baptist Committed*, March 2006, 19.

30. Trevizo, "Mexican Americans and Religion," 4:675–76; Storey, "Religion," 5:526– 27; Clyde McQueen, *Black Churches in Texas, A Guide to Historic Congregations* (College Station: Texas A&M University Press, 2000), xvii–xviii.

31. Storey, *Texas Baptist Leadership*, 91–121; McQueen, *Black Churches in Texas*, 17; Paul Harvey, *Redeeming the South, Religious Cultures and Racial Identities among Southern Baptists, 1865–1925* (Chapel Hill: University of North Carolina Press, 1997), 243–50; *Baptist Standard*, November 19, 2001, p. 2.

32. Storey, *Texas Baptist Leadership*, 131–43, 172–200; *Baptist Standard*, February 18, 2002, p. 9; *Houston Chronicle*, November 12, 2005, pp. F1, 4.

33. Johnson, *Churches and Church Membership, 1971*, p. 11; Jones, *Religious Congregations*, 38; and *Houston Chronicle*, May 27, 2006, pp. F1, 4.

34. Jeffrey K. Hadden, "Religious Broadcasting," in *Religion*, 39–43.

35. Jeanne Halgren Kilde, *When Church Become Theatre, The Transformation of Evangelical Architecture and Worship in Nineteenth Century America* (New York: Oxford University Press, 2002), 215–20.

36. *Houston Chronicle*, February 4, 2006, pp. F1, 3, July 24, 2005, pp. D1, 8; *Dallas Morning News*, March 19, 2002, p. 24A; *Texas Monthly*, August 2005, 104–13, 167–75; James B. Twitchell, *Branded Nation, The Marketing of Megachurch, College Inc., and Museumworld* (New York: Simon & Schuster Paperbacks, 2004), 81–84; John N. Vaughn, *Megachurches and American Cities, How Churches Grow* (Grand Rapids: Baker Books, 1993), 120–36; Os Guinness, *Dining With the Devil, The Megachurch Movement Flirts with Modernity* (Grand Rapids: Baker Books, 1993), 9–40.

37. *Newsweek*, May 24, 2004, 44–50; *Texas Monthly*, July 2004, 50–54.

38. Elaine J. Lawless, *Handmaidens of the Lord, Pentecostal Women Preachers and Traditional Religion* (Philadelphia: University of Pennsylvania Press, 1988), 3–13; Matt Costella, "The Role of Women in the Local Church," *Foundation*

Magazine, July–August 2001, 2–3, http://www.fundamental biblechurch.org/Foundation/fbcrollof.htm (accessed June 19, 2006); Vicki Brown, "Church Marks 50th Anniversary of Full Clergy Rights for Women," *Women Clergy*, 1–2, http://archives.umc.org/interior.asp?mid=1021 (accessed June 19, 2006).

39. *Baptist Standard*, May 15, 2006, 10; *Texas Monthly*, July 2004, 87, 161; *Beaumont Enterprise*, September 20, 2003, http://www.southeasttexaslive.com/site/news.cFm?newsid=101968; Katie Sherrod, "Texas Time Warp," *Women's Ministries*, August 11, 2004, http://www.ecusa.anglican.org/41685_49492_ENG_HTM.htm (accessed June 18, 2006); PC (USA), Research Services-Statistics-FAQ/Interesting Facts, http://www.presbyterianchurch.org/research/statistics_Faq.htm (accessed June 19, 2006); 2005 General Council on Finance and Administration, United Methodist Church, Clergy Membership 2004, Gender, Racial/Ethnic Distribution; *Houston Chronicle*, October 7, 2006, F1.

40. *Texas Monthly*, July 2004, 85–86, 161–66; *New Yorker*, April 17, 2006, 54–65; *Houston Chronicle*, May 6, 2006, p. A8; May 7, 2006, p. A3.

41. Jones, *Religious Congregations*, 38.

Over Here

Texans on the Home Front

Ralph A. Wooster

MUCH HAS BEEN WRITTEN about the courage and heroism of Texans in battle. The impact of war upon Texas culture and society, especially in the twentieth century, has received less attention. While the exploits of Texas military units such as the 90th Division in the Meuse-Argonne Forest in 1918 and the 36th Division at Salerno and the Rapido River in 1943–44 and individual Texas soldiers and seamen such as John W. Thomason, Chester W. Nimitz, Audie Murphy, Sam Dealey, and William H. Walker have been described in various books and films, little attention has been paid to the effect that twentieth-century wars, both hot and cold, have had upon cultural and social developments in the state.[1]

The First World War, 1914–1918, or the Great War as it was called by contemporaries, had a profound impact upon Texans. Nearly 200,000 Texans saw military service, many overseas in the trenches of France. The war also affected those Texans who remained at home. Hundreds of new jobs were created in constructing camps for training soldiers, building ships, drilling for and refining oil, and increasing production of cotton and other agricultural commodities. The war developed a new sense of national patriotism among many Texans, most of whom thought of themselves more as southerners than Americans when the conflict began.[2]

164

The outbreak of war in Europe in 1914 surprised most Texans. Local matters such as the extremely hot weather, the bumper cotton crop, and the political and military turmoil in Mexico seemed of greater interest. This changed when the German submarine campaign brought the United States into the war in April 1917. The impact upon American, and Texan, society was enormous. Thousands of Texans entered military service through mobilization of the Texas National Guard as the 36th Infantry Division. Others volunteered or were conscripted into units such as the 90th Division made up primarily of Texans and Oklahomans. Thousands of other Texans were employed in the building of new military camps such as Camp Bowie in Fort Worth, Camp Travis in San Antonio, Camp MacArthur in Waco, Ellington Field, near Houston, and Kelly and Brooks Fields in San Antonio.[3]

Economic mobilization immediately affected Texas culture and social life. In addition to building the two dozen training camps and military airfields located in the state, Texans were soon working in war production, particularly shipbuilding and oil refining in cities such as Houston, Beaumont, and Port Arthur. Greater production of all agricultural commodities, especially cotton, wool, and foodstuffs, required the employment of many additional workers. Unemployment almost disappeared as thousands of Texans were soon involved in production of the materials of war.[4]

In an effort to mobilize resources for the war effort, the United States Congress created the National Council of Defense. Every state, including Texas, established councils of defense to assist in wartime mobilization. The Texas state council was divided into ten statewide committees designed to mobilize production, conservation, and support for the war effort. To assist the state council, 240 county and 15,000 community councils were created. These local groups sold government war bonds and stamps, supported conservation of food and materials, and generated patriotism and support for the war effort.[5]

To encourage increased production and conservation of the nation's food resources Congress created the Federal Food Administration headed by future president Herbert Hoover. Under Hoover's leadership each state created an organization for food production and conservation. Headed by Houston businessman E. A. Peden, the Texas Food Administration conducted a vigorous educational program aimed at encouraging Texans to observe meatless Tuesdays and Thursdays, wheatless Mondays and Wednesdays, and porkless Saturdays. At the same time the Food Administration encouraged Texans to save surplus garden and orchard produce by canning and drying. Demonstrations were given throughout the war with "victory kitchens" set up in public schools where women were given instruction in canning and drying.[6]

At the same time that Texans were making sacrifices for the war effort, criticism of anyone who opposed government policies grew. In June 1917 Congress passed the Espionage Act, which provided severe penalties for anyone who obstructed the war effort or directed others to do so. Under this act, and the Sedition Act passed the following year, the government was given far-ranging power to curb those opposed to the war effort. Two Texans in the Wilson cabinet, Postmaster General Albert Sidney Burleson and Attorney General Thomas Watts Gregory, played major roles in enforcing these acts and dealing with anyone suspected of disloyalty.[7]

The Espionage Act gave Postmaster General Burleson authority to exclude from the mail any material designed to obstruct the prosecution of the war. Under this measure Burleson exercised wide discretionary power to determine what constituted "willful obstruction" and to withhold such material from the mail. Since most newspapers and periodicals at the time depended upon the mail for delivery, this amounted to virtual censorship. Secretary Burleson was vigorous in enforcing the Espionage Act. Within a few weeks his Post Office Department excluded from the mail fifteen major publications, most of which were deemed socialist. Civil libertarians protested Burleson's actions, but President Wilson upheld the Texan in his policies.[8] Tom Hickey, an Irish immigrant who lived in Hallettsville in south Texas, was one of the first to feel the effects of Burleson's crackdown on political dissent. A fiery speaker and tireless worker for socialist-labor causes, Hickey, labeled "Red Tom" because of his radical political views as well as his ruddy complexion, was editor of a weekly newspaper, *The Rebel*, which was the official organ of the Socialist Party in Texas. In June 1917 *The Rebel* became the first victim of Burleson's crackdown when the Post Office refused to accept it for mail, effectively suppressing the paper. At the same time Hickey, along with leaders of another suspected socialist organization, the Farmers' and Laborers' Protective Association, was arrested on charges of opposing selective service registration.[9]

During 1917–1918 the U.S. government arrested numerous Texans for opposing the war effort. In northeast Texas twenty-four men were charged with organizing resistance to the draft. In west Texas fifty-five men attending a Farmers' and Laborers' Protective Association meeting were arrested on similar charges. In both instances most of the accused were later released, but three officers of the Protective Association were found guilty and sentenced to prison.[10]

Failure to support the war effort was not tolerated in much of Texas. In the town of Mineola in northeast Texas organizers of the Nonpartisan League, a militant midwestern farmers' organization critical of government policies, were arrested and imprisoned. In Wichita County a local citizen was tarred and feathered for not supporting the war effort. In another instance a Texan was arrested for saying President Wilson "is a wooden-headed son a bitch" and declaring "I wish Wilson was in hell, and if I had the power I would put him there." In Brenham townsmen flogged a man for refusing to support a Red Cross drive. A federal district judge in south Texas, Walter T. Burns, declared that traitors should be executed.

Burns believed that those convicted of disloyalty should be stood up against an adobe wall and "given what they deserve."[11]

Schools and colleges were expected to support the war effort. The state legislature required all public schools to devote at least ten minutes a day to teaching patriotism, to fly a flag in each school yard, and to include Texas history in the course of instruction. Governor William P. Hobby vetoed the appropriation for the German Department at the University of Texas, and many schools dropped the German language from their curriculum. College instructors frequently wrote patriotic pamphlets and gave lectures on Americanism. A popular instructor at the University of Texas, Lindley M. Keasbey, was dismissed for alleged antiwar activities.[12]

Texans of German descent were suspect. Ella Behrens, a young nurse who was the daughter of German immigrants, was removed from her duties at Fort Worth's Camp Bowie on suspicion of spreading influenza germs in the food of patients. Arrested and held incommunicado for eight days, Behrens was eventually released, but dishonorably discharged by the War Department. She lived with this stigma for the next thirty years. With the aid of a local congressman she finally secured an honorable discharge in January 1949.[13]

While most German Texans did not suffer physical abuse they were often the objects of suspicion and distrust. The state legislature required that all classes in public schools be taught in English. The playing of German music and reading of German prose and poetry were discouraged. The names of some food items were changed; hamburgers became "liberty sandwiches," frankfurters "liberty pups," and sauerkraut "liberty cabbage." The San Antonio city council temporarily renamed King William Street in the city's fashionable German district Pershing Avenue.[14]

Congressmen, led by Texas United States Senator Morris Sheppard, who favored national prohibition of alcoholic beverages, criticized German control of the brewing industry. In December 1917 Congress passed a constitutional amendment prohibiting the manufacture, sale, and transportation of alcoholic beverages. In February 1918 the Texas legislature ratified the prohibition amendment, which became effective when approved by three fourths of the states in January 1919. Even before ratification of the Eighteenth Amendment, the Texas legislature passed a law prohibiting alcoholic beverages within ten miles of a military installation, making much of the state "dry."[15]

The struggle for woman suffrage gained momentum during the war. Suffragists pointed out that the disfranchisement of women contradicted the democratic principles for which Americans were fighting and dying in France. They noted that women had demonstrated their patriotism and loyalty through work in the Red Cross, Liberty Loan drives, food conservation programs, and war industries. As a consequence, the 1918 governor's election helped Texas women gain the right to vote. Former governor James Ferguson, an opponent of woman suffrage, was attempting to regain the seat he had lost when impeached by the state legislature the previous year. Supporters of his successor, William P. Hobby, pushed a bill through the state legislature giving women the right to vote in the state Democratic primary. In the election Texas suffragists, led by Minnie Fisher Cunningham, head of the Texas Equal Suffrage Association, worked for and helped Hobby win the primary, which assured his reelection in November.[16]

Although Texas women did not gain the right to vote in general elections until ratification of the Nineteenth Amendment in August 1920, World War I significantly impacted their lives. The majority of Texas women remained homemakers, but an increasing number found employment outside the home. There was also a shift in patterns of employment for those women working outside the home. Many who had worked as charwomen, cleaners, laundresses, dressmakers, seamstresses, and household servants found new employment opportunities as stenographers, typists, bookkeepers, cashiers, teachers, telephone operators, and nurses.[17]

World War I was a period of frustration and disappointment for the 700,000 African Americans living in segregated Texas. In the hope that the war might bring improvements at home, many black leaders saw the conflict as an opportunity to illustrate their patriotism. They encouraged African Americans to purchase Liberty Bonds and stamps, participate in Red Cross drives, assist in food conservation, and take part in patriotic rallies and parades. Unfortunately, these efforts brought few improvements in the lives of most Texas African Americans.[18]

The training and stationing of African-American soldiers in Texas during the war caused tension and in one instance a major riot. When construction began on two new army training camps in Texas (MacArthur at Waco and Logan at Houston), the War Department sent two battalions of the all-black (except for officers) 24th Infantry Division to serve as security guards during the work. Almost immediately trouble occurred. At Waco a small skirmish between black soldiers and white police officers took place. Six soldiers found guilty of assault were sentenced to dishonorable discharge, forfeiture of pay and allowances, and five years imprisonment. An uneasy truce prevailed between soldiers and civilians in Waco until the battalion departed a few days later.[19]

The troubles in Houston were more serious, and deadly. Tensions in the city grew steadily following the first arrival of a battalion of the 24th Infantry in late July 1917. On the evening of August 23, after nearly a month of racial insults, humiliating encounters with civilians, and physical assaults from white police officers, black soldiers armed with rifles and bayonets marched into town. In an exchange of gunfire with police and civilians, the black troops killed fifteen whites, including an army officer, and wounded twelve others. Two black troopers were killed in the disturbance; two others died a few days later. Following the death of the white army officer, the mutineers began quarreling among themselves and decided to return to their camp. Sergeant

Vida Henry, leader of the mutineers, stayed behind and apparently killed himself.[20]

Local authorities, assisted by the Texas National Guard and troops from the 5th Illinois National Guard, which had recently arrived in Houston for training, soon restored order. The army moved quickly to transfer the black regiment back to New Mexico. In a series of court- martials held later that autumn, twenty-nine black soldiers were sentenced to be hanged and sixty-five others received lengthy prison sentences.[21]

Mexican Texans fared somewhat better than black Texans during the war. Historian Carole Christian believes that World War I "represented a crucial stage in the assimilation of Hispanics into the political and social life of Texas and the nation." She points out that prior to the war most Texas Mexicans, or *Tejanos*, lived as tenants or peons on ranches and farms in south Texas. The war brought more Tejanos into the mainstream of society and into the interior of Texas in greater numbers than before.[22]

The demand for Mexican labor, both resident and migratory, during the war was greater than ever. The National Immigration Act of 1917, which imposed literacy requirements and an eight-dollar head tax on immigrants, temporarily reduced the influx of Mexicans. However, the law permitted the secretary of labor to set aside the restrictions if convinced of a labor shortage. Under pressure primarily from southwestern businessmen and farmers, the secretary exempted Mexican workers from the requirements. Consequently, thousands of Mexicans entered Texas during the war as temporary workers.[23]

Although jobs were plentiful in wartime Texas, organized labor made few advances in improved working conditions and union recognition. Workers received slightly higher wages but they often found that prices for food, housing, clothing, and other commodities increased more rapidly than their wages. In an effort to secure higher wages, an eight-hour day, and union recognition, several thousand oil field workers went on strike. The chair of the President's Mediation Committee, Vernon S. Reid, supported the workers' demands. However, oil producers, led by Ross Sterling, head of Humble Oil & Refining, rejected Reid's recommendations. The oil producers hired strikebreakers looking for work as a result of the west Texas drought and convinced the public that the strikers were unpatriotic. In late January 1918 the strikers gave in and accepted an agreement that was a complete victory for the producers.[24]

The war had some effect upon Texas higher education. Since young men under the age of twenty-one were not liable for the draft until the last three months of the war, deferment for college students was not a serious issue. Enrollments declined slightly, however, as many college-age males enlisted for service. In 1917 Texas A&M, at the time an all-male college, held a special commencement exercise at Camp Funston in central Texas, where most of the seniors had gone for advanced training. In the course of the war 1,233 Aggies served as commissioned officers. Nearly five thousand students or former students of the University of Texas saw military service in the war.[25]

Organized sports felt the effect of the war. The Texas League, the only professional sports organization in Texas at the time, cut short its 1918 baseball schedule when it became obvious that many of its players were either in the military or subject to conscription. Attendance dropped, causing the Galveston and Beaumont clubs not to field teams in 1918. The other six clubs continued to play until the government announced that players would be subject to the draft. League officials halted play in July with the league-leading Dallas Submarines declared champion.[26]

Texas colleges continued to play football during the war although many players and coaches were in military service. Texas A&M won the 1917 championship of the young Southwest Intercollegiate Athletic Conference (later shortened to Southwest Conference) with an undefeated and untied team. Even with many of their players and coach in military service the Aggies won the first six games of the 1918 season, but lost in the final game to rival University of Texas, which won all of its nine games and the conference title.[27]

Texas high school football was still in its infancy in the First World War. In the early twentieth century, teams organized with little regard to age, academic status, or school attendance. In 1913 the Texas Interscholastic Athletic Association (later the Interscholastic League) attempted to bring some order into the sport. Member schools agreed that high school athletes must be amateurs, not over twenty-one years of age, and have attended the schools represented for at least three months with passing grades. A state championship game was not played until 1921, a contest in which Cleburne and Houston Heights played to a scoreless tie.[28]

In addition to sporting events, Texans found various ways to entertain themselves during the war. Hunting and fishing continued to be the most popular forms of relaxation. Adults enjoyed traditional entertainments such as dancing, attending parties, and playing dominoes, bridge, and other card games. Young Texans played "hide and seek," "drop the handkerchief," and "farmer in the dell." Swimming, either in creeks and rivers or the Gulf of Mexico, continued to be a favorite way to beat the torrid Texas summer heat. A new family treat, an afternoon or Sunday automobile drive, was becoming fashionable, although the government encouraged conservation of (but did not ration) oil and gasoline.[29]

Going to the movies was an increasingly popular form of entertainment for Texans during the First World War. Both the movie houses and films were improving in quality as well as quantity. In the larger cities such as Dallas, Houston, and San Antonio, new "deluxe" theaters replaced the old nickelodeons. More serious efforts at storytelling improved the quality of the films; newsreels and animated cartoons were added features. Films such as *A Daughter of France, The Slacker, The Eagle's Wings, To Hell With the Kaiser,* and *The Woman The Germans Shot* praised America and its allies and condemned the German enemy.[30]

Texas Catholic and Protestant churches, with nearly 1,800,000 members, supported the war effort. They sent their ministers and priests abroad as chaplains or YMCA workers, encouraged young male members to enlist and fight, and urged their female members to engage in voluntary organizations such as the Red Cross. Journals of the state's largest Protestant denominations, the *Baptist Standard* and the Methodist *Christian Advocate,* endorsed the war effort and called upon their members to support the government's efforts "to make the world safe for democracy." Texas Catholics, under the leadership of the National Catholic War Council, contributed to the war effort in various ways including the maintenance of recreation and worship centers at various military installations.[31]

In the closing days of the war the great influenza epidemic that swept across the world hit Texas. The first wave of the epidemic arrived in the spring of 1918, but the major impact occurred in the latter part of 1918. Thousands of Texans, both in the military and at home, contracted the disease. San Antonio, with 571 influenza deaths and 543 related pneumonia deaths, and El Paso, with 507 influenza and 297 pneumonia deaths, were particularly hit hard in 1918. Other Texas cities suffered heavy loss of lives that same year. The influenza epidemic eased somewhat in 1919, but even so El Paso had 338 deaths due to the flu and related pneumonia that year; Houston 278; Dallas, 268; and San Antonio, 266. In all, 479,000 Americans died from flu and related pneumonia in 1918; 189,000 in 1919.[32]

By 1920 the great influenza epidemic had ended. In the next decade life in Texas returned to what President Warren G. Harding referred to as "normalcy." The armies disbanded, the training camps closed, the programs for building ships and planes ended, and the wartime efforts to limit consumption of grains, meat, and sugar discontinued. The Texas oil industry continued to grow with new discoveries in the Permian basin and east Texas, making Texas the largest oil-producing state in the nation. Cotton remained king of agriculture with expansion from east and central Texas to the High Plains and the Rio Grande Valley. [33]

The economic growth and prosperity of the 1920s came to an end with the Great Depression of the 1930s. Unemployment figures rose, salaries and wages declined or remained static, and prices of agricultural and industrial commodities dropped. The New Deal programs of the Roosevelt administration seemed to help the state's economy, but full economic recovery came only with the Second World War.[34]

World War II had a major impact upon life in Texas. Nearly 750,000 Texans, 12,000 of whom were women, served in the armed forces during the war. Texas became the site of more military training camps, airfields, and naval stations than any other state. By the end of the war in 1945 thirty-five major army airfields, twelve major army training camps, five naval air stations, five army general hospitals, and three naval hospitals were located in the state. Over one and a half million Americans received military training in Texas.[35]

In addition to the men and women trained in the state during wartime, thousands of others came to work in military camps and defense installations spawned by the war. Some areas experienced tremendous population growth. Orange County, which became a center for shipbuilding, had a population of 17,382 in 1940; four years later over 60,000 people lived in the county. Farther down the coast, Brazoria County increased from 27,056 residents in 1940 to 45,439, largely due to the building of the Dow Chemical plant. The population of Moore County in the Texas Panhandle doubled due to expansion of petroleum and government construction of a nitrogen plant nearby. Harris County, with shipbuilding and oil refining, increased over 70,000 residents; Bexar, 48,425; Dallas, 44,496; and El Paso, 10,305. Some regions lost population, how-

ever, as thousands of rural Texans moved to the cities to find war
work. Of the state's 254 counties, 194 declined during the war.
Seventeen of these (ten in east Texas) had a population loss of over
30 percent.[36]

The thousands who moved to work in defense plants or to be
near family members stationed at training camps found housing to
be a major problem. In many instances local residents helped by
taking boarders in spare rooms or dividing their homes into small
apartments. The National Housing Authority attempted to help by
building new, modestly priced dwellings or with federally insured
mortgages to private builders. But the demand was always
greater than the number built. The lack of adequate housing remained one of the state's, and nation's, greatest domestic needs
during the war.[37]

Housing was only one of many shortages that faced Texans in
the Second World War. Early in the war the U.S. War Production
Board banned manufacture of new automobiles for civilian use as
factories turned to production of planes, ships, trucks, and weapons. Soon thereafter the Production Board halted manufacture of
radios, phonographs, refrigerators, vacuum cleaners, washing machines, and sewing machines for civilian purchase. Other commodities, such as automobile tires, coffee, sugar, meats, cheese, fats, and
processed and canned foods, were rationed. Shortages of unrationed
items, such as brand-named cigarettes, soft drinks (especially Coca
Cola), chewing gum (especially Wrigley's), candy bars (especially
Hershey's), toilet paper, diapers, cotton shirts, and nylon hose, became commonplace.[38]

Gasoline rationing was one of the most unpopular restrictions
for wartime Texans. In a state with an abundance of oil and gasoline
and where traveling distances were great, many Texans failed to see
the need for gasoline rationing to save natural rubber no longer
available after the Japanese overran the East Indies. Although massive drives to collect rubber were conducted in Texas and elsewhere,

they did not produce enough rubber to meet national needs. In autumn 1942 President Roosevelt ordered nationwide gasoline rationing, a ban on all pleasure driving, and a 35-mile per hour speed limit.[39]

Although Texans, like other Americans, complained about gasoline rationing, most learned to make do with their gasoline allotment. About half of the registered drivers received an "A" sticker, which entitled them to purchase four gallons per week (later three). Individuals employed in vital war work received a "B" sticker, which allowed them to purchase additional gasoline dependent on their distance to work. A "C" sticker, which permitted the individual to purchase even more gasoline, was given to ministers, doctors, dentists, police, and others engaged in essential work.[40]

Gasoline rationing meant that most long-distance travel was by other means. Air travel, still limited to the larger cities, was too expensive for most Texans. Travel in Texas by rail and bus increased dramatically during the war, from seventeen million bus riders in 1941 to eighty-eight million in 1943, and from four million who traveled by rail in 1941 to twenty-five million in 1943.[41]

For the first time since the advent of the Great Depression there was full employment for any Texan who wished to work. The expansion of war industries and the departure of husbands, brothers, and other young men for military service created the need for additional workers. More Texas women worked outside the home than ever before. By 1944 slightly over one-fourth of all Texans engaged in essential war industries and military establishments were women. They performed a variety of jobs formerly reserved for men. In coastal shipyards women worked as welders, packers, burners, tool checkers, and layout workers. In aircraft factories in Dallas and Fort Worth they operated machines, rivet guns, and welding torches. In other industries women were timekeepers, storeroom helpers, chemists, crane operators, electricians, and machinists.[42]

Unidentified female welder, Pennsylvania Shipyard, Beaumont, Texas. Courtesy Tyrell Historical Library, Beaumont, Texas.

There were limited improvements in opportunities for Texas ethnic minorities during the Second World War. There were increases in the number of Mexican Americans and African Americans employed, but generally for lower pay than for Anglo Americans and usually as unskilled laborers. The Federal Employment Practices Commission in the Southwest, headed by Carlos E. Castañeda and Leonard M. Brin, made efforts to eliminate discriminatory practices, but with little real improvement. Discrimination against Mexican migrants in Texas led the government of Mexico to exclude Texas from the *bracero* program that brought additional Mexican workers into the United States during the war. Even so, hundreds of Mexicans entered the state illegally as migrant workers during the conflict.[43]

Although not subjected to the rigid Jim Crow laws that excluded African Americans from the same public facilities as other Texans, Mexican Americans endured various forms of discrimination. In 1943 Governor Coke Stevenson issued a proclamation directing Texans to adhere to a policy of non-discrimination of all Caucasians, but some restaurants, cafes, and clubs were closed to Mexican Texans and in some districts Mexican and Anglo children attended separate schools.[44]

African Americans suffered even more discrimination than Mexican Texans. The rigid code of segregation kept African Americans from using the same public facilities and attending the same public schools as Anglo Americans. Some industries refused to hire African-American workers; others employed them only in a non-skilled capacity and often kept them separated from white workers. A major riot occurred in Beaumont in June 1943 when a white woman claimed she had been raped by a black man. Word of the alleged assault led to a riot by several thousand shipyard workers. The mob violence went on all evening as whites unsuccessfully sought the rapist. Several hundred blacks were injured, homes, stores, and restaurants in the African-American community were looted, and automobiles and buildings were set afire. At least three persons, two black and one white, were killed in the affair. State and local authorities called out the Texas State Guard, Texas Rangers, local police, and county lawmen. Beaumont remained under martial law for the next four days while authorities took steps to establish order. Fear persisted that other riots might occur, but the only other disturbance in Texas took place at Fort Bliss in El Paso where African-American troops retaliated against white soldiers who earlier attacked black soldiers.[45]

Texans of Japanese ancestry experienced considerable prejudice as a result of the attack on Pearl Harbor. Although they were not forced to relocation centers like Japanese Americans on the West Coast, they were subjected to a good deal of intimidation and harassment, particularly in the early days of the war. Federal agents searched their homes and sometimes took residents in for further questioning. Japanese businessmen were often required to close their shops or change their names. For example, the Jingo family, which had operated a Japanese tea garden at Brackenridge Park in San Antonio for twenty years, was forced to leave. A Chinese couple replaced them and the site was renamed the Chinese Tea Garden, later changed to the Sunken Gardens.[46]

The antagonism toward German Texans that existed in the First World War was not openly expressed in the Second World War. In part this was due to efforts by national and state leaders to make a distinction between the German people and the government controlled by the Nazi Party. This was helped by lessons learned in the First World War and in part because Texans of German background such as Admiral Chester W. Nimitz, General Dwight D. Eisenhower, and Lieutenant General Walter Krueger were leading American military forces in Europe and the Pacific.[47]

Texans on the home front followed events of the Second World War through letters from family members and friends, newspapers, motion picture newsreels, and the radio. The radio was particularly important in keeping Texans informed during the war. There were fifty-six radio stations operating in the state, twenty-eight of them owned wholly or in part by newspapers. In a nationwide poll taken during the war, 67 percent of the respondents put radio at the top of all media for news of the war. Newspapers, ranked highest by 17 percent of all respondents, were second, followed by motion pictures and magazines.[48]

The radio and motion pictures provided a major source of entertainment for Texans during the Second World War. Jack Benny, Red Skelton, Fred Allen, and Bob Hope were successful in both forms of media. Movies with a war theme, such as the 1942 Academy Award winner *Mrs. Miniver* and the 1943 winner *Casablanca*, were extremely popular early in the war. By the latter years of the war moviegoers sought something lighter, such as the 1944 Academy Award winner *Going My Way* starring Bing Crosby as a happy-go-lucky Catholic priest.[49]

Texans continued to have a major interest in sports during the Second World War. High school football had become much better organized than in the First World War. The Texas Interscholastic League had a well-run state playoff system for the larger schools leading to a state championship game in late December. The first round of playoff games in 1941 was played on December 6, the day before the Japanese attack at Pearl Harbor. Three weeks later the Wichita Falls Coyotes won the state championship by defeating the Temple Wildcats, 13–0. High school football continued to be played throughout the years of the Second World War with the Austin Maroons crowned champion in 1942, the San Angelo Bobcats in 1943, and the Port Arthur Yellow Jackets in 1944.[50]

College football, particularly games played in the Southwest Conference, remained a major attraction for Texans during the war, although an increasing number of athletes were in military service. The University of Texas Longhorns won the Southwest Conference championship in 1942 and 1943, but lost the title in 1944 to Texas Christian University. Some military installations, especially Randolph Air Field, had strong teams that competed with college teams for public interest.[51]

Although the major league baseball leagues continued to operate during the war, the Texas League again suspended operations. League owners voted to continue play in 1942, but after the season ended they suspended play for the duration of the war.[52]

Other sports, including college and high school basketball, baseball, track and field, and tennis, continued during the war, but schedules were often limited due to travel difficulties. Texans' interest in golf grew during the war. In part this was due to the success of Texas golfers such as Byron Nelson and Mildred "Babe" Didrikson Zaharias. Nelson won eleven consecutive Professional Golf Association events and was named Athlete of the Year in 1945 by the Associated Press. Zaharias was the outstanding female golfer of the era, winning seventeen consecutive tournaments, including the British Women's

Amateur championship and playing in several events with professional male golfers. She was named Woman Athlete of the Year in 1945.[53]

Even though most Texas colleges continued to field athletic teams, enrollment in higher education was adversely affected by the war. The first Selective Service Act set twenty-one as the minimum age for conscription, but in 1942 this was lowered to eighteen years. The larger schools such as the University of Texas and Texas A&M offset the loss of regular students somewhat with special initiatives such as pre-flight training programs and Women's Army Corps administrative schools. Even so, total college enrollment dropped statewide.[54]

The firing of University of Texas president Homer P. Rainey was the biggest controversy in Texas higher education during World War II. Rainey, a native of Clarksville and a highly respected educator, assumed the presidency of the university in 1939. During his tenure as president, composition of the Board of Regents changed dramatically. Terms of regents appointed by liberal Governor James V. Allred (1935–1939) expired and they were replaced by regents chosen by conservative governors W. Lee O'Daniel (1939–1941) and Coke R. Stevenson (1941–1947).[55]

For several years the regents and President Rainey quarreled over a variety of issues. The regents were convinced that the university was overrun by subversive individuals who threatened to destroy the social, political, and economic structure of the state. When President Rainey refused to fire several tenured faculty members, the Board of Regents voted on November 1, 1944, to dismiss him. The firing of Rainey, an administrator popular with most faculty, students, and alumni, set off a firestorm of protest, which continued throughout the next several years. The American Association of University Professors censured the university and the Southern Association of Colleges and Universities placed the university on probation for a year. Rainey himself was an unsuccessful candidate for governor in 1946.[56]

Homer P. Rainey, President, University of Texas. Courtesy Center for American History, University of Texas at Austin.

Texans everywhere welcomed the end of the Second World War in September 1945. The thousands of veterans who returned home found the state changed in some ways but the same in others. The Servicemen's Readjustment Act, passed by Congress in 1944 and popularly known as the "G.I. Bill," offered educational, housing, employment, and medical benefits to ease the transition of veterans back into civilian life. Returning African-American and Mexican-American veterans, however, found that racial prejudice and segregation had not disappeared and would face years of struggle to achieve equal rights. For example, in 1949 a funeral home in Three Rivers, Texas, refused to conduct a funeral service for Felix Longoria, a Mexican-American war hero.[57]

Texas veterans had barely resumed civilian life when North Korean military forces invaded South Korea, forcing the state and the nation back into military conflict in June 1950. In response to a resolution passed by the United Nations Security Council to render assistance to the South Koreans, the United States joined fifteen

other nations in sending troops to repel the invaders. Once more
the impact of war was felt in Texas. Thousands of Texans eventually
participated in the American military commitment in Korea. The
state was again a major site for training the young men who would
fight in the war. The government reactivated or expanded World
War II facilities such as Fort Hood, Fort Bliss, Ellington Field,
Goodfellow Air Force base, and Hondo Army Airfield to provide
training for Americans sent to the Far East.[58]

Unlike during World War II compulsory rationing was not instituted in Texas or the nation during the Korean conflict. Although
selective service, or the draft, was resumed, many young Texans,
especially those attending colleges and universities, managed to obtain military deferments to complete their education. Once again
the radio and newspapers brought Texans firsthand knowledge of
the war. A new medium, television, for the first time brought pictures of the war to Texas homes.[59] Many Texans were critical of the
failure of the Truman administration to prosecute the war in Korea
more vigorously. When the president removed General of the Army
Douglas MacArthur from his Far Eastern command for his criticism
of administration efforts to limit the scope of the war, many Texans
voiced support for MacArthur. After his return from the Far East,
MacArthur addressed the United States Congress and then made
a triumphal speaking tour, which included an address to the Texas
legislature and stops at the state's larger cities.[60]

The removal of General MacArthur from Far Eastern command
came at a time when Texans were increasingly concerned about the
federal government's attempts to control oil resources in the coastal
tidelands. In the presidential election of 1952, Governor Allan Shivers, a Democrat, led a movement in support of Republican Dwight
D. Eisenhower who pledged the return of tidelands oil to the states.
For the first time since 1928 the Republicans carried the state. Once
elected, Eisenhower took steps to ensure state control of tidelands oil
and to secure an armistice in the fighting in Korea.[61]

During the Korean conflict many Texans worried about the growing threat of communism, both at home and abroad. Chapters of the Minute Women of the U.S.A., an organization dedicated to fighting communism in government and education, appeared in Houston, Dallas, San Antonio, and Wichita Falls. The Houston chapter of Minute Women was particularly active in school board elections. Working with a group of Houston businessmen, they formed an organization known as the Committee for Sound American Education (CSAE), which supported conservative candidates in the 1952 elections for the Houston school board. In the contest for four open seats, two CSAE candidates, Dr. Henry Peterson and Dallas Dyer, were elected.[62]

Although the CSAE members constituted a minority on the Houston school board, they were able to stir up a controversy within the city that led to a number of resignations and firings, including the deputy superintendent, George W. Ebey. The so-called Red Scare reached its peak just as the fighting in Korea came to an end. In October 1953 the *Houston Post* carried an exposé that brought about an investigation of the Houston school system. The report coincided with national criticism of the tactics of Senator Joseph McCarthy and momentarily improved relations between the United States and the Soviet Union. Thereafter, organizations like the Minute Women remained active, but their influence diminished.[63]

While the concerns over communism at home abated somewhat during the late 1950s, the Cold War between the western nations led by the United States and the Communist bloc, headed by the Soviet Union and China, continued. Soon after the fighting in Korea ended, the United States became involved in efforts to prevent South Vietnam from coming under the domination of the Communist government in North Vietnam. Beginning in the Eisenhower administration, gradually increasing under John F. Kennedy, and reaching over half a million United States troops under Lyndon B. Johnson, the American commitment in Southeast Asia grew.[64]

Most Texans supported the early American involvement in Southeast Asia. Opposition to the war increased in 1965–1966 as the size of the American commitment, including larger draft calls, and the loss of American lives grew. Although public opinion polls showed that the majority of Texans continued to support American involvement, opposition to the war increased, particularly after the Tet offensive in 1968. Students and professors at colleges and universities were among the leaders in voicing this concern. At first they limited their criticism to "teach-ins" and peaceful demonstrations, but the incursion into Cambodia and the 1970 killing of four student demonstrators by the National Guard at Kent State University in Ohio led to large protests against the war at Texas colleges and universities. The largest of these occurred at the University of Texas in Austin. Following an antiwar protest on campus the day after the Kent State shooting, several hundred protestors marched to the state capitol. When protestors threw rocks at the capitol building, police fired tear gas at the demonstrators. During the next several days growing unrest escalated on campus as student leaders planned a larger march. This event, which attracted a crowd estimated at between 10,000 and 25,000, took place on March 8 but was relatively peaceful and without violence. Although the largest antiwar demonstrations took place in Austin, additional marches and protest demonstrations occurred at other Texas campuses, including North Texas State University (now the University of North Texas), Texas Tech University, the University of Houston, San Antonio College, Southern Methodist University, and Baylor University.[65]

In spite of student protests, most Texans continued to support the war in Southeast Asia. In the 1970 Democratic primary, Texas millionaire and former congressman Lloyd Bentsen, Jr., who supported American policy in Southeast Asia, defeated incumbent United States Senator Ralph W. Yarborough, who had been sympathetic with those opposed to the war.

That same year peace negotiations between American and

North Vietnamese representatives began and President Richard Nixon announced plans for the gradual American withdrawal from Vietnam. Most Texans continued to support the president despite the number of casualties, including 3,414 Texans killed. In January 1973 a ceasefire agreement was signed whereby the United States pulled its remaining troops out of Vietnam. That same month the Nixon administration announced an end to the draft.[66]

The conflict in Southeast Asia was the last prolonged military action in which Americans, and Texans, participated in the twentieth century. Although American troops took part in peacekeeping efforts in the Caribbean, Somalia, and Kosovo, as well as Operation Desert Storm in which Iraqi invaders were driven from Kuwait in 1991, these military operations were short-lived and had little impact upon the lives of most Texans. Of greater concern to Texans on the home front in the late twentieth century were the efforts of the federal government to reduce spending through the closing and realigning of military installations throughout the country. This process, known originally as Base Readjustment and Closure and later as Defense Base Closure and Realignment, had its origins in the early 1960s when President John Kennedy directed Secretary of Defense Robert S. McNamara to develop a plan of military cost reduction. Military needs, particularly the Vietnam War, delayed the efforts until the 1980s. Four successive base closure commissions, in 1988, 1991, 1993, and 1995, made recommendations resulting in the closing or realigning of over 300 military bases throughout the country.[67]

Among the bases closed in Texas were naval stations at Galveston, Dallas, Corpus Christi, and Beeville, Bergstrom Air Force Base (Austin), Kelly Air Force Base (San Antonio), and Red River Army Depot (Texarkana). This process, while economically painful to the communities affected, resulted in saving over sixteen billion dollars nationally through 2001. The process continued into the twenty-first century with additional closures and realignments in 2005.[68]

As the twentieth century closed few could see that in the first decade of the twenty-first century the nation would be involved in major military undertakings in Afghanistan and Iraq that would have major ramifications for all Americans.

Selected Bibliography

Barry, John M. *The Great Influenza: The Epic Story of the Deadliest Plague in History.* New York: Viking, 2004.

Baskin, Lawrence M., and William B. Strauss, *Chance and Circumstance: The Draft, the War, and the Vietnam Generation.* New York: Knopf, 1978.

Carleton, Don E. *Red Scare!: Right-Wing Hysteria, Fifties Fanaticism, and Their Legacy in Texas.* Austin: Texas Monthly Press, 1985.

Fairchild, Louis, ed. *They Called It the War Effort: Oral Histories From World War II Orange, Texas.* Austin: Eakin, 1991.

Haynes, Robert V. *A Night of Violence: The Houston Riot of 1917.* Baton Rouge: Louisiana State University Press, 1976.

Lee, James Ward et al. *1941: Texas Goes to War.* Denton: University of North Texas Press, 1991.

Luckingham, Bradford. *Epidemic in the Southwest, 1918 and 1919.* El Paso: Texas Western Press, 1984.

McKay, Seth M., and Odie Faulk. *Texas after Spindletop.* Austin: Steck-Vaughn, 1965.

Wooster, Ralph A. *Texas and Texans in World War II.* Austin: Eakin, 2005.

Zamora, Emilio. *The World of the Mexican Worker in Texas.* College Station: Texas A&M University Press, 1993.

Endnotes

1. For the Texas military heritage, see Joseph G. Dawson III, ed., *The Texas Military Experience From the Texas Revolution through World War II* (College Station: Texas A&M University Press, 1995).

2. Ralph W. Steen, *Twentieth Century Texas: An Economic and Social History* (Austin: Steck, 1942), 285; Walter L. Buenger, *The Path to A Modern South: Northeast Texas between Reconstruction and the Great Depression* (Austin: University of Texas Press, 2000), 127–31; *Second Report of the Provost General to the Secretary of War on the Operations of the Selective Service System to December 20, 1918* (Washington, D.C.: U.S. Government Printing Office, 1919), 468.

3. Lonnie J. White, *Panthers to Arrowheads: The 36th (Texas-Oklahoma) Divi-

sion in World War I (Austin: Presidial Press, 1984), 2–84; White, *The 90th Division in World War I: The Texas-Oklahoma Draft Division in the Great War* (Manhattan, Kan.: Sunflower University Press, 1996), 1–47; Bruce L. Brager, *The Texas 36th Division: A History* (Austin: Eakin, 2002), 27–48.

4. Robert S. Maxwell and Robert D. Baker, *Sawmill Empire: The Texas Lumber Industry, 1830–1940* (College Station: Texas A&M University Press, 1983), 184–95; *Order of Battle of the United States Land Forces in World War I*, 3 vols. (Washington: Center of Military History, United States Army, 1988); Robert H. Hays, Jr., "Military Aviation in Texas, 1917–1919," *Texas Military History* 3 (Spring 1963): 1–13. The army camps in Texas are described in Ron Tyler et al., eds., *New Handbook of Texas*, 6 vols. (Austin: Texas State Historical Association, 1996).

5. Oran Elijah Turner, "History of the Texas Council of Defense" (master's thesis, University of Texas, 1926), 20–21; Steen, *Twentieth Century Texas*, 293–94.

6. Henry George Hendricks, "The Federal Food Administration in Texas, 1917–1919" (master's thesis, University of Texas, 1925), 32–56, 165–66.

7. Geoffrey R. Stone, *Perilous Times: Free Speech in Wartime* (New York: W. W. Norton, 2004), 146–53.

8. Adrian Anderson, "Albert Sidney Burleson: A Southern Politician in the Progressive Era" (Ph.D. dissertation, Texas Technological College, 1967), 226; Paul L. Murphy, *World War I and Civil Liberties in the United States* (New York: Norton, 1979), 97–98; Donald Johnson, "Wilson, Burleson, and Censorship in the First World War," *Journal of Southern History* 28 (February 1962): 47–48; Woodrow Wilson to Burleson, July 13, 1917, Burleson to Wilson, July 16, 1917, in Arthur S. Link, ed., *The Papers of Woodrow Wilson*, 69 vols. (Princeton: Princeton University Press, 1961–1994), 43:164, 187–88.

9. James R. Green, *Grass-Roots Socialism: Radical Movements in the Southwest, 1895–1943* (Baton Rouge: Louisiana State University Press, 1978), 45–46, 355–56; James R. Green, "Tenant Farmer Discontent and Socialist Protest in Texas, 1917," *Southwestern Historical Quarterly* 81 (October 1977): 137–39; William R. Hunt, "Thomas Aloysius Hickey," *New Handbook of Texas*, 3: 585.

10. H. C. Peterson and Gilbert C. Fite, *Opponents of War, 1917–1918* (Madison: University of Wisconsin Press, 1957), 38–39; Jeanette Keith, *Rich Man's War, Poor Man's Fight: Race, Class, and Power in the Rural South during the First World War* (Chapel Hill: University of North Carolina Press, 2001), 96.

11. First quote, Peterson and Fite, *Opponents of War, 1917–1918*, 141; second quote, *Congressional Record*, 65th Congress, 1st sess., October 6, 1917, 7878. See also Seth M. McKay and Odie Faulk, *Texas after Spindletop* (Austin: Steck-Vaughn, 1965), 73.

12. William E. Nicholas, "World War I and Academic Dissent in Texas," *Arizona and the West* 14 (Autumn 1972): 215–30; William F. Pilcher, "Lindley Miller Keasbey," *New Handbook of Texas*, 3: 1043. Joe B. Frantz, longtime professor of history at the University of Texas, later wrote that he had heard at least

a dozen University of Texas professors say that Keasbey "was the most profound influence in their lives." One of those was Walter Prescott Webb, author of numerous books on frontier history and later president of the American Historical Association. Joe B. Frantz, *The Forty Acres Follies* (Austin: Texas Monthly Press, 1983), 35.

13. Oliver King, *Fort Worth: Outpost on the Trinity* (Norman: University of Oklahoma Press, 1953), 192–94.

14. Glen Lich, *The German Texans* (San Antonio: Institute of Texan Cultures, 1981), 110, 138; McKay and Faulk, *Texas after Spindletop*, 74; Bera Flach, *A Yankee in German- America Texas Hill Country* (San Antonio: Naylor, 1973), 72; Christopher Long, "King William Historic District," *New Handbook of Texas*, 3: 1116; Benjamin Paul Hegi, "'Old Time Good Germans': German-Americans in Cooke County, Texas, during World War I," *Southwestern Historical Quarterly* 109 (October 2005): 235–57; Mark Sonntag, "Hyphenated Texas: World War I and the German-Americans of Texas" (master's thesis, University of Texas at Austin, 1990).

15. Lewis L. Gould, *Progressives and Prohibitionists: Texas Democrats in the Wilson Era* (Reprint, Austin: Texas State Historical Association, 1992), 227–33; *Journal of the House of Representatives of the Fourth Called Session of the Thirty-Fifth Legislature* (Austin: Von Boeckmann-Jones, 1918), 42, 90–91, 141–42; *Journal of the Senate, Fourth Called Session of the Thirty-Fifth Legislature* (Austin: Baldwin & Sons, 1918), 60–61, 262–63; Steen, *Twentieth Century Texas*, 229–38.

16. A. Elizabeth Taylor, "The Woman Suffrage Movement in Texas," *Journal of Southern History* 17 (May 1951): 207; Judith N. McArthur, *Creating the New Woman: The Rise of the Southern Woman's Progressive Culture in Texas, 1892–1918* (Urbana: University of Illinois Press, 1998), 136–37; Judith N. McArthur and Harold L. Smith, *Minnie Fisher Cunningham: A Suffragist's Life in Politics* (New York: Oxford University Press, 2003), 61–64; *Journal of the House, Fourth Called Session*, 325; *Journal of the Senate, Fourth Called Session*, 355; Seth S. McKay, *Texas Politics, 1906–1944: With Special Reference to German Counties* (Lubbock: Texas Tech Press, 1952), 76–79.

17. Maurine Weiner Greenwald, *Women, War, and Work: The Impact of World War I on Women Workers in the United States* (Westport, Conn.: Greenwood, 1980), 5, 13, 15, 21, 93.

18. Steven A. Reich, "Soldiers of Democracy: Black Texans and the Fight for Citizenship, 1917–1921," *Journal of American History* 82 (March 1996): 1478–1504; Margaret B. Baker, "The Texas Negro and the World War" (master's thesis, University of Texas, 1938), 44–45, 53–54.

19. Garna L. Christian, "The Ordeal and the Prize: The 24th Infantry and Camp MacArthur," *Military Affairs* 50 (April 1986), 65–70.

20. Robert V. Haynes, "The Houston Mutiny and Riot of 1917," *Southwestern Historical Quarterly* 76 (April 1973): 420–31. C. Calvin Smith, "The Houston Riot of 1917 Revisited," *Houston Review* 13, no. 2 (1991): 96, argues that

the claim that Henry led the men in the conspiracy is not supported by reliable evidence.

21. The National Association for Colored People appealed to President Wilson for clemency; sentences of ten men were commuted to life imprisonment. Robert V. Haynes, *A Night of Violence: The Houston Riot of 1917* (Baton Rouge: Louisiana State University Press, 1976), 171–96; Garna L. Christian, *Black Soldiers in Jim Crow Texas, 1899–1917* (College Station: Texas A&M University Press, 1995), 154–60. In spite of the troubles at Waco and Houston several hundred black troops later were trained in Texas at Camp Bowie (Fort Worth) and Camp Travis (San Antonio). They were separated from white troops by high fences and were cautioned about their activities outside the posts.

22. Quote, Carole Christian, "Joining the American Mainstream: Texas' Mexican Americans during World War I," *Southwestern Historical Quarterly* 92 (April 1989): 559.

23. Otey M. Scruggs, "The First Mexican Farm Labor Program," *Arizona and the West* 2 (Winter 1960): 319–25; Lawrence A. Cordoso, "Labor Emigration to the Southwest, 1916–1926: Mexican Attitudes and Policy," *Southwestern Historical Quarterly* 79 (April 1976): 400–6; Emilio Zamora, *The World of the Mexican Worker in Texas* (College Station: Texas A&M University Press, 1993), 38–39.

24. James C. Maroney, "The Texas-Louisiana Oil Field Strike of 1917," in Gary M. Fink and Merl E. Reed, eds., *Essays in Southern Labor History* (Westport, Conn.: Greenwood, 1976), 161–72.

25. John Q. Adams, Jr., *We Are the Aggies: The Texas A&M University Association of Former Students* (College Station: Texas A&M University Press, 1979), 103–5; Henry C. Dethloff, *A Centennial History of Texas A&M University*, 2 vols. (College Station: Texas A&M University Press, 1975), 1: 282–83; John A. L. Scarborough, "The University of Texas and the Great War" (master's thesis, University of Texas, 1927), 114, 428.

26. Bill O'Neal, *The Texas League, 1888–1987: A Century of Baseball* (Austin: Eakin Press, 1987), 46–50.

27. Kern Tips, *Football—Texas Style: An Illustrated History of the Southwest Conference* (Garden City, N.Y.: Doubleday, 1964), 21; Harold Classen, comp., *Ronald's Encyclopedia of Football*, 3rd ed (New York: Ronald Press, 1963), 254, 262.

28. Harold V. Ratliff, *Autumn's Mightiest Legions: History of Texas Schoolboy Football* (Waco: Texian Press, 1963), 2–3, 8–10, 16–18.

29. Steen, *Twentieth Century Texas*. 161–62, 270.

30. Richard Schroeder, *Lone Star Picture Shows* (College Station: Texas A&M University Press, 2001), 47; Larry Wayne Ward, *The Motion Picture Goes to War: The U. S. Film Effort During World War I* (Ann Arbor, Mich.: UMI Research, 1985), 52–54; Daniel Blum, *A Pictorial History of the Silent Screen* (New York: Putnam's, 1953), 153.

31. U.S. Department of Commerce, Bureau of Census, *Religious Bodies,*

1916, 2 parts (Washington, D.C.: U.S. Government Printing Office, 1919), pt. 1:224–25; Ray H. Abrams, *Preachers Present Arms: The Role of American Churches and Clergy in World War I and II*, rev. ed. (Scottsdale, Penn.: Herald Press, 1969), 86–87, 171–76.

32. Mortality statistics for Texas cities may be found in U.S. Department of Commerce, Bureau of Census, *Mortality Statistics, 1918* and *Mortality Statistics, 1919* (Washington, D.C.: U.S. Government Printing Office, 1920, 1921). Unfortunately statistics are given only for several cities of the state, not the entire state. There are numerous works describing the influenza epidemic of 1918. See especially Alfred W Crosby, Jr., *Epidemic and Peace, 1918* (Westport, Conn.: Greenwood, 1976); Crosby, *America's Forgotten Pandemic: The Influenza of 1918* (Cambridge, Eng.: Cambridge University Press, 2003); John M. Barry, *The Great Influenza: The Epic Story of the Great Influenza Pandemic of 1918 and the Search for the Virus That Caused It* (New York: Simon & Schuster, 1999); Bradford Luckingham, *Epidemic in the Southwest, 1918 and 1919* (El Paso: Texas Western Press, 1984).

33. Randolph M. Campbell, *Gone to Texas: A History of the Lone Star State* (New York: Oxford University Press, 2003), 360–64.

34. For the impact of the Great Depression in Texas, see two works by Donald W. Whisenhunt, *The Great Depression in Texas: The Hoover Years* (New York: Garland, 1983), and Whisenhunt, ed., *The Depression and the Southwest* (Port Washington, N.Y.: Kennikat Press, 1980).

35. The impact of military expansion on Texas life during World War II is described in Ralph A. Wooster, *Texas and Texans in World War II* (Austin: Eakin, 2005), especially chapters 2, 5, and 6.

36. *Texas Almanac and Industrial Guide, 1945–1946* (Dallas: Belo, 1945), 109–112; Louis Fairchild, ed., *They Called It The War Effort: Oral Histories from World War II Orange County* (Austin: Eakin, 1991) is a particularly thorough account of the impact of the population growth in one Texas coastal community.

37. Wooster, *Texas and Texans in World War II*, 84–85; Geoffrey Perrett, *Days of Sadness, Years of Triumph: The American People, 1939–1945* (Baltimore: Penguin Books, 1974), 342–43.

38. Richard R. Lingeman, *Don't You Know There's A War On: The American Home Front, 1941–1945* (New York: Putnam's, 1970), 235–47; Ronald H. Bailey, *The Home Front: USA* (Alexandria, Va.: Time-Life Books, 1977), 110.

39. *Houston Post*, June 5, 11, 20, 1942; *Liberty Vindicator*, October 19, 1942; Lingeman, *Don't You Know There's A War On*, 237–39.

40. Lingeman, *Don't You Know There's A War On*, 242–43.

41. *Texas Almanac, 1945–1946*, 281, 299.

42. *Ibid.*, 273–74; Julia Kirk Blackwelder, *Now Hiring: The Feminization of Work in the United States, 1901–1955* (College Station: Texas A&M University Press, 1997), 123–24, 136–38; Cynthia Guidici, "Women at War," in James Ward Lee et al., *1941: Texas Goes to War* (Denton: University of North Texas Press, 1991), 150–63; Charlotte A. Holliman, "Beaumont Women During World War

II," *Texas Gulf Historical and Biographical Record* 31 (November 1995): 59–60; Gary L. Rabalis, "Humble Women at War: The Case of Humble's Baytown Refinery," *Houston Review of History and Culture* 2, no. 2 (Spring 2005): 33–36, 58. As noted earlier twelve thousand Texas women served in the armed forces of the United States in World War II. Oveta Culp Hobby, wife of former governor William P. Hobby, was director of the Women's Army Corps.

43. Johnny M. McCain, "Texas and the Mexican Labor Question, 1942," *Southwestern Historical Quarterly* 85 (July 1981): 52–53; Felix D. Almaráz, Jr., *Knight Without Armor: Carlos Eduardo Castañeda, 1896–1958* (College Station: Texas A&M University Press, 1999), 213–62.

44. McCain, "Texas and the Mexican Labor Question," 52–53; Emilio Zamora, "The Failed Promise of Wartime Opportunity for Mexicans in the Texas Oil Industry," *Southwestern Historical Quarterly* 95 (January 1992): 323–50.

45. James A. Burran, "Violence in an 'Arsenal of Democracy': The Beaumont Riot of 1943," *East Texas Historical Journal* 14 (Spring 1976): 39–47; James S. Olson and Sharon Phair, "Anatomy of a Race Riot: Beaumont, Texas, 1943," *Texana* 2, no. 1 (1973): 66–71; Pamela Lippold, "Recollection, Revisiting the Beaumont Race Riot of 1943" (Paper, McNair Scholar Program, Lamar University, 2005); Harvard Sitkoff, "Racial Militancy and Interracial Violence in the Second World War," *Journal of American History* 58 (December 1971): 672–74; Alwyn Barr, *Black Texans: A History of Negroes in Texas, 1528–1971* (Austin: Pemberton Press, 1972), 108.

46. Thomas K. Walls, *The Japanese Texans* (San Antonio: Institute of Texan Cultures, 1987), 151–58; Gwendolyn Wingate, "The Kishi Colony," in Francis E. Abernethy, ed., *The Folklore of Texan Cultures* (Austin: Encino, 1974), 327–37.

47. David M. Kennedy, *Freedom From Fear: The American People in Depression and War, 1929–1945* (New York: Oxford University Press, 1999), 749–50; Lingeman, *Don't You Know There's A War On*, 332–33.

48. *Texas Almanac and Industrial Guide, 1941–1942* (Dallas: Belo, 1941), 257; Richard Schroeder, *Texas Signs On: The Early Days of Radio and Television* (College Station: Texas A&M University Press, 1998), 12, 95–96; Gerd Horton, *Radio Goes to War: The Cultural Politics of Propaganda during World War II* (Berkeley: University of California Press, 2002), 22–38, 89–90.

49. Horton, *Radio Goes to War*. 140; Dawn Duncan, "Entertainment At Home & Abroad," James Ward Lee et al., *1941: Texas Goes to War* (Denton: University of North Texas Press, 1991), 203–4.

50. Bill McMurray, *Texas High School Football* (South Bend, Ind.: Icarus Press, 1985), 18–20.

51. Tips, *Football—Texas Style*, 104–108.

52. O'Neal, *The Texas League*, 93–97.

53. Curt Sampson, *Texas Golf Legends* (Lubbock: Texas Tech University Press, 1984), 88–100; Donald Steel and Peter Ryde, *Encyclopedia of Golf* (New York: Viking, 1975), 269–70; Susan E. Cayleff, "Mildred Ella Didrikson Zaharias," in Tyler, ed., *New Handbook of Texas*, 6: 1138–39. For more on Zaharias, see Cayleff,

Babe: The Legend and Life of Babe Didrikson Zaharias (Urbana: University of Illinois Press, 1998).

54. *Texas Almanac, 1945–1946,* 81, 373–75; Dethloff, *Centennial History of Texas A&M,* 2: 456–61; Fredericka Meiners, *A History of Rice University: The Institute Years, 1907–1963* (Houston: Rice University Studies, 1982), 134–35.

55. Don E. Carleton, *A Breed So Rare: The Life of J. R. Parten, Liberal Texas Oil Man, 1896–1992* (Austin: Texas State Historical Association, 1998), 210–11, 244–45, 301–2; George H. Green, *The Establishment in Texas Politics: The Primitive Years, 1938–1957* (Westport, Conn.: Greenwood Press, 1979), 83–84.

56. Carleton, *A Breed So Rare,* 302–6, 312; Frantz, *Forty Acre Follies,* 82–85; "Trouble in Texas," *Time,* November 13, 1944, p. 54, and "In the Lone Star State," *Time,* November 27, 1944, p. 44; John Moretta, "The Battle for the Texas Mind: The Firing of Homer P. Rainey and the Fight for the Survival of Academic Freedom and New Deal Liberalism at the University of Texas," *Houston Review of History and Culture* 2, no. 2 (2005): 40–44, 59–66. For Rainey's story, see his *The Tower and the Dome: A Free University Versus Political Control* (Boulder, Colo.: Pruett, 1971).

57. Michael Hobbs, "Coming Home," in Lee, *1941: Texas Goes to War,* 217–38; Patrick J. Carroll, *Felix Longoria's Wake: Bereavement, Racism, and the Rise of Mexican American Activism* (Austin: University of Texas Press, 2003), 54–85.

58. For military installations in Texas during the Korean War, see various entries in Tyler, ed., *New Handbook of Texas,* especially 2: 827–28, 1089, 1104–5, and 3: 238, 680.

59. Martin Gilbert, *A History of the Twentieth Century* (New York: Harper Collins Publishers, 2001), 367.

60. D. Clayton James, *The Years of MacArthur,* 3 vols. (Boston: Houghton-Mifflin, 1985), 3: 642–43; "Eyes on MacArthur," *Newsweek,* June 25, 1951, p. 17; "A Delightful Trip," *Time,* January 2, 1951, pp. 21–22; "Not So Deep in the Heart of Texas," *Nation,* June 30, 1957, pp. 605–606.

61. Campbell, *Gone to Texas,* 416–17; T. R. Fehrenbach, *Lone Star: A History of Texas and Texans* (New York: MacMillan, 1968), 659–60.

62. Don E. Carleton, *Red Scare! Right-Wing Hysteria, Fifties Fanaticism, and Their Legacy in Texas* (Austin: Texas Monthly Press, 1985), 154–78; Carleton, "McCarthyism in Local Elections: The Houston School Board of 1952," *Houston Review: History and Culture of the Gulf Coast* 3 (Winter 1981): 168–77.

63. Don E. Carleton, "McCarthyism in Houston: The George Ebey Affair," *Southwestern Historical Quarterly* 80 (October 1976): 163–76; Carleton, *Red Scare,* 179–254.

64. For the story of American involvement in Vietnam, see Guenter Lewy, *America in Vietnam* (New York: Oxford University Press, 1980) and Marvin E. Gettleman et al., *Vietnam and America: A Documentary History* (New York: Grove Press, 1985).

65. *Austin Statesman*, May 6–9, 1970; *Dallas Morning News*, May 5–9, 1970; Campbell, *Gone to Texas*, 430; Mostafa Bahloul, "Student Protest Against the Vietnam War on the Baylor Campus Between April 1967 – January 1971" (master's thesis, Baylor University, 1988), 61–68, 92–93, 100–1.

66. Robert A. Calvert, Arnoldo De León, and Gregg Cantrell, *The History of Texas* (Wheeling, Ill.: Harlan Davidson, 2002), 409; Campbell, *Gone to Texas*, 436; Lawrence M. Baskin and William B. Strauss, *Chance and Circumstance: The Draft, the War, and the Vietnam Generation* (New York: Knopf, 1978), 28; Gilbert, *History of the Twentieth Century*, 485, 494. For number of Texas deaths in Vietnam, see http://members.aol.com/warlibrary/vwc/4 htm (accessed February 6, 2006).

67. David S. Sorenson, *Shutting Down the Cold War: The Politics of Military Base Closure* (New York: St. Martin's, 1998) provides the best overall survey of base closures. Reports of the various base closure commissions may be found online under various headings.

68. The number of job losses as a result of base closures is debatable. Sorenson, *Shutting Down the Cold War*, 166–69, for example, notes that the *New York Times*, July 10, 1997, originally estimated 20,000 jobs lost at Kelly Field, but this figure was later reduced to approximately 5,000.

From Yellow Roses to Dixie Chicks

Women and Gender in Texas Music History

Gary Hartman

DURING THE PAST FEW years there has been a groundswell of scholarly interest in the musical history of Texas, as historians, ethnomusicologists, and cultural anthropologists increasingly acknowledge the importance of music in shaping and reflecting the complex history and ethnically diverse culture of the American Southwest. As a vital part of the cultural vocabulary for so many immigrant communities in Texas over the centuries, music has helped ethnic groups communicate information, pass along traditions from one generation to the next, and articulate a sense of individual and collective identity. One reason music has been so effective as a means of cultural expression is that it is so democratic. It allows virtually everyone, regardless of race, ethnicity, gender, age, educational background, or socioeconomic status, to participate in the cultural dialogue of the local community. In the Southwest, where most ethnic groups had a relatively low rate of literacy until after World War II, music has played a particularly important role in helping people communicate ideas, information, and folk culture. [1]

Despite the historical and cultural significance of music in the Southwest, there has been very little published information available regarding women and gender in Texas music. This is somewhat surprising, considering that music has played a vital role in the lives of women in the Southwest in several ways. For one thing, music has given women a "voice" within their local communities that they otherwise might not have had. Through music, women have been able to address issues and concerns, demonstrate their creative skills, and share their knowledge and folk culture with others. Secondly, music has presented women with opportunities for economic and social advancement by providing employment and allowing women to gain greater prestige and social standing within their communities. Finally, music has served as an important cultural medium through which ethnic communities have articulated their views on such issues as male-female relationships, gender identity, and notions of "femininity" and "masculinity."

Music certainly has provided a more public voice through which Texas women have been able to articulate their beliefs, concerns, and culture. Historically, most women in the Southwest have not had equal legal, political, economic, or educational status with men, nor, for the most part, have they had the ability to speak as openly in public. In fact, prior to the 1950s and 1960s, when civil rights legislation finally began to bring improvements for women and minorities, females from most ethnic groups in Texas could face serious consequences for being too outspoken. As a result, music sometimes served as an outlet through which women could express frustrations over the daily hardships they faced, complain about unhappy relationships, or simply communicate ideas and information to others in a socially acceptable format. Since they still had to be careful about speaking too candidly regarding certain matters, women sometimes relied on song lyrics that included euphemisms or indirect references to more serious issues as a way in which to express themselves without risking retribution from others within the community.

There are many examples of Texas women using music to address their concerns publicly. One older song that remained popular across the Southwest at least as late as the 1930s, "Gee, I Wisht I Was a Single Girl Again," tells of a bad marriage in which the wife takes in extra washing to try and feed her hungry children, only to find that the husband has been stealing the family's money. Lydia Mendoza, the most popular Tejana singer of the 1930s and 1940s, also criticized what she considered errant male behavior in such songs as "Mal Hombre (Evil Man)" and "Dime, Mal Hombre (Tell Me, Evil Man)." In both songs, Mendoza complains of men who seduce innocent young women and then abandon them later to a life of shame and dishonor within the local community. In the 1950s Texas-based blues singer Willie Mae "Big Mama" Thornton used humor to chastise men in the Jerry Lieber-Mike Stoller song "(You Ain't Nothing But A) Hound Dog," later popularized by Elvis Presley. During the following decade, Port Arthur native Janis Joplin stole the show at the 1967 Monterey Pop Festival with her stunning rendition of Big Mama Thornton's "Ball and Chain," another commentary on relationships between men and women, which helped launch Joplin's career as the leading female vocalist of the 1960s "acid rock" era.[2]

Also, in the late 1960s Jeannie C. Riley from Anson, Texas, had a smash hit on both the country and pop charts with the Tom T. Hall song "Harper Valley, P.T.A," which told of an angry mother who confronts prominent figures within her community after they accuse her of being an unfit parent. By exposing the town leaders' dishonesty, infidelity, and corruption, the heroine in this story demonstrated a growing willingness among women at the time to challenge authority figures and question traditional gendered roles in American society. More recently, other female artists have used music to speak out on a variety of social and political issues. Dallas-born Michelle Shocked gave up a lucrative recording career with Mercury Records in the 1980s in order to write and record more politically oriented songs on an independent label. California transplant Eliza Gilkyson also has used her music to address a variety of social and political issues. The Dixie Chicks, whose members hail from Dallas and Lubbock, tackled the problem of spousal abuse in their humorous but hard-hitting song, "Goodbye, Earl," and their recent criticism of the Iraq war ignited a contentious debate among country music fans regarding U.S. foreign policy.[3]

Women also have used music in the community church to address certain issues, exercise leadership roles, and gain greater prestige among their peers by demonstrating their musical skills. For women who spent much of their lives confined to the family home, the weekly church meeting was an important chance to escape the isolation and drudgery of daily life, showcase their creative talents through music, and reaffirm their position within the local religious hierarchy. This certainly can be seen in African-American churches throughout the Southwest in which black women often took a leading role in the congregation's musical services as a way to gain respect and to contribute to the cultural development of their communities. In fact, many well-known female African-American singers, including Beulah "Sippie" Wallace from Houston, first gained prominence singing in their own neighborhood churches before going on to build successful professional careers.[4]

Music also has been important for women in terms of courtship, marriage, and motherhood. Dancing to music, a particularly integral part of the courtship and mating process in virtually all societies, is rooted in older rituals designed, at least in part, to allow participants to evaluate the physical and intellectual qualifications of a prospective mate. By demonstrating their strength, agility, intellectual ability, and emotional sensitivity through music and dance, and by looking for the same traits in others, participants can identify themselves as desirable mating partners. The importance of music, and especially dance, as a cultural ritual for virtually all ethnic communities in Texas is evident in the state's remarkable array of dance halls and other musical venues that feature a broad variety of ethnic music.[5]

As couples move from courtship to marriage, music continues to play an important part in their lives. In fact, most cultures have acknowledged the central role of music in the mating and marriage process by formally institutionalizing it through the wedding ceremony, which typically includes a ceremonial "first dance" reserved for the newly wed couple, followed by a "father-daughter" or "mother-son" dance, in which parents symbolically release their children to begin their married lives. After these initial rituals, the entire wedding party of friends, family, and others close to the bride and groom join together for an extended period of music, dancing, and celebration. As newlyweds become parents, music takes on new importance within the family, especially as a means of nurturing and communicating with the couple's offspring. Pediatric specialists have long known that lullabies, nursery rhymes, and other musical interaction between parents and children are vital to early childhood development and continue to affect the psychological and physiological well-being of humans well into their adult years. Because women traditionally have had the primary responsibility for raising children, music has been particularly important to them in helping educate and nurture their offspring. In the Southwest, where literacy rates among most ethnic groups were relatively low until the mid-twentieth century, mothers have relied on folk songs and other oral music traditions to pass along family and community beliefs, values, and history to succeeding generations.[6]

Music also has been important to women in the Southwest by providing them with economic opportunities they otherwise might not have had. A number of Texas-based women have had significant commercial and critical success in music over the years, including Olga Samaroff, Sippie Wallace, Lydia Mendoza, Big Mama Thornton, Victoria Spivey, Dale Evans, Vicki Carr, Mary Martin, Lavelle White, Chelo Silva, Janis Joplin, Barbara Mandrell, Tanya Tucker, Laura Canales, Lee Ann Womack, Selena Quintanilla, Shawn Colvin, Le Ann Rimes, Beyoncé Knowles, Kelly Willis, the Dixie

Ruthie Foster. Courtesy Don Anders.

Chicks, Tish Hinojosa, Norah Jones, Eliza Gilkyson, Ruthie Foster, Cindy Cashdollar, Edie Brickell, Lisa Loeb, and many others.[7]

In addition to these performers, there are many women who have been important "behind the scenes" in the music business. One of the more influential was the late Cindy Walker, born in Mart, Texas, who wrote hit songs for such popular singers as Bob Wills, Gene Autry, Dale Evans, Elvis Presley, Ray Charles, George Jones, and Roy Orbison. Grammy Award-winning Terri Hendrix, born and raised in San Antonio but currently living in San Marcos, not only is a critically acclaimed musician and songwriter, but also has helped pioneer the new "independent artist" movement in Texas by writing, performing, publishing, and marketing her own music. Several others, including Carlyn Majer, Susan Antone, Marsha Milam, Nancy Coplin, Roggie Bear, Robin Shivers, Denise Boudreaux, Cash Edwards, Ginger Shults, Dalis Allen, Victoria Castillo, Nancy Fly, Val Denn, Gigi Benno, Robin Devin, Debora Hanson, Vickie Lucero, Barbara Martin, Robin Dickson, and Kath-

Terri Hendrix. Courtesy Don Anders.

leen O'Keefe, have worked as managers, booking agents, promot-
ers, club owners, festival producers, and recording agents, helping
build the vibrant Texas music scene and making possible the successful careers of others.[8]

Of course, there are thousands of other women who may never
be famous, but for whom music has represented at least some degree of economic opportunity that otherwise would not have been
available to them. One very interesting example of Texas women
and the important economic role music has played in their lives
is that of the *cantineras*, Mexican-American women who work in
cantinas, or working-class neighborhood bars. In addition to being
paid by the bar owner to socialize with patrons and encourage them
to buy drinks and "feed" the jukebox, *cantineras* often hire themselves out to dance with men, usually charging a nominal fee for
each dance. The *cantinera* is a long-standing tradition within Mexican-American society throughout the Southwest, and, for a significant number of women, it has been one of the few available means

of earning an adequate income in a limited labor market. However, working as a *cantinera* also is a controversial occupation that carries a negative social stigma and reflects many underlying gender, class, and economic issues within Texas-Mexican society. Although most of these women do not cross the line into prostitution, some do, and the very fact that all of them essentially are renting out their bodies for the physical gratification of men is simply unacceptable to many others within the Mexican-American community.[8]

Clearly, the broader implications of the *cantinera* and her place within Mexican-American society are complex and far-reaching. Most of these women probably were not eager to become *cantineras*, but only did so out of economic necessity. Many are recent immigrants, widows, or have been abandoned by their husbands and often have children to raise. Since well-paying jobs are difficult to find for many Mexican-American females in the Southwest, these women have few options. Working as a *cantinera* allows them to provide for themselves and their families in a way that certainly brings some negative social consequences, but, ultimately, gives them a degree of economic autonomy. In the end, the *cantineras*, as marginalized figures within their communities, risk public humiliation for themselves and their families in order to take advantage of the economic opportunities available through music.

Another important area to consider involves the portrayal of women and gender-related issues in Texas music. In many cases the ways in which men and women are represented in musical culture can provide insight into how various groups and individuals view gender identity, male-female relations, and the concepts of "femininity" and "masculinity." In the folk music of many ethnic communities throughout the Southwest, men and women often are cast in rather idealized and even stereotyped "masculine" or "feminine" roles, which frequently portray them in either positive or negative ways. For example, men often are represented as either virile, heroic figures, or weak and cowardly villains, while women are seen as either loving, nurturing (and generally submissive) sweethearts, wives, and mothers, or they are portrayed as treacherous and deceitful "Jezebels." In any case, the characters in the folk music of Texas and the Southwest sometimes reflect a highly idealized understanding of what it means to be "good" or "bad," as well as what it means to be "masculine" or "feminine." By examining how various ethnic communities articulate notions of good and evil or masculinity and femininity through the lyrics and characters of songs, it is possible to better understand how these groups conceptualize the appropriate roles of men and women in society.

One example of how both positive and negative images of women and men are sometimes woven into the musical culture of the Southwest can be found in the story surrounding the famous ballad, "The Yellow Rose of Texas." Although this tune originated in the nineteenth century, it grew in popularity throughout the twentieth century and became such a powerful part of the state's folk culture that it provides important insight into issues of gender and race that continue to resonate throughout Texas society today. It is unclear exactly when and how the song originated, but it has become linked to a larger folk mythology involving the exploits of a mulatto woman named Emily D. West (or Emily Morgan), a free black who came to Texas in 1835 to work on Colonel James Morgan's plantation near New Washington (present-day Morgan's Point). Soon after the Texas war for independence began in March 1836, the Mexican General Antonio López de Santa Anna and his forces, having defeated the rebel Texas troops at the Alamo on March 6, moved eastward, capturing Morgan's estate and confiscating several black servants, including Emily. Santa Anna reportedly kept her as his sexual companion during the weeks preceding the decisive Battle of San Jacinto, which took place on April 21, 1836. Legend says that Emily West kept Santa Anna distracted with sexual favors on that day so that Sam Houston's army could surprise and capture the Mexican general and his troops. Because of her efforts, this "Yellow Rose of Texas" became a hero in the Texas war for independence, and the myth and the song honoring her soon began to take shape.[9]

The following verses, taken from the earliest known written copy of "The Yellow Rose of Texas," date from around 1836. There are no direct references in the song to Emily West's relationship with Santa Anna or the events at the Battle of San Jacinto, and, in fact, some scholars believe the song originated outside the Southwest and actually has no direct connection to the Texas war for independence. Nevertheless, by the mid-twentieth century the tune and the legend of Emily West had become woven together as part of a larger folk mythology.

> There's a Yellow Rose in Texas
> That I am going to see
> No other darky [*sic*] knows her
> No one, only me
> She cryed [*sic*] so when I left her
> It like to broke my heart
> And if I ever find her
> We nevermore will part
>
> She's the sweetest rose of color
> This darky ever knew
> Her eyes are bright as diamonds
> They sparkle like the dew
> You may talk about dearest May
> And sing of Rosa Lee
> But the Yellow Rose of Texas
> Beats the belles of Tennessee[10]

Throughout the twentieth century "The Yellow Rose of Texas" grew increasingly popular and was repeatedly modified to reflect changing social and cultural circumstances. In 1906 a bilingual English-German version, also known as "Die Gelbe Rose von Texas," appeared and became part of the repertoire of many Texas-German singing groups throughout the state. In 1936 famed Texas composer David Guion published a more racially neutral version in which he substituted the word "fellow" for "darky" and made no mention of Emily West as a "rose of color." In 1955 the nationally popular singer Mitch Miller released his hit version of the song, which had been altered even further by changing "beats the belles of Tennessee" to "the only girl for me."[11]

In certain ways the mythology surrounding Emily West reflects underlying issues regarding race, gender, and the role of women in Texas society. For one thing, she became a hero for engaging in what, for most white women at the time, would have been considered unacceptably promiscuous sexual behavior. While it is true that Santa Anna forced West to be his companion, legend suggests that she willingly used her sexual charms to distract the general, helping lead to the defeat of his troops. Although her actions helped Texas win its independence, similar sexual behavior by a white woman undoubtedly would have seriously compromised her standing within the local community as a "respectable" female. The willingness of white Texans over the years to celebrate rather than criticize West for her "sexual improprieties" may be largely a result of common racial misperceptions that persisted well into the twentieth century. Because many whites had long considered blacks unable to restrain their sexual appetites, they may have been inclined to forgive West, whereas a white woman who had done the same thing might have been appreciated on some level for helping win the war, but most likely would have faced significant criticism from within her own community for her actions.[12]

By broadening this notion of non-whites as being incapable of restraining their sexual appetites, one can see how the racial and gender implications of "The Yellow Rose of Texas" mythology also apply to men and other ethnic groups. After all, the legend suggests that Santa Anna, president of Mexico and commander of Mexican forces in Texas, became so caught up in his pursuit of carnal pleasures that he abandoned his leadership responsibilities and allowed Houston and his Texan fighters to surprise and defeat the Mexican troops at San Jacinto. For some white Texans, such dereliction of duty and the resultant loss of a major military campaign by Santa Anna in pursuit of baser physical gratification fit their preconception that Mexicans, like Africans, were inherently more bestial and, therefore, incapable of rising to the level of sophistication and responsibility of whites. The caricature of Santa Anna as an unsavory and undisciplined tyrant, along with the image of his Mexican troops as marauding hooligans, is reinforced in various twentieth-century accounts of Emily West and the Texas war for independence, in which some authors have described the general as a "haughty dictator" who was lecherous, drank excessively, and even had a fondness for wearing silk underwear. Unfortunately, such negative stereotypes of Hispanics persisted throughout much of the twentieth century and helped bolster widespread discrimination against Texas Mexicans, or *Tejanos*.[13]

In a somewhat different vein, other examples can be found of how gender identity and the dynamics of male-female relationships are represented in southwestern folk culture, especially in regard to the ways in which women often are portrayed in either positive or negative terms in Texas music. Of course, the notion of wicked women causing the downfall of virtuous men is deeply rooted in western culture, dating back at least as far as the biblical story of Adam and Eve. Likewise, the concept of female goodness is embodied in the biblical Virgin Mary, a woman so near to perfection that God chose her to bear his son. This dichotomy of the "good" versus "evil" female appears in the music of virtually all ethnic genres in the Southwest. During the 1920s and 1930s, for example, Blind Lemon Jefferson and other Texas blues singers frequently sang of malicious and untrustworthy women who seemed intent on causing men heartache and misery. Jefferson's 1927 "I Labor So Far From Home" describes a wife who is a cunning and deceitful adulteress, cleverly taking advantage of her husband's trusting nature. The song's underlying theme, that appearances can be deceiving, perhaps carried even greater meaning for Jefferson as a blind singer.

> Old man went the other night his loving wife to see,
> What did he see but someone's horse where his horse ought to be.
> Oh wife, oh wife, dear loving wife, come quickly and tell to me,
> Whose horse is this hitched in my rack where my horse ought to be?
>
> You old fool, blind fool, old man, can't you see?
> That's nothing but a milk cow that my mother sent to me.
> Ten thousand miles I've traveled, ten thousand more I go,
> I never saw a milk cow with a saddle on before.[14]

In other instances Jefferson demonstrated feelings of tenderness and love toward women, while at the same time expressing anger and a desire for retribution. In his 1928 "Money Tree Mama Blues," he sings of a "good gal" who once treated him well, but now that she has left him for someone else he fantasizes about killing her.

> She sure was a good gal, could get money anywhere,
> Sometimes she'd come home to me with money sticking in her hair.
>
> As long as I had this woman, I didn't know what it was to be broke,
> But somebody stole my money tree, and believe me it ain't no joke.
>
> I'm going to buy an ax, and search all over this town,
> When I find that woman, I'm gonna chop my money tree down.[15]

Images of "good" and "bad" women are found throughout Texas country music as well. Lefty Frizzell's hit song "That's the Way Love Goes," co-written with fellow Texan Whitey Shafer and later recorded by Merle Haggard, Johnny Rodriguez, and others, praises a woman who has stuck by her man despite his lifelong inclination to "chase rainbows." By contrast, Willie Nelson's classic tune "Crazy" complains of a lover who uses men and then abandons them without remorse. "Good Hearted Woman," Nelson's 1976 duet with fellow Texan Waylon Jennings, tells of a long-suffering wife who loves her husband "in spite of his wicked ways that she don't understand." Singer-songwriter Kinky Friedman has taken a somewhat more humorous, albeit controversial, approach to commenting on gender roles through such songs as "Get Your Biscuits in the Oven and Your Buns in the Bed."[16]

Texas rock and rollers also have addressed the dynamics of male-female relationships through their music. Buddy Holly's "That'll Be the Day," first released in 1957, expresses a somewhat exaggerated sense of self-confidence when he claims that, despite his lover's repeated threats to leave him, he is sure she would never actually do so. By contrast, in his 1964 hit "Oh, Pretty Woman," Roy Orbison, whose thick glasses, short stature, shy demeanor, and falsetto voice made him the antithesis of Elvis Presley and other contemporary rock and roll idols, fantasizes about capturing the attention of a female passerby who, apparently, has little or no interest in him. Orbison's lyrics, which vacillate between self-doubt and cautious optimism, reflect the ambivalence he feels as he wonders whether such a "pretty woman" could ever be attracted to him. Texan Don Henley, a founding member of the rock supergroup the Eagles, sang about a "Witchy Woman" who held him "spellbound" but ultimately could not be trusted because she had been "sleeping in the devil's bed."[17]

Texas music also includes instances in which the concepts of "good" and "evil" and notions of "femininity" and "masculinity" are used to portray men in either positive or negative ways. For example, there are some songs in which male characters use lyrical imagery to portray their opponents as weak, cowardly, or even effeminate, in order to suggest that they are somehow "unmanly." By using such lyrics the heroic male character in the song can figuratively "emasculate" his adversary by "feminizing" him, or attributing to him supposedly feminine characteristics. This allows the hero to call into question his opponent's masculinity and, by implication, his very worth as a man. Some of the best examples of this "emasculation through feminization" can be found in *corridos*, the Spanish-language ballads of the Texas-Mexican border region. These *corridos*, which generally relate epic tales of heroic figures from within local Mexican-American folklore, often addressed the ongoing tensions between Anglos and Tejanos, which remained high in the Southwest throughout the first half of the twentieth century. As Tejanos faced growing discrimination, they sometimes used *corridos* to express their sense of anger and alienation, frequently portraying Anglo lawmen and other white authority figures as abusive, corrupt, dishonorable, and "unmanly" in a variety of ways.[18]

"The Ballad of Gregorio Cortez," perhaps the best known of all the border *corridos*, is a good example of how this type of gendered imagery has been used within Mexican-American folk culture to articulate notions of good and evil or masculinity and femininity. In 1901 Gregorio Cortez, a south Texas ranch hand, was wrongly accused of stealing a horse. When the local sheriff tried to arrest him, a scuffle broke out during which Cortez killed the sheriff and then fled. He eluded authorities for several days, but was finally captured and served time in prison, although he eventually was released. For many Tejanos, Cortez came to symbolize their ongoing struggle against what they considered to be an unjust, Anglo-dominated legal system. The corrido that celebrates his exploits not only carries a great deal of political and cultural significance regarding Anglo-

Tejano relations in the region, but it also includes gendered imagery intended to portray the principal male characters in either positive or negative ways. For example, "The Ballad of Gregorio Cortez" describes Cortez as a brave, honest, "godlike" man, while portraying his Anglo pursuers, especially the Texas Rangers (or *rinches*), as weak, cowardly, and somewhat effeminate. The following selected verses, translated into English from the original Spanish, highlight the sharp contrast between Cortez's "manly" actions and the Anglo posse's decidedly "unmanly" behavior.[19]

> The Americans were coming; they were whiter than a poppy
> From the fear that they had of Cortez and his pistol.

> They let loose the bloodhounds so they could follow the trail
> But trying to overtake Cortez was like following a star.

> He struck out for Gonzales, without showing any fear:
> "Follow me, cowardly *rinches*, I am Gregorio Cortez."

> From Belmont he went to the ranch, where they succeeded in surrounding him,
> Quite a few more than three hundred, but he jumped out of their corral.

> Then said Gregorio Cortez, with his pistol in his hand,
> "Don't run, you cowardly *rinches*, from a single Mexican."

> Then said the Major Sheriff, as if he was going to cry,
> "Cortez, hand over your weapons; we do not want to kill you."

> Then said Gregorio Cortez, speaking in his godlike voice
> "I won't surrender my weapons until I'm inside a jail."[20]

Another *corrido*, "The Corrido of Kiansis," tells of Mexican *vaqueros*, or cowboys, who demonstrate their "manliness" by outperforming Anglo cowboys on a cattle drive.

> Five hundred steers there were, all big and quick;
> Thirty American cowboys could not keep them bunched together.

> Then five Mexicans arrive, all of them wearing good chaps;
> And in less than a quarter-hour, they had the steers penned up

> Those five Mexicans penned up the steers in a moment,
> And the thirty Americans were left staring in amazement.[21]

For the Texas-Mexican community such tales of bravery and physical prowess were not simply idle boasting. In truth, many Tejanos, especially men, felt psychologically "emasculated," as they found themselves increasingly marginalized politically, socially, and economically during the first half of the twentieth century. Because some Mexican-American civil rights organizations, such as *La Raza Unida*, would not appear until the 1960s, Hispanics in the Southwest prior to World War II had limited opportunities to speak openly about their experiences as an ethnic minority. So, by living out such heroic exploits vicariously through *corridos*, Tejanos could, at least symbolically, preserve a sense of pride, dignity, and power, despite the difficulties they faced as a community.

A more recent event underscores several of the points made earlier about women and gender-related issues in Texas music. During a concert in London on March 10, 2003, Natalie Maines, lead singer for the internationally renowned Texas group, the Dixie Chicks, announced from the stage her opposition to American military involvement in Iraq, saying, "Just so you know, we're ashamed the president of the United States is from Texas." Although her comments regarding George W. Bush did not include any specific references to the impending war in Iraq or the status of U.S. troops, her remarks brought an almost immediate and overwhelming response from both critics and supporters, highlighting a wide political chasm within country music. Many fans enthusiastically agreed with Maines, but those who did not voiced their criticism loudly. Numerous radio stations boycotted the group, and the women were publicly vilified in newspapers and on radio with such labels as "Saddam's Angels" and "Dixie Sluts." Although the Dixie Chicks admitted in later interviews that their criticism of the president could have been expressed in a more constructive manner, they did not back down on their opposition to his policies, and they reiterated their belief that they had every right to address such issues openly.[22]

This incident involving the Dixie Chicks and their political outspokenness is revealing in several ways. First of all, it demonstrates clearly just how powerful a public voice women have gained through music, especially in terms of addressing controversial political issues. The fact that Maines' remarks, although actually rather benign, could cause such immediate and profound repercussions reflects the influence that music, as a cultural medium, can have on shaping and reflecting public opinion. There are certainly economic implications to this story as well. The band's unprecedented commercial success prior to the event, which included numerous industry awards and record-breaking album sales, placed them among the top-earning female artists in the business. However, the radio station boycotts, CD burnings, and other protests that followed Maines' comments cut into the band's earnings and highlighted the fact that expressing one's views publicly through music can carry financial risks as well as rewards. The incident also challenged the popular perception that all country music fans are socially and politically conservative. Although the Dixie Chicks faced widespread criticism from conservative groups, the groundswell of support from millions of their fans is a reminder that many in the country music world are politically and socially progressive.[23]

Finally, the fact that such sexually charged epithets as "Dixie Sluts" were commonly used to deride the women reveals lingering attitudes regarding the acceptable parameters of "femininity" and the "proper" behavior of women in public. Although Maines' comments were purely political in nature, the use of such sexually suggestive language seems to have been an attempt by critics, at least on a subconscious level, to divert attention from the band's original message regarding governmental policy and, instead, call into question the women's very moral character. It is doubtful that any such connection between political outspokenness and deviant sexual behavior would have been made if it had been an all-male band criticizing an American president. However, for at least some critics, the Dixie Chicks had stepped outside the bounds of "acceptable" female behavior by openly challenging the nation's chief executive. By violating the more traditional codes of social behavior for women, which included everything from deference to authority figures to sexual chastity, the band members had breached the boundaries of "ideal womanhood" and could now be considered not only ideologically suspect but also morally deficient.

Despite lingering controversy, the Dixie Chicks seem to have rebounded completely from the 2003 incident. The group's 2006 release, *Taking the Long Way Home*, which featured the hit song "Not Ready to Make Nice," a reaffirmation of the band's progressive social and political views, has sold millions of copies and won an impressive five Grammy Awards at the 2007 Country Music Awards program.

In a variety of ways music has played an important part in the lives of virtually everyone living in the Southwest over the years. For women, music has provided opportunities to communicate ideas, information, and cultural traditions and to advance socially and economically. Music also has been a vital part of our cultural vocabulary, in terms of how we define and articulate notions of "femininity," "masculinity," and other gender-related issues. By examining the musical history of Texas, one can gain valuable insight into the complex social and cultural dynamics of the American Southwest and better understand the role of women and gender in the development of Texas society.

Selected Bibliography

Barkley, Roy, Douglas E. Barnett, Cathy Brigham, Gary Hartman, Casey Mona-
    han, Dave Oliphant, and George B. Ward, eds. *The Handbook of Texas Music.*
    Austin: Texas State Historical Association, 2003.
Bufwack, Mary A., and Robert K. Oermann. *Finding Her Voice: Women in Coun-
    try Music, 1800–2000.* Nashville: Country Music Foundation Press & Vander-
    bilt University Press, 2003.
Burr, Ramiro. *The Billboard Guide to Tejano and Regional Mexican Music.* New
    York: Billboard Books, 1999.
Clayton, Lawrence and Joe Specht, eds. *The Roots of Texas Music.* College Station:
    Texas A&M University Press, 2003.
Hartman, Gary. *The History of Texas Music.* College Station: Texas A&M Univer-
    sity Press, 2008.
Joplin, Laura. *Love, Janis.* New York: Villard Books, 1992.
Peña, Manuel. *Música Tejana: The Cultural Economy of Artistic Transformation.*
    College Station: Texas A&M University Press, 1999.
San Miguel, Jr., Guadalupe. *Tejano Proud: Tex-Mex Music in the Twentieth Cen-
    tury.* College Station: Texas A&M University Press, 2002.
Turner, Martha Anne. *The Yellow Rose of Texas: The Story of a Song.* El Paso: Texas
    Western Press, University of Texas at El Paso, 1971.
Wood, Roger. *Down in Houston: Bayou City Blues.* Austin: University of Texas
    Press, 2003.
Wyman, Bill. *Blues Odyssey: A Journey to Music's Heart and Soul.* New York: DK
    Publishing, 2001.

Endnotes

1. The author presented an earlier version of this chapter as a paper at the Texas State Historical Association's Annual Conference held on March 5, 2004, in Austin. For the most complete online bibliography of Texas music history, see

the Center for Texas Music History's Web site at: www.txstate.edu/ctmh. For a more generalized overview of Texas music history, see Gary Hartman, *The History of Texas Music* (College Station, Texas: Texas A&M University Press, 2008); Lawrence Clayton and Joe Specht, eds., *The Roots of Texas Music* (College Station: Texas A&M University Press, 2003); Roy Barkley, Douglas E. Barnett, Cathy Brigham, Gary Hartman, Casey Monahan, Dave Oliphant, and George B. Ward, eds., *The Handbook of Texas Music* (Austin: Texas State Historical Association, 2003); *The Journal of Texas Music History* (published by the Center for Texas Music History, Texas State University, San Marcos); and Rick Koster, *Texas Music* (New York: St. Martin's, 1998).

2. William A. Owens, *Tell Me a Story, Sing Me a Song: A Texas Chronicle* (Austin: University of Texas Press, 1983), 72–79; *Lydia Mendoza: A Family Autobiography*, compiled and introduced by Chris Strachwitz with James Nicolopulos (Houston: Arte Público Press, 1993), 18–21, 333–35; Ramiro Burr, *The Billboard Guide to Tejano and Regional Mexican Music* (New York: Billboard Books, 1999), 151–152; Carlos B. Gil, "Lydia Mendoza: Houstonian and First Lady of Mexican American Song," *Houston Review* 3 (Summer 1981): 249–57; Louis Barbash and Frederick P. Close, "Lydia Mendoza: The Voice of the People," *Texas Humanist* 6 (November–December, 1983). See also Allan Turner, Jay Brakefield, and David Cavasos interview with Lydia Mendoza, January 28, 1978, Allan Turner Oral History Collection, Center for American History, University of Texas at Austin. For a good overview of women in Texas-Mexican music (a.k.a. *música Tejana*), see John Koegel, "Crossing Borders: Mexicana, Tejana, and Chicana Musicians in the United States and Mexico," in Walter Aaron Clark, ed., *From Tejano to Tango: Latin American Popular Music* (New York: Routledge, 2002), 97–125; Robert Santelli, *The Big Book of Blues: A Biographical Encyclopedia* (New York: Penguin, 1993), 404–5; Alan Lee Haworth, "Willie Mae Thornton," in Barkley, ed., *Handbook of Texas Music*, 324–25; Bill Wyman, *Blues Odyssey: A Journey to Music's Heart and Soul* (New York: DK Publishing, 2001), 268; Roger Wood, *Down in Houston: Bayou City Blues* (Austin: University of Texas Press, 2003), 28, 195, 200; Alice Echols, *Scars of Sweet Paradise: The Life and Times of Janis Joplin* (New York: Metropolitan Books, 1999), 164–69; Patricia Romanowski and Holly George-Warren, eds., *Rolling Stone Encyclopedia of Rock and Roll* (New York: Rolling Stone Press, 1995),. 523–24; Richard B. Hughes, "Janis Lyn Joplin," Barkley, ed., *Handbook of Texas Music*, 167–69, and Jerry Rodnitzky, "Janis Joplin: The Hippie Blues Singer as Feminist Heroine," *Journal of Texas Music History* 2, no. 1 (Spring 2002): 7–15. For additional readings on Joplin, see Laura Joplin, *Love, Janis* (New York: Villard Books, 1992), Myra Friedman, *Buried Alive: The Biography of Janis Joplin* (New York: William Morrow, 1973), and Ellis Amburn, *Pearl: The Obsessions and Passions of Janis Joplin* (New York: Warner Books, 1992).

3. Don Rhodes, "Jeannie C. Riley," in Paul Kingsbury, ed., *The Encyclopedia of Country Music: The Ultimate Guide to the Music* (New York: Oxford University Press, 1998), 446; Mary A. Bufwack and Robert K. Oermann, *Finding Her Voice: Women in Country Music, 1800–2000,*(Nashville: Country Music Founda-

tion Press & Vanderbilt University Press, 2003), 278–79, 495–98; Richard Carlin, *Country Music: A Biographical Dictionary* (New York: Routledge, 2003), 342; Romanowski and George-Warren, *Rolling Stone Encyclopedia*, 893–94; author's conversation with Eliza Gilkyson, June 12, 2005; Richard Skanse, "Eliza Gilkyson," *Texas Music*, no. 24 (Fall 2005) 40–47; Robert J. Elster, ed., *International Who's Who in Popular Music 2004* (London: Europa Publications, 2004), 364.

4. Alan Lomax, *Land Where the Blues Began* (New York: New Press, 1993), 46–48, 70–84; Glenn Appell and David Hemphill, *American Popular Music: A Multicultural History* (Belmont, Calif.: Thomson Higher Education, 2006), 313–18; Owens, *Tell Me a Story,*. 255–93; Donna P. Parker, "Sippie Wallace," Barkley, ed., *Handbook of Texas Music*, 349–50.

5. For examples of the importance of dance to the musical culture of the Southwest, see Solveig A. Turpin, "Native American Music," Barkley, ed., *Handbook of Texas Music*, 225–28; Brenda M. Romero, "Cultural Interaction in New Mexico as Illustrated in the Matachines," in Kip Lornell and Anne K. Rasmussen, eds., *Musics of Multicultural America: A Study of Twelve Musical Communities*, (New York: Schirmer Books, 1997), 155–85; Geronimo Treviño III, *Dance Halls and Last Calls: A History of Texas Country Music*, (Plano: Republic of Texas Press, 2002); José E. Limón, *Dancing With the Devil: Society and Cultural Poetics in Mexican-American South Texas* (Madison: University of Wisconsin Press, 1994), 141–49, 154–67; and Gertrude Prokosch Kurath, "Panorama of Dance Ethnology," in *Garland Library of Readings in Ethnomusicology*, Kay Kaufman Shelemay, ed., (New York: Garland, 1990), 71–92.

6. Kenneth L. Stewart and Arnoldo De León, "Literacy Among *Immigrantes* in Texas, 1850–1900," *Latin American Research Review* 20, no. 3, (1985): 180–87. In addition to these social and anthropological implications, music serves an important physiological purpose. It triggers specific psycho-physiological responses in humans, such as the release of endorphins, which induce a sense of euphoria and contribute to good physical and mental health. See Anne J. Blood and Robert J. Zatorre, "Intensely Pleasurable Responses to Music Correlate With Activity in Brain Regions Implicated in Reward and Emotion," Montreal Neurological Institute, McGill University, Montreal, Quebec, Canada, H3A 2B4, accessed at: www.pnas.org.

7. For more on the lives and careers of these women, see Barkley, ed., *Handbook of Texas Music*, Hartman, *History of Texas Music*, Koster, *Texas Music*, and the Center for Texas Music History's online bibliography.

8. There is little published scholarship on cantineras, but the following sources provide some helpful information: Keith Plocek, "Addicted to Love: Romance Resides at the Bottom of a Bottle in Local Cantinas," *Houston Press*, June 30, 2005, www.houstonpress.com (accessed May 1, 2006). See also H. Hammill and Angela Mora, "Effective HIV and Health Intervention for 'Cantineras' (Barmaids)," presented at the 1999 National HIV Prevention Conference, www.aegis.com/conferences (accessed May 1, 2006).

9. Emily West was a mulatto of mixed black and white heritage, and white

southerners commonly considered mulattos to be "yellow" in skin color. James Lutzweiler's "Emily D. West and the Yellow Rose of Texas: A Primer on Some Primary Documents and Their Doctoring," in Frances Edward Abernethy, ed., 2001: *A Texas Folklore Odyssey*, (Denton: University of North Texas Press, 2001), 295–315, offers compelling evidence that Emily West may, in fact, have been with Santa Anna at the Battle of San Jacinto. See also Juan Carlos Rodriguez, "Yellow Rose of Texas," Barkley, ed., *Handbook of Texas Music*, 364; Margaret Swett Henson, "Emily D. West," *Handbook of Texas Online*, www.tsha.utexas.edu/handbook/online/articles (accessed April 20, 2006).

10. F. E. Abernethy, "The Elusive Emily D. West, Folksong's Fabled 'Yellow Rose of Texas,'" in Frances Edward Abernethy, ed., 2001: *A Texas Folklore Odyssey*, 318–329, argues that the tune probably was composed as a minstrel song in the Northeast during the 1850s and originally had no connection to Emily West. Martha Anne Turner, *The Yellow Rose of Texas: The Story of a Song*, (El Paso: Texas Western Press, University of Texas at El Paso, 1971), 6–7.

11. Henson, "Emily D. West," *Handbook of Texas Online*; Turner, *The Yellow Rose of Texas*, 10–19.

12. The notion that blacks somehow had "overactive" sexual libidos was a commonly held belief among many whites as late as the mid-twentieth century. During slavery, this argument was sometimes used by white masters to excuse their physical involvement with slave women, insisting that it was the slave herself who had initiated sexual contact. See, for example, Melton A. McLaurin, *Celia, A Slave: A True Story*, (Athens, Ga.: University of Georgia Press, 1991).

13. See Arnoldo De León, *They Called Them Greasers: Anglo Attitudes Toward Mexicans in Texas, 1821–1900*, (Austin: University of Texas Press, 1983), especially 11, 24–48, 78, and David Montejano, *Anglos and Mexicans in the Making of Texas, 1836–1986*, (Austin: University of Texas Press, 1987), 82–85, 220–34; Anita R. Bunkley, *Emily, The Yellow Rose* (Houston: Rinard Publishing, 1989), 190–98. Although this is a semi-fictional account of Emily West's experiences, it still employs many of the common stereotypes used by others to portray Santa Anna as devious, cowardly, and incompetent.

14. Luigi Monge and David Evans, "New Songs of Blind Lemon Jefferson," *Journal of Texas Music History* 3, no. 2 (Fall 2003): 15.

15. Ibid., 23–24.

16. Daniel Cooper, "Whitey Shafer," Chet Flippo, "Waylon Jennings," and Bob Allen, "Willie Nelson," in Kingsbury, ed., *The Encyclopedia of Country Music*, 476–77, 263–64, 374–76; Jan Reid, *The Improbable Rise of Redneck Rock*, rev. ed., (Austin: University of Texas Press, 2004), 179–92.

17. Martin Donell Kohout, "Buddy Holly" and George B. Ward, "Roy Kelton Orbison," Barkley, ed., *Handbook of Texas Music*, 139–42, 236–37; *Buddy Holly: A Rock and Roll Collection*, MCA Records, 1979. See also Peter Lehman, *Roy Orbison: The Invention of an Alternative Rock Masculinity*, (Philadelphia: Temple University Press, 2003); *The Eagles*, Asylum Records, 1972.

18. Guadalupe San Miguel, Jr., *Tejano Proud: Tex-Mex Music in the Twentieth*

Century, (College Station: Texas A&M University Press, 2002), 22–23; For more on the corrido tradition, see Manuel Peña, *Música Tejana: The Cultural Economy of Artistic Transformation*, (College Station: Texas A&M University Press, 1999), 37–43, 69–82.

19. Américo Paredes, *A Texas-Mexican Cancionero: Folksongs of the Lower Border*, foreword by Manuel Peña, (Austin: University of Texas Press, 1995), 31, 53–55, 64–71.

20. Ibid., 66–67.

21. Ibid., 53–55.

22. Associated Press, "Bush backers smash Dixie Chicks disks," March 16, 2003, www.celiberal.com/linkcache (accessed April 15, 2006); Chris Willman, "Stars and Strife," *Entertainment Weekly*, no. 708, May 2, 2003, pp. 22–29. See also Erika Waak, "Celebrities Counter the War," *The Humanist* 63, no. 4 (July–August 2003): 20–24.

23. Bufwack and Oermann, *Finding Her Voice*, 495–98; Robert W. Van Sickel, "A World Without Citizenship: On (the absence of) Politics and Ideology in Country Music Lyrics, 1960–2000," *Popular Music and Society* 28, no. 3 (July 2005): 313–31. There are many examples of this political and ideological schism in country music. For instance, western swing musicians of the 1930s and 1940s defied contemporary racial mores in order to blend African-American and Anglo-American cultural traditions. During the 1970s, progressive country artists not only borrowed from Mexican-American, African-American, and other diverse ethnic influences, but they also often expressed progressive social and political viewpoints through their songs. For more on this, see Cory Lock, "Counterculture Cowboys: Progressive Texas Country of the 1970s and 1980s," *Journal of Texas Music History* 3, no. 1 (Spring 2003): 14–23.

Goodbye Ol' Paint, Hello Rapid Transit

Texas Literature in the Twentieth Century

Mark Busby

STRETCHING FROM THE PINEY woods of east Texas to the Gulf Coast, across the rolling Texas Hill Country to the deserts of the Trans-Pecos West, Texas offers an immensely varied and complex landscape, one that has been creatively and imaginatively probed by twentieth-century writers. Traditional stories have included such stock elements as laconic cowboys, nasty outlaws, greedy oil barons, saucy bar girls, leering *bandidos*, Texas Rangers, blind heifers, horny boys, or conspicuous Cadillacs. Other stories— those with more lasting literary appeal—examined the state's diversity and moved beyond stereotypes, reflecting and transforming elements that defined the region with originality, supple language, and humanity.[1]

Twentieth-century writers responded to the realities of Texas' natural environment, as well as to the themes and qualities those events induce. Historically, writers journeying across Texas—from explorers such as Cabeza de Vaca to twentieth-century nature writers such as Roy Bedichek and John Graves—attempted to capture their responses to the natural and cultural phenomena they encountered. Much of the writing emphasized coming to terms with a variety of cultures, but just as often the literature explored the aesthetic and pragmatic challenges posed by the region's natural conditions, where lush pine forests give way to empty plains that sometimes stretch so far that the eye yearns for even the slightest hill to lean against (as Roy Bedichek commented in his 1951 *Adventures with a Texas Naturalist*), where most of the indigenous vegetation is thorny and fruitless, and where often insufficient water exists to sustain cities or livestock. Texas landscapes are both as beautiful and appealing as they are dangerous and frightening—arid Chihuahuan desert, jutting Guadalupe Mountains, eroding Caprock canyon-lands, and rolling Llano Estacado.[2]

Traveling occurs naturally in a state as large as Texas—266,807 square miles—801 miles from the north in the Panhandle to Brownsville in the south and 773 miles from the Sabine River's easternmost bend to the Rio Grande's westernmost point near El Paso. From 1853–1854 Frederick Law Olmsted, later known for designing New York City's Central Park, traveled by horseback across Texas, then published *A Journey through Texas*. With all this territory, journeying continues to be necessary for the state. Several twentieth-century titles by Texas writers reflected the fundamental importance of journeying: *Waltz across Texas; North to Yesterday; North Toward Home; Moving On; Horseman, Pass By; Leaving Cheyenne; Dead Man's Walk; The Trail to Ogallala; Goodbye to a River; Pale Horse, Pale Rider; Rafting the Brazos;* and *Trip to Bountiful.* Many Texas stories use journeys for structure, with searching as a metaphor for the existential reality of contemporary life. From Saul on the road to Damascus, Oedipus on the way to Thebes, Odysseus headed home, Huck on the river, Gus and Call going up the trail, and John Grady Cole crossing the Rio Grande, the journey's power as archetype gains emphasis where expanse beckons and hinders.

Much of the state's literature also reflects the frontier mythology central to the larger American experience. Frontier mythology refers to a cluster of images, values, and archetypes that grew out of the confrontation between the "uncivilized" and the "civilized" world, what Frederick Jackson Turner called the "meeting point between savagery and civilization." Civilization is associated with the past, with Europe, and with society: its institutions, laws, demands for compromise and restriction, cultural refinement and emphasis on manners, industrial development, and class distinctions. The wilderness with which civilization collides offers individuals freedom to test themselves against nature without demands for social responsibility or compromises of a community.

Texas mythology, which matured in the twentieth century, draws from frontier mythology, particularly the emphasis on the Southwest as a land of freedom and opportunity, where individuals can demonstrate those values that the Anglo myth reveres: courage, determination, ingenuity, and loyalty. The most recognizable indigenous American hero—the cowboy—is a product of Texas' frontier legacy. But the Southwest's frontier history and geography produce deep feelings of ambivalence. On one hand, the vastness of the area seems to negate borders; on the other, the region's location on the edge of southern and western culture and along the long Rio Grande border with Mexico reinforces an awareness of borders. As Tom Pilkington pointed out in *My Blood's Country* (1973), Texas is a land of borders: "Men have always been fascinated by rims and borders, ends and beginnings, areas of transition where the known and the unknown merge. In the Southwest one feels something of this fascination." Both borders and the frontier suggest a line where differing cultures, attitudes, and factions meet. In fact, one of the major features of twentieth-century Texas fiction is ambivalence—the act of being torn in several directions at once. Early settlers who both conquered nature and simultaneously felt at one with it began the feelings of ambivalence that Larry McMurtry admitted to in *In a Narrow Grave* (1968), which still cut him "as deep as the bone." These mixed feelings are also central to McMurtry's epigraph for *Lonesome Dove* (1985) from T. K. Whipple's *Study Out the Land*

(1943): "All America lies at the end of the wilderness road, and our past is not a dead past, but still lives in us. Our forefathers had civilization inside themselves, the wild outside. We live in the civilization they created, but within us the wilderness still lingers. What they dreamed, we live, and what they lived, we dream."[3]

The duality of being drawn simultaneously toward such opposing forces as civilization/wilderness, rural/urban, individual/community, and past/present is central to the Texas legend, and it intensified in the twentieth century as the schism between old and new tore more strongly at the human heart. Often Texas writers examined the sharp division between the frontier myth that lives inside and the diminished, transformed natural world outside, especially as the old, often romanticized rural world gave way to a complicated urban one. Larry Goodwyn identified three other important elements of the Texas myth in an essay titled "The Frontier Myth and Southwestern Literature." According to Goodwyn, the frontier legend was pastoral, masculine, and racist. It dealt with courageous men who subdued, but at the same time were in harmony with nature, overlooked the presence of women, and relegated Mexicans, blacks, and Indians to a status decidedly below that of Anglos.[4]

Although Goodwyn described the legend as nineteenth-century writers had defined it, much of the ambivalence that twentieth-century writers exhibit stems from these older elements. Because the pastoral primitivism of the legend emphasizes the positive values of living close to the land, it increases the ambivalence. Instead of riding out under a high sky, bookish people hunker down in libraries or in front of computers. And these writers know that well before the end of the twentieth century, the majority of Texans—over 82 percent—lived in urban areas. They also realize that many of the region's remaining natural areas along rivers and coastlines were being threatened by some of the foulest polluters, who were free to exercise the liberty that a "guvment"-hating territory allowed.

As for sexism and racism, many twentieth-century authors, especially women and ethnic minorities, challenged these ugly legacies. Examples abound: Gloria Anzaldua, Sarah Bird, Sandra Cisneros, Mary Karr, Naomi Shihab Nye, Carolyn Osborn, Katherine Anne Porter, Dagoberto Gilb, Rolando Hinojosa, J. California Cooper, and Reginald McKnight. In 1968 Larry McMurtry, in a collection of essays entitled *In a Narrow Grave*, urged Texas writers to turn away from the harsh physical landscape of the Southwest to the "emotional experience [that] remains largely unexplored." The "ideal place to start," he suggested, was "with the relations of the sexes, a subject from which the eyes of Texas have remained too long averted." Increasingly, Texas fiction writers focused on male-female relationships. [5]

With these elements of Texas mythology—landscape diversity, journeying, frontier, ambivalence, primitivism, racism, and sexism—another ambiguous element continued from the frontier past: violence. In an *Atlantic* essay in 1975 McMurtry excoriated Texas, noting that the frontier emphasis on violence was one of the few vestiges of the old world still hanging on: "If frontier life has left any cultural residue at all, it is a residue of a most unfortunate sort—i.e., that tendency to romanticize violence which is evident on the front page of almost every Texas newspaper almost every day." Richard Slotkin examined the myth of violence in three books—*Regeneration through Violence: The Mythology of the American Frontier, 1600–1860* (1973), winner of the Albert J. Beveridge Award of the American Historical Association; *The Fatal Environment: The Myth of the Frontier in the Age of Industrialization, 1800–1890* (1985); and *Gunfighter Nation: The Myth of the Frontier in Twentieth-Century America* (1992). Slotkin identified an American archetypal pattern: the American hunter journeying into the wilderness, confronting the Indian violently, and regenerating himself and his people. The long history of Texas and its literature demonstrates the sad reality of this dubious legacy. [6]

Media guru Marshall McLuhan noted in the 1960s that "[w]e look at the present through a rear-view mirror. We march backwards into the future." Twentieth-century Texas literature began to look back at Texas' frontier past and its dominant figure on horseback. The cowboy is the frontier myth's ascendant icon. As Henry Nash Smith demonstrated in *Virgin Land* (1950), the story of the cowboy began in dime novels toward the end of the nineteenth century. At the turn of the twentieth century the cowboy became the principal embodiment of frontier values as Americans, led by Frederick Jackson Turner's famous 1893 address, feared that the closing frontier signaled the end of the traits that had defined the country. Dime novels gave way to such serious literary treatments as Owen Wister's *The Virginian* (1902) and a trail-drive novel with significant Texas connections, Andy Adams' *The Log of a Cowboy* (1903). In the short story, William Sydney Porter (O. Henry) drew from his own experiences on sheep ranches in south Texas, especially in *Hearts of the West* (1907), to create stories with the author's distinctive surprise endings, such as "The Hiding of Black Bill" and "The Last of the Troubadours," which J. Frank Dobie called "the best range story in American fiction." Some early women writers also wrote about cowboys. Mollie E. Moore Davis' *The Wire-Cutters* (1899) predates the books by Wister and Adams, usually identified as the beginnings of the western. Range wars involving cowboys cutting fences to gain access to water provided the backdrop for Davis' stories about ranch life, romance, gunplay, and murder.

One twentieth-century writer who extended the cowboy story's reach was J. Frank "Pancho" Dobie, who almost single-handedly brought Texas literature to respectability. Neither a fiction writer nor a scientific folklorist, Dobie was a raconteur, a collector of stories. Still, most collectors of Texana begin with Dobie's books. His correspondence from 1925 to 1928 with John Young, an old cowboy, formed the basis for Dobie's first book, *A Vaquero of the Brush Country* (1929), which told of Young's life as a cowboy. Dobie collected stories of cowboys throughout his career, especially in *The Longhorns* (1942) and *The Mustangs* (1952), and also mined the Spanish Southwest for stories of searches for ancient treasure in such works as *Coronado's Children* (1931), one of the first books by a non-Eastern writer to be selected by the Literary Guild. Throughout his career Dobie published twenty-two books and edited numerous others. His main themes defined much of Texas literature as he identified himself—a tireless enemy against anyone who attempted to exercise tyranny over human freedom, particularly the rich and powerful, the cruel and pretentious. He extolled a vigorous humanity and celebrated living in the natural world.

Dobie was one of the "Texas Triumvirate," the "Big Three" of Texas literature, which also included historian Walter Prescott Webb and naturalist Roy Bedichek. In the fall of 1994 a statue of these three famous Texans was placed near Barton Springs in Austin's Zilker Park. Webb's *The Texas Rangers* (1935) helped establish the Ranger myth that still infuses popular culture, as evidenced by the success of *Lonesome Dove* (1985) and the television series *Walker, Texas Ranger*. Webb glossed the racism attributed to the Rangers in border wars, and his *The Great Plains* (1931) tended to stereotype Indians and Mexican Americans. Still, surveys of Western historians identified it as the most influential book in shaping their views of western history.

Bedichek, the third member, was director of the University Interscholastic League for years and began to write after he retired. As Tom Pilkington noted about Bedichek:

> A lifetime of observing nature and of wide and intelligent reading had produced a truly remarkable understanding of the working of the natural order. His *Adventures with a Texas Naturalist* (1947) is a quiet statement of joy in the observation and appreciation of the state's plant and wildlife; it is at once a philosophical treatise, a celebration

The "Three Philosophers" statue by sculptor Glenna Goodacre at Barton Springs in Austin. Roy Bedichek is on the left, J. Frank Dobie in the middle, and Walter Prescott Webb with rolled pants legs and cigarette on the right. Courtesy Dick Heaberlin.

of life, and a minor classic in the field of natural history. *Karankaway County* (1950) and *The Sense of Smell* (1960), sequels to his first book, are on only a slightly lower level of achievement.[7]

Like Aldo Leopold and John Van Dyke, Bedichek served as a forerunner to the outpouring of environmental literature in the 1960s.

Early twentieth-century Texas women affected literary history, but not all celebrated the region as Dobie did. Katherine Anne Porter (1890–1980), one of Dobie's contemporaries, grew up in Kyle, five miles north of San Marcos. Almost all college anthologies of

American literature include a Porter story, such as "The Grave" or "The Jilting of Granny Weatherall." Porter shaved four years off her age and claimed to have been brought up among a Southern, "white pillared" crowd. Porter's Texas past was unhappy, and she "got out of Texas like a bat out of hell" as soon as she could. But her strong, ambivalent women like Sophia Jane Rhea of *The Old Order* (1935) come from that past, and through these characters Porter comments on the strengths and weaknesses of her regional heritage. Like other twentieth-century Texas writers, for instance, she demonstrated a strong ambivalence about her home territory, excoriating yet embracing it. She created strong female characters that challenged southwestern sexism. Porter lived a similarly independent life, traveling widely and boasting once of having had "thirty-seven lovers," yet she highly prized more traditional female values of beauty and cooking. [8]

Katherine Anne Porter in Notre Dame de Champs apartment, Paris, between the spring of 1935 and winter of 1935–36. Courtesy Papers of Katherine Anne Porter, Special Collections, University of Maryland Libraries.

Although Porter kept coming back to Texas in her fiction, she was thwarted in her desires to return with her literary archive later in life. She thought Harry Ransom, who was building the archive that became the Humanities Research Center at the University of Texas, was going to name a library for her. Porter went to Austin to lecture and left believing she had been promised a library in her name. She made plans to be buried underneath the library in a brightly painted Mexican wooden coffin, but when the plans never materialized she gave her materials to the McKeldrin Library in Maryland. Still, on a last, late trip, Porter decided that her own remains would be interred next to her mother's in Indian Creek. So it is fitting that her literary remains—including that coffin—are in Maryland, but her ashes are in Texas.

Like Porter, Dorothy Scarborough (1878–1935) in *The Wind* (1925) presented a less than favorable view of Texas. Made into a now-classic silent film with Lillian Gish in 1927, the work presents a harsh west Texas environment with an unrelenting wind and an unsupportive community that drive its main character insane. Scarborough received a Ph.D. in folklore from Columbia University and taught at Columbia and Baylor universities.

Notable African-American and Hispanic writers born in Texas also were published during this period. Sutton E. Griggs was educated at Bishop College in Dallas. Such works as *Imperium in Imperio* (1899) and *Unfettered* (1902) foreshadowed themes that dominated subsequent African-American literature by calling for full rights for black citizens, examining the possibility of revolt, and indicating the need for an organization to champion black rights. J. Mason Brewer (1896–1975) achieved success primarily through his folklore collections, many of which appeared in the annual volume of the Texas Folklore Society edited by Dobie. Dobie also encouraged Mexican-American writers, especially Jovita Gonzalez, who with Dobie's support served as president of the Texas Folklore Society, 1931–1932. With Eve Raleigh, Gonzalez wrote a novel in the 1930s, *Caballero*, eventually published in 1996.

Several other Texas writers before 1960 achieved success, including Loula Grace Erdman, George Sessions Perry, Fred Gipson, Tom Lea, and Ramsey Yelvington. Erdman taught for many years at West Texas State University in Canyon and published a series of novels set in the Panhandle. George Sessions Perry's Pulitzer Prize-winning novel, *Hold Autumn in Your Hand* (1941), about a year in the life of a central Texas sharecropper, explores the demise of small family farms, documenting an era when many people led rural lives in constant conflict with changing climates. Famed French filmmaker Jean Renoir adapted it as *The Southerner* in 1945. In 1957 Gipson's most famous novel, *Old Yeller* (1956), was made into a Disney movie starring Fess Parker and Dorothy McGuire. Lea, who was both a painter and a writer, published a lengthy history of the King Ranch (1957), two important novels, *The Brave Bulls* (1949) and *The Wonderful Country* (1952), lived into the twentieth-first century, and was lauded by George W. Bush in his acceptance speech for the Republican presidential nomination in 2000. A significant regional playwright of the early and mid-twentieth century, Yelvington (1913–1973) studied with Paul Baker at Baylor in the 1930s. His *A Texian Trilogy*, produced in the 1950s, includes *Women and Oxen, A Cloud of Witnesses*, and *Shadow of an Eagle*, and was significant because the plays focused on regional material.

Among the important writers who achieved acclaim in the 1950s were three from east Texas, which physically and historically has strong ties to the South. Many early east Texas settlers came from the South and brought slavery and cotton farming, and their influence led Texas to join the Confederacy. East Texas writers often claim Southern heritage, especially since the influence of William Faulkner looms heavily over American literature. Among the most important east Texas writers are three Williams—William Humphrey, William Goyen, and William Owens. Humphrey is probably the best known, primarily because his novel *Home from the Hill* (1958) was filmed starring Robert Mitchum. Goyen's novel *The House of Breath* (1950) and Owens' *Fever in the Earth* (1958) concern the importance of oil to east Texans.

A resurgence in Texas literature began in the 1960s and continued through the end of the century. Fiction, much still about the cowboy and frontier past, continued to be the major genre, but drama, poetry, and particularly environmental literature demonstrated a vital presence. The dominant name in Texas letters for forty-five years, Larry McMurtry, who grew up in the small town of Archer City, just south of Wichita Falls, published his first novel in 1961. By 2006 the prolific McMurtry had published thirty novels, ten books of non-fiction, several screen and teleplays, and hundreds of book reviews. Several of his novels have been made into movies or television miniseries. His most important works are *Horseman, Pass By* (1961), *Leaving Cheyenne* (1962), *The Last Picture Show* (1966), *In a Narrow Grave* (1968), *Terms of Endearment* (1975), *Lonesome Dove* (1985), *Texasville* (1987), *Duane's Depressed* (1999), and *Walter Benjamin at the Dairy Queen* (1999). In 1994 McMurtry published his first collaborative novel, *Pretty Boy Floyd*, with Diana Ossana, and in 2006 he and Ossana won the Academy Award for best-adapted screenplay for their script of Annie Proulx's *Brokeback Mountain*.

Throughout his career McMurtry has alternated between writing about the frontier and cowboys past and present, calling for urban novels, then returning to the frontier for a series of novels at the beginning of the twenty-first century. Drawn to the power of place, his career demonstrates the mythic pattern of escape and return. After garnering initial celebrity writing about the passing Southwest of the cowboy, McMurtry soon scorned the work his critics praised and praised the work his critics scorned: urban novels cut off from the old Southwest. Then in the 1980s McMurtry returned to the settings and themes he had rejected, and the critical fame he previously enjoyed came back as well. (*Lonesome Dove*, his most important novel, won the Pulitzer Prize and was later made into a highly regarded television miniseries.) In fact, McMurtry's novels and his life demonstrate that traveling is an axiomatic part of both, especially the mythical pattern of escape and return. Throughout much of his life McMurtry has found his home territory an awkward, uneasy place. Like the well-cinched bucking strap on a good rodeo horse, growing up in west Texas created productive tension between his love for the land that nourished him and an equally strong aversion to the narrow-minded elements of his heritage.[9]

Although not as well known as McMurtry, another prominent west Texan who has written primarily about the cowboy Southwest is Elmer Kelton. Where McMurtry has criticized traditional Texas writing as "country and Western literature," Kelton has taken the traditional western genre novel and moved beyond it in several important novels about Texas: *The Day the Cowboys Quit* (1971), *The Good Old Boys* (1978), *The Man Who Rode Midnight* (1987), *The Time It Never Rained* (1973), among others. He has won the Texas Institute of Letters fiction award and is widely respected as a historical novelist. Although his work has been compared to Louis L'Amour's, Kelton notes that whereas L'Amour's western heroes are six foot two and courageous, his main characters are five foot eight and scared.

Robert Flynn is another noted west Texas writer. Until the mid 1980s his modest reputation rested on a little-known novel titled *North to Yesterday* (1967), a black humor novel of the Southwest. Although he had won the Western Heritage Award, Flynn stopped publishing in the 1970s, and *North to Yesterday* went out-of-print. But the novel's supporters continued to praise it, and Flynn began to publish again in the mid-1980s. He is now one of the more important writers in Texas and is a former president of the Texas Institute of Letters. With *Wanderer Springs* (1988) and *Tie Fast Country* (2001) Flynn returned to his mythical west Texas town.

Recently, Cormac McCarthy is the most important Texas writer focusing on the cowboy, and he is arguably the most important twentieth-century American author. His powerful novels demonstrate a strong revision of the traditional western story. His enigmatic southwestern novels, including *Blood Meridian* (1985), *No Country for Old Men* (2005) and the Border Trilogy—*All the Pretty Horses* (1992), *The Crossing* (1994), and *Cities of the Plain* (1998)—are united through border crossings, a repeated metaphor for a complex and oxymoronic melding of nihilism and optimism, good and evil, illusion and reality, and others that intertwine positive and negative forces to present a world view suggesting a nihilistic optimism. McCarthy's border metaphor creates a world that is not simply black or white, good or evil, life or death, but is an ongoing dialectic between the forces of death and life, end and beginning, and other dualities the border symbolizes. With *The Road* (2006), winner of the Pulitzer Prize, McCarthy moves away from the border and returns to his roots in the Piedmont Southeast. The geographical specificity is blurred, almost insignificant, because the story is universalized. Still, this new novel travels the oxymoronic landscape of McCarthy's earlier work. If some of the earlier novels place more emphasis on nihilism, *The Road* enters into a nihilistic world and ultimately travels through the blackened cinders into a brightly human, compassionate and paradoxical world where "they can't go on; they went on" obtains.

Another emerging trend in the 1960s reflected the growing awareness of the state's changing natural environment. In 1960 the primary inheritor of the Dobie-Bedichek-Webb mantle, John Graves, now the dean of Texas letters, published *Goodbye to a River*. What makes Graves a memorable writer is his subtle, distinctive style, an amalgamation of fiction, folklore, philosophy, history, nature, personal experience, anecdotes, and allusion presented with repeated use of sentence fragments, ellipses, dashes, parenthetical remarks, and dialogue. Graves achieves a balance of high and low, moving from a quotation by Shakespeare or Thorstein Veblen to regional dialect. In his four major works, *Goodbye to a River, Hard Scrabble* (1974), *From a Limestone Ledge* (1980), and *Myself and Strangers* (2004), he builds upon the Old Order's concern with the passing Southwest, but approaches it with a complex blend of nostalgia and acceptance built from a cosmopolitan understanding of the world and a powerful emphasis on the value of preserving nature.[10] Other Texas nonfiction writers mirrored these concerns as well, including Rick Bass, Ray Gonzalez, Susan Hanson, Stephen Harrigan, and Arturo Longoria.

While nature continued to receive emphasis, so did the growing world of Texas cities. Important Texas writers who staked out urban Texas were Billy Lee Brammer and Edwin "Bud" Shrake. Brammer's one published work, *The Gay Place* (1961), has become the classic Texas political novel. (The title reflects its time, not ours, and refers to a happy place.) Brammer, who served as a press aide to Lyndon Johnson when he was Senate majority leader, imagined what Texas would have been like had a character like Johnson, Arthur "Goddam" Fenstemaker, become the state's governor. A Brammer contemporary, Shrake wrote two novels set in Texas cities, *But Not for Love* (1964) and *Strange Peaches* (1972). An acquaintance of Jack Ruby, Shrake was a Dallas sportswriter when John Kennedy was assassinated, and his work bears the mark of that fatal day. Later, Shrake wrote two important novels about the nineteenth-century Southwest, *Blessed McGill* (1968) and *The Borderland* (2000).

Many Texas writers in the later part of the century focused on a specific region of the state. The Texas Gulf Coast stretches from the Louisiana bayous to the salt marshes leading to Brownsville, including the oil refining areas around Beaumont/Port Arthur, the urban port of Houston, and the tourist-rich areas of Galveston, Port Aransas, and Corpus Christi. Several Texas writers hail from this region, notably James Lee Burke, Stephen Harrigan, and Mary Karr. Although best known for his Louisiana detective Dave Robicheaux,

Burke draws from his Texas background as well. Harrigan, who now lives in central Texas, grew up along the coast, and his novel *Aransas* (1980) is one of the better books about that area. His *The Gates of the Alamo* (2000) has been hailed as the definitive novel about the fated Texas mission. With *Challenger Park* (2006), Harrigan returned to the coast, concentrating on the NASA program. Mary Karr's memoir, *The Liars' Club* (1995), about her troubled childhood in the Golden Triangle of Beaumont-Port Arthur-Orange was a *New York Times* bestseller for over a year. She recalled a memorable mishearing of the region's weather cliché as "It ain't the heat; it's the stupidity."[11]

Another important part of the Texas literary landscape is south Texas, which reflects the changing demographics of the state with the growth of Mexican-American literature. Since mid-century Mexican-American writers have become increasingly recognized, led initially by Américo Paredes, who taught folklore at the University of Texas for years, Paredes collected the *corridos,* Mexican border folk ballads, about Gregorio Cortez in *With His Pistol in His Hand* (1958). The legend was made into a film, *The Ballad of Gregorio Cortez* (1982), set at the turn of the century in south Texas. It concerns a vaquero named Gregorio Cortez, who, due to a misunderstanding, killed Sheriff W. T. Morris when the sheriff accused him of stealing a horse. Cortez fled from the authorities, was captured, tried, and sentenced to life imprisonment, but was pardoned after twelve years. Paredes' book demonstrated the power both of the story and of Mexican-American storytelling, which is also apparent in Paredes' fiction, *George Washington Gomez* (1990) and *The Hammon and the Beans and Other Stories* (1994). Continuing this tradition was Tomás Rivera (1935–1984), whose one book, *. . . y no se lo tragó la tierra (And the Earth Did Not Part)* (1971), was filmed by Severo Perez as *And the Earth Did Not Devour Him.* It is a loosely connected series of vignettes about a migrant family moving from Texas to Minnesota in 1952. Both the book and Rivera were highly influential, as he became chancellor of the University of California, Riverside, in 1979.

Other recent Mexican-American writers, including novelists, poets, and dramatists, have also published significant works. Influenced by Rivera's life and work, Rolando Hinojosa focused on a fictional county in the lower Rio Grande Valley through a generational narrative called the Klail City Death Trip Series: *Estampas del valle y otras obras* (*Sketches of the Valley and Other Works*) (1973), *Klail City y sus alrededores* (*Klail City and its Environs*) (1976), *Mi Querida Rafa* (*My Dear Rafe*) (1981), *The Valley* (1983), and *The Useless Servants* (1993). Dagoberto Gilb, a journeyman El Paso carpenter with an M.A. in art history, began writing and has now published two story collections, *The Magic of Blood* (1993) and *Woodcuts of Women* (2001), and a novel, *The Last Known Residence of Mickey Acuña* (1995). Gilb won the PEN/Hemingway Award, a Whiting Award, and was a PEN/Faulkner finalist.

Looking back at Texas poetry at mid-century, J. Frank Dobie declared it "mediocre,"[12] but throughout the last half of the century Texas poetry flourished among the diverse groups that constitute the Southwest. Among the most accomplished poets are William Barney, Vassar Miller, Naomi Shihab Nye, and Walt McDonald. Barney's work reveals Robert Frost's influence in *Kneel from the Stone* (1952), *The Killdeer Crying* (1977), and *A Cowtown Chronicle* (1999). Miller's poems, collected in *If I Had Wheels or Love* (1991), are often philosophical and religious and reflect the author's lifelong affliction with cerebral palsy. Nye of San Antonio began to reach a national audience after a television profile by Bill Moyers. Her works include *Different Ways to Pray* (1980) and *Hugging the Juke Box* (1982). McDonald of Lubbock is one of the more prolific Texas poets over the last three decades of the twentieth century. An Air Force pilot, he taught at the Air Force Academy before moving to Texas Tech University. His work focuses on both Vietnam and west Texas, juxtaposing the harsh landscapes in such collections as *Caliban in Blue and Other Poems* (1976), *Rafting the Brazos* (1988), *Counting Survivors* (1995), and *Blessings the Body Gave* (1998).

Texas produced other notable poets as well. Dave Oliphant, who is also a critic, translator, and publisher, wrote *Lines & Mounds* (1976), *Footprints* (1978), *Maria's Poems* (1987), and *Austin* (1985); Betty Adcock authored *Beholdings* (1988); and Jerry Bradley penned *Simple Versions of Disaster* (1981). R. S. Gwynn of Beaumont combines humor with a fine feeling for form in such works as *Bearing & Distance* (1977), *The Narcissiad* (1982), a satirical poem (1982), and *No Word of Farewell: Poems 1970–2000* (2001). *The Drive-In* (1986) won the Breakthrough Award from the University of Missouri Press in 1986.

Accompanying the growing interest in multiculturalism has been the recent outpouring of poetry by ethnic poets, especially Mexican Americans. Many of these writers publish in various genres, such as Sandra Cisneros, who won early fame for a book about growing up in Chicago. She later moved to San Antonio and turned to the Southwest in *Woman Hollering Creek and Other Stories* (1991). Her books of poetry include *My Wicked Wicked Ways* (1992) and *Loose Woman* (1994). Other Chicano poets draw from specific cultural experiences, many easily merging English and Spanish. Tino Villanuevo's *Scene from the Movie* Giant (1993) is a long meditation about the effect of watching a major film that deals with ethnicity at a theater in Villanuevo's hometown, San Marcos, in the 1950s. Ray Gonzalez is primarily a poet, publishing *The Heat of Arrivals: Poems* (1996), *Cabato Sentora: Poems* (1999), and *Turtle Pictures* (2000). He is also an editor, *After Aztlan: Latino Poetry of the Nineties* (1998); a memoirist, *Memory Fever: A Journey Beyond El Paso Del Norte* (1999), and a short-story writer, *The Ghost of John Wayne, and Other Stories* (2001).

Cultural mix is also important to some Texas poets, such as Ai, who was initially identified as African American. She has since described herself as "1/2 Japanese, 1/8 Choctaw, 1/4 Black, and 1/16 Irish."[13] Born Florence Anthony in Albany, Texas, in 1947, Ai grew up in Tucson, Arizona, and later changed her name to "Ai" ("love" in Japanese). Her poetry is edgy, often confronting violent themes. *Vice* (1999) won the National Book Award for Poetry. Her other books are *Killing Floor* (1979), which won the 1978 Lamont Poetry Award of the Academy of American Poets; *Sin* (1986); and *Greed* (1993).

Since 1960, American drama has demonstrated a variety of elements, primarily the result of the Broadway stranglehold on American theater. Two developments—the growth of powerful regional theaters such as the Dallas Theater Center and Houston's Alley Theatre and the emergence of Off-and Off-Off-Broadway playhouses—allowed several Texas dramatists to gain national prominence with plays that often looked critically at their state. However, Texas drama, like American drama in general, diminished after the 1980s. Beginning in the 1990s Broadway became dominated by big budget musicals and revivals of classic plays, resulting in a decline in new plays as playwrights turned to film and television to reach audiences.

One particular stand-out in the 1970s was Preston Jones, who established himself as a significant American playwright. Jones' plays are generally comic examinations of small-town Texas life presented realistically with stock characters speaking recognizable dialect. Jones got his start with Paul Baker at the Dallas Theater Center. Like other Texas writers, Jones demonstrated a deep ambivalence toward the impermanence of the values of the mythic West. His plays concern the loss of heroic ideals and coherent values that the American West formerly represented. His three plays comprising *A Texas Trilogy*—*The Last Meeting of the Knights of the White Magnolia, The Oldest Living Graduate,* and *Lu Ann Hampton Laverty Oberlander*—began at the Dallas Theater Center in 1973–1974, where he had been an actor since 1960. After their successful Texas performances, the three plays were presented in 1976 at the Kennedy Center in Washington, D.C., to receptive audiences, but tepid reviews greeted them when they opened in repertoire on Broadway. Jones went back to Texas, continued to write plays, and died in 1979 at age 43 from complications of bleeding ulcers. His strength was the realistic Texas comic language of his characters and the depiction of the contemporary Southwest as often effete, enervated, or materialistic. Old patterns embracing racism, sexism, and corrupted individualism hang on in unsympathetic ways.[14]

Horton Foote, one of the more acclaimed writers of small-town America, and especially Wharton, Texas, his hometown, influenced Jones' emphasis on small-town Texas. Foote wrote about Wharton in a nine-play series about four generations of his Texas ancestors. Several of these plays have been made into films: *The Trip to Bountiful* (1985); *1918* (1986), for which Geraldine Page won the Best Actor Oscar; *On Valentine's Day* (1986); and *Convicts* (1991). Besides adapting his own work for the screen, Foote adapted Harper Lee's *To Kill a Mockingbird* (1962) and won his first Oscar for Best Screenplay. He added another Academy Award for his original screenplay, *Tender Mercies* (1982), the portrait of a country singer that won a Best Actor Oscar for Robert Duvall. Foote's *The Young Man from Atlanta* won the 1995 Pulitzer Prize.

Other Texas playwrights found greater acceptance for their work in the 1970s. Jack Heifner's *Vanities* (1977) focuses on three Texas girls at various stages of their lives. James McLure, trained at Southern Methodist University in Dallas, received acclaim for *Pvt. Wars* (1980), *Laundry and Bourbon* (1981), and *Lone Star* (1979). First presented by the Actors Theater of Louisville, *Lone Star* combines light, folksy humor with a weightier analysis of the effects of war on a Vietnam veteran. D. L. Coburn, a Dallas friend whom Preston Jones encouraged to write, won a Pulitzer Prize for *The Gin Game* (1977), an unsentimental play about old people in a nursing home that could be anywhere.

Texas chic aided Larry L. King and Peter Masterson with *The Best Little Whorehouse in Texas* (1978). *Whorehouse* grew out of a *Playboy* article that Texas journalist King had done about the closing of the legendary Chicken Ranch, a brothel outside La Grange. Using the traditional western theme of individual freedom versus the constraints of civilization represented by a meddling television journalist, this musical, with songs by Carol Hall, enjoyed an extended Broadway run and a less successful film version with Dolly Parton and Burt Reynolds. King went on to write several other plays, including *The Night Hank Williams Died* (1990), *The Kingfish* (1992), and *Golden Shadows Old West Museum* (1993). He also published several noteworthy nonfiction collections, especially *Confessions of a White Racist* (1972), for which he earned a National Book Award nomination.

Toward the end of the twentieth century and into the next, Texas crime fiction gained a significant following, with writers finding a setting for their tales in particular parts of the state.[15] Their stories often featured a hybrid protagonist, a detective with a rural background who pursues justice in the dark urban underbelly of the state. For Susan Wittig Albert, Mary Willis Walker, and Kinky Friedman, central Texas provided literary inspiration. Albert uses Hill Country herb storeowner China Bayles in many of her works. Walker's detective is Austin journalist Molly Cates in *The Red Scream* (1994), *Under the Beetle's Cellar* (1995), and *All the Dead Lie Down* (1998). Friedman, originally an over-the-top musician with the Texas Jewboys, later became private eye Kinky Friedman in such mysteries as *A Case of Lone Star* (1987) and *Road Kill* (1997). In 2006 Friedman turned gadfly politician and ran for Texas governor against incumbent Rick Perry using the slogan, "How Hard Could It Be?"

East Texas was the backdrop for Bill Crider, Joe Lansdale, and David Lindsey. Crider is author of dozens of mysteries, mostly set along the Texas Gulf Coast, such as *One Dead Dean* (1988),

The Prairie Chicken Kill: A Truman Smith Mystery (1996), and *A Knife in the Back* (2002). Nacogdoches resident and acclaimed horror/fantasy writer Lansdale has a mystery series featuring Hap Collins and Leonard Pine in such mysteries as *Mucho Mojo* (1994) and *Rumble Tumble* (1998). And Lindsey traces Stuart Haydon, a Houston high society homicide detective, in *A Cold Mind (1983)* and *Spiral* (1986).

Clay Reynolds of Denton and McKinney and A. W. Gray and Doug Swanson of Dallas turned to north Texas for their setting. Reynolds has written literary fiction about his hometown of Quanah in The Sand Hill Chronicles. The second in the series, *Agatite* (1986), republished as *Rage* in 1994, concerns a series of crimes in Reynolds' fictional town. Gray is the author of a series with a hard-boiled, six-foot-six-inch albino lawyer from Dallas in *Bino* (1988), *Size* (1989), and *Bino's Blues* (1995). Swanson's Dallas detective Jack Flippo appears in *Big Town* (1994) and *House of Corrections* (2000).

Looking southward were Jay Brandon, Rick Riordan, Jim Sanderson, Rolando Hinojosa, and Max Martinez. Brandon is the author of several courtroom suspense novels based in San Antonio, such as *Fade the Heat* (1991) and *Angel of Death* (1998). Riordan's San Antonio detective is Tres Navarre, who has an enchilada-eating cat and a Ph.D. in medieval literature. Sanderson's literary mysteries feature Dolph Martinez, a pudgy, myopic Border Patrol cop in *El Camino Del Rio* (1998) and *La Mordida* (2002). In *Safe Delivery* (2002), set in San Antonio, Sanderson carefully weaves together the stories of three characters: a Mexican writer and former priest, a private investigator, and an aging Texas Ranger. Hinojosa, discussed above for his best-known literary fiction and poetry about the Valley, is also author of the Rafe Buenrostro mysteries in *Partners in Crime* (1985) and *Ask a Policeman* (1998). Martinez, another Chicano author of literary fiction, published crime novels also set in south Texas, including *White Leg* (1996) and *Layover* (1997).

Among the more acclaimed mystery writers of west Texas are James Crumley and D. R. (Doris) Meredith. Crumley's novels include *The Mexican Tree Duck* (1993), *Bordersnakes* (1996), and *The Final Country* (2001). Using the Texas Panhandle for her setting, former librarian Meredith features Sheriff Charles Matthews, reference librarian Megan Clark, and attorney John Lloyd Branson in *The Sheriff and the Branding Iron Murders* (1985), *Murder by Reference* (1991), and *Murder Past Due* (2001).

As the conclusion of the twentieth century, Texas literature had emerged as a major regional American literature with its emphasis on the Texas mystique. But even as Texas letters gained recognition, a countermovement arose. More recently critics have pointed out that too many Texas writers drew from a Texas past that reveres wild nature and often romanticizes wilderness and ethnic minorities, and these critics have called for writers to recognize the reality of an urban Texas where ethnic divisions trouble city dwellers and where the revered wilderness has almost disappeared. Indeed, some writers began to move in those directions, writing diverse, urban works that still echo recognizable themes: landscape diversity, journeying, frontier, ambivalence, primitivism, racism, sexism, and violence. The new works indicate the new directions for Texas literature and demonstrate the ongoing vitality of the region's literature.

Selected Bibliography

Busby, Mark, ed., with David Mogen and Paul T. Bryant. *The Frontier Experience and the American Dream: Essays on American Literature.* College Station: Texas A&M University Press, 1989.

———. *Larry McMurtry and the West: An Ambivalent Relationship.* Denton: University of North Texas Press, 1995.

Clifford, Craig, and Tom Pilkington, eds. *Range Wars: Heated Debates, Sober Reflections, and Other Assessments of Texas Writing.* Dallas: Southern Methodist

University Press, 1989.

Davis, Steve. *Texas Literary Outlaws: Six Writers in the Sixties and Beyond.* Fort Worth: Texas Christian University Press, 2004.

Goodwyn, Larry. "The Frontier Myth and Southwestern Literature." In *Regional Perspectives: An Examination of America's Literary Heritage,* edited by John Gordon Burke, 175–206. Chicago: ALA, 1973. Originally published in *American Libraries,* February 1971, 161–67; April 1971, 359–66.

Graham, Don. *Giant Country: Essays on Texas.* Fort Worth: Texas Christian University Press, 1999.

Graham, Don, James W. Lee, and William T. Pilkington, eds. *The Texas Literary Tradition: Fiction/Folklore/History.* Austin: College of Liberal Arts, University of Texas, 1983.

Grider, Sylvia Ann, and Lou Halsell Rodenberger, eds. *Texas Women Writers: A Tradition of Their Own.* College Station: Texas A&M University Press, 1997.

Lee, James Ward. *Adventures with a Texas Humanist.* Fort Worth: Texas Christian University Press, 2005.

McMurtry, Larry. *In a Narrow Grave.* Austin: Encino, 1968.

Paredes, Américo. *"With His Pistol in His Hand": A Border Ballad and Its Hero.* Austin: University of Texas Press, 1958.

Pilkington, William T. *Imagining Texas: The Literature of the Lone Star State.* Boston: American, 1981.

Endnotes

1. This essay draws from my introductions to *New Growth/2* (San Antonio: Corona Press, 1993) and *Greenwood Encyclopedia of American Regional Cultures: The Southwest* (Westport, Conn.: Greenwood, 2004).

2. Roy Bedichek, *Adventures with a Texas Naturalist* (Austin: University of Texas Press, 1951), 115.

3. William T[om] Pilkington, *My Blood's Country* (Fort Worth: Texas Christian University Press, 1973), 3.

4. Larry Goodwyn, "The Frontier Myth and Southwestern Literature," *American Libraries,* February 1971: 161.

5. Larry McMurtry, *In a Narrow Grave* (Austin: Encino, 1968), 54.

6. Larry McMurtry, "The Texas Moon and Elsewhere." *Atlantic* 235, no. 3 (March 1975): 31.

7. William T[om] Pilkington, *Imagining Texas: The Literature of the Lone Star State.* (Boston: American, 1981), 31.

8. See "Katherine Anne Porter and the Southwest: Ambivalence as Deep as the Bone" in *From Texas to the World and Back: Essays on the Journeys of Katherine Anne Porter,* eds. Mark Busby and Dick Heaberlin (Fort Worth: Texas Christian University Press, 2001), 133–47.

9. See Mark Busby, *Larry McMurtry and the West: An Ambivalent Relationship* (Denton: University of North Texas Press, 1995).

10. See Mark Busby and Terrell Dixon, eds., *John Graves, Writer* (Austin: University of Texas Press, 2007).

11. Mary Karr, *The Liars' Club: A Memoir* (New York: Penguin, 1998), 44.

12. J. Frank Dobie, *Life and Literature of the Southwest*, http://www.oldcardboard.com/lsj/olbooks/dobie/dobie33.htm.

13. "Ai (Florence Anthony) (1947 –)" http://www.poetryfoundation.org/archive/poet.html?id=80637.

14. See Mark Busby, *Preston Jones*, Western Writers Series, (Boise, Idaho: Boise State University, 1983).

15. See Bill Cunningham, Steven L. Davis, and Rollo K. Newson, eds., *Lone Star Sleuths: An Anthology of Texas Crime Fiction* (Austin: University of Texas Press, 2007).

Lone Star Cinema

A Century of Texas in the Movies

Don Graham

FILM IS A LITTLE over a century old, and films about Texas are almost exactly a century old. As early as 1898 traces of future Texas content appeared in some Thomas Edison-produced segments of film depicting typical ranching activities. The titles told all: *Branding Cattle*, *Cattle Leaving the Corral*, *Lassoing Steer*, and *Cattle Fording Stream*. These pioneering cinematic moments were documentaries rather than fictional stories, but they were also the raw material around which plots could be developed. Since populations largely ignorant of western landscapes primarily viewed these early scenes in urban centers, the footage must have served, whether intentionally or not, as travelogues to faraway places, namely, the West. After all, in 1898 the frontier had been "closed" for only eight years, and travel to those distant sites was still expensive and time-consuming.[1]

Film footage came early to Texas, which in the late nineteenth century was still a lot closer to the frontier than New York and New Jersey. In February 1897 Thomas Edison's Vitascope showed various scenes to Dallas audiences, including a Mexican duel, a fire rescue, Niagara Falls, and a lynching. In 1900 in Austin citizens were able to see projected film footage in a tent show. The first actual filming to take place in Texas occurred at Galveston that same year. A series of Edison newsreels depicted scenes from the Galveston Flood, which killed thousands. The segments were shot on September 24, 1900, against the will of the city authorities, who tried to forbid moving pictures of the stricken community. They bore titles like *Panorama of East Galveston*; *Panorama of Orphans Home, Galveston*; and *Panoramic View, Wreckage along Shore, Galveston*. The purpose of each piece of footage was to show the devastation and damage to buildings caused by the hurricane and subsequent tidal wave. Oddly, the image of Texas in the movies began with a documentary of a disaster, not with the soundless puffs of smoke from blazing six-guns.[2]

In the first decade of the new century, the movie as a coherent narrative art form began to take shape in such early classics as *The Great Train Robbery* (1903) and *A Corner in Wheat* (1909). At the same time, because moving pictures were still a novelty, mere footage was enough to attract the curious. Exhibitors in Austin, for example, as late as 1910 advertised "2,000 feet of moving pictures" with no definition of content. The emergence of genres, popular subjects for plots, and movie stars was a slow but steady process, and the development of specific Texas materials in the movies to a degree paralleled these currents in the newest entertainment industry.

The genre most closely aligned with Texas was, of course, the western—and that meant the cowboy. The working cowboy held no more interest for mass audiences than he did for the most important mythologizers of the cowboy era. Frederic Remington, Owen Wister, and Theodore Roosevelt—painter, novelist, and cowboy president—were the three who did more than anybody else to transform the hired man on horseback into a national hero. They saw—and made the nation see—the cowboy as a picturesque figure, a man of action as well as repose, and perhaps above all, a paragon of American qualities that included physical prowess, courage, and a sense of moral rectitude. The cowboy became the American par excellence, and the Texas cowboy became preeminent among cowboys, at least in the number of westerns made with Texas in the title or with Texas associations. It has been estimated, for example, that 6 percent of all the dime novels of the nineteenth century dealt with Texas, a remarkable statistic in that no other state attained even 1 percent of such dubious popularity. Additionally, over 600 films concerned Texas, well over half of them westerns.[3]

Where did screenwriters, or scenarists as they were called then, turn for their stories of cowboys? The sources were varied, but authentic historical records were seldom among them. One influence was Buffalo Bill's Wild West shows. Immensely popular throughout the 1880s and 1890s and on into the new century, the shows provided strong visual motifs, including trick shooting, a stagecoach pursued by howling Indians, and a timely rescue by the cavalry. There were also Texas associations. From the beginning of the Wild West shows in 1883, one of the stars was a Texan, "Buck" Taylor, an authentic cowboy born near Fredericksburg. In 1887 Texas Jack Omohundro was among the cast of stars to perform at the Madison Square Garden in New York City, the first time the Buffalo Bill show played in that major venue. The black cowboy, Bill Pickett, from Travis County, made a name for himself in Buffalo Bill's arena with his rodeo skills in what later would be known as bulldogging. Pickett developed a technique of bringing the animal to the ground by biting its lips.[4]

Another influence on the early films was dime novels. These cheap precursors of pulp fiction gave early movies not so much specific stories as they did a general romantic feeling for the West and for western heroes. One of the staples of the dime novels was the Texas Ranger story. They had ridiculous titles and similarly ridiculous plots: *Single Hand, the Comanche Attila; or the Chaparral Rangers* (1872); *The Prairie Queen; or Tom Western, the Texas Ranger* (1871); *The Quadroon Spy; or The Ranger's Bride* (1870).

This body of popular literary culture became the stuff of early films with such Ranger titles as *The Ranger and His Horse* (1912). The first western serial, *Liberty*, starring Jack Holt as a Texas Ranger, appeared in 1916. In the silent and talkie eras, Texas Rangers appeared in western after western. In World War II a Texas Ranger went to the Philippines to fight the Japanese in *Texas to Bataan* (1943).[5]

Stage plays were a third source for the early scenarists. In *The Scouts of the Prairie, or Red Deviltry As It Is* (1872), a character named Texas Jack played a major role. The character was repeated in other spin-off plays. A more interesting and influential play was Charles Hoyt's farce *A Texas Steer* (1890), popular at the time and still produced into the 1940s. It featured a Texas cattleman named Maverick Brander who hailed from Red Dog, Texas, "where men are men and the plumbing is improving." Brander was elected to Congress and had to deal with crooked Washington politicians. It is funnier than *The Best Little Whorehouse in Texas*, but also incredibly racist and could not be produced today. The play was filmed twice, in 1915 and again in 1927, when Will Rogers gave the definitive performance.[6]

A fourth source, coming a bit later, was western pulp novels. From the 1910s onward, this type of fiction provided a steady stream of stories that could be made into films. Popular sellers such as Clarence E. Mulford and Zane Grey saw their works filmed repeatedly in the early days and later. Grey's *Last of the Duanes* was filmed four times, and *Lone Star Ranger* and *Riders of the Purple Sage* each enjoyed multiple remakes over many decades. Although *Riders of the Purple Sage* was set in Utah and dealt with Mormons, its famous gunslinger hero, Lassiter, was a Texas Ranger. Grey even formed his own motion picture company to produce Zane Grey films in hopes of maximizing his profits.[7]

On occasion other sources from popular culture supplied plot material. Frank Desprez's popular poem, "Lasca: The Story of a

Texas Cowboy," dating from 1882, is a good example. The poem told a wildly romantic story of a Mexican beauty who sacrificed her life during a raging stampede in order to save her lover, a stalwart Texas cowboy. According to J. Frank Dobie, the poem was so beloved that it "was recited on Friday afternoons in country schoolhouses from Montana to the Gulf of Mexico."[8]

Scenarists also invented stories of their own, and not surprisingly these tended to be very similar to the outlandish, melodramatic plots of dime novels, popular stage plays, and the pulps. This is certainly the case with the first non-documentary Texas film, in 1908. Fittingly enough, it was titled *Texas Tex* and it was filmed in Copenhagen, Denmark. Many Texas-based films have been filmed elsewhere. *Texas Tex* made use of a troupe of touring Wild West performers that included some authentic American Indians. Billed as an "American story for Americans," the film mixed colorful elements of western life, such as capturing and taming wild horses, with rousing melodrama. The plot concerned a bad cowboy and his sidekick, a Sioux Indian—not a Comanche or Kiowa, but a Sioux! The cowboy steals Tex's horse and abducts his sweetheart. In the woods the cowboy tries to kiss the girl, and she resists, whereupon the Sioux kills his partner, hoping to have the girl to himself. But Tex arrives just in time to coldcock the Indian and reclaim his sweetheart. *Texas Tex* had about as much to do with actual Texas cowboy life as did the scores of singing westerns with Texas titles made in the 1930s and 1940s by Gene Autry, Roy Rogers, and Tex Ritter.[9]

Another factor in popularizing the Texas cowboy in the early days was the public persona of Tom Mix. Mix began making movies in 1910, and he, Broncho Billy Anderson, and William S. Hart became the first major western stars. By the late 1920s Mix eclipsed even Hart, whose grim allegories such as *Hell's Hinges* (1916) were masterpieces of the silent era. Mix's titles often bore unmistakable Texas brands. *The Man from Texas* (1915), *The Heart of Texas Ryan*

(1917), and *The Texan* (1920) are three in this vein, though the
name Texas Ryan actually referred to the heroine, not to the cowboy hero. Mix's frequent movie identification with Texas cowboys
was reinforced by the perception that he was a native Texan, born
in El Paso, and that he had been a Texas Ranger at one time—all
excellent credentials for a celluloid hero, but all false. Mix was born
in Mix Run, Pennsylvania, and he was never a Texas Ranger. Like
Davy Crockett, Sam Houston, and many another legendary Texas
hero, Mix was a Texan because he either chose to be or studio management thought it was good box office.[10]

Mix's success in portraying the Texas cowboy of historical legend and pulp novel popularization can be seen in a contemporary
review of *The Texan*. The movie portrays a Texas cowboy who rides
over to New Mexico to straighten out a bad situation and save a
couple of damsels in distress in the bargain. *Motion Picture News*
stated: "Tom Mix is offering propaganda for Texas here and the
theme is based upon the specie of male which is raised in the Lone
Star state. In other words, he appears as a rip-snorting, 'up and at
'em,' hard-riding, six-shooting cowboy who will show the neighbors over in New Mexico just what constitutes a regular he-man!"
As a Texas cowboy specializing in trick riding, wearing spangled,
tailor-made outfits, and performing high deeds of derring-do, Tom
Mix operated at considerable distance from the workaday cowboy
life recorded in those pre-1900 Edison documentaries.[11]

But lest anyone blame solely the movies for glamorizing and
falsifying the Texas cowboy beyond all recognition, it is helpful
to remember that historians themselves liked to portray the Texas
cowboy as a demigod rather than a hired hand. Even such devotees of realism as J. Frank Dobie and Walter P. Webb considerably romanticized the lives of cowboys and Texas Rangers in books
like Dobie's *A Vaquero of the Brush Country* (1929) and Webb's
The Texas Rangers (1935). The process of glamorizing the Texas
cowboy began with the earliest writing about the new vocation. In

Tom Mix in a characteristically spectacular action shot, this one from *The Texan* (Fox, 1920). Courtesy Academy of Motion Picture Arts & Sciences.

Joseph McCoy's *Historic Sketches of the Cattle Trade of the West and Southwest* (1874), the granddaddy of trail-driving histories and a work widely regarded as a primary source for later historians, Texas cowboys were described in language befitting a movie prologue or a gaudy poster. McCoy declared them to be "a hardy self-reliant, free and independent class, acknowledging no superior master in the wide universe." With historical hyperbole of this sort, no wonder the movies polished the Texas cowboy image to a high gloss.[12]

As the western genre maintained its standing throughout the 1910s and 1920s, only one kind of western film came close to expressing the realism of the cowboy's actual life and work. These were the cattle-drive films, and in 1924 two of the best were released: *North of 36* and *Sundown*. Both were filmed on location in Texas, the first on a ranch thirty miles from Houston, the second on the open prairie near El Paso. Both drew praise from contemporary reviewers for their accurate pictures of cattle, and both were criticized for contrived plots and superfluous male-female romance. In short, the bovines were better than the beauties. Years later J. Frank Dobie recalled how impressed he had been by the serenity of the cattle in *North of 36*. He said he could read the brands on the steers and that it was the only western he had ever seen in which the cattle walked at their natural gait instead of being forced to run all the way to Kansas.[13]

Apart from the scenarists' search for western materials throughout the West, Texas provided a unique site of major tropes and myths. Texas history was in some ways the equivalent of stories from ancient Britain in Shakespeare's day. The Matter of Britain, as it is called in English studies, has its parallel in the Matter of Texas. The major and most fecund sources of stories, images, lore, and legend arising from Texas are the Alamo and the triad of Alamo heroes (Crockett, Travis, and Bowie), the trail drives, the Texas Rangers, ranching, and the ubiquitous cowboy who recurs from *Texas Tex* to John Travolta's *Urban Cowboy*.

Other familiar Texas subjects surfaced first in the silent era, to be resurrected again and again when the talkies took over. Oil, for example, entered the lexicon of Texas moviemaking in the 1920s with *Mr. Potter of Texas* (1922) and *Flowing Gold* (1924). Both were, at best, precursors of stereotypes of sudden wealth and bumpkin manners. Another subject received a more artistic treatment, and that was the plight of women of a cultivated sensibility suddenly thrust into the frontier conditions of nineteenth-century west Texas. *The Wind* (1928), directed by Victor Seastrom, starred Lillian Gish as the young heroine of Dorothy Scarborough's controversial novel of the same title, published three years earlier. In the novel Letty succumbs to the madness induced by the harsh environment and dies, but in the film she accepts her lot and lives.

Pioneering filmmakers saw the possibilities of using Texas history early in the century. The first Alamo film, *The Immortal Alamo*, was shot in San Antonio in 1911 at the Star Film Ranch, a film company operated by Gaston Mélies, brother of the famous French filmmaker Georges Mélies. The second, *Martyrs of the Alamo*, was released in 1915, and re-released in the 1920s under the title *The Birth of Texas*. So racist in its depiction of Mexican Americans, it was boycotted in Corpus Christi by Hispanics. There were other silent Alamo offerings, and as the years rolled by other attempts to make the Alamo story into film followed one after the other, all disappointing to various degrees. The Alamo story in film should be the foundation movie of the Texas myth, but no Alamo movie has truly captured the Texas mystique. John Wayne's *The Alamo* (1960) came closest, but nobody is likely to argue that this film is remarkable in any sense except its great running time and Wayne's presence—which is considerable. The film is didactic and filled with historical bloopers.[14]

One has to look elsewhere to find the greatest of the Texas films, the most iconic, the ones that most powerfully defined the state as a mythic site. The first three appeared between 1948 and

Splendid action sequence from *The Alamo*, John Wayne's big-budget epic about America. United Artists, 1960. Courtesy Library of the Daughters of the Republic of Texas at the Alamo.

1963, the arc of national ascension that marked the rise of Texas as a Super-State, to adapt the title of John Bainbridge's 1961 book on Texans, *The Super-Americans*. The films are *Red River* (1948), *Giant* (1956), and *Hud* (1963), with *The Last Picture Show* (1971) acting as a coda on the Big Three. No Texas films before or afterwards, are as rich as these, though some academics would plump for John Sayles' *Lone Star* (1996).

Taken together as a continuous narrative of myth-making, the Big Four define the founding, the growth of empire, the ironic decline, and the death of the central trope of Texas mythology: the cattle kingdom in all its glory. *Red River*, which began the cycle, is the story of the founding of a world from an Anglo viewpoint. Tom Dunson (John Wayne) crosses the Red River, abandoning his sweetheart, leaving her for land. Land is more important than any human tie, more important even than the love of a good woman. Of course, she was supposed to join him later, but was killed in an Indian attack before doing so. South of Red River, 200 miles from the Rio Bravo, Dunson performs the primal act. He takes the land away from its owner, a Mexican grandee. The Mexican owns too much land for any man to possess, says Old Groot, Wayne's side-kick, and besides, as Groot explains, the Mexican had taken it away from somebody else anyway.

What follows is the story of expansionism and of a changing world, a new phase of distant markets and finance capitalism, a world that Dunson does not understand. It remains for his ad-opted son (Montgomery Clift) to lead the trail herd to the new site of capitalism, the railheads at Abilene, Kansas. There Joseph McCoy had prepared the ground for the mass marketing of cattle bound for the Chicago slaughterhouses and their transformation into expensive steaks at Delmonico's in New York City or into tins of Vienna sausage for cowboys back in Texas. Through some tricky plot manipulations, Wayne and Clift are reconciled, securing the empire's line of succession. The ranch will be passed on to the next generation, which has proved itself worthy. No later movies are as confident of the line of succession as *Red River*. As a side note, Jane Tompkins, in her little book of criticism, *West of Everything: The Inner Life of Westerns*, offers a vegetarian reading of the film. With a straight face, Tompkins argues that the "red" of the title refers to the blood of the slaughtered cattle. It could just as easily refer to menstrual blood or the Red Sea, and it certainly does refer to the river that happens to separate Texas from Oklahoma, where, incidentally, red Indians lived.[15]

In *Giant* the ranch founded by Wayne—symbolically speaking—is now a huge feudal patriarchy with its lord—Bick Benedict (Rock Hudson)—its lady, Leslie Benedict (Elizabeth Taylor)—and a work force of cowboys and peasants, the latter all having one thing in common: they are of Mexican ancestry. *Giant* is a kind of dream-scape of the ranching tradition as it would like to see itself, and it embodies every element of the archetypal Texas movie: cowboys, wildcatters, cattle (chattel), empire, wealth, crassness of manners, garish taste, drawling speech, and barbecue. But the world of *Giant* is undergoing tremendous pressures to change, and the conditions for change are imminent. Unlike *Red River*, in which the woman is a purely symbolic figure, in *Giant* the woman is vitally present, representing both a criticism of Texas patriarchy and a grudging accommodation with Texas' provincial power. Leslie Benedict challenges the old ways but eventually, through her long-running marriage, makes a number of concessions to the weight of tradition.

But the biggest challenge to the wholeness of the ranching way of life is irresponsible materialism as represented by the beguiling and ruthless young wildcatter, Jett Rink (James Dean). Oil and the glittering, easy wealth that it engendered was the force that reshaped modern post-war Texas. The ranchers resist the incursions of oil, and then, once found on their land, appreciate its capacity for generating great sums of money. At the same time, *Giant*'s feudalism—specifically in the form of oppressive racial injustice—remains painfully intact, despite Leslie's attempts to improve the lot of Mexican-American laborers, and her son's marriage to a Mexican woman and his decision to become a doctor and practice medicine among the disadvantaged living in the very shadow of Reata. Bick Benedict's rousing fight in the diner is an important moment in the film and in Texas film history when, though defeated physically, he achieves a moral triumph by publicly acknowledging the fact that his grandson, of mixed descent, is a Benedict. (In the novel, Bick is not present in this scene and no fight occurs.) *Giant* was a huge favorite in Texas for at least two generations and did more than any other single film to define what Texas looked like for the rest of the world, especially those who had never been to the state.

Just seven years later, the year of the assassination of President John F. Kennedy, a much darker western, *Hud*, undercut or collapsed every optimistic assumption underlying *Red River* and *Giant*. In fact, *Hud* is a kind of stripped-down version of both films. The John Wayne trail-driver figure is replaced by Homer Bannon, an 82-year-old stubborn and honest rancher who can remember the trail drives of his youth. Only now he lives in a dying world. His cattle become infected with hoof-and-mouth disease and they have to be exterminated. This is where the trail drives end, in a mass grave into which the cattle are driven, shot, and buried—thus, the *Red River* connection. From *Giant*, *Hud* borrows the iconography of the house, the patriarchal structure of the family, and the empty landscape. Only this time the landscape is even emptier, and the family is a grotesque parody in that the boy Lonnie has no father or mother, and the only loving maternal figure is the white housekeeper, Alma, who is threatened with rape. In the novel her name is Halmea, she is black, and she is brutally raped. Hud is a version of Jett Rink in that he wants to drill for oil and will do anything it takes to gain control of the land. Thus, once again the lust for quick wealth is at war with the pastoral virtues embodied in the older generation, just as in *Giant*.[16]

Although *Hud* seemed to represent the final stage in the movement from expansive imperial optimism beginning with *Red River* and receiving its apotheosis in *Giant*, the final *coup de grace* to the Texas frontier/cattleman myth actually appeared in 1971 with *The Last Picture Show*, also based on a Larry McMurtry novel. In this Academy Award-winning film, *Red River* (in the novel the last movie was actually an Audie Murphy western, *The Kid From Texas*) reappears as cinematic legend, with the last picture show at the Royal Theater in Anarene (Archer City), Texas. *The Last Picture Show* is a western without cowboys. The young boys in the film hope to work in the oil fields or enlist in the military during the Korean War. They have no dreams of becoming cowboys or ranchers. The only character with any western ties is Sam the Lion, who now lives (and will die) in the little town where he operates a pool hall and owns both the café and the movie theater. Sam the Lion used to be a rancher, but those days belong to a distant, long-ago time that holds little interest for the current generation of oil drillers and high school boys. Western movies are the only connection with that storied past. The fact that two of the major Texas movies were based on novels by Larry McMurtry, not to mention the award-winning film *Terms of Endearment* and the hit miniseries, *Lonesome Dove*, both also based on McMurtry novels, adumbrates his importance in Texas literary and film culture. After the big Texas movies came many Texas-based films of interest, but none that possessed the size, the scale, and the impact of the Big Four.

The western maintained its centrality to the Texas film tradition, and in the late 1960s two of the more violent and influential American films of the era had explicit Texas themes and, in the case of one of them, detailed location shooting in Texas: Sam Peckinpah's *The Wild Bunch* (1969), shot in Mexico, and Arthur Penn's *Bonnie and Clyde* (1967), filmed in Texas. Each found innovative ways to present gunfire and its effects. Over the years *The Wild Bunch* has retained its greatness, but *Bonnie and Clyde*, probably because of Warren Beatty's "cuteness," has become more mannered with each passing year.

A subset of Texas-based films is the oil film, dating back to the first one, *Flowing Gold* (1922). Set in west Texas, the movie depicted the disastrous effects of instant wealth upon a simple rural family. They get rich, move to Dallas, and are threatened with urban corruption, especially the two grown children. At the end they return to their pastoral origins, *but they keep the money*. All the oil movies had essentially this same premise. *Boom Town* (1940) showed not only the rags-to-riches climb of wildcatters, but also the deterioration of traditional values along the way. *Written on the Wind* (1956) developed the theme of moral corruption in a lurid, over-the-top melodrama that still has a following among some film aficionados. *Waltz Across Texas* (1982) was a low-budget production that tried to tell the story of a small-time wildcatter, but the film was little seen and did not pack much punch. All of these story lines were developed in the west Texas oilfields, except for hints in *Written on the Wind* that east Texas was also a site for big oil pools.[17]

Another tradition of Texas movies—one that was always overshadowed by the western side of the southwestern equation—was the southern or east Texas-based films. For those films set ostensibly in east Texas, one of two things usually happened. Either the film translated east Texas pines into west Texas cactus, or it blurred east Texas into the Old South. In either case, the specific sense of east Texas was lost. Examples of the "westernization" of east Texas are plentiful. In *American Empire* (1942) Richard Dix operates a gigantic ranch along the Sabine River, just a few miles from the Louisiana border. Yet lofty, snow-clad mountains, the high Sierras, surround his ranch. In *A Walk on the Wild Side* (1962), Laurence Harvey gets off a train in the middle of a desert and sees a sign beside the track that says: "Beaumont One Mile." And then a tumbleweed tumbles past. Almost all movies supposedly set in east Texas are not.

The prime example of the second tendency of redefining east Texas as the South is *The Southerner*, Jean Renoir's 1945 film based on George Sessions Perry's Texas novel, *Hold Autumn in Your Hand* (1941). The film's title gives the game away. A 1952 film entitled *The Return of the Texan* even better illustrates the point of Texas' identification with the West and the western. The film was based on a novel by Fred Gipson entitled *The Home Place*, but the title was changed to specify the identity of the protagonist. However, the filmmakers outsmarted themselves because audiences of the day expected to find themselves in a western instead of on the family farm. After the dust settled, studio boss Daryl F. Zanuck cautioned director Delmer Daves with this simple truth: "If you go to Texas, go on a horse with a gun." Zanuck knew that *Texas* and *Texan* were permanently branded in the audience's mind as western to the core.[18]

A setback in the representation of Texas in the movies was the assassination of President John F. Kennedy. In a bit of historical irony that reveals a great deal, a comedy about Texas stereotypes premiered in Dallas on November 20, two days before the fatal attack. The film, *The Wheeler Dealers* (1963), starred James Garner as a fake Texan, a Yale graduate with a degree in Romance languages who impersonates a Texas oilman in order to get rich. The film is consistently funny and presents three colorful stereotypes: Texan good-ol'-boy oilmen named R. J., Ray Jay, and J. R. In the 1890s' play *A Texas Steer* they were named Yell, Bragg, and Blow, monikers that indicate similar functions in *The Wheeler Dealers*. During the month leading up to the premiere, the *Dallas Morning News* ran ads featuring Texas-brag jokes that presented Texans as rich, loveable, and harmless.[19]

Two days after the film's release nobody was laughing, and Texans were no longer comic or heroic figures. Now they were the people who had killed the president, and a long decade of anti-Texan movie portrayals set in. Films like *Dr. Strangelove* (1964), *Billion Dollar Brain* (1967), and *Executive Action* (1973) depicted Texans as dangerous buffoons, rightwing fanatics, and threats to American democracy. It was not until 1980 that *Urban Cowboy* redeemed Texas from years of opprobrium, and Texans could once again be seen on screen as cowboys and not as murderous ideologues. The TV show *Dallas*, which started in 1978, was also important in rehabilitating and re-establishing many of the old stereotypes. J. R. Ewing's name echoes the initials of the famous wildcatter from *Giant*, Jett Rink, as well as the oilman in *The Wheeler Dealers*. Texas was back in the saddle again, as Gene Autry might have sung.

Following in the wake of *Urban Cowboy* were several films of uneven quality. *Hard Country* (1981) starred Kim Basinger as a west Texas cowgirl who at film's end is headed to Los Angeles to try her hand as a flight attendant. The inevitable movie version of the long-running popular musical, *The Best Little Whorehouse in Texas* (1982), starred Burt Reynolds and Dolly Parton to no particular advantage. The film was noisy, obvious, and boring. The best of the music-based films about Texas, without question, was *Tender Mercies* (1983), with Robert Duvall doing a convincing turn as a country-western singer trying to rebuild his career and his life. Nobody has achieved a better Texas accent than Duvall. Certainly this film was far superior to Willie Nelson's *Honeysuckle Rose* (1980), the first of several attempts, all unsuccessful, to put Nelson forward as a cinema star. This includes the brooding western that he made with Gary Busey, *Barbarosa* (1982). Another musical-based film that should not be overlooked is *Selena* (1997), which brought Tejano music to a larger audience than it had previously known and launched the career of Jennifer Lopez.

From the early 1980s until quite recently, several Texas-based films have attempted, with considerable success, to set their plots and action in the most contested region of the state, the area along the Rio Grande separating Texas from Mexico. Tony Richardson's *The Border* (1982), starring Jack Nicholson as a border patrol officer from California reassigned to El Paso, was an honorable attempt to highlight the corruption and injustices on both sides of the law in the trafficking of illegals in a border city. *The Ballad of Gregorio Cortez* (1982), based on the groundbreaking book by Américo Paredes, was an independent production. Edward James Olmos played Cortez effectively, but for whatever reasons this story of bilingual misunderstanding with tragic results was not widely seen in this country, although it did fare better in some parts of the Third World. Two other border-related films of the 1980s were *Flashpoint* (1984), an interesting film with a John F. Kennedy assassination plot thrown in for good measure, and *Extreme Prejudice* (1987), an ultra-violent depiction of drug trafficking along the border.

The most ambitious of the border-related films was John Sayles'
Lone Star (1996). Set in Frontera, an imaginary border town, *Lone
Star* contained too many plot lines and too many ethnic subplots to
be compelling. Seemingly written by a committee of identity-poli-
tics professors, though it was director Sayles who actually authored
the script, the film contained some good riffs on Texas history with
"Forget the Alamo" being the most famous line in the movie. But
eventually it collapsed of its own thematic weight. Only academics
truly loved this film, chiefly because it gave them plenty of racism
and marginalization to write about.

John Lee Hancock's *The Alamo* (2004) was the most disappointing of the few latter-day attempts to make a big Texas movie.
Like *Lone Star*, its agenda of political correctness, coupled with an
obsession with historical accuracy, produced a tepid, prolix, and essentially boring epic that was anything but an epic. The familiar
triad of Bowie, Travis, and Crockett were portrayed with many personal failings rooted in some factual historical records, but in the
end nobody in the audience much cared what happened to them.
In his zeal for accuracy, director Hancock even went so far as to
have differing levels of Spanish spoken in the film, so as to reflect
various regions and classes. And in trying to tell the whole complex
story, the film wasted valuable time on Sam Houston, played with a
kind of stupefied blankness by Dennis Quaid. Similarly, in footage
that did not survive the cutting-room floor, Sam Houston's meeting with the Cherokees in east Texas was conducted in their native
language. The film has a few good moments, most of them be-
longing to Billy Bob Thornton's turn as Crockett—once, when he
fiddles on the Alamo wall, for which there is no historical evidence,
and then when he is executed after having surrendered to Santa
Anna's officers, which is also disputed by historians.[20]

Since the 1980s, with the exception of flawed ambitious films
like *Lone Star* and *The Alamo*, there has been a spate of minor films.
Some of the earlier ones are not bad. In fact, the Coen brothers'

first film, *Blood Simple* (1984), is an excellent noir outing set in Austin and nearby fields. It contains one of the best Texas-themed narrative prologues ever to appear in film: "Now, in Russia, they got it mapped out, so that everyone pulls for everyone else . . . . That's the theory, anyway. But what I know about is Texas, an' down here . . . . you're on your own." Other smaller films of the 1980s include *Raggedy Man* (1981); *Places in the Heart* (1984); *Nadine* (1987); and *Fandango* (1985), interesting for its homage to *Giant*.

From the 1990s to the present the films have seemed to shrink even further. *A Perfect World* (1993) and *Flesh and Bone* (1993) have their moments, for example, but *Secondhand Lions* (2003), *Happy, Texas* (1999), and *The Good Girl* (2002) are pretty slow going. One film that enjoyed far more attention than it deserved was *Dancer, Texas, Population 81* (1998). It told the story of four boys and a girl who are the only graduates of a tiny high school in far west Texas. Their goal in life—for the boys, anyway—was to visit Los Angeles when they finish high school, and to achieve this goal they buy bus tickets at the age of nine and make a "sacred vow" (repeated endlessly, it seems) to make the trip together. That is the premise of the film. All the adults are cretinous, and the high school kids are as sexless as newts. This is the nadir of the small-town-Texas movie, although it does have a rival in another ridiculous film set in Down Home, Texas, *Hope Floats* (1998), starring Austin sweetheart Sandra Bullock. Finally, though it takes place in a big city, namely Dallas, *Dr T and the Women* (2000), starring Richard Gere as a gynecologist, must not be overlooked in any survey of bone-dumb Texas movies. [21]

One small film that was well done, and was something of a surprise hit, at least locally in Texas, was the documentary *Hands on a Hard Body* (1997). This film captured the lives, hopes, dreams, and voices of actual people who take part in a contest held in Longview in east Texas. The contestants try to win a truck by outlasting their competitors in touching the truck continuously until everybody but one, the winner, is left. There is more truth about people's real lives in this film than in most that deal with small-town Texas.[22]

The best recent Texas film is one that goes to the heart of the Texas film tradition. Tommy Lee Jones's *The Three Burials of Melquiades Estrada* (2005) fashions a compelling narrative out of elements of the western, the border film, and ethnicity in the Southwest. In it Jones plays a hard-bitten ranch hand named Pete Perkins, who befriends an illegal vaquero, Melquiades Estrada. When Estrada is accidentally killed by a border patrol agent, Perkins sets out on a one-man journey to return his friend's body to Mexico, to the village and family that Estrada has spoken of but which in fact may not even exist. The film has a stark originality, great visual honesty in its depiction of the material culture of the Southwest, and a sure sense of character and redemption.

A much-anticipated Texas film of 2007 with excellent blood lines was *No Country for Old Men*, in which the Coen brothers (Ethan and Joel) returned to Texas to lens Cormac McCarthy's 2005 novel of the same name. Early promotional trailers promised a revival of the wild beauty of the border country of far west Texas and a character-driven narrative grounded in the old-fashioned premise that evil exists and has its own inherent and bloody logic. But films like this, which draw upon traditional Texas tropes and images, are likely to remain few and far between. In a century of Texas in the movies the state has changed drastically, and many of its regional characteristics seem to have largely disappeared. Students from cities and suburbs do not know the difference between a farm and a ranch, and many of them think that chopping cotton means to chop the cotton (not the weeds). With 82 percent of its population residing in cities and suburbs, and with its steady influx of citizens from other parts of the U.S., the Texas that is seen in films like *Red River*, *Giant*, and *The Last Picture Show* seems to belong to another age.

Selected Bibliography

Bryant, Keith L. *Culture in the American Southwest: The Earth, the Sky, the People.* College Station: Texas A&M University Press, 2001.

Busby, Mark. "Film and Theater," in *The Greenwood Encyclopedia of American Regional Cultures: The Southwest,* edited by Mark Busby, 175–210. Greenwood, Conn.: Greenwood, 2004 .

Graham, Don. *Cowboys and Cadillacs: How Hollywood Looks at Texas.* Austin: Texas Monthly Press, 1983.

—————. "The Cinematic Texas Cowboy," *Texas Libraries* 44 (October 1983): 131–36.

—————. "The Comic Texan in Film: A Regional Stereotype in the National Imagination," in *New Directions in American Humor,* edited by David E. E. Sloane, 51–58. Tuscaloosa: University of Alabama Press, 1998

—————. "Moo-vie Cows: The Trial to Hollywood," in *Giant Country: Essays on Texas,* by Don Graham. Fort Worth: Texas Christian University Press, 1998, 213–26.

—————. "A Short History of Texas in the Movies: An Overview," *Literature/Film Quarterly* 14 (1986): 71–81.

————— and William T. Pilkington, eds. *Western Movies.* Albuquerque: University of New Mexico Press, 1980.

Mitchell, Lee Clark. *Westerns: Making the Man in Fiction and Film.* Chicago: University of Chicago Press, 1996.

Thompson, Frank. *Alamo Movies.* East Berlin, Penn.: Old Mill Books, 1991.

Endnotes

1. Don Graham, "Moo-vie Cows: The Trial to Hollywood," in *Giant Country: Essays on Texas,* by Don Graham (Fort Worth: Texas Christian University Press, 1998), 213.

2. Mark Busby, "Film and Theater," in *Greenwood Encyclopedia of American Regional Culture,* ed. Mark Busby (Greenwood, Conn.: Greenwood, 2004), 187; and Don Graham, *Cowboys and Cadillacs: How Hollywood Looks at Texas* (Austin: Texas Monthly Press, 1983), 11.

3. Philip Durham, introduction to *Seth Jones and Deadwood Dick on Deck* (New York: Odyssey, 1966), vii.

4. Don Graham, "A Short History of Texas in the Movies: An Overview," *Literature/Film Quarterly* 14, no. 2 (1986): 74; Busby, 176.

5. Graham, *Cowboys and Cadillacs,* 17.

6. *Ibid.,* 18–19.

7. Graham, "A Short History of Texas in the Movies," 74.

8. J. Frank Dobie, *The Longhorns* (Austin: University of Texas Press, 1980), 128.

9. Graham, *Cowboys and Cadillacs*, 11; and "Texas Tex," *Motion Picture World* 2 (June 27, 1908): 546.

10. Graham, "A Short History of Texas in the Movies," 75.

11. "The Texan," *Motion Picture News* (November 27, 1920): 4159.

12. Joseph McCoy, *Historic Sketches of the Cattle Trade of the West and Southwest* (Columbus, Ohio: Long's College Book Company, 1951), 146.

13. Graham, *Cowboys and Cadillacs*, 30.

14. For extensive discussion of the Alamo story in film and literature, see Don Graham, "Remembering the Alamo: The Story of the Texas Revolution in Popular Culture," *Southwestern Historical Quarterly* 89 (July 1985): 35–67. For a full discussion of the making of John Wayne's *The Alamo*, see Don Graham, "Wayne's World," *Texas Monthly* (March 2000): 108–13, 144–45.

15. Quoted in Graham, "Moo-vie Cows: The Trail to Hollywood," 221.

16. The discussion of these films in a somewhat different context appears in Graham, "A Short History of Texas in the Movies," 78–80.

17. Don Graham, "The Displacement of East Texas in Movies about Texas," *East Texas Historical Journal* 25, no. 1 (1987): 20. For a further discussion of the oil tradition, see Don Graham, "*Dallas*: Oil's Final Triumph in Texas Mythology," *The Texas Gulf Historical and Biographical Record* 37, no. 2 (November 2001): 83–85.

18. Delmer Daves Collection, Department of Special Collections, Stanford University.

19. Graham, *Cowboys and Cadillacs*, 73.

20. For a longer discussion of the making of Hancock's film, see Don Graham, "Alamo Heights," *Texas Monthly* (December 2003): 132, 144, 214, 216, 218, 220, 234. For a tongue-in-cheek piece on the difficulties of filming the Alamo story, see Don Graham, "Mission: Impossible," *Texas Monthly* (February 2002): 83–85.

21. For further discussion of this film, see Don Graham, "Schmaltz across Texas: On the Lonesome Trail with the New Western Movies," *Texas Observer* 90, no. 11 (June 5, 1998): 29–31.

22. For a selective list of films set in the Southwest, see Busby, "Film and Theater," 207–10. For a rundown of the best Texas movies on video, see Don Graham, "'Time-Traveling Through Texas': A Half-Century of Lone Star Movies on Video," *Giant Country: Essays on Texas*, 265–85.

"Wider Than the Limits of Our State"

Texas Art in the Twentieth Century

Michael R. Grauer

IN 1983 THE HIGHLY esteemed and lauded American studies professor William H. Goetzmann described Cadillac Ranch, an art installation west of Amarillo, as "perhaps the best symbol of the new, true art establishment in Texas." This writer disagrees with Goetzmann's definition of what constitutes Texas art. Amarillo arts patron Stanley Marsh 3 commissioned the Ant Farm, a California group, to create Cadillac Ranch. Thus, Cadillac Ranch is a work of art depicting a symbol of Texas and placed in Texas, but a depiction of something Texan does not make that depiction a piece of Texas art. Likewise, neither Donald Judd nor Robert Smithson should be considered "Texas artists" as their works in Texas are merely matters of geography. Claude Monet painting in a Houston museum does not make Monet a Texas artist. Now if Monet had painted bluebonnets . . . or perhaps some other environmental feature associated with Texas . . .

Actually, early artists found Texas an inhospitable environment. For most of the nineteenth century the pioneers "were too occupied with the development of material resources . . . to have any leisure for the enjoyment of beauty." As one observer complained in 1877, Texas had "artists of genuine merit, with reputations wider than the limits of our state," but fellow Texans paid them scant notice. Even so, by the 1880s, with memories of secession and the Civil War fading, radical Republican rule overthrown, and the Indian frontier subdued, Texas prepared to commemorate its past, especially the founding period. In 1888 the Texas legislature commissioned portraits of the presidents of the Republic and governors of the state. For Frances Battaile Fisk, author of *A History of Texas Artists and Sculptors*, that year signaled the beginning of Texas art history. Actually, the course for the twentieth century was set earlier by three major figures who had arrived in the state in the 1870s. German sculptor Elisabet Ney (1833–1907) had settled near Hempstead in 1873, Charles Franklin "Frank" Reaugh (1860–1945) had moved with his family from Illinois to a farm near Terrell in 1876, and Robert Jenkins Onderdonk (1852–1917), originally from Maryland, had located in San Antonio in 1879. To this talented triumvirate twentieth-century Texans are deeply indebted.[1]

Often called the "Dean of Texas Painters," Reaugh was the only artist in the nation to paint the Texas trail-driving industry during its heyday. Beginning in 1883, probably near Wichita Falls and Henrietta, he sketched and painted the only images of true Texas longhorns before they were crossbred with European cattle. About 1890 he started using a camera as a sketching tool and was, if not the first, among the earliest artists to photograph in Palo Duro Canyon. The camera allowed him to capture on film "whole Texas steer[s]" as well as landscape views. And his *plein-air* pastels, usually painted along the Red, Wichita, Brazos, and Concho rivers, exemplify his drive to "preserve" the region before it was overgrazed or plowed under. "It is the beauty of the great Southwest as God has made it," Reaugh remarked, "that I love to paint."[2]

Never a self-promoter, Reaugh enjoyed his greatest critical acclaim from about 1890 to 1915. He had one of the more prestigious national exhibition records in Texas history, with solo exhibitions in Chicago and Colorado Springs in 1895 and 1897, respectively. After

Frank Reaugh (1860–1945), *Watering the Herd,* 1889. Pastel on paper mounted on canvas, 18 ⅛ x 34 ⅜ in. Courtesy Panhandle-Plains Historical Museum, Canyon, Texas, Frank Reaugh Estate.

joining the Society of Western Artists in 1897, he exhibited his work through the society all over the United States. He also toured his paintings with much success, especially in the upper Midwest, and he exhibited regularly in Dallas and Fort Worth from 1890 to 1939. Then, in 1900 he urged Dallas, his adopted city since 1890, to build the city's first art gallery. At Reaugh's suggestion, the State Fair of Texas began hosting an American art exhibition about 1900, which led to local displays of the works of some of the nation's leading artists. In 1903 he helped found the Dallas Art Association, which eventually became the Dallas Museum of Art. His substantial contributions notwithstanding, Reaugh was forgotten as the Dallas Art Association grew, a sad commentary for a man who for almost half a century had shaped the careers of artists all across the state and had cultivated an appreciation for southwest Texas.[3]

Onderdonk had an equivalent impact, albeit cut short by his untimely death in 1917. Unlike Reaugh, whose work as artist *and* teacher affected Texas art, Onderdonk's legacy is largely that of a teacher, evidenced primarily through his artist son, Julian, and his artist and art historian daughter, Eleanor. He had come to San Antonio hoping to paint portraits of affluent San Antonians, but they preferred European artists, or at least more established Americans. As a result, much of Onderdonk's early work focused on Hispanic life around San Antonio, for which "there was little market locally," forcing the transplanted Marylander to turn to teaching "in order to survive." In 1886 he helped found the Van Dyke Art Club, the first formal art organization in the Alamo City, which was limited to women. Although the art world began to prosper in San Antonio, Onderdonk ventured to Dallas in 1889, then later to St. Louis, Missouri, before returning permanently to San Antonio near the end of the nineteenth century when the State Fair of Texas Association hired him part-time, along with Reaugh, to organize the annual art exhibition at the fair. About the same time Texas historian James T. DeShields commissioned Onderdonk to do *David Crockett's Last Stand (The Fall of the Alamo)* (1901), which joined H. A. McArdle's *Dawn at the Alamo* and *The Battle of San Jacinto* and William Henry Huddle's *Surrender of Santa Anna as* the most important paintings of Texas' revolutionary history.

But Robert Onderdonk made his greatest contributions as a teacher. Mary Bonner, considered one of the finest etchers in the 1920s, studied with him, as did Edward G. Eisenlohr, Seymour Thomas, the first great Texas expatriate artist, and Rolla Taylor. His greatest protégé, however, was his own son Julian, whose impressionist paintings of the Texas landscape inflamed Texas art in the first third of the twentieth century and inspired the cottage industry known as the bluebonnet school. Onderdonk's daughter, Eleanor, also carved her own niche as an art curator at the Witte Museum in San Antonio, where she almost single-handedly saved historic Texas art from the ash heap of history.[4]

European immigrant-artists contributed not only to Texas painting but also to sculpture, and arguably the finest sculptor to work in

Texas in the nineteenth century was Elisabet Ney. In the early 1880s this transplanted German began modeling portraits of wealthy Texans, and in the 1890s she was commissioned to sculpt figures of Sam Houston and Stephen F. Austin for the 1893 World's Columbian Exposition in Chicago. These marbles now flank the entrance to the rotunda of the Texas Capitol, and Ney's Austin studio, Formosa, built to sculpt the figures of Austin and Houston, is now a historic landmark and museum for her work, as well as the first headquarters for the Texas Fine Arts Association, founded in 1911.[5]

Following in Ney's path, fellow German Frank Teich (1856–1939) came to Texas in 1883 to carve stone for the new Texas Capitol and the Tarrant County Courthouse. By the mid-1890s he began receiving commissions and "became primarily a sculptor of the South." His work in 1899 on the Confederate monument for the Texas Capitol grounds brought Italian sculptor Pompeo Coppini (1870–1957) to Texas. Coppini lived in San Antonio from 1901 to 1916, then moved to Chicago and later to New York, before returning to San Antonio in 1937 and building a special studio to complete the Alamo heroes cenotaph. Today his studio houses the Coppini Academy of Fine Arts, founded originally in 1945. Coppini's native-Texan protégé, Waldine Tauch (1892–1986), continued into the 1960s the traditional sculptural convention in Texas begun by Ney.[6]

From 1927 to 1929 Julian Onderdonk's landscapes inspired exhibitions of Texas wildflower paintings in San Antonio and ultimately gave rise to the ubiquitous bluebonnet school. During this period San Antonio reached its zenith as an art center, and the city's Art League hosted the exhibition first called the Texas Wildflower Competitive Exhibition, which became the San Antonio Competitive Exhibition in 1928. Wealthy oilman Edgar B. Davis of Luling, enamored of the state's wildflowers, sponsored the exhibitions, which not only popularized the bluebonnet school, but also helped make the flower a state symbol. And when President Lyndon B. Johnson hung the works of San Antonio painter Porfirio Salinas in the White House, bluebonnet painting reached a national stage. Salinas and his mentor Robert Wood subsequently helped push central Texas and Hill Country landscapes to their current place at the top of *juste-milieu* painting in Texas today.[7]

One of the more significant cultural events in the United States in the 1930s, the Texas Centennial Exposition, which marked the apogee of Texas art in the twentieth century, opened in Dallas in June 1936 following a fierce competition between Dallas, Houston, and San Antonio. The Exposition included exhibitions at the newly opened—and air-conditioned—Dallas Museum of Fine Arts, to which the national arts magazine, *Art Digest*, dedicated nearly its entire June 1936 issue. Over 600 works of art comprised the general exhibition. Although European art was on display, American art was more prominent. The Texas Section itself included 164 paintings, prints, watercolors, and drawings, ostensibly by the state's most important artists at that time. The works of women dominated the Texas Section, constituting over 60 percent of the exhibit, yet the introductory essay to the catalog for the Department of Fine Arts at the Exposition made no mention of them. It was left for Jerry Bywaters to give the women their due, writing in the *Southwest Review* that the Texas Section contained the work of nineteen women, who "through their continued development during the past ten years, have achieved a distinct and valuable mode of expression." And one contributor to *Art Digest*, which for the most part also ignored the ladies, openly acknowledged that "almost all" of the state's sculptors were women.

From the 1920s on, exhibitions of Texas art became increasingly common at the local, state, and national levels. The Texas General, for instance, commenced in 1940. Renamed the Annual Texas Exhibition of Painting and Sculpture in 1950, this was a collaborative exhibition of contemporary Texas art that traveled regularly between Dallas, Houston, and San Antonio until 1963. Twenty-two Texas artists displayed their work at the World's Fair in New York in 1939, and in 1943 the American Federation of Arts asked the Dallas Museum of Fine Arts to organize Texas Panorama for a national tour to six states. The following year the exhibition, Six Texas Painters, opened at New York's cutting-edge Weyhe Gallery, by which time a significant shift had occurred in the Texas art world. Regionalism had emerged, and a discussion in *The Dial* magazine had been at least partially responsible.[8]

In articles for *The Dial*, Van Wyck Brooks, John Dewey, and George Santayana, along with writers in the *Southwest Review*, sounded a call for regionalism. In 1918 Brooks urged American artists to draw on the nation's "communal experience" as a "usable past" and to create works reflective of their own communities. Two years later Dewey elaborated that art depicting local themes could be used to explore universal values. A bit later Santayana chimed in, asserting that art was not to be found in museums, which he likened to mausoleums, but in the normal occurrences of everyday life. And the nation's artistic strength, he felt, was to be found in its regional diversity. Paraphrasing Santayana, Henry Nash Smith, a leader of regionalist literature in Texas, challenged artists to focus on their own environments in order to create "an art which is firmly enough rooted in its own earth to command attention from the world."[9]

West Texas, or everything west of Fort Worth in the Texas vernacular, also inspired a number of artists during the first half of the twentieth century. Georgia O'Keeffe was in Canyon from 1916 to 1918, although she had yet to decide if teaching or painting was her life's direction. Printmaker Margaret Seewald and painters Isabel Robinson, Ben Carlton Mead, and Emma Hendricks led art activities in the Amarillo area in the 1920s. H. D. Bugbee of Clarendon became the Charlie Russell of the southern plains, painting Native Americans, cowboys, and the flora and fauna of the region. He also worked as an illustrator for southwestern histories and pulp westerns. Lloyd Albright at Dalhart, Maurice Bernson at Canadian, and Russell Vernon Hunter at Farwell also achieved acclaim outside the Panhandle. Urbici Soler, Tom Lea, Lewis Woods Teel, Lois Denton, and

Fern and Eugene Thurston were prominent among El Paso artists and exhibited in some of the Texas art exhibitions "down state," including during the 1920s the San Antonio Competitive Exhibitions, which ended with the beginning of the Great Depression. In 1931 Fort Worth artists Blanche McVeigh and Evaline Sellors helped found the Fort Worth School of Fine Arts. Not until 1939, however, did the Fort Worth Art Association reorganize and adopt a policy for exhibiting local artists' work.[10]

A group of Dallas artists, all under thirty years of age, also heeded the call, and in 1932 nine of them—Jerry Bywaters, John Douglass, Otis Dozier, Lloyd Goff, William Lester, Charles McCann, Perry Nichols, Everett Spruce, and James Buchanan—held an exhibition that caught the attention of *Art Digest*. Joined by Alexandre Hogue, the Dallas Nine, as they were dubbed, soon founded the Dallas Artists League and began sponsoring the Alice Street Carnivals, complete with a Mexican orchestra and an African-American band. Modeled after Greenwich Village's Washington Square art festivals, these carnivals served notice that the young Turks of Dallas were to be taken seriously.[11]

In a sense, the emerging regionalism of north and west Texas was accentuated by the Great Depression and the New Deal. While artists in the Dallas area turned their brushes toward the land, believing that a return to local agrarian roots—even if only through art—would restore America, certain New Deal programs gave momentum to an exceptionally dynamic period in American and Texas art. One result was a coalescence of regionalism and public art. American artists had produced little public art until after 1875, when centennial celebrations across the nation spawned massive architectural projects, murals, and prominent commemorative sculpture. Bringing to mind the Italian Renaissance, this burst of public art was christened the "American Renaissance." Although short-lived, it gave impetus to the idea that public art contributed to the health of the nation, a belief that reached the White House in the early 1930s through a former schoolmate of President Franklin Roosevelt at Groton, painter George Biddle. It was Biddle who envisioned a federally funded mural program to promote the ideals of the New Deal and to provide relief for struggling artists.[12]

The New Deal subsequently produced four programs to put artists to work for the good of the nation: the Public Works of Art Project (PWAP); the Treasury Department's Section of Painting and Sculpture (The Section); the Treasury Relief Art Project (TRAP); and the Works Progress Administration's Federal Art Project (WPA/ FAP). By the time it ended on June 30, 1934, the PWAP had employed 3,749 artists nationwide, forty-four in Texas. Texas received 125 Section works, of which thirty-two have been unaccounted for and seventeen destroyed. At its peak the WPA/FAP employed some 5,300 artists. In 1934 the PWAP commissioned artists across the state. Harold Dow Bugbee of Clarendon (1900–1963) and Ben Carlton Mead (1902–1986) of Amarillo completed two murals for the newly opened Pioneer Hall of the Panhandle-Plains Historical Museum in Canyon. The PWAP's successor, The Section, sponsored large-scale, multi-panel mural competitions in bigger Texas cities, such as Amarillo, Dallas, Fort Worth, Houston, El Paso, and San Antonio. The 1939 regional mural competition for the new Amarillo post office illuminates this process for a large-scale Section commission. Open to "All American Artists Resident of or Attached to the States of Louisiana, Mississippi, Arkansas, Missouri, Kansas, Oklahoma, Colorado, New Mexico, and Texas," the competition required entrants to pay a larger fee and submit anonymously. Making these competitions particularly attractive to artists was the greater exposure for the winner and the prospect of "consolation" commissions for other entrants. After selecting the finalist for the Amarillo post office, for example, officials invited eight other artists whose Amarillo proposals were "of vitality and distinction" to submit designs for smaller murals for post offices in Brownfield, Center, Livingston, and Rockdale, as well as in Idabel, Madill, Sayre, and Wewoka, Oklahoma.[13]

Florence McClung (1894–1992), *Ellis County Landscape*, 1936. Oil on canvas, 23⅞ x 29⅞ in. Courtesy Panhandle-Plains Historical Museum, Canyon, Texas, gift of the artist.

Two Texas muralists were particularly noteworthy. El Paso artist Tom Lea's Section commission for the Odessa post office resulted in one of the greater pieces of Texas art ever produced, *Stampede.* Inspired by the cowboy song, "Little Joe, the Wrangler," Lea believed *Stampede* "especially appropriate for Odessa, a town out on the wide plains near the old Goodnight Cattle Trail and not far from the Horsehead Crossing of the Pecos." Likewise, the murals of Julius Woeltz (1911–1956), a San Antonio painter, have become a source of great pride to the citizens of Amarillo, who recognize their high quality and importance. However, this was not the opinion at the time of noted Texas folklorist J. Frank Dobie, whose harsh criticism of New Deal art echoed the assertion of a *New York Times* art critic that "perfectly terrible art" had "been brought into existence under the WPA." The views of Dobie and others notwithstanding, New Deal art in Texas was genuinely outstanding.[14]

Schools are essential to the cultivation of art appreciation and for the training of aspiring artists. Accordingly, beginning in the 1880s schools of art became increasingly influential in Texas as citizens endeavored to bring culture to the frontier. European-trained artists introduced the academic tradition to various art schools in Austin, Galveston, Houston, and San Antonio. Many of the earlier schools were private, such as that founded in 1884 by Frank Reaugh at Terrell, where women populated his classes. Of course, Reaugh taught at a number of schools in the Dallas area, and he advanced the art community there by establishing the Dallas School of Fine Arts in 1899. Other private artists followed suit, including Vivian Aunspaugh, who established Aunspaugh Art School in Dallas in 1902, and Olin and Kathryne Hail Travis, who started the Art Institute of Dallas (AID) in 1926, modeling it after the Art Institute of Chicago where they both had studied. After the reorganization of the AID in 1940, the Dallas Museum of Fine Arts School became integral to the mission of the museum. In San Antonio in the 1920s Jose Arpa began operating the San Antonio Art School, which offered both arts and crafts classes and held exhibitions. At the same time, German-trained Hugo Pohl from Detroit offered the academic tradition at his San Antonio Academy of the Fine Arts. And in 1942 the San Antonio Art League partnered with Marion Koogler McNay to form the San Antonio Art Institute, succeeding the Witte school.

Without minimizing the significance of these private ventures, the proliferation of public art schools touched the lives of far greater numbers of Texans. By the end of World War II, many high schools and virtually every college or university in the state had an art department of some sort. Kidd-Key College, founded in 1866, had one by 1868. Texas University at Georgetown opened with an art department in 1873, as did Southwest Texas Normal School at San Marcos (now Texas State University) in 1903. This quickly became standard procedure, and whether attending Mary Hardin-Baylor, Southern Methodist University, Texas Christian University, Sam

Houston Normal Institute, Rice Institute, Stephen F. Austin, Texas Technological College, or Lamar College, students had access to an array of artistic opportunities. Perhaps the most cutting-edge and controversial art school in Texas in the 1930s was at Sul Ross State Teachers College at Alpine, where Xavier Gonzales held forth. So by the early twentieth century instruction for future teachers of art had come of age in the Lone Star State.[15]

The late 1930s and 1940s were a time of flux in Texas art circles. Stylistically, as the American-scene movement began to wane, the harder edges of social realism, which heretofore had never really caught on in Texas, began to appear. The arrival of artists from the national art centers influenced the isolationist atmosphere created by the Lone Star regionalists. Among those artists with the greatest influence were Donald Vogel, who came to Dallas from Chicago in 1942, Henry Lee McFee, and Boyer Gonzales, Jr., a native Texan schooled in New York, who arrived in San Antonio from New York in the late 1930s. By 1945 American art in general and Texas art in particular saw dramatic changes. The domination of the Lone Star regionalists ended when Everett Spruce and William Lester assumed teaching positions at the University of Texas in 1940, followed by Jerry Bywaters' promotion to the director of the Dallas Museum of Fine Arts in 1941 and Alexandre Hogue's departure for the University of Tulsa in 1945. By 1950 the center of Texas art had shifted to Houston with the establishment of a more abstract school of painting.

Serving as something of a bridge between Dallas' waning regionalism and Houston's upcoming non-representational school were a group of Fort Worth artists and "an extraordinary circle of independent artists," mostly women in Denton. While Fort Worth and Denton shared the art center for Texas from about 1940 to 1950, the antagonism between Fort Worth and Dallas produced an "anti-regionalist" vision in the former city. This spawned a hybrid style, ranging between surrealism and abstract expressionism, a "magic realism," if you will. The power of the Fort Worth school culminated in the Six Texas Painters exhibition at New York's Weyhe Gallery in late 1944. This exhibition by five Fort Worth artists–Flora Blanc, Bill Bomar, Veronica Helfensteller, Dickson Reeder, and Bror Utter, along with Donald Vogel from Dallas, who felt a closer kinship with the Fort Worth school than with the Dallas regionalists—broke the hegemony enjoyed by the Dallas Nine and their Circle since 1930.

Meanwhile, during the late 1930s and early 1940s Denton's North Texas State College, now the University of North Texas, and the Texas State College for Women (TSCW), now Texas Woman's University, became hotbeds of artistic dialogue, largely due to the powerful personas and work of their female instructors, such as Coreen Mary Spellman, Edith Brisac, Toni LaSelle, Marie Delleney, Carlotta Corpron, and Thetis Lemmon. Corpron, for example, came to Texas in 1935 to teach at TSCW and was "one of the first artists in Texas to adopt the program of the New Bauhaus." And LaSelle was perhaps even more remarkable since she was the only Texas artist in the 1930s "committed to nonobjective abstraction."[16]

World War II also caused a seismic shift in Texas art. Along with the loss of federal patronage, many artists put aside their careers for service in the military. The Dallas printmaking group, Lone Star Printmakers, for example, went out of existence. The post-war era brought additional alterations in American art. A good many European artists had fled the carnage and destruction of war, and many of them settled in the East where they were quickly hired to teach their avant-garde ideas. Some Texas artists studied under many of these émigrés, such as Vaclav Vytlacil at the Art Students League and Viktor Lowenfeld at Hampton Institute. And many returning veterans, taking advantage of the G.I. Bill, studied art and affected art movements across the country. Texas artists in Austin, Dallas, Fort Worth, Houston, and San Antonio struggled to keep pace with this changing scene. In San Antonio, for instance, the Villita Street Artists organized in 1936, followed by the River Art Group in 1947 and the Texas Watercolor

Society in 1949. More importantly for avant-garde art, the Men of Art Guild was established in 1952 "to join together the serious paint-ers in San Antonio for mutual aid, to promote art interests and activi-ties in the state, [and] to keep the public advised on new art forms." To counteract their perceived dismissal of academic/traditional art, another group of San Antonio artists, led by Pompeo Coppini, cre-ated the Coppini Academy of Fine Arts in 1952. This was followed two years later by the opening of the McNay Art Institute and its extensive collection of European modernism.[17]

Other Texas cities followed San Antonio's lead. The formation of the Contemporary Arts Association (CAA) in Houston in 1948, the Fort Worth Art Center in 1951, and the Dallas Museum for Contem-porary Arts in 1956 "offered important challenges to the regional scene." Simultaneously, contemporary American art exhibitions at the Museum of Modern Art and the Whitney Gallery (now Museum of American Art) provided opportunities for Texas artists. Never-theless, Fort Worth and Denton held sway in Texas painting largely through the 1940s.

While two of the more prominent sculptors in the 1940s were based in Fort Worth, Evaline Sellors and Charles Williams, Texas sculptors in general were not limited to a particular locale. Octavio Medellin, for example, one of the first Latino artists in Texas to achieve recognition, taught in Denton, Dallas, San Antonio, and Bandera. The direct carving and more tactile connection to materi-als, espoused by William Zorach, became *de rigeur* in Texas with sculptors such as Bess Bigham Hubbard in Lubbock, Ione Ruth Franklin in Commerce, and Dorothy Austin and Mimi Murphey in Dallas. Figurative sculptors such as Charles Umlauf of Austin, Hari Bartscht of Dallas, and Ishmael Soto of San Antonio and Austin found their muse in expressionism and northern European Gothic art. Still, Texas sculpture, like paintings and prints, marched steadily toward abstraction. As one authority observed, by "the 1950s the long uninterrupted dominance of the figure in Texas sculpture was being challenged, as sculptors increasingly turned to new ideas and new materials."

As Cold War tensions gripped the nation and fed the paranoia of the 1950s, many artists sought novel modes of expression. In Texas after World War II, artists often fell into one of two categories: those attached to Texas and/or "Texanness," and those who worked in the state with an almost phobic intensity not to be seen as Texas artists. This schizophrenic approach "to be or not to be" Texan is almost comical, particularly today, given the cross-pollination that has occurred. By the 1950s Houston had become "the hub of art activity in the Southwest," and the city's artists, like those associated with the McNay Institute in San Antonio, embraced European modernism. Largely through exhibitions at the CAA, brought in by more cosmopolitan directors such as Jermayne MacAgy and the patronage of John and Dominique de Menil, Houston was thrown into the maelstrom of modernism, like it or not. Still, artists in Houston, as well as those in San Antonio and Dallas, generally lagged about ten years behind New York and San Francisco, the great filters and disseminators of abstract painting.

While cutting-edge exhibitions and the avant-garde patronage of the Menils were critical, one scholar has offered another, quieter protagonist for modernism in Houston. In a 2006 essay, "Was Mrs. Cherry the Mother of Modernism in Houston?," Randolph Tibbits answers in the affirmative, arguing that Mrs. E. Richardson Cherry literally hid her modernist leanings under the surface pigment on her paintings, concealing the "underlying [cubist] structure with detail" and "sheer prettiness," aware that many people did not like modernism. After all, said Tibbits, she wanted to sell her paintings. Consequently, it was through the teachings of Cherry's protégé, Ola McNeill Davidson, that non-representational painting gained a toehold in Houston. Davidson acknowledged as much in an undated [1950?] letter to Cherry: "Without you and the showing of the way there would be no Robert [Preusser], Carden [Bailey], Gene [Charlton],

Harley [Brubaker] and a number of others [including Frank Dole-jska] on their way to the top in their field that you do not know."[18]

There were several artists—transitional figures of a sort—who contributed to Houston's emergence as a focal point of modernism. Fort Worth native Jack Boynton journeyed from Fort Worth and Denton to the Bayou City in the 1950s. In Fort Worth in the 1940s he exhibited as "Jack Boynton," but in Houston in the early 1950s he became "James Boynton" and led the charge toward non-representational art. John Biggers came to Houston in 1949 from North Carolina via Pennsylvania State University, and from his position at Texas State College for Negroes (now Texas Southern University), he painted social realist murals dealing with southern blacks in the best tradition of Jacob Lawrence. He later moved more and more toward his ancestral roots in Africa. Forrest Bess was another key figure. Working in a thick impasto, heavily influenced by Vincent Van Gogh and Maurice de Vlaminck, he began painting seriously in 1934 while supporting himself as a shrimp fisherman. After World War II he exhibited at the famed Betty Parsons Gallery in New York, which also showed the works of Jackson Pollock, Mark Rothko, and Barnett Newman. Through its "visionary potency and abstract simplicity," Bess's work had a profound effect on contemporaries and subsequent generations of Texas artists. Finally, after being away from her native Houston for nearly two decades, Dorothy Hood returned in 1961. She brought European modernism filtered through and blended with Latin American movements. Her exposure to expatriate European surrealists in Mexico armed her for the rest of her career. Although not a part of the Houston art scene, Temple artist Ben L. Culwell deserves mention here, for his experimentations with abstraction and action painting were quite advanced, and Dallas co-opted him as "their" first representative in this type of painting.

The new ground in non-representational painting plowed by the likes of Boynton and Hood flowered in Houston in the 1960s. Joseph Glasco, Dick Wray, Richard Stout, and Charles Schorre were all devotees of this new style, "comprising a small nucleus . . . attracted to the sense of romance, independence, isolation, and open space that Houston proffered." Unfortunately, "the audience for a serious painter in Houston during the sixties was essentially nonexistent." But James Johnson Sweeney, director of the Museum of Fine Arts, prodded the city "to take a broader view of the art world." He brought a major exhibition of fauvist Andre Derain to Houston, but jettisoned the somewhat sacred "local" in favor of a juried regional competition. He also pushed for the acquisition of pre-Columbian objects and a major collection of surrealist sculptures by Jean Tinguely. Sweeney moreover afforded "Houston artists the opportunity to have their works judged in a larger context." While Houston may not have been ready for Sweeney, or MacAgy and his successor "Lefty" Adler, artists certainly were "keyed into [their] spirited aggressiveness and international sophistication." These men showed Texas artists that their work did not exist in a vacuum and had the potential to hold its own with art anywhere in the world.

Similarly, as director of the Dallas Museum of Contemporary Art (DMCA), Douglas MacAgy "brought modern art to Dallas." The DMCA gave the first museum exhibition in the United States to Rene Magritte and presented the Museum of Modern Art's exhibition "The Art of the Assemblage." MacAgy also invited Claes Oldenburg to Dallas and staged the DMCA's first art "happening." The activities of the DMCA in the late 1950s and early 1960s also influenced heavily the work of three sculptors who came to the fore at this time—Jim Love, Roy Fridge, and David McManaway. Initially swayed by Dadaist humor and the attraction of the found object, these artists had "digested the prevalent ideas of art in the country and devised their own [but related] responses." The Amarillo-born Love, whose career took him into theater arts initially, turned to sculpture in the mid-1950s. Called an "urban archeologist" by one scholar, he came to Houston in 1953. In 1958 CAA director Jermayne MacAgy "discovered" Love through the latter's theater work and hired him to install two major exhibitions at the CAA. Soon thereafter Love began to weld steel sculpture, influenced by David Smith and Richard Stankiewicz.

While living in Dallas, Fridge began trekking to Port Aransas, collecting bones and beach detritus, before moving to the coastal city in 1961. This period of self-imposed relative isolation resulted in totemic assemblages that eventually morphed into boat shapes, given Fridge's own practical need for utilitarian boats. McManawy met Love and Fridge at the DMCA in 1959. He followed the found-object aesthetic and tapped into the same mysticism that intrigued Fridge. He also shared Fridge's wont for isolation, although not to the extent of becoming a hermit. McManaway juxtaposed disparate objects in old Coca-Cola bottle boxes to create tensions. Rather than interpret each object individually, however, he preferred to search for understanding "through the gestalt of the work."[19]

Commercial galleries assumed a greater responsibility for much of the art growth by the 1960s. In Houston, for example, the New Arts Gallery and Cushman Gallery emphasized local cutting-edge work and often provided the first solo exhibitions for avant-garde Houston artists in the late 1950s and early 1960s. Likewise, in Dallas the Betty McLean galleries, and particularly Valley House Gallery, focused on area artists "even when the tangible returns … were nebulous." By the late 1960s, of course, social and cultural unrest gripped the nation, and American art, perhaps reflecting the troubled times, began to spin in multiple directions. In Texas, the hegemony Houston had held since about 1950 diminished and artists all over the state attempted to find their own way. Consequently, the idea of an "art center" in the state, so clearly defined in earlier times, became somewhat obsolete. Texas art was now centered anywhere and everywhere. And instead of Houston, or Dallas, or San Antonio, it had now become "Texas art," an idea nurtured and cultivated in the late 1960s by native Texan art critic Dave Hickey. Hickey ran Austin's A Clean Well Lighted Place gallery from 1967 to 1971 and featured

> this monster called 'Texas Art' and it nearly devoured the whole [art] scene [in Texas]. We had begun by trying to convince people that there was something special happening in the visual arts here, and reaching for the metaphor at hand, we invoked the *mythos* of Texas... . Talk about waking the sleeping tiger! Before you could say 'Look out!' the art was touted as special *because* it was being done in Texas, because it was *about* Texas. Which was absolute bullshit. It was special because it was good art.

Hickey encouraged his artists to "not make a profession of portraying Texas, per se." Art historian William H. Goetzmann calls these artists "pre post-moderns."[20]

Meanwhile, the Oak Cliff Group shared "a love of humor and low-art aesthetics that came to be known as Texas Funk. Jack Mims, George Green, Jim Roche, and Bob Wade attempted in their work to "out Texan" Texas. It seemed Texas was made to order for pop art and op art. This was never truer than in the art of Luis Jimenez. The son of a neon-sign maker, Jimenez returned to his roots, both culturally and structurally, to put a new and controversial spin on not only Texas' mythos, but also the spirit of the American West. Among Jimenez' countless accomplishments as an artist, and perhaps his greatest impact in Texas, the sheer genius of his art notwithstanding, are the doors he opened as the first major Latino artist to be recognized and honored in the almost exclusively white fraternity of Texas artists. Jimenez spent the bulk of his career in Texas, but in the last several years he lived and worked in Las Cruces, New Mexico.

The 1960s were tumultuous for this nation, as the civil rights and American Indian movements and the National Farm Workers Association mobilized Americans across the country in protests against racism and other forms of discrimination, protests which often turned violent. The emergence of the Houston school and the Oak Cliff Group at this time was symptomatic of the broader effort within society to break with the establishment. The nation's diversity was becoming more obvious, and in the realm of art the National Endowment for the Arts encouraged the trend through its grants. The impact on Texas was immense.

On the other hand, other branches of Texas art rarely given serious consideration by scholars also became ingrained in the state's cultural fabric during the 1960s. These movements include the cowboy school, the bluebonnet school, and what Goetzmann pejoratively calls the "Last Picture Show" school. Generally, studies of Texas art have taken an anachronistic—if not downright insulting—view of these forks in the road, if they even consider them at all. To be sure, much of this work is pedestrian at best, but some deserves consideration. Representative of the cowboy school was H. D. Bugbee of Clarendon. He plugged away as a "prophet in his own country" from 1915 or so until his death in 1963. Bugbee exhibited and sold his work in New York in the early 1930s, and his pen-and-ink drawings for pulp magazines such as *Ranch Romances* and *Western Stories* inspired many a budding cowboy artist. His followers in Texas helped form the Cowboy Artists of America in the 1960 and the short-lived Texas Cowboy Artists in the 1970s. Today, cowboy artists from Texas are whipping and spurring in national and international exhibitions, but are never considered mainstream artists.

Porfirio Salinas led the charge in the 1950s and 1960s with his ubiquitous paintings of Texas wildflowers, which received national attention during the presidency of Lyndon B. Johnson. The natural heir to Julian Onderdonk and the San Antonio competitives, Salinas was an exemplary landscape painter with a loaded brush. However, he suffered from the pressures of too many patrons and too little paint on the canvas in the latter part of his career. Salinas' successors are legion today, as thousands of Sunday painters attempt to emulate him. Perhaps this is why there is nothing more damning to a Texas artist than to be called a "bluebonnet painter." Equally ubiquitous is the nostalgic (some might say passé) school with its abandoned barns and crumbling historic buildings. Among the highly skilled artists practicing in this vein since the 1950s have been Ancel Nunn, E. M. Schiwetz, and J. B. Erwin.

By the late 1970s Texas artists had "learned to acknowledge the exhaustion of modernism with its quaint cubists, futurists, synchromists, and abstract expressionists." They recognized that there was "nothing really stylistically new; not op, pop, structural, minimal, sculpted (hard and soft), mixed media, collage, or happening." To Goetzmann, the future for Texas artists in the 1980s and 1990s appeared grim and pointless. Even so, he saw in some of the art of the 1980s "a startling reprise of the 1840s and 50s when explorers from the metropolis ventured out into unknown Texas … struggling to comprehend its vastness and vagueness." In Goetzmann's judgment, mid-1980s Texas art was fully "under the scrutiny of the postmoderns," for whom "fantasy is reality." They were "seeing Texas for what it is." Goetzmann's archetype was the Cadillac Ranch near Amarillo, which he considered "the best symbol of the new, true art establishment in Texas."[21]

The natural world of Texas, abstracted as it was in Texas art between 1980 and 2000, still provided the major launching pad for most postmodernism in this state. The collision of the natural with the manmade world also provided fuel. And, finally, spirituality invested much of the work created during this period. Beginning in the 1970s artists such as Roger Winter in Dallas and Robert Levers in Austin explored the possibilities of placing the human figure in altered realities, bordering on fantasy. This baton was carried forward through the 1990s by Houston artists Derek Boshier, Kermit Oliver, Earl Staley, and Richard Thompson; Dallas artists Barnaby Fitzgerald, Bill Kommodore, and Lee Smith, the former two with their quasi-mythological scenes, the latter with his "suburban realism"; and Fort Worth's Ed Blackburn.

All coming of age at about the same time in the 1970s and 1980s, David Bates, James Surls, and John Alexander focused on the unique, non-western, Old South feel of east Texas. The paintings of Bates, a direct stylistic descendant of the Lone Star regionalists in Dallas, combine the rawness of Everett Spruce with the theatricality of German expressionist Max Beckmann. Surls and Alexander "had their closest parallels to William [T.] Wiley's hallucinogenic depictions of the northern California landscape." Every bit as much a neo-regionalist as Bates, Surls produced strongly anthropomorphic early works. His mature style allowed the spirit within the materials to dictate the direction of the piece, rather than vice versa. This recognition of natural spirituality was further underscored by the power of New Mexican carvers in Cordova and Taos, such as Jose Dolores Lopez and Patrocino Barela, respectively. Tapping into the "spirit of place" of the Southwest, their approach resembled that of the regionalists sixty or seventy years earlier.

The natural landscape continued to inspire other artists. Although living in Amagansett, Long Island, John Alexander maintained his Texas roots. After studies at Lamar University and Southern Methodist University, he took a teaching position in Houston. His move from Houston to Soho, then to Long Island, prompted a return to nature. His paintings after 1980 frequently used the human figure, but landscape remained the point of departure. Houston's Melissa Miller and Fort Worth's Julie Bozzi also select from nature—albeit a large dehumanized nature—as their vehicles. Miller's canvases are cousins to Bates' neo-regionalist works in style. And while several of the Dallas regionalists painted animals, notably Otis Dozier and Everett Spruce, there are rarely the violent dioramas of animal angst Miller favors. Although this renders Miller's work unappealing to some, it is nevertheless true to its source: nature. Drama and artifice also play starring roles in Bozzi's landscape environments. Her obsessively arranged, almost hermetically sealed "specimen boxes," complete with quasi-scientific labeling of her landscapes, place her squarely in the company of Texas artist-explorers such as George Catlin and Vincent Colyer. Moreover, her encased *assemblages* recall Joseph Cornell and David McManaway. The collision of the natural and manmade worlds saturates the work of signal figures in Texas art such as Vernon Fisher, who "brought a Postmodern sensibility to his musings on Western identity." By "layering narratives (literal words) over photographs over often-beautifully rendered drawings, often installed with three-dimensional objects intruding outside the picture plane into the viewer's personal space," Fisher mined "the histories of [his] personal landscapes."

Spirituality, particularly the dialogue with the transition between the earthbound realm and the domain of souls, infuses the work of Michael Tracy and Sharon Kopriva. Christianity is essential to Tracy and his art. Years of Catholic studies and travels in Egypt fortified him before he settled in Galveston in the mid-1970s. Moving to San Ygnacio on the Mexican border in 1978, he continued his studies on the role and evolution of Christianity in the conquest of Mexico. His encrusted shrines, altars, and *reredos* are "beautiful, violent, reflective, potent. [They are] of this world, yet [suggest] another." A kindred spirit, Kopriva also explores the mysticism of Latin America. Choosing instead to interpret pre-Columbian attitudes toward death as regenerative, Kopriva's sculptures appear to have been excavated rather than created.

Latin American tactics of faith and belief systems in the early 1980s and through the 1990s presaged the rapidly changing demographics of Texas and influenced the state's art through the influx of Latino artists. The Mexican muralists of the 1920s heavily influenced Jerry Bywaters, Otis Dozier, and their circle in the 1930s, spawning the Greater Texas and Pan American Exposition in Dallas in 1937. This connection has prevailed through 2000. As Michael Ennis has opined: "The Pan-Americanism of Texas art is less a matter of appropriated imagery and beliefs than it is a fundamental attitude about making art, an attitude in which Houston and Mexico City are more

Sharon Kopriva, *From Dust Thou Art,* 1997. Mixed media, 54 x 23 x 39 in. Collection of Nancy Kienholz.

closely linked than Houston and New York City." Ennis further believes that the Mexican "emphasis on communication and content appealed [not only] to the Lone Star Regionalists," but also to Texas artists who matured in the 1980s. According to one authority, exhibitions of Hispanic art in Texas in 1987 and 1990 tipped the balance of recognition for Latino artists. Particularly noteworthy of this trend are Benito Huerta, Kathy Vargas, and Celia Alvarez Munoz, whose works demonstrate "their appropriation of religious iconography [which] yield[s] to a range of meaning, reflecting not only the artists' shared heritage, but also their individual pursuits."[22]

Texans are woefully ignorant of their art history, and most historians have offered a skewed view of Texas art. Fortunately, recent studies have attempted to correct that, emphasizing that Texas has one of the nation's richest art heritages. Hopefully, these re-examinations will force the state's public institutions to set aside fears of provincialism and dust off those pieces of Texas art languishing in storage areas across the state and put them on exhibit. Furthermore, these recent publications encourage not only much-needed research on Texas artists, but also tear down Texas myths. Actually, something of a love-hate relationship has evolved—the more forceful the criticism, the more tightly they embrace Texas. So that which makes Texas art unique defies definition. Texas art is literally all over the map. No better example would suffice than to cite one of the consummate anti-Texas Texans, Larry McMurtry, who capitalizes on Texas while poking Texas in the eye with his novels and screenplays. With regard to Texas art of the twentieth century, and taking considerable liberty with two of the great characters of fiction and film, *Lonesome Dove's* Woodrow and Gus, it probably would have been lost on Woodrow, but Gus would have known that Texas had "artists of genuine merit, with reputations wider than the limits of our state."

Selected Bibliography

Bywaters, Jerry. *A Century of Art and Life in Texas*. Dallas: Dallas Museum of Fine Arts, 1961.

Bywaters, Jerry, Cantey, Sam B. III, Chillman, James Jr., Mozley, Loren, and Utterback, Martha. *Texas Painting & Sculpture: 20th Century*. Dallas: Southern Methodist University, 1971.

Goetzmann, William H. and Reese, Becky Duval. *Texas Images and Visions*. Austin: University of Texas at Austin, 1983.

Grauer, Michael R. *Women Artists of Texas, 1850–1950*. Canyon: Panhandle-Plains Historical Museum, 1993.

Grauer, Paula L., and Grauer, Michael R. *Dictionary of Texas Artists, 1800–1945*. College Station: Texas A & M University Press, 1999.

Greene, Alison de Lima. *Texas: 150 Works from the Museum of Fine Arts, Houston*. Houston: Museum of Fine Arts, Houston, 2000.

Hendricks, Patricia D., and Reese, Becky Duval. *A Century of Sculpture in Texas, 1889–1989*. Austin: University of Texas at Austin, 1989.

Kalil, Susie. *Fresh Paint: The Houston School*. Houston: Museum of Fine Arts Houston, 1985.

Parisi, Philip. *The Texas Post Office Murals: Art for the People*. College Station: Texas A&M University Press, 2004.

Reaves, William E., Jr. *Texas Art and a Wildcatter's Dream: Edgar B. Davis and the San Antonio Art League*. College Station: Texas A&M University Press, 1998.

Steinfeldt, Cecilia. *Art for History's Sake: The Texas Collection of the Witte Museum*. Austin: Texas State Historical Association, 1993.

Stewart, Rick. *Lone Star Regionalism: The Dallas Nine and Their Circle*. Austin: Texas Monthly Press for the Dallas Museum of Art, 1985.

Endnotes

1. *Austin Daily Democratic Statesman*, July 8, 1877; Frances Battaile Fisk, *A History of Texas Artists and Sculptors* (Abilene: Frances Battaile Fisk, 1928), 4. For a complete study of art in Texas prior to 1900, see Samuel Deshong Ratcliffe, *Painting Texas History to 1900* (Austin: University of Texas Press, 1992).

2. Frank Reaugh, *Biographical*, (Dallas: publisher unknown, 1936). A contemporary of Charles M. Russell and Frederic Remington, in 1936 Reaugh described how his art took a different trail from theirs: "Remington and Charlie Russell came a few years later. Remington in the '90s, painted the Indian and his pony. He knew little about cows, and was principally interested in the cowboy as a wild man. Russell painted the cowboys of the Northwest." Reaugh, Remington, and Russell all began painting in the West between 1882 and 1883, and enjoyed national recognition as artists of the American West between 1890 and 1915.

Reaugh photographed Palo Duro Canyon, on the J A Ranch, and Charles Goodnight's ranch in October 1893. He is probably the first artist to paint and photograph the geological feature in the canyon today known as "The Lighthouse."

Reaugh's photographs are especially historically significant as not long after the 1890s the land was altered drastically through farming and ranching and longhorns were crossbred with European cattle by the 1880s. However, it is clear Reaugh almost never transferred a photographic image directly to a painting. I have only seen one Reaugh painting based directly on a Reaugh photograph, *Grazing the Herd*; otherwise it seems he used his photographs more as reminders than images to copy.

3. See Reaugh, *Biographical*. Reaugh exhibited at most of the major U.S. venues. He also showed at the World's Columbian Exposition (1893) and the Louisiana Purchase Exposition (1904). He even had a two-man show at the Saint Louis Museum of Fine Arts and the Art Institute of Chicago in 1902 and 1903, respectively.

Reaugh's popularity in Chicago culminated in the Armour Meat Packing Company commissioning him to paint a calendar for them in 1904.

Because he was not invited to exhibit in the major exhibition at the new Dallas Museum of Fine Arts at the Centennial Exposition, at first Reaugh applied for a vendor's license along with hawkers of cotton candy and hot dogs. He withdrew his application, probably out of humiliation, and eventually exhibited some paintings in the Texas Ranger Building.

Furthermore, he promised to donate 50 percent of his picture sales to an acquisition fund for the DAA.

4. Cecilia Steinfeldt, *The Onderdonks: A Family of Texas Painters* (San Antonio: Trinity University Press): 12–26. Interestingly, Steinfeldt says Onderdonk "was the logical selection for a leader when the art-oriented citizens made the decision to organize and form an Art Students' [*sic*] League." A fire at DeShield's Dallas home destroyed another Onderdonk history painting, *The Surrender of Santa Anna,* and other pieces of early Texas art. See Ratcliffe for a thorough discussion of these Texas history paintings.

5. For the seminal essay on early sculpture in Texas, see Patricia D. Hendricks, "Texas Sculpture in the Figural Tradition," *A Century of Sculpture in Texas, 1889–1989* (Austin: University of Texas, 1989), 3–86. See also Emily F. Cutrer, "Ney, Elisabet," *Handbook of Texas Online.*

6. Teich sculpted Confederate monuments in Dallas, Gainesville, Gonzales, Longview, Marshall, and Scottsville, and in Louisiana and Mississippi. He also produced sculptural monuments in Austin, Blessing, Houston, Orange, Navasota, and San Antonio. See Hendricks, "Texas Sculpture in the Figural Tradition," 20.

In addition to Coppini's collaboration with Teich for the Capitol monument, between 1901 and 1911 he completed Confederate-themed sculpture in Paris, Victoria, and Palestine and two others on the Capitol grounds, including the equestrian monument to Terry's Texas Rangers. *Handbook of Texas Online.*

Among his better-known works are the Littlefield Memorial Fountain at the University of Texas, Austin, and the Hall of State bronze statues of Stephen F. Austin, Thomas J. Rusk, William B. Travis, James W. Fannin, Mirabeau B. Lamar, and Sam Houston. For his numerous contributions to art in Texas, Baylor University awarded Coppini an honorary doctorate of fine arts in 1941.

7. While many have acknowledged Porfirio Salinas, the general feeling of this writer is that Salinas merely aped his mentor, Robert Wood, and there is considerable condescension given his—almost stereotypical—struggles with alcoholism.

8. The Texas General became the Annual Texas Exhibition of Painting and Sculpture with the January 22–February 12, 1950, exhibition. Ellen Buie Niewyk to author, August 23, 2006, Jerry Bywaters Collection on Art of the Southwest, Southern Methodist University, Dallas, Texas (hereafter referred to as Bywaters Collection). The participating cities were Dallas; Houston; San Francisco and Stockton, California; Denver, Colorado; St. Paul, Minnesota; Bozeman and Great Falls, Montana; and Williston, North Dakota. Paintings by twenty-seven Texas artists were selected for "the first representative group of paintings by contemporary Texas artists to go on the road on its own merits as an art exhibition." Jerry Bywaters, *Texas Panorama* (Dallas: Dallas Museum of Fine Arts, 1945).

9. Van Wyck Brooks, one of many prominent contributors to *The Dial,* urged American artists to draw on the nation's "communal experience" as a "usable past" and to create works reflective of their own communities. In 1920 philoso-

pher and educator John Dewey extended Brooks' views, arguing that art depicting local themes could be used to explore universal values. Two years later George Santayana chimed in, asserting that art was not to be found in museums, which he called mausoleums, but in the natural occurrences of everyday life. See also Henry Nash Smith, "Culture," *Southwest Review* 8 (January 1928): 249–55.

10. For a complete discussion of the San Antonio Competitives, see William E. Reaves, Jr., *Texas Art and a Wildcatter's Dream: Edgar B. Davis and the San Antonio Art League* College Station: Texas A & M University Press, 1998.

Allie Tennant, who came to Texas as a child, studied at the Art Students League before she created *Tejas Warrior* to go above the portal to the Hall of State for the Centennial Exposition. A Dallas native, Austin also studied at the Art Students League before returning home to embark on a sculpture career. After giving up her art in the 1940s, partly due to sexism, Austin recently had a major exhibition at an important Dallas gallery, which nearly sold out. See Dorothy Austin Retrospective, 14 July–21 August 1999, Valley House Gallery, Dallas. Evaline Sellors helped found the Fort Worth School of Fine Arts. She exhibited in the Texas Centennial and the Fort Worth Annual. Her work was included in recent exhibitions, Beyond Regionalism (1986) and One Hundred Years of Sculpture in Texas (1989).

Both Fort Worth and Austin held art exhibitions including Texas artists. However, the former was mainly focused on western art. Texas artists included H. D. Bugbee, Edward G. Eisenlohr, Clinton King, J. M. "Tex" Moore, Elisabet Ney (posthumously), and Hughlette "Tex" Wheeler. The University Centennial Exposition occurred in two parts with twenty-eight artists in the first and thirty-three in the second. See Paula L. Grauer and Michael R. Grauer, *Dictionary of Texas Artists*, 1800–1945 (College Station: Texas A & M University Press, 1999), 225.

11. In March 1932 *Art Digest* noted the exhibition of nine artists all under thirty years of age, including Jerry Bywaters, John Douglass, Otis Dozier, Lloyd Goff, William Lester, Charles McCann, Perry Nichols, Everett Spruce, and James Buchanan Winn. Notably, Alexandre Hogue, whose work has become synonymous with the Dallas Nine, was not in the exhibition.

12. For additional information on the American Renaissance, see *The American Renaissance, 1876–1917* (New York: Brooklyn Museum, 1979). President Roosevelt's former schoolmate, painter George Biddle, told Roosevelt that "the Federal government has the same obligation to keep an artist alive during the Depression as to keep a farmer or carpenter alive." Biddle envisioned a federally funded mural program to promote the ideals of the New Deal as well as provide relief to suffering artists modeled after the Mexican government's promotion of the ideals of the Mexican Revolution through murals on public buildings in Mexico City in the 1920s. George Biddle, quoted in Janet Marquesee, *Painting America: Mural Art in the New Deal Era* (New York: Midtown Galleries, 1988): 4.

13. For an excellent and well-researched look at the New Deal art programs, see Belisario R. Contreras, *Tradition and Innovation in New Deal Art*, (Lewisburg, Pa.: Bucknell University Press, 1983).

The PWAP divided the United States into sixteen regions overseen by committees headed by chairpersons chosen by Edward Bruce. Each regional committee evaluated applications and chose artists for their regions. Artists were steered to depict the American Scene in their PWAP work, thus the program was representational by its very nature. Furthermore, Bruce insisted that the PWAP maintain high standards of quality instead of relying on financial need as the sole criterion for work.

The goals of "the Section," as it was known popularly, were "to secure the best quality art to embellish public buildings; to stimulate the development of American art in general; to employ local talent where possible; to secure the cooperation of the art world in selecting artists for this work; and to encourage competition project proposals where practicable, although certain established artists were entitled to commissions *hors concours*." One percent of a new building's appropriation was to be used for decoration, usually in the form of murals. Artists were chosen through anonymous competitions rather than from relief rolls. The majority of the works completed under the Section were done for new post offices. However, during its nine-year history the Section sponsored 2,500 murals, 17,000 sculptures, and 108,000 easel paintings, nationally. Contreras, *Tradition and Innovation*, 51.

Edward Bruce also headed the Treasury Relief Art Project (TRAP), founded in July 1935 to decorate already-existing public buildings. Unlike the Section's emphasis on murals and sculpture, TRAP allowed artists to create easel paintings, posters, portraits, and decorative hangings. Funded by the Works Progress Administration, TRAP selected artists directly from relief rolls, although Bruce attempted to enforce the high aesthetic standards of the Section. However, WPA administrator Harry Hopkins insisted that TRAP select 90 percent of its artists from relief rolls, thus thwarting Bruce's insistence on high standards. Fortunately, Secretary Morgenthau successfully lobbied for a reduction to 75 percent. Nevertheless, the Artists' Union criticized TRAP for not providing enough relief for artists. This conflict persisted throughout TRAP's existence without any clear resolution between quality and relief. Unfortunately, Treasury Department officials, insisting that Treasury was not a relief agency, forced TRAP's cancellation in June 1939. Contreras, *Tradition and Innovation*, 56.

14. In August 1935 administrators for the first New Deal art programs attempted to solve the dilemma of quality versus relief by creating the Works Progress Administration Federal Art Project (WPA/FAP). Its director, Holger Cahill, selected regional directors to administer all programs on the state level, hoping to decentralize. Moreover, the WPA/FAP discarded Edward Bruce's emphasis on the American Scene and allowed more artistic freedom. As part of the second New Deal, the WPA/FAP also developed programs to employ as many destitute artists as possible. Cahill sought to combine the fine and practical arts under the WPA/FAP and to elicit local support for the projects. The WPA/FAP established community art centers in which to exhibit the creations of the program, compiled the Index of American Design, and encouraged and funded the creative arts. The mis-

sion of Cahill's agency was to employ as many artists as possible with the greatest impact on local communities, a tall order to say the least. *Texas Post Office Murals of the New Deal, A Traveling Photo Exhibit, 1990-1991* (Austin: Texas Historical Commission, n.d.).

The president's Reorganization Act of 1939 placed the WPA/FAP under the FWA and transferred control to the states, where the program came to be called the WPA Art Program. In 1941 the WPA urged all programs to focus on the defense effort, getting "the artists right down in the front line trenches." (As cited in Contreras, *Tradition and Innovation*, 231, 234 n 85.) In March 1942 the WPA reorganized its Art Program as the Graphics Section of the War Services Program with Cahill as its national consultant in March 1942. However, presidential decree finally scraped the WPA/FAP from the national canvas on April 30, 1943.

New York Times, September 20, 1936, as quoted in Contreras, *Tradition and Innovation*, 156, 158 n 25; *Time*, September 7, 1936, 35, as quoted in Contreras, *Tradition and Innovation*, 156, 158 n 25. For a more complete discussion of New Deal art on the Texas Plains, see Michael R. Grauer, "The Artistic Legacy," *Panhandle-Plains Historical Review* (1993). For an enlightening discussion of New Deal murals, see Karal Ann Marling, *Wall to Wall America: A Cultural History of Post Office Murals in the Great Depression* (Minneapolis: University of Minnesota Press, 1982).

Suggested subjects for post office murals included "The Post; local history, past or present; local industry; pursuits or landscape" and the committee was to judge the "appropriateness to the use and design" of the place decorated. These "suggestions" were fairly standard for all Section competitions. Artists were advised that "the primary requirement [was] a distinguished and vital design." The Section suggested subject matter, although submitting artists were "free to select other material" more appealing or consistent with his/her design. *Competition for the Mural Decoration of the Amarillo, Texas, Post Office and Court House*, 1939, broadside, Bywaters Collection.

For the best study on New Deal murals for Texas post offices, see Philip Parisi, *The Texas Post Office Murals: Art for the People* (College Station: Texas A & M University Press, 2004). See also Grauer, "The Artistic Legacy," PPHR (1993), 1541. Most single-panel murals painted for Texas post offices were consolation commissions, a few of which were outstanding.

Lea received the Odessa commission as a consolation for a larger regional competition. Other New Deal murals by Lea can be found in the Pleasant Hill, Missouri, post office; the Seymour, Texas, post office; the El Paso Federal Courthouse; New Mexico State University, Las Cruces; and the Post Office Department Building, Washington, D.C. Non-New Deal murals can also be found at the Hall of State, Dallas, and the Branigan Cultural Center (formerly the public library), Las Cruces, N.M.

Stampede was reproduced on the dust jacket of J. Frank Dobie's *The Longhorns* in 1941.

For a complete analysis of the Woeltz mural commission, see also Grauer, "The Artistic Legacy," PPHR.

15. According to Powers, Kidd-Key had 110 studio students and ninety art history students in 1910. Evangeline Fowler taught drawing, teacher training, design, and art history. Dallas artist Frank Klepper became director in 1932 and the school closed in 1935, "notwithstanding its excellent reputation." John and Deborah Powers, *Texas Painters, Sculptors & Graphic Artists* (Austin: Woodmont Books, 2000), 576. Ed Bearden, Elizabeth Walmsley, and Jerry Bywaters taught at SMU, and under Stella Lodge LaMond's leadership, the school achieved regional acclaim.

Frances Battaile Fisk writes that the first art school in Dallas was founded in 1868; however, Diana Church indicates the Dallas Art Academy was the first. Diana Church's *Guide to Early Dallas Artists, 1890–1917* (Dallas: Diana Church, 1987) shows the first art school listed in a Dallas city directory in 1884. Richard Lentz was the art instructor at the academy from 1884 to 1886, when he began teaching at the German-American high school and in his studio. Lentz became an architect by 1890 and left Dallas by 1895. See *Memorial & Biographical History of Dallas County, Texas* (n.p.: publisher unknown, 1892), 318–19.

From 1926 to 1953 Samuel Ziegler taught at Texas Christian University and at Texas Wesleyan College in Fort Worth, followed by Sallie Gillespie in the early 1940s. The site of the first West Texas Art Exhibitions, Abilene offered art instruction at Simmons College (now Hardin-Simmons University) by 1902 and Abilene Christian College (now Abilene Christian University) by 1912. Another boost came with the opening of McMurry College (now University), which offered art instruction under Sweetwater painter Lois Hogue beginning in 1923. Trained at Mary Hardin-Baylor College in Belton, Hogue also taught at Abilene Christian and at Mary Hardin-Baylor. She also studied at the Art Students League under John Sloan and the Art Institute of Chicago.

Among the steady stream of art instructors at WTSNC was Georgia O'Keeffe, who was in Canyon from 1916 to 1918. A provision in O'Keeffe's contract with WT required her to take classes from Arthur Wesley Dow at the Art Students League in New York. Dow was the leading proponent of modern art in the United States at the time. For a school traditionally considered one of the more conservative in one of the more conservative parts of Texas, this requirement to be conversant with modern art tenets is simply amazing for the time.

Directed by WT professor Isabel Robinson, the PDSA brought instructors in from all over the United States to teach in the Palo Duro Canyon, including Texans Adele Brunet, A. W. Mack, Amy Jackson, and H. D. Bugbee. Students lived in tents or in stone cabins build under the New Deal and painted from Coronado Lodge on the rim or down in the canyon bottom. World War II suspended the PDSA. See James C. Chillman, "Houston," *Texas Painting & Sculpture: 20th Century* (Dallas: Brodnax Printing, 1971), 15.

16. Alexandre Hogue, with his Dust Bowl series, provided the only really confrontational social statements in his work. Others of that circle occasionally ven-

tured into social realism, albeit tentatively. Most of the Texas regionalists aligned nicely with their midwestern counterparts who "nurse[d] illusions of an innocent, promise-laden agrarian past." However, while most members of the circle only ventured tentatively into social realism, Hogue provided the only truly confrontational social statements through his "Erosion" series. Ironically, Hogue did not see the series as social commentary: "It was a complete surprise to me when critics began referring to these paintings as social comment . . . . Social comment is negative; my interest in conservation is positive." See Lea Rosson DeLong, *Nature's Forms/Nature's Forces: The Art of Alexandre Hogue* (Norman: University of Oklahoma Press, 1984), 22–27, 104.

Other contemporaneous and kindred Fort Worth artists included Cynthia Brants, Jack Boynton, Sallie Gillespie, Marjorie Johnson, and others.

Working in photography through her design studies, Corpron moved into abstract photography due to the influence of Lazlo Moholy-Nagy, who conducted summer workshops at TSCW in 1942 and 1943, Gyorgy Kepes who began teaching at North Texas State in 1944.

LaSelle came to TSCW in 1928 from the University of Chicago. She later studied further with Moholy-Nagy in Chicago (and helped bring him to Denton) and with Hans Hofmann at Provincetown.

Provincetown proved to be attractive to several Denton artists, including Delleney and Brisac. My own research indicates that most female art professors in Texas, and across the United States for that matter, spent virtually all their time away from their respective schools enrolled in art classes somewhere, usually taught by avant-garde instructors. Art colonies in particular seemed especially attractive to these artists, including Taos and Santa Fe, New Mexico; Santa Barbara, California; and Woodstock, New York.

17. Patricia Peck, "At the Museums: Printmakers Guild Season," *Dallas Morning News*, October 21, 1943. Three of the artists represented in Texas Panorama served in the armed forces: Boyer Gonzales, Jr., Ward Lockwood, and Julius Woeltz. See also Martha Utterback, "San Antonio," *Texas Painting & Sculpture: 20th Century* (Dallas: Southern Methodist University Press, 1971) 10–11.

The Coppini Academy is still active today and remains committed to its original mission.

Greene, Alison de Lima. *Texas: 150 Works from the Museum of Fine Arts, Houston* (Houston: Museum of Fine Arts, Houston, 2000) 24. These institutions became the Contemporary Arts Museum, the Modern Art Museum of Fort Worth, and part of the Dallas Museum of Art, respectively.

18. Hendricks, "Texas Sculpture in the Figural Tradition," 57; Susie Kalil, "Dynamic Pioneers: A Brief History of Painting in Houston, 1900 to the Present," *Fresh Paint: The Houston School* (Houston: Museum of Fine Arts Houston, 1985): 24. Greene, *Texas*, 43–46, 124; Randolph K. Tibbits, "Houston Art, 1900–1965: Some New Questions Raised by Old Paintings," *Houston Art from Houston Collections: Works from 1900–1965* (San Marcos: Center for the Advancement and Study of Early Texas Art, 2006), 45–48. This catalog was printed for an exhibition of the same title

at The Heritage Society Museum, Houston, May 2 through June 25, 2006.

19. Bywaters, "Dallas," 8; Kalil, 27-28; Becky Duval Reese, "Experiment and Idea in Contemporary Texas Sculpture," A *Century of Sculpture in Texas, 1889–1989* (Austin: University of Texas, 1989): 93. "The Trojan Horse: The Art of the Machine" and "Totems Not Taboo: An Exhibition of Primitive Art." See Reese, 9497.

20. Ron Gleason, "Interview: Dave Hickey," *Arts and Architecture* 1, no. 2 (Winter 1981): 33. As quoted in Greene, "A Sense of Place," *Texas*, 46; Goetzmann, 39–40. The stable of artists in A Clean Well Lighted Place included Terry Allen, Jack Boynton, Barry Buxkamper, Mel Casas, Jim Franklin, Steve Gosnell, George Green, Luis Jimenez, Bobbie Moore, June Robinson, Jim Roche, Gilbert Shelton, Early Staley, Bob Wade, and Fred and Glenn Whitehead. Greene, 46. Tragically, earlier this year Jimenez was crushed to death by a piece of sculpture on which he was working. Texas lost one of its few geniuses that day.

21. James Boren, Tom Ryan, and Melvin Warren were all early members of the CAA.

TCA founding members included Jack Bryant, Clay Dahlberg, George Kovach, Bob Moline, Don Ray, Mark Storm, Jim Thomas, Jim Ward, Tom Warren, and Kenneth Wyatt.

Goetzmann, 40.

22. For the best and most understandable discussion of post-modernism, see Greene, "This State I'm In," *Texas*, 51, 57, 105, 173–205; Reese, 105; Ennis 48.

The Games Texans Play

Bill O'Neal

TEXAS BOASTS A RICH heritage as a hotbed of sports in America. For nineteenth-century Texans, who were members of a predominantly agricultural society with deep frontier roots, athletic activities provided a natural cultural expression. Texans reveled in physical competitions, and team sports came readily to people who worked together at log rollings, barn raisings, crop harvests, cattle roundups, and other commercial efforts. As the twentieth century progressed, urbanization and industrialization afforded Texans more time for leisure and recreation, and organized sports subsequently took on added importance in towns and communities across the state. Texans identified with their local teams, attending Friday night football games, rooting for their alma maters, or following the professional franchises. By century's end the games Texans played, whether amateur or professional, had become another measure of community pride.

The first team sport in Texas, along with the rest of America, was baseball. Originating in eastern cities, baseball was first witnessed by Texans who traveled north in the 1850s, and the Houston Baseball Club was organized before the Civil War. During the Civil War thousands of soldiers learned the game of baseball at hundreds of army camps, and after the war these young veterans brought the sport home to a multitude of towns and country villages. In Texas a game was reported in detail in 1867: on San Jacinto Day, April 21, 1867, the Stonewalls of Houston crushed the R. E. Lees of Galveston, 35–2.[1]

Amateur nines flourished in Texas during the next few years, playing on vacant lots and in cow pastures across the state. An amateur club from New Orleans, the Robert E. Lees (the name already was immortalized across the South), came to Texas in 1872 and played teams in Dallas, Waco, and Austin, traveling the dusty roads of the frontier state by stagecoach. By the 1880s some of the better baseball clubs in Texas cities were hiring skilled pitchers, catchers, and sometimes a shortstop to bolster local talent. Beginning in 1887 major league teams barnstormed through Texas, and a player-promoter known as "Honest John" McCloskey recognized opportunity. By the spring of 1888 McCloskey brought together baseball enthusiasts who organized a "State Base Ball League."[2]

When the Texas League began play in 1888, only a few other minor leagues were in operation around the United States. While the National League had been playing since 1876, the American League did not commence until 1901. Thus, the Texas League is one of the older leagues in professional baseball, and in the late nineteenth century it began most seasons with six teams. Independently owned by local sportsmen, teams often failed before the end of the season. Sometimes a franchise was shifted to another city to finish the schedule, or the league would try to limp to the end of the season with four teams. Occasionally, the last part of the league schedule had to be cancelled, and at times the Texas League skipped an entire season. But there were natural rivalries between Dallas and Fort Worth, San Antonio and Austin, and Houston and Galveston.

Other Texas towns entered a team from time to time. In 1895 Shreveport, Louisiana, played its first season in the Texas League. Seven years later the Corsicana Oilers stormed to the championship with a historic performance that included a twenty-seven-game winning streak that stood for eighty-four years as the record in professional baseball. A 51–3 victory over Texarkana featured fifty-three hits by the Oilers, including eight home runs from future major league catcher J. J. Clarke. The runs, hits, and Clarke's eight homers all are organized baseball records, which still stand.

From 1920 through 1925 the Fort Worth Cats dominated the Texas League with one of the greater dynasties in the history of minor league baseball. As an independent club, the Cats kept their roster intact season after season, including slugging first-baseman Otto "Big Boy" Kraft, who blasted fifty-five home runs with 196 runs batted in (RBIs) in 1924. Southpaw Joe Pate anchored the pitching staff and twice won thirty games, while right-handed spit-baller Paul Wachtel led the league on two occasions with twenty-six victories. During the reign of the Cats, the Texas League and the Southern League began playing the Dixie Series, a best-of-seven "World Series of the South" between the champions of the two leagues. Fort Worth won five of the first six Dixie Series, with fans chartering a "Dixie Special" train to out-of-state games. The Dixie Series was played through 1957, with a one-year resurrection in 1967.

Texas League fans saw future Hall-of-Famer Tris Speaker from Hubbard win the 1907 batting championship while playing center field for Houston. He went on to compile a .344 lifetime batting average in twenty-two big-league seasons. Another future Hall-of-Fame member, Dizzy Dean, won a pitcher's triple crown with the Houston Buffs in 1931 (26–10, 1.53 ERA, 303 Ks), the only time in baseball history that a pitcher has posted the best season record in victories, earned run average, and strikeouts for every league in organized baseball. Other future Hall of Famers who showed their skills as young stars in the Texas League included Carl Hubbell and Hank Greenberg with Beaumont, Duke Snider with Fort Worth, Al Simmons and Bill Terry with Shreveport, Brooks Robinson with San Antonio, and Frank Robinson with Tulsa. Indeed, a steady parade of future major leaguers entertained Texas League crowds through the seasons.

Rogers Hornsby of Winters, who compiled the highest life-time batting average (.359) of any right-handed hitter, was one of a number of native Texans who achieved major-league stardom without playing in the Texas League, although the "Rajah" managed in the Texas League after his long-playing career and inserted himself into the lineup a couple of times. Hall-of-Fame shortstop Ernie Banks of Dallas blasted 512 home runs and won back-to-back Most Valuable Player (MVP) awards with the Chicago Cubs. Born in Refugio, Nolan Ryan pitched for an incredible twenty-seven seasons in the major leagues, including long stints with the Houston Astros and the Texas Rangers. Ryan is the all-time major-league strikeout leader (5,714), and he twirled a record seven no-hitters en route to 324 victories and the Hall of Fame.

During the heyday of the minor leagues, from early in the twentieth century through mid-century, there were numerous other leagues of lower classification than the Texas League. The East Texas League, for example, featured such teams as the Longview Cannibals, Jacksonville Jax, Kilgore Drillers, Palestine Pals, and Paris Red Peppers. In 1946 Monty Stratton, a Greenville native who had been an American League All-Star pitcher before losing a leg in a hunting accident, went 18–8 in the East Texas League in a courageous comeback, which inspired a motion picture starring James Stewart. Other Texas-based leagues included the Texas Association, Rio Grande Valley League, Lone Star League, Big State League, Longhorn League, Gulf Coast League, Sophomore League, Panhandle-Pecos Valley League, Southwest Texas League, Texas-Oklahoma League, Middle Texas League, and Central Texas Trolley League. Over one hundred Texas cities and towns—far more than in any other state—have hosted minor league franchises.[3]

Major league baseball came to Texas in 1962 with the addition of the Houston Colt .45s to the National League. Colt Sta-

dium provided a temporary home for three seasons, until the Astrodome, the "Eighth Wonder of the World," opened on April 9,
1965. The Colts then became the Astros, playing in the world's
first domed stadium, which established a new standard for sports
stadiums. Future Hall-of-Famer Joe Morgan starred at second base
from 1963–1971, and again in 1980, while Nolan Ryan demonstrated his spectacular talents as an Astro from 1980–1988. A new
downtown stadium was opened in 2000, and the Astros finally won
their first National League pennant in 2005, although the Chicago
White Sox took the first World Series involving a Texas team.

The American League arrived in Texas in 1972 when the Washington Senators' franchise was moved to Dallas-Fort Worth. The
Texas Rangers played in Arlington Stadium, an enlarged minor
league park, until 1994, when the Ballpark at Arlington opened, a

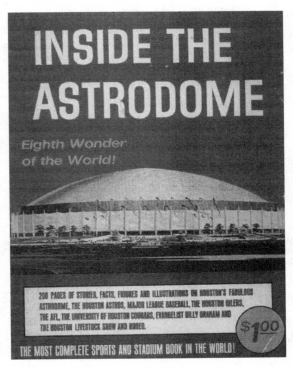

Cover of the opening-
day program for the
world's first domed
stadium. The Houston
Astros hosted the New
York Yankees in an ex-
hibition game on April
9, 1965. Yankee star
Mickey Mantle hit the
first home run in the
Astrodome. Courtesy
Bill O'Neal.

state-of-the-art facility that was admired throughout baseball. Future Hall-of-Fame pitcher Ferguson Jenkins won twenty-five games in 1974, his first season with the Rangers, establishing an all-time Ranger record for season victories. Nolan Ryan spent the last five seasons of his record-setting career, 1989–1994, as a Ranger. The Rangers were more famous for slugging home runs than for pitching, but they have made only three brief playoff appearances, following division titles in 1996, 1998, and 1999.

Far more successful in playoff action was the University of Texas (UT) baseball team. A perennial conference champion for decades, the Longhorns have won the National Collegiate Athletic Association (NCAA) World Series six times, in 1949 and 1950 behind Coach Bibb Falk, in 1975 and 1983 under Coach Cliff Gustafson, and in 2002 and 2005 with Coach Augie Garrido. In 2003 Rice University won a national title behind Coach Wayne Graham, who had already claimed five National Junior College Athletic Association (NJCAA) World Series championships with San Jacinto Community College. Indeed, during the forty-eight NJCAA World Series played since the 1958 inaugural, one of every three—sixteen—has been won by ten different Texas community colleges. Texas sports fans have long enjoyed quality baseball at every level.

Despite baseball's long head start in Texas, football was to become the sport that triggered the deepest response from Texans. The rugged game reached Texas by 1893, when the University of Texas eleven twice defeated the Dallas Foot Ball Club. Texas A&M opened play in 1894, beating Ball High School of Galveston before losing to Texas, 38–0. Soon Sam Houston High School of Houston and Dallas High fielded football teams, and so did Baylor University and Texas Christian University (TCU). Early in the twentieth century a few more high schools and colleges began to try football, usually playing only two to four games per season. But in 1914 Texas, Texas A&M, Baylor, Rice, Southwestern University, and three out-of-state institutions formed the Southwest

Conference (SWC), which provided the highest level of Texas collegiate athletics for the next eight decades. For much of its history the SWC was made up of A&M, Baylor, Rice, Southern Methodist University (SMU), UT, TCU, and Arkansas; Texas Tech joined in 1958, Houston in 1972.

In 1913 the University Interscholastic League (UIL) was organized to regulate high school competitions, from football to debate. It grew out of a merger of two earlier organizations and operated as a part of the University of Texas at Austin. Although the UIL supervised an increasing number of high school football programs, the game remained primitive, with scant equipment or coaching. In 1919 the UIL limited its membership to white participants, which continued until desegregation in 1965. As the oldest and largest high school association in the nation, it has expanded its competitive programs to include both curricular (debate, journalism, and academics) and extracurricular (football, basketball, and track and field) activities.

In the 1920s an exceptional coach, Paul Tyson, turned Waco High School into a football powerhouse. His 1921 team scored 526 points while allowing none for the opposing teams. From 1922 through 1927 Tyson and his Tigers won four state championships, scoring more than 100 points nine times. The 1927 champs went 14–0, averaged over fifty-six points per game, and traveled to Ohio to defeat a Cleveland team, 44–12, for the mythical national championship. At a time when most Texas high schools had only one coach and fewer than twenty players, Tyson regularly suited up more than one hundred athletes, and he was provided with assistant coaches. Waco took enormous pride in Tyson's superb teams, and 20,000 to 30,000 fans turned out for Tiger games.[4]

Texas towns increasingly pursued the community pride associated with victorious high school football teams. Such towns began providing better equipment and facilities, and instead of assigning an agricultural or industrial arts teacher to be the football coach, administrations sought out dedicated professionals such as Paul Tyson. Blair Cherry guided the Amarillo Golden Sandies to three consecutive state championships, 1934–1936, and in 1950 he led the Texas Longhorns to the Southwest Conference title—the only coach ever to win a Texas high school state crown and the SWC championship. Johnnie Pierce, coach of Corsicana's 1932 state champs, was the founding father of the Texas High School Coaches Association, which greatly elevated the professionalism of its members through clinics conducted by top college coaches. Chuck Moser, a disciplined and organized professional, coached Abilene to a forty-nine-game winning streak and three consecutive state titles, 1954–1956. In a legendary coaching career that extended from the 1930s through the 1980s, Gordon Wood won nine state championships at Stamford and Brownwood. These men set a standard for coaching excellence that was embraced by other Texas high school coaches, who established professional programs and accomplished their own superb feats.

Booty Johnson, an elusive running back who could drop-kick a field goal fifty yards, was Paul Tyson's greatest player at Waco, but injuries cut short his college career at Baylor. Although Kenneth Hall established an all-time national record with 11,232 rushing yards, along with 899 points, during a spectacular career at Sugar Land, he was used sparingly by Coach Bear Bryant at Texas A&M. While Johnson and Hall represent the vast number of Texas players whose football careers, for one reason or another, peaked in high school, other schoolboy stars improved and excelled at the next level.

Sammy Baugh, for example, was a football and baseball star at Sweetwater High School. At TCU the Horned Frog offense was built around the uncanny passing prowess of "Slingin' Sammy," who led the team to the Sugar Bowl and, in 1937, to a victory in its first Cotton Bowl visit. Then, in a sixteen-year Hall-of-Fame career with the Washington Redskins, Baugh transformed the National Football League (NFL) as the first true passing quarterback. He was followed at TCU by diminutive Davey O'Brien, All-City at Woodrow Wilson High in Dallas and All-American for the Horned Frogs. O'Brien propelled TCU to the 1938 national championship and was awarded the Heisman, Maxwell, and Walter Camp trophies. Another national championship came to Texas the next year, when a bruising All-American fullback from Haskell, "Jarrin' Jawn" Kimbrough led the Texas Aggies to victory.

During the 1940s teammates Bobby Layne and Doak Walker took the Highland Park Scotties deep into the playoffs, then went on to star in college and the NFL. At the University of Texas Layne enjoyed a spectacular career as a pitcher and was an All-American quarterback before going on to a Hall-of-Fame career with Detroit and Pittsburgh in the NFL. The gifted, versatile Walker was an All-American three times at SMU, won the Heisman Trophy in 1948, then earned Hall-of-Fame recognition in the NFL. SMU, winner of back-to-back Southwest Conference championships, moved from its campus stadium to the Cotton Bowl, which was expanded to host crowds that wanted to see Walker and such talented teammates as Kyle Rote. Rote was All-State at Thomas Jefferson High School in San Antonio, All-American at SMU, and All-Pro in the NFL.

Several exceptional high school linemen of the 1950s became college standouts and professional players. E. J. Holub of Lubbock was a two-time All-American center at Texas Tech before launching a long and distinguished career in professional football. Bob Lilly of Throckmorton was an All-American tackle at TCU and a Hall-of-Fame defensive lineman for the Dallas Cowboys. Scott Appleton of Brady was a superb tackle at the University of Texas, and Caldwell tackle Charles Milstead was equally intimidating at Texas A&M, as well as in the NFL.

Another noted Aggie was Jack Pardee, perhaps the best player to come out of Texas six-man football. After dominating the opponents of tiny Christoval High School, Pardee became a rugged fullback for Bear Bryant, and then enjoyed a long career as a linebacker and coach in the NFL. Bryant, already famous for coaching an intimidating brand of hard-nosed football, took over the Aggies in 1954 and staged a rigorous training camp in Junction. Two-thirds of the squad quit, but the thirty-five "Junction Boys" who stuck it out formed the nucleus of the best Aggie team since the Kimbrough clubs of 1939 and 1940. In 1957 Bryant's rugged halfback, John David Crow, won a Heisman Trophy before departing for a stellar NFL career.[5]

Bryant left Texas A&M after four seasons to return to his alma mater, the University of Alabama. But even before his departure in 1957, another superstar coach had entered the Southwest Conference. Thirty-two-year-old Darrell Royal was named coach of the Texas Longhorns late in 1956, and during twenty memorable seasons he won three national championships, eleven Southwest Conference titles, and took the Horns to sixteen bowl games. Personable and innovative, Royal coached twenty-six All-Americans and introduced the wishbone formation, after which his teams won thirty consecutive games and six straight SWC championships. National championships came in 1963, 1969, and 1970. Royal's most memorable victory was a 15–14 thriller over Arkansas in 1969 when the Horns and Razorbacks were ranked number one and two nationally during the centennial season of college football.

Texas has boasted several outstanding Heisman winners. Royal recruited massive running back Earl Campbell, who led John Tyler High School to a state championship, won the 1977 Heisman Trophy at UT, then starred for the Houston Oilers. Billy Sims, like the "Tyler Rose," was a two-time All-American, and was awarded the 1978 Heisman Trophy. In a spectacular high school career at Hooks, Sims gained 7,738 yards, second only to Kenneth Hall, including 2,885 as a senior, before taking his enormous talents to the

University of Oklahoma. Quarterback Andre Ware of the Houston Cougars also won the 1982 Heisman Trophy.

With more than 1,100 high schools and superb coaching, Texas was a target for college recruiters from across the nation. Texas schoolboys stocked college programs from Division I to the community college level, and legions of high school stars—like Billy Sims—played college ball in other states. Many excellent programs in Texas fell below the Division I level, and through the years there have been numerous National Association of Intercollegiate Athletes (NAIA) and NJCAA champions. Most notably, Coach Gil Steinke led the Texas A&I Javelinas (now Texas A&M at Kingsville) to six NAIA titles between 1959 and 1976, recording a superb 182–61–4 record overall.

The quality of Southwest Conference football accelerated with the addition of black athletes to team rosters. The Prairie View Interscholastic League (PVIL), originally known as the Texas Interscholastic League of Colored Schools (TILCS), was organized by twenty-one black high schools in 1940, with the membership growing until there were three classifications playing to a state championship. Headquartered at Prairie View A&M College, PVIL administered the football program along with the state basketball tournament, track meet, and baseball playoffs. The PVIL produced a stream of talented athletes, but if they played beyond high school they matriculated out of state or at small black colleges in Texas. In 1964, however, Coach Hayden Fry of SMU recruited Jerry Levias of Beaumont's Hebert High School. The fleet receiver set SMU records and was named an All-American, prompting other colleges to integrate. Desegregation brought the demise of the PVIL and the league ceased to exist after 1967.

One episode that severely marred collegiate football in Texas was the play-for-pay scandal that eventually became known as "Ponygate." In 1987 SMU received the harshest penalty allowable for providing payments to athletes, a violation of NCAA rules. The incident involved Governor William Clements, who served as chairman of the SMU governing board at the time and had authorized the payments. The NCAA "death penalty" abolished the school's football program for a year and the Mustangs voluntarily sat out the 1988 season due to additional NCAA sanctions. No school before or since has received such severe discipline, although the University of Houston, TCU, and Texas A&M have received NCAA sanctions of varying degrees.

Football took on a new dimension in Texas during the 1960s. An NFL franchise, the Dallas Texans, started play in 1952, but the winless team generated little fan support and finished the season as the Baltimore Colts. In 1960 two wealthy sportsmen, Lamar Hunt of Dallas, who had played football at SMU, and Bud Adams of Houston, were instrumental in organizing the American Football League (AFL) after being unable to obtain NFL franchises. The Houston Oilers, bolstered by such Texas stalwarts as Longhorn All-American Scott Appleton and Baylor quarterback Don Trull, won the first two AFL championships, while the Texans, with E. J. Holub from Texas Tech and running back Abner Haynes from North Texas State, took the third AFL title.

The NFL countered in 1960 by awarding an expansion franchise to Dallas. Managing partner Clint Murchison hired an innovative, experienced executive, Tex Schramm, as general manager. Schramm was a University of Texas graduate, and so was his head coach, Tom Landry. Landry, who had been a star quarterback at Mission High School, interrupted his Longhorn career to pilot B-17s over Germany, then became an All-Pro defensive back in the NFL. A brilliant analyst of the game, Landry soon was a player coach for the New York Giants, and by 1960 he was regarded as the NFL's best defensive coach. The Dallas Cowboys signed Bob Lilly of TCU, who anchored the defensive line for fourteen seasons, and quarterback Don Meredith, an All-State selection in both football and basketball at Mount Vernon High School and a two-time All-

American at SMU. Following nine years in the NFL, "Dandy Don" became a media celebrity as a witty commentator on Monday Night Football alongside Howard Cosell and Frank Gifford.

The Cowboys were badly outmanned during their early seasons, but Schramm and Landry built solidly, and soon the club was a regular winner. Landry's twenty-nine years as coach of the Cowboys produced five Super Bowl appearances, including championships in 1972 and 1978. Quarterback Roger Staubach, who led the two Super Bowl championship teams, delivered the speech in 1990 when Landry was inducted into the Pro Football Hall of Fame. During the Landry years the Cowboys moved from the Cotton Bowl to state-of-the-art Texas Stadium, which became a popular site for high school playoff games.

Wealthy oilman Jerry Jones purchased the Cowboys in 1989 and unceremoniously fired Landry. Jones soon dumped Schramm as well, preferring to manage his own club. To head the Cowboys on the field Jones hired a teammate from the University of Arkansas, Jimmy Johnson, a highly successful college coach and a former high school standout from Port Arthur's Thomas Jefferson High School. Johnson built the new Cowboy offense around quarterback Troy Aikman, receiver Michael Irvin, running back Emmitt Smith, who established the all-time NFL running record, and mammoth lineman Larry Allen. The Cowboys won Super Bowls in 1992 and 1993, but Jones angrily fired Johnson after the back-to-back championships. Barry Switzer, a former University of Oklahoma head coach, replaced Johnson and led the Cowboys to another Super Bowl victory in 1995. He resigned two years later after a lackluster 6–10 season.

Although the Cowboys slumped after their Super Bowl triumphs of the 1990s, Texas has continued to enjoy national championship football. In 2004 and 2005 Southlake Carroll was ranked as the best high school team in the United States after Coach Todd Dodge, another high school standout from Port Arthur, won back-to-back state titles. Although the venerable Southwest Conference dissolved in 1996, such crowd-pleasing intrastate rivalries as Texas A&M versus UT continued, even as Division I schools in Texas began playing in conferences that encompassed numerous out-of-state universities. The University of Texas produced another Heisman Trophy winner, Ricky Williams, in 1998, and a succession of highly ranked teams. In the 2006 Rose Bowl the Longhorns, behind a magnificent quarterback from Houston, Vince Young, defeated Southern Cal for their fourth national title.

Cheerleader squads and drill teams enhance most college, high school, and junior high football games in Texas. The Texas A&M yell leaders were the first to encourage their team from the sidelines, but cheerleader squads grew rapidly, and in 1940 Gussie Nell Davis trained the first Rangerettes at Kilgore Junior College. The high-kicking Rangerettes became internationally famous and were emulated by numerous high school and college drill teams—and by the Dallas Cowboy Cheerleaders, the first precision team to represent a professional franchise. Not surprisingly, Texas invented cheerleading camps, a popular enterprise that has grown into a $150,000,000 industry.

In most Texas high schools and colleges, basketball has been regarded as a second-tier sport. Even so, Texas has produced many outstanding basketball teams. In 1921 El Paso High School defeated San Antonio High, 25–11, for the first UIL basketball championship. El Paso High finished second the next three years. An even better program was put together at Athens High School, which won five state championships between 1927 and 1934. The Athens Hornets also were designated national high school champions in 1929 and 1930, even though they failed to record a state title in the latter year. Still, basketball long remained an afterthought at most Texas high schools, except for rural schools too small to field a football squad.

In 1942 Slater Martin, a five-foot-ten-inch, sharp-shooting, ball-handling wizard, led Houston's Jefferson Davis High School to the state championship. Martin's collegiate career at UT was interrupted by two years in the Navy, but he sparked the Longhorns to a 26–2 season and third place in the NCAA tournament, followed by two consecutive appearances in the National Invitation Tournament (NIT) finals. The Texas All-American later played eleven seasons in the NBA.

E. O. "Doc" Hayes played high school basketball in Krum, and then led the North Texas State Teachers College Eagles to the 1926 championship of the Texas Intercollegiate Athletic Association (TIAA). Three times Hayes was named to the All-TIAA squad. As a high school coach he was a perennial winner at Crozier Tech of Dallas, including the 1946 state championship. Two years later Hayes began twenty years as head coach at SMU, winning or sharing eight SWC titles.

Wiley College of Marshall won the 1945 Negro National Championship. In 1960 Southwest Texas University recorded an NAIA title, followed by Prairie View in 1962 and East Texas State in 1965. Men's and women's teams from Texas community colleges have won numerous NJCAA championships. The most unique women's squad represented Wayland Baptist College from Plainview. The Flying Queens have enjoyed repeated success, traveling to games courtesy of an ardent fan who runs a flying service. The University of Texas, under highly respected coach Jody Conradt, won the NCAA women's championship in 1986 with a sparkling 34–0 record. The Texas Tech Lady Raiders claimed a national championship in 1993, and in 2005 new coach Kim Mulkey-Roberts brought a national title to Baylor University.

Coach Don Haskins of Texas Western in El Paso (now the University of Texas at El Paso) earned the only NCAA men's championship ever won by a Texas college or university. The 1966 triumph was a sporting event of historic proportions. When appointed head coach in 1961, Haskins found it difficult to entice players to the small El Paso college. He succeeded by recruiting black athletes, and in 1963 and 1964 the Miners made it to the NCAA tournament. This opened the door to more prospects, and in 1966 the Miners stormed to the NCAA finals, where they opposed legendary coach Adolph Rupp and his Kentucky Wildcats, starring future National Basketball Association (NBA) coach Pat Riley. Although segregation had legally ended, southern colleges like Kentucky still fielded all-white teams. Throughout the championship game Haskins played an all-black roster, and after the Miners won, the bars to athletic segregation in the South rapidly disappeared. In 2006 a motion picture, *Glory Road*, portrayed the story of these 1966 champions.[6]

The American Basketball Association (ABA) secured franchises in several Texas cities. In 1967 the Dallas Chaparrals enjoyed winning seasons on the court, but fan support was weak. Consequently, a San Antonio group purchased the franchise, and the San Antonio Spurs first appeared in the 1973–74 season. Two years later the ABA ceased to exist and the Spurs merged into the NBA. The Spurs brought the NBA title back to Texas three times in seven years—1999, 2003 and 2005. The Houston Rockets joined the NBA in 1971 after the franchise was transferred from San Diego. Elvin Hayes, a two-time All-American at the University of Houston, starred for the first Rockets team. The Rockets recorded back-to-back NBA championships in 1994 and 1995. When Dallas acquired an NBA franchise in 1980, the Mavericks completed the trio of professional basketball teams in the state. Generously financed by colorful owner Mark Cuban, the Mavericks became a crack defensive outfit under their intense new coach, Avery Johnson, and charged to the NBA finals in 2006.

Although less familiar than football or basketball, track and field has a long and distinguished record by Texas athletes. Clyde Littlefield of Beaumont, who starred in football, basketball, and track at the University of Texas and earned twelve varsity letters (1912–1916), was most responsible for its early success. In 1920

Littlefield returned to his alma mater as head track-and-field coach, serving for forty-one years and winning twenty-five Southwest Conference championships. Doubling as a cross-country coach for twenty years, he recorded fifteen SWC titles, and in five years as football coach he won two championships. Co-founder of the famous Texas Relays, he coached ten NCAA championship holders and three Olympic performers, including sprinter Eddie Southern from Sunset High School of Dallas.

Littlefield's counterpart at Texas A&M was Frank Anderson, often called "Colonel Andy." In 1920 Coach D. X. Bible brought the World War I veteran to the campus as an assistant in football, basketball, and track. Although Anderson soon concentrated on track, especially cross-country, he put his coaching career on hold for a decade, serving first as a dean, then as an artillery colonel during World War II. Anderson won nine track-and-field championships in the Southwest Conference, along with nine cross-country titles and two co-championships. Aggie quarter-miler Art Harnden won a gold medal in the 1948 Olympics in London, and four years later repeated the feat in Helsinki. Buddy Davis of Nederland High School, who became a star on the Aggie basketball team, set an Olympic record in the high jump. A later Aggie champion, massive shot-putter Randy Matson of Pampa, won the 1968 Olympics in Mexico City and took first-place honors in seventy competitions over a seven-year career.

As an athlete at Abilene Christian College, Oliver Jackson played quarterback and ran the 220- and 440-yard dashes, with time out for service in the Air Force during World War II. After graduation Jackson joined the coaching staff, and by the 1950s he had built a nationally known track program. Beginning in 1952 Abilene Christian hosted the first of four NAIA championships. Jackson's squads won NAIA titles in 1952, 1954, and 1955, before advancing to the NCAA in 1957. Jackson's superb relay teams won seventy-eight championships at major events, including twenty-eight at the Texas Relays. His greatest athlete was rangy Bobby Morrow, a two-time state champ in the 100-yard-dash at San Benito who was 23–0 in competition during his senior year. At Abilene Christian, Morrow won eighty events as a sprinter and starred as a sophomore in the 1956 Olympics at Melbourne. In Australia Morrow claimed three gold medals and the title "World's Fastest Human," winning the 100- and 200-meter dashes and anchoring the 400-meter relay team. Johnny "Lam" Jones of Lampasas High School performed a fabled exploit in the 1976 Texas Relays. As anchor of the Lampasas mile relay team, Jones took the baton trailing six other runners and forty meters behind the leader. He raced past the field to win the state championship, and then won a gold medal in the 400-meter relay at the 1976 Olympics. Jones later played football at the University of Texas and was a speedy receiver in the NFL for six seasons.

Another legendary track star was Mildred Ella Didrikson, a tomboy from Beaumont who so excelled at physical activities that her friends nicknamed her after Babe Ruth. A superb basketball player, teenager Babe Didrikson went to Dallas as a typist for an insurance company. The five-foot-seven-inch, 115-pound athlete subsequently became a three-time All-American on the company's Amateur Athletic Union (AAU) basketball team. Witnessing her first track meet in 1931, Didrikson persuaded the company to sponsor her in track competitions. As a one-woman team at the 1932 women's AAU championships, she won six of the eight events, setting three world records and piling up thirty points (the second-place *team* totaled only twenty-two points). Her performance earned a trip to the 1936 Olympics in Los Angeles, where she was permitted to enter just three events, setting Olympic records in the javelin and 80-yard hurdles (her first place in the high jump was disallowed because she used a western roll technique that became legal by the next Olympics).

Although Didrikson excelled in track and field, she was an all-around athlete. She pitched exhibition baseball against major leaguers. She won championships in tennis, swimming, cycling, shooting, billiards, speed skating, and squash, before mastering golf as an adult. A founder of the Ladies Professional Golf Association (LPGA) tour, she won eighty-two amateur and professional tournaments, including every major golfing event at least once. Later stricken with cancer, Didrikson continued to win LPGA events before her untimely death at forty-two in 1956. Six times the Associated Press named her Woman Athlete of the Year: 1932, 1945, 1946, 1947, 1950, and 1954. An AP poll proclaimed Babe Didrikson Zaharias the greatest woman athlete of the first half of the twentieth century, and fittingly she is honored by a museum in Beaumont.[7]

The second woman to be inducted into the Texas Sports Hall of Fame after Babe Didrikson Zaharias was golfer Betty Jameson of Dallas. As a teenager she won four Texas Women's Amateur Championships and was the first girl to letter on a boys' golf team, at Sunset High. Twice she won the Women's United States Amateur crown. One of the first women golfers to turn pro with Babe and nine other women, Jameson helped organize the LPGA and toured successfully into the 1960s.

Texas produced a dazzling lineup of male counterparts to such female champions as Babe Didrikson Zaharias, Betty Jameson, and amateur Polly Riley. Texas natives have won thirty-nine major golf championships, including twenty-three of the sixty-six majors played from 1937–1956 and twelve more from 1965–1984. Byron Nelson from Waxahachie posted fifty-two titles on the tour, including five majors. In 1945 Nelson, famed for consistent play, set all-time records with eighteen tour victories and eleven consecutive championships—one of the greatest feats in sports history. The popular champ presided genially over the Dallas tournament bearing his name into his 90s. Ralph Guldahl of Dallas won back-to-back U.S. Open titles in 1937 and 1938, and then took the Masters in 1939. Flamboyant Jimmy Demaret of Houston became the first golfer to win three Masters, in 1940, 1947, and 1950. Although born in Dublin, Texas, Ben Hogan made his home in Fort Worth. Cool and analytical, "Bantam Ben" was a fierce competitor who carefully studied golf swings. Hogan's sixty-four tour victories included nine majors. In 1949, while returning from a tour event his body was shattered in a near-fatal auto crash. A year later "The Hawk" limped back onto the tour and, although limiting his number of appearances, resumed his winning ways. Hogan posted one of the best seasons in golf history in 1953. Entering only seven tournaments, he won five, including three majors—the Masters, U.S. Open, and British Open. Hogan had no chance for the Grand Slam because the PGA Championship conflicted with the British Open.[8]

Other professional and college players made names for themselves in the golfing world. The irrepressible Lee Trevino of Dallas won six majors in a career that began as a golf hustler. After claiming his first major victory at the 1968 U.S. Open, "Super Mex" brandished his check and laughed: "I'm so happy I'm gonna buy the Alamo and give it back to Mexico!" During three consecutive weeks in 1971 Trevino won his second U.S. Open, the Canadian Open, and the British Open. Ben Crenshaw of Austin won the Masters in 1984 and 1995. Crenshaw was a product of the University of Texas golf program, which was prominent nationwide during the late 1960s and early 1970s. From 1956 through 1985 the University of Houston won sixteen national golfing titles, and during the late 1940s and early 1950s North Texas State was a national power. Such sustained success by a college program is unlikely in the future, since talented players turn professional at younger ages.

Rodeo is the only major American sport to evolve from a business—the range cattle industry. Closely identified with Texas cattle ranching and cowboys, the rodeo began in 1883 at the Pecos Fourth of July celebration. As a boy growing up near Taylor, Bill Pickett, a descendant of African and Native Americans, observed that bulldogs handled longhorns by biting their upper lips. Young Pickett tried the feat himself, seizing the horns and sinking his teeth into a steer's lip. Soon he demonstrated this unique method at local fairs. Later billed as "Bulldoggin' Bill" and the "Dusky Demon," Pickett popularized bulldogging to rodeo audiences and became the only performer to originate a rodeo event. In 1971, four decades after his death, he became the first African American elected to the National Rodeo Hall of Fame. Pickett's contemporary Samuel "Booger Red" Privett of Williamson County rode more than 25,000 bucking horses during his cowboy career. In 1975 he was voted into the National Rodeo Hall of Fame along with legendary calf roper Clay McGonagill of Lavaca County. Many other rodeo stars have been native Texans, and a growing number of college rodeo teams help perpetuate this popular sport.

Since frontier days Texans have also enjoyed prize fighting. In 1896 the colorful Judge Roy Bean staged a heavyweight championship bout that Progressive reformers had attempted to block. A special train brought sportsmen and the pugilists to tiny Langtry, where challenger Bob Fitzsimmons knocked out Peter Maher in the first round. The next year a strapping African-American teenager from Galveston, Jack Johnson, began fighting professionally. The "Galveston Giant" was an expert at feinting and packed enormous power in his punches. Johnson was outspoken and married several white wives, but he was unable to get a title fight until 1908, when he was thirty. He knocked out Tommy Burns, and then defended his title for seven years. Hulking Jess Willard felled Johnson in 1937, but the ex-heavyweight champ fought exhibitions until he was 67.[9]

A Texas cowboy, George "Tex" Rickard, proved to be a brilliant boxing promoter. Working with Jack Dempsey, Rickard promoted boxing's first million-dollar gate and the first two-million-dollar gate. Rickard enriched himself and many associates; he was instrumental in popularizing boxing; and he was voted into the Texas Sports Hall of Fame. George Foreman of Marshall won an Olympic gold medal in the heavyweight division in Mexico in 1968. Turning pro, he claimed the heavyweight championship in 1973 with a second-round knockout of "Smokin' Joe" Frazier. Foreman lost the title the next year to Muhammad Ali, but he continued to fight into middle age, reclaiming his title at the age of forty-five with a 1994 knockout of Michel Moorer. Texas champs in lighter divisions included welterweight Curtis Cokes of Dallas and high-living lightweight Lew Jenkins, the "Sweetwater Swatter."

Throughout the twentieth century Texans have participated in all forms of racing. Cyclist Lance Armstrong of Plano won the prestigious Tour de France an unprecedented seven times, 1999–2006. Another spectacular racing champion was A. J. Foyt of Houston, who won more auto races than anyone in the history of the sport. Foyt won the Indianapolis 500 four times (1961, 1964, 1967 and 1977) and the USAC stock car title three times (1968, 1978 and 1979). He also was the first man to win auto racing's Triple Crown (Indianapolis, Ontario, and Pocono). In another sport—horse racing—diminutive Willie Shoemaker of Fabens became the winningest jockey of all time, visiting the winner's circle more than 8,000 times.

There have been other champions and other great teams. In 1999 the Dallas Stars of the National Hockey League won the coveted Stanley Cup, and beginning in 1997 the Stars claimed seven division titles in nine seasons. The Dallas Stars, formerly the Minnesota North Stars, is the only NHL franchise in Texas. But minor league hockey, surprisingly, dates back to the 1940s, when Dallas, Fort Worth, and Houston played in the Western Division of the United States Hockey League. Similarly, Dallas and Houston began fielding professional soccer teams in 1966. Although most of the players were foreign, in 1972 Kyle Rote, Jr., son of the former SMU and NFL star, became a feature player of the Dallas Tornado, and after seven seasons he was traded to the Houston Hurricane.

Great numbers of Texas boys and girls now don Little League uniforms and play organized sports. Many youth play on soccer fields across the state and continue their careers on high school squads and select teams. A growing number of Texas universities also field soccer teams, or "football," as the rest of the world calls it. Children as young as five begin playing baseball and softball, then progress to high school and select teams, and perhaps to the community college or university level. Other Texas children take up swimming or tennis or basketball. Summer football, basketball, baseball, and softball camps are available to young athletes. If many young players stop participating because of burnout, others learn how to achieve excellence through discipline and hard work and long-term commitment. Such athletes carry on the sports traditions of their high schools and colleges, and build community pride with championship performances. The Texans who played primitive versions of baseball, football, and basketball more than a century ago would be astounded at the resources and attention poured into modern sports. But they would understand the sheer physical joy of participating in the wide variety of games Texans play.

Selected Bibliography

The "Babe": A Record of Achievement, Mildred (Babe) Didrikson Zaharias, 1914–1956. Pamphlet available at Babe Didrikson Zaharias Museum, Beaumont, Tex.

Cashion, Ty. Pigskin Pulpit: A Social History of Texas High School Football Coaches. Austin: Texas State Press, 1999.

Dent, Jim. The Junction Boys. New York: St. Martin's, 1999.

Fleischer, Nat, and Sam Andre. A Pictorial History of Boxing. New York: Citadel, 1993.

Johnson, Lloyd, and Miles Wolff, eds. The Encyclopedia of Minor League Baseball. Durham, N.C.: Baseball America, 1993.

McComb, David G. Houston: The Bayou City. Austin: University of Texas Press, 1969.

McMurray, Bill, ed. Texas High School Football. South Bend, Ind.: Icans, 1985.

O'Neal, Bill. "The East Texas Baseball League, 1916–1950." East Texas Historical Journal 36, no. 1 (1998).

————. *The Texas League, 1888–1987: A Century of Baseball.* Austin, Tex.: Eakin, 1987

Texas Sports Hall of Fame: Its Members and Their Deeds. Grand Prairie: Texas Sports Hall of Fame, n.d.

Endnotes

1. David G. McComb, *Houston: The Bayou City* (Austin: University of Texas Press, 1969), 43; Bill O'Neal, *Texas League, 1888–1987: A Century of Baseball* (Austin, Tex.: Eakin, 1987), 1–2, 251.

2. O'Neal, *Texas League,* 2. The history of the first century of the TL is detailed in this volume.

3. Lloyd Johnson and Miles Wolff, eds. *Encyclopedia of Minor League Baseball.* For the East Texas League, see Bill O'Neal, "The East Texas Baseball League, 1916–1950" *East Texas Historical Journal* 36, no. 1 (1998).

4. Ty Cashion, *Pigskin Pulpit: A Social History of Texas High School Football Coaches* (Austin: Texas State Press, 1999), 69–73; Bill McMurray, ed., *Texas High School Football* (South Bend, Ind.: Icans, 1985). These books cover all aspects of high school football in Texas.

5. Jim Dent, *The Junction Boys* (New York: St. Martin's, 1999).Facts about college and pro achievements are readily available on individual Web sites. Information about star players and coaches also may be found online. Almost all Texas athletic notables are included in *Texas Sports Hall of Fame: Its Members and Their Deeds* (Grand Prairie: Texas Sports Hall of Fame, n.d.).

6. Dave Kindred, In '66, the champs couldn't sing their song," *Sporting News,* January 20, 2006, 56; "Don Haskins, Unwitting Pioneer," *Dallas Morning News,* November 25, 2005.

7. *The "Babe": A Record of Achievement, Mildred (Babe) Didrikson Zaharias, 1914–1956,* Pamphlet available at Babe Didrikson Zaharias Museum, Beaumont, Tex.; Frank Luksa, "A Footnote? No, Babe Was a Sensation," *Dallas Morning News,* February 22, 2003; Brad Townsend, "Golden Girls—50 Years Ago, 13 Trailblazing Women Created the LPGA," *Dallas Morning News,* May 7, 2000.

8. Bill Nichols, "Has Texas' Golf Well Dried Up?" *Dallas Morning News,* May 9, 2004.

9. The boxing champions from Texas may be studied in *Texas Sports Hall of Fame* and in Nat Fleischer and Sam Andre, *A Pictorial History of Boxing* (New York: Citadel, 1993).

Private Wealth, Public Good

Texans and Philanthropy

Mary L. Kelley

TEXANS, LIKE CITIZENS FROM many other states, have participated fully in the American philanthropic tradition. Beginning in the nineteenth century and continuing to the present, they have repeatedly performed numerous acts of charity and mutual helpfulness. During the frontier period, the problems involved in settling a hostile land promoted neighborly cooperation in times of need and friendly assistance to confront unexpected dangers. Many risked their lives in epidemics of diseases such as yellow fever and cholera to tend to the sick and dying. Others formed mutual aid societies to assist families and disabled Civil War veterans, organized benevolent associations to help the poor and the orphaned, and established disaster-relief organizations such as the Howard Association—the first charitable organization in the Republic of Texas.[1]

Such unselfish attributes, or "habits of the heart," continued into the twentieth century. But as more wealthy benefactors accumulated vast profits from land, livestock, and crude oil, many charitable-minded Texans turned to philanthropy to improve the quality of human life. Steel master Andrew Carnegie prescribed this concept in his classic essay, "Wealth," published in 1889. Carnegie believed that the accumulation of wealth was inevitable within a capitalist system, and the inequality between the rich and poor was the price society paid for competition and material comfort. As a proponent of Social Darwinism, which justified ruthless competition and "survival of the fittest" in the marketplace, he assumed that wealth was proof of individual fitness, while poverty was a sign of inferiority. To bestow charity on the "unreclaimably poor" caused more injury by encouraging "the very evils which it proposes to mitigate or cure." Instead, Carnegie reasoned, the responsibility of the "man of wealth" was not to provide monetary handouts, but to return surplus wealth to society in a manner calculated to do the most good. To the steel tycoon this meant endowing museums, libraries, and scholarships, institutions that the "fit" could use to advance themselves. Or, as Carnegie put it, he and other wealthy individuals should establish "ladders upon which the aspiring can rise."[2]

In the late nineteenth and early twentieth centuries many *nouveau riche* Texans continued the Carnegie tradition. Armed with the notion of civic stewardship and *noblesse oblige*, which linked the duties of the rich to the society that had enriched them, they practiced individual benevolence, giving both time and money to favorite causes. For example, civic-minded businessmen regularly donated their profits to fund needed city projects, while wives of prominent men contributed to the support of orphanages and hospitals. But beginning in 1920 a fundamentally different philanthropic vehicle emerged in Texas—the general purpose foundation. Rather than the more traditional "retail" style of individual giving, "wholesale philanthropy" enabled wealthy donors to rationally and dispassionately distribute their private wealth for the public good. Although individual giving has always far outstripped organized philanthropy, increasingly wealthy Texans established private foundations, which have significantly contributed to the social and cultural development of the state.[3]

During the first decades of the twentieth century several factors converged to produce a climate conducive to the creation of philanthropic foundations. Most significantly, the oil discovery at Spindletop started an economic boom that became the linchpin of Texas prosperity. From oil profits flowed enormous revenue that lined the pockets of enterprising businessmen, as well as promoting related industries throughout the state. In the absence of state or federal regulation, hundreds of independent operators made quick fortunes in the petroleum business, thereby providing much of the necessary seed money to endow philanthropic endeavors. At the same time the preexistence of institutional antecedents, such as the private foundations created by Andrew Carnegie (1905, 1910, and 1911), heiress Margaret Olivia Sage (1907), and oil baron John D. Rockefeller, Sr., (1913), also promoted organized giving by example. Overwhelmed by the magnitude of their fortunes, made possible by the *laissez-faire* economics of the day, these Gilded Age millionaires (and billionaires such as Rockefeller) turned to organized philanthropy, which provided a systematic approach to the disposal of their charitable dollars.[4]

Progressive Era (1900–1920) reforms to reorder and improve society also led many Texans to seek long-term solutions to the major social problems of the day. A rising middle class worked to bring about more responsive government, restore competition to the marketplace, upgrade the quality of public schools, create more humane treatment of prisoners and the mentally ill, outlaw alcohol and other moral threats, and build safer, cleaner communities. In particular, Texas women, who were disenfranchised until 1920, espoused a wide variety of reforms. Through their club activities, they mobilized their ranks to successfully lobby for pure food inspection laws, campaign against child labor, and establish kindergartens where none existed. As a consequence, some wealthy Texans applied the Progressive Era approach of efficiency and order to their giving and converted to "wholesale philanthropy" as a more effective vehicle to "do good" and achieve lasting reform.[5]

Industrialization, diversification, and urbanization in the twentieth century also promoted organized philanthropy. Expanding
economic opportunities, especially after Spindletop and the resulting oil boom, triggered demands for cheap labor as industrial
production replaced agricultural output as the state's main source
of wealth by the end of the 1920s. New industries located in the
state, including meat packing, flour milling, lumbering, publishing, cottonseed, and construction, thereby adding to the available
private wealth for the public good. And greater numbers of people
moved to large metropolitan areas such as Dallas, San Antonio,
and Houston, so that by the 1940s more Texans lived in the cities
than on the farms. Political and military events such as the Mexican
Revolution (1910–1920), World War I (1917–1919), and World
War II (1941–1945) also fostered modernization by embroiling the
state in world affairs, broadening the industrial base, and attracting
outsiders, all of which accelerated its transition to an urban environment. In the latter half of the twentieth century, tourism, the bio-
medical and aerospace industries, and computer technology combined to ease the shock of collapsing oil prices and, in the process,
created another class of *nouveau-riche* Texans with surplus income
to endow private foundations.[6]

With the advent of urban Texas came a shift in social concerns
from the rural areas to the cities and towns, which was where most
newcomers concentrated. This dramatically increased demands on
infrastructure, schools, and health care. With a less rural, more
diverse society, Texans suffered from many of the same afflictions
of older northeastern cities, namely persistent poverty, inadequate
social services, and poor health care. Pernicious segregation and
flagrant discrimination further compounded these problems. While
government at all levels provided some measure of assistance, escalating growth and budgetary constraints outstripped its ability to
respond satisfactorily. In turn, many Texans looked to the private
sector—churches, charities, and families—for help. But many times

traditional resources—both public and private—were inadequate. Significantly after 1920, many socially conscious elites that wanted to improve Texas society, as well as take advantage of tax incentives, increasingly broke from Victorian-era charity and "retail philanthropy" to practice large-scale philanthropy. Consequently, in every region of the state, from the Piney Woods and Gulf Coast to the west Texas high plains and Rio Grande Valley, Texans established approximately 3,500 private foundations by century's end.[7]

Organized philanthropy emerged in Texas during the second stage (1910–1930) of national development. Its "founding moment" was the creation in 1920 of the George W. Brackenridge Foundation in San Antonio through a bequest in his will. As the first modern Texas philanthropist, publisher-banker Brackenridge had benefited financially from Gilded Age *laissez-faire* economics, as well as from his unpopular Unionist activities in Texas during the Civil War. Both he and his father profited from the cotton trade, thus initiating his fortune, sometimes at the expense of his neighbors. Believing that "profit is one of the essential things," he further enlarged his holdings as president of the San Antonio National Bank, owner of the San Antonio Water Works Company, director of the Express Publishing Company, founder of the San Antonio Loan and Trust, and owner of numerous land parcels throughout the state. By age fifty Brackenridge had become a self-made "man of wealth."[8]

Influenced by the example of philanthropist Andrew Carnegie, as well as Social Darwinism, which justified vast accumulations of wealth through ruthless competition and "survival of the fittest," Brackenridge supported numerous worthy causes during his life, but none more assiduously than the University of Texas. His many grants included funds to construct a men's dormitory, Brackenridge Hall in Austin, as well as land donated for a recreational park in San Antonio and money to build a new public high school that bore his name. In later years, however, Brackenridge became convinced

George W. Brackenridge, the first modern Texas philanthropist. From UTSA's Institute of Texan Cultures, No. 3334-F, San Antonio *Light* Collection.

that his most enduring legacy would be "the education of poor boys and girls equally as may be without reference to the school or college they attend." He therefore purposefully left the bulk of his $3 million estate to a more permanent institution, a foundation, to fulfill his wishes. Although his trust did not become a reality until after his demise in 1920, he was, according to biographer Marilyn Sibley, "one of the pioneers in the establishment of philanthropic foundations."[9]

After a four-year legal battle, the trustees of the Brackenridge estate at last initiated the George W. Brackenridge Foundation—the first of its kind in Texas. Education received the lion's share of his largesse. A scholar by instinct, Brackenridge had demonstrated his commitment to higher learning by serving as a regent to the University of Texas for more than twenty-five years. Furthermore, in 1917, in response to a veto by Governor James E. Ferguson of the school's biennial appropriations bill, he offered to underwrite its expenses out of his own private funds. He therefore directed in his final will that "benefactions of an educational nature" be the recipient of his altruism. Specifically, all remaining funds after payment of individual bequests, estate taxes, and administrative expenses, would benefit the education of deserving young Texans—one- half to the "Anglo-Saxon race" and one-half to the "Negro race."[10]

From its inception in 1920 to the present, the Brackenridge Foundation has provided loans, grants, and scholarships not only to Anglo Texans, but also to minorities—especially black and female students. Brackenridge believed that the only practical solution to the race problem was "to educate the Negro up to the highest citizenship he was capable." Rather than challenge the existing social relations in Jim Crow Texas, which mandated "separate but equal" facilities for the races, he worked for the betterment of both races within the state's segregated system. His gifts therefore supported both the all-white University of Texas, as well as Prairie View Normal School, a historically black institution. At the same time Brackenridge advocated female education. He had long supported equal rights for women and endorsed the suffrage campaign waged by his sister Eleanor. Constrained by Texas law and custom, women in the early twentieth century could not vote, control their separate property if married, make contracts or write a will without their husband's consent, or serve on juries (until 1955). Nevertheless, Brackenridge encouraged women to pursue professional careers by financing the Women's Building at the University of Texas Medical Branch at Galveston, donating funds for a school of home economics, and establishing a loan program for coeds to study medicine, law, and architecture.[11]

The pioneering efforts of Brackenridge served as a model for other wealthy Texans, who were similarly concerned about the rightful distribution of their fortunes. Like Brackenridge, they regarded charitable gifts and almsgiving as misguided good intentions that benefited neither the individual nor society, destroying self-reliance and ignoring long-term solutions. They too viewed permanent trust funds as a way to channel their money to favorite causes that benefited society as a whole. Consequently, by the end of the decade eight new foundations resulted from the large fortunes of Texas families. Only the Brackenridge Foundation, conceptualized in 1913, four years before federal revenue acts allowed charitable deductions from personal income, however, escaped the possible taint of tax avoidance for financial advantage.[12]

In 1929 a new vehicle for philanthropic giving emerged in Texas—the community trust. This unique form of organized philanthropy offered a distinct alternative to the larger, private endowments created by individual donors such as Brackenridge. By consolidating many large and small gifts to benefit a particular city or region, community foundations had a more localized focus, thereby readily responding to the immediate needs of citizens. Additionally, they offered a respected and reliable place for donors of more modest means to pool their resources with others for greater investment with minimal risk. It also had the effect of "democratizing philanthropy" by expanding the number of donors while providing "incomparable good" for Texas communities.[13]

The first community trust arose in Dallas, the state's second largest city with a population of 158,976 in 1920. After the railroads reached the town in the early 1870s, Dallas developed into a major trade center for the redistribution of goods and merchandise in the Southwest. Thereafter, the city prospered and boasted two major universities, a federal reserve bank, numerous national and state banks, an insurance center, a complex transportation network, over forty theaters, a symphony orchestra, and "the largest inland cotton market in the nation." Spearheading these cultural and economic developments was a group of business and civic leaders who shared a commitment to their community and eagerly sought to promote the economic fortunes of their city. At the same time they recognized the value of this new form of philanthropy, which had its beginnings in Cleveland, Ohio, in 1914, and its potential for Dallas.[14]

The establishment of the Dallas Foundation resulted from a combination of "business progressivism" and the leadership of *Dallas Morning News* publisher George B. Dealey. By the early twentieth century the Dallas civic culture was composed of young, public-spirited entrepreneurs who encouraged progress though efficient government and better public services. Typically, these Dallas boosters implemented their vision through municipal reform, civic organizations, and volunteer activities. Their efforts led to a citywide blueprint, a Dallas Citizens Council, and a Community Chest, a federated, charitable giving campaign. In a spirit of collective leadership one group in particular, the Critic Club, an exclusive fifteen-member fraternity of Dallas leaders, met regularly to discuss ideas, investigate problems, and support solutions to improve the city. They believed that Dallas had suffered from a lack of public benefactions that other, more fortunate cities enjoyed. Consequently, after investigating this new instrument of philanthropy, Critic Club members unanimously endorsed the creation of a community foundation to benefit the citizens of Dallas.[15]

George B. Dealey soon became aware, and then convinced, of the merit of community foundations. As a wealthy steward who believed that newspaper publishers should "involve themselves wholesomely in public and civic affairs," he unleashed a media campaign through his newspaper columns to "help push along the idea of the Dallas Community Trust." For example, he contacted government officials who supported the plan and then printed at least "one or two letters a day" of their endorsements. He also produced hundreds of brochures at his own expense, explaining the benefits of this new community philanthropy to potential donors. By unrelentingly keeping the issue before the public, Dealey, by then in his seventies, hoped to see the project firmly established before he "passed out of the picture."[16]

On June 25, 1929, the Dallas Community Trust, later renamed the Dallas Foundation, became a reality. Created just four months before the onset of the Great Depression, it suffered from the devastating effects of the crash. By January 1931, with many fortunes diminished and the future uncertain, there were "no contributions of any sort." The next year only deepened the crisis, with 532 firms in bankruptcy statewide during the first six months and business failures occurring at the rate of fifteen per month. Estimates placed the number of unemployed Texans at 350,000 to 400,000, with 25 percent without any kind of financial resources. Dealey, however, refused to become dispirited. Like many other Texans, he rejected the belief that the economic crisis would be long-lasting. He was also encouraged by the news that several Dallas citizens had already written bequests to the foundation in their wills. Then, on March 21, 1935, following the death of Sigmund Mayer, a local retailer, the Dallas Foundation recorded its first gift of $10,000. Four years later, on April 13, 1939, the board of governors authorized its first grant of $1,000 to benefit a West Dallas neighborhood. By the end of the decade, according to Waverly Briggs, who had earlier delivered a paper to the Critic Club endorsing a community foundation, the Dallas Foundation was now "a going concern." Thereafter, most large and many mid-size Texas cities established community foundations to enhance the quality of life for their citizens.[17]

During the next stage (1930–1945) philanthropic activity in Texas waxed and waned. In the early years of the Great Depression, 1930–1935, economic uncertainty discouraged planned, charitable giving by Texans who did not know what the prospective value of their estates would be at the time of their deaths. Furthermore, the 1935 Tax Act with its "soak the rich" progressive assessments on the wealthy also contributed to a decrease in private and public gifts. Gradually, however, after 1936 with rising, but unwarranted, optimism that the Depression was over, as well as new legislation allowing corporate charitable deductions, several new grant-making organizations emerged. Most resulted from private family fortunes, which had either rebounded with the ebbing of the Depression or surged due to wartime production. Consequently, by the end of World War II over ninety philanthropic foundations existed throughout the state, a tenfold increase since 1929.[18]

In Texas and elsewhere the Depression revealed the inadequacies of local resources to cope with an economic disaster. Initially, private and civic charities, such as churches, the Community Chest, the Red Cross, and the Salvation Army shouldered the burdens of the poor and destitute. Cities augmented private efforts by authorizing public works projects to expand job opportunities for those out of work. But by late 1931 most cities could not continue their relief efforts and began eliminating personnel and curtailing some city services. Private organizations also announced that their funds were exhausted and unable to meet the demands of massive unemployment. Texans therefore looked to new solutions: the New Deal programs of Franklin D. Roosevelt and the resources of private philanthropy.[19]

One of the hallmarks of philanthropy is to augment programs and services overlooked or under-funded by national, state, and local governments. During the Great Depression, Texas benefited from the infusion of federal money authorized under the New Deal (1933–1938), but even those efforts failed to restore prosperity. The problems of a modern, complex society in the throes of a depression were too vexing even for Roosevelt and his promises of "relief, recovery, and reform." One Texan, Jesse H. Jones of Houston, who exercised greater power than even Vice President John Nance Garner as Reconstruction Finance Commission chairman, as well as numerous other New Deal appointments, recognized that the severity of the Depression had redefined both the role of the federal government and private philanthropy. Henceforth, government would intervene on a far larger scale in the welfare of its citizens, playing an expanded role in areas traditionally considered the province of the private sector. While many naysayers decried the en-croachment of big government and prophesied the decline—even destruction—of private philanthropy, Jones understood the limita-tions of the federal bureaucracy. Rather than scaling back assistance, he contended that individual efforts must continue to supplement government programs.[20]

During the Great Depression Jesse and Mary Gibbs Jones were among a minority of Texans financially able to fund a new philan-thropy. Shrewd financial practices, opportunistic banking buyouts, and "aggressive lending to the oil industry" permitted the Joneses in 1937 to establish one of the largest foundations in Texas. Named for the city they called home, the Houston Endowment resulted from the profits of their commercial and financial empire. Eschewing the typically unstable Houston commodities of cotton, chemicals, and oil, Jesse Jones pursued building, real estate, and finance. Possessed with an uncanny business acumen, he assiduously acquired a di-verse network of commercial enterprises, from banks and mortgage companies to newspapers and skyscrapers. Ambitious, energetic, at times even autocratic, Jones prided himself on owning the biggest newspaper, the highest building, the richest bank—and residing in "the largest state in the Union." He even designed and erected "the tallest man-made memorial in the world," the San Jacinto Monument (1936–1939), eclipsing the Washington Monument by more than fourteen feet. As a New Deal administrator he continued his commanding role by brokering million-dollar deals, control-ling important patronage, and authorizing "more money than any man in history." Little wonder then that when he decided in 1937, along with wife Mary, to practice "wholesale philanthropy," Jones established an institution of considerable magnitude—the Houston Endowment—and began plans to transfer much of their income-producing properties to this new philanthropic institution.[21]

The decision to institutionalize his philanthropy arose from a long-standing tradition of private, charitable giving. As a youth

Jones had inherited not only his standards of good business conduct, but also his values of social responsibility. While working in the tobacco fields and warehouses, he had frequently observed numerous acts of generosity by his father, whose smokehouse was always open "to those who needed a little tiding over until harvest time." Jones therefore modeled this pattern of private giving by dispensing numerous often-unpublicized gifts. As his wealth increased, his largesse multiplied as well. For example, he frequently gave sizeable monetary handouts, "big enough to choke a dog," to needy recipients and established a $10,000-a-year trust fund to ease the financial burden of former President Woodrow Wilson.[22]

As prominent members of Houston's ruling elite, the Joneses initially made education the primary object of their philanthropy. Jesse, a school dropout who claimed that he had read only one book in his entire life—a biography of Sam Houston—nonetheless recognized the importance of learning. "My own educational training was decidedly limited," he wrote in 1924, "and I have keenly felt it a great handicap." He resolved, along with wife Mary, who had attended college in Waco, "to assist other ambitious young men and women in equipping themselves for life's problems with a college training." Not limited to Texas recipients, as were other private foundations in the state, the Houston Endowment aided more than 4,000 students on fifty-seven campuses nationwide by the time of Jones's death in 1956.[23]

Akin to their interest in education and mindful of the Carnegie model of philanthropy, which supported libraries throughout Texas and the nation, the Joneses also built free libraries, thereby creating "ladders upon which the aspiring can rise." Beginning in 1940 the Houston Endowment generously contributed to numerous funds such as the A&M College library in College Station and the construction of the Gibbs Memorial Library in Mexia, the birthplace of Mary Jones. Erected on the Gibbs family homestead, the library was of continuing interest to Mary, who regularly supplied books for its shelves. These institutional gifts, the Joneses believed, ful-filled their intention to benefit local communities while improving the general condition of Texas society.[24]

During the first half of the twentieth century Texas minorities played less prominent roles as philanthropists. Low wages, few op-portunities, and inadequate education more often made Hispanic and black Texans grant recipients rather than wealthy donors. In addition, discrimination, segregation, and poverty precluded their participation in organized, large-scale giving. Besides, the needs of minority communities necessitated immediate relief to improve basic living conditions rather than long-term solutions to social problems. As a consequence, minority patterns of giving differed significantly from the Carnegie model practiced by predominately white, male philanthropists. Rather than utilizing institutional tools such as foundations, trusts, and endowments, Mexican Texans tra-ditionally donated their funds in more informal ways to churches, family members, and mutual aid societies, known as *mutualistas.* Black Texans, legally separated from mainstream institutions since 1896, also adopted a more personal approach; they supported local religious groups and created their own self-help organizations.[25]

Texas women, constrained by law and custom, were also con-spicuously absent as philanthropic donors. Since few females in the first half of the twentieth century held public office or exercised financial power apart from their spouses, they used "organized womanhood," such as voluntary associations, church guilds, and women's clubs to improve their communities. Through these fe-male institutions they aided the less fortunate by volunteering their time, organizing charity events, lobbying the legislature, and raising needed funds. Gradually, by the late 1960s, as social and economic restrictions eased, as more women gained access to education, and as additional career options became available, more Texas women accumulated capital and began to practice philanthropy on a large scale.[26]

Despite the many obstacles, a few Texas women did establish philanthropic institutions. While their male counterparts earned their fortunes through business entrepreneurship, women used their inherited wealth or marital estate to establish private foundations. They too recognized the need for a more systematic approach to the allocation of charitable dollars. Once engaged in philanthropy, Texas women became active donors, bringing an enlarged social consciousness and a unique set of female values. Hence, better child care, improved city services, adequate health care, and expanded education received their attention. At the same time, organized philanthropy provided women with leadership opportunities and meaningful work outside their traditional roles as mothers, teachers, or nurses.[27]

One of the first Texas women to practice large-scale philanthropy was Ima Hogg, daughter of Governor James S. Hogg. Raised with a sharp sense of *noblesse oblige*, "Miss Ima," sometimes referred to by journalists as "the first lady of Texas," regarded inherited wealth as a public trust. "I was taught that every citizen has an obligation to serve humanity according to his talents and privileges." Like other Texas women, she had already volunteered her time and money to a wide range of projects, including the Houston Child Guidance Center, the Houston Symphony, and the Houston Community Chest. Gradually, however, she came to exercise public influence and private authority otherwise denied her. As heir to the family oil fortune and trusted confidante to brothers Will and Mike, Ima, at the age of fifty-eight, leveraged her private wealth for the public good by establishing the first professionally managed, philanthropic institution associated with the University of Texas—the Hogg Foundation for Mental Health (1940).[28]

The death of Will Hogg on September 12, 1930, and the disposal of his sizeable estate created the corpus of the Hogg Foundation. He had expressed in his will a desire to combine his funds with those of his sister, Ima, for some future endeavor that would bring

Ima Hogg, ca. 1940.
Courtesy Hogg (Ima)
Papers, 1824–1977,
CN 11344, Center
for American History,
University of Texas at
Austin.

"far-reaching benefit to the people of Texas." But the final use of his approximately $2.5 million gift remained ambiguous. While a legal battle over inheritance and transfer taxes ensued, Mike, along with "the good judgment and opinion" of his sister, Ima, considered several options for the money. Following considerable discussion, they chose to leave the principal part of the estate to the University of Texas for mental health care, commonly referred to as "mental hygiene" at the time.[29]

The selection of mental health as the mission of the Hogg Foundation generated considerable speculation and conjecture. The emotional and mental anguish of many Texans during the Depression years focused national and state attention on mental illness and its effects, especially insanity and suicide rates. Some suggested that Ima's own severe bouts of depression and insomnia, particularly after the deaths of her parents and the emotional afflictions of younger brother Tom, contributed to her own interest in a mental health program with an emphasis on education and prevention. Others cited her enduring interest in psychology—a relatively new discipline at the University of Texas—where she had studied as an undergraduate with A. Caswell Ellis, a leading authority in the field. Whatever the reason, Ima Hogg vowed to do something positive about the problem when time and resources permitted.[30]

In 1940 Ima Hogg, following Mike's death after a two-year bout with cancer, pioneered the creation of the Hogg Foundation for Mental Health. Anxious that "her brother's estate be put to a cause of such potential benefit to human welfare," she necessarily assumed control of the family fortune and its philanthropic mission. She envisioned a statewide program that would be both "preventive and therapeutic," as well as provide educational information to rural and urban areas. In particular, she wanted to target Texas youth. Mental health intervention, she maintained, "must start at the roots," that is, at the early stages of life. Child-guidance programs in the schools and mental health centers, rather than research, were more likely to curb juvenile delinquency and prevent broken families. This determination, Miss Ima believed, amply fulfilled her "Brother Will's aspirations and intentions."[31]

From its inception Miss Ima played an active and innovative role in the Hogg Foundation. She grasped the consequences of mental illness as an often-concealed social problem and the importance of early intervention and treatment. She also purposefully restricted grant recipients to Texas residents, according to her brother's wishes. "I believe every state should take care of its own," she asserted. Furthermore, in 1964 Ima Hogg added her own financial resources to the foundation by creating a separate fund to promote mental health among the children in the Houston area, especially the Child Guidance Center, the Children's Mental Health Services, and the Hope Center for Youth. Advancing age notwithstanding, she never wavered from her commitment. "My first obligation," she reminisced in 1967 at age eighty-five, "is to this Foundation." Then a year later, she reiterated: "My interest in mental health is as strong as ever." Until her death in 1975, she continued to provide "intelligent inspiration of a broad nature" to set the agenda and guide the course of the Hogg Foundation to benefit the mental health of Texans.[32]

Another distinguishing characteristic of private philanthropy is a desire to improve society, especially the local communities from which donors heralded. Most Texas philanthropists identified with a particular city or geographical region and sought to return a portion of their good fortune to their hometowns or state. None was more assiduous in the support of his beloved city of Fort Worth than Amon G. Carter. Born on December 11, 1879, in Crafton, Texas, Carter relocated to "the city of his boyhood dreams" in 1905. The settlement of the West, especially the Anglo occupation of Texas with its "horse and gun" culture, left an indelible imprint on him. Justly proud of Fort Worth's history, traditions, and seemingly unlimited prospects, he became convinced that his chosen hometown, often hailed as "the Queen City of the Prairie," offered the best opportunity to escape from the dreary mesquite and scrub oak plains of north Texas and begin his life's work.[33]

As a successful businessman and newspaper publisher of the *Fort Worth Star-Telegram*, Carter was an ambitious and generous man, especially concerning projects that would improve and promote Fort Worth. He had inherited from his mother a strong sense of regard for the less fortunate, engaging in numerous early private acts of charity—what biographer Jerry Flemmons called "fits of philanthropy." For example, he paternalistically provided liberal benefits, annual bonuses, and emergency assistance to his newspaper employees. At the annual Thanksgiving dinners Carter remembered the corner news carriers by giving each a silver dollar, a sizeable sum at the time, and awarded scholarships to the paperboys with the highest high school grades. During the hot summer months Carter also sponsored a free milk-and-ice fund for the needy, while during the Christmas season he provided toys and candy to disadvantaged children. Believing that west Texas suffered from a lack of recognition, he consistently channeled his energy and wealth into airports, schools, and hospitals for the region. At the same time he was an indefatigable fundraiser who directed capital campaigns to benefit the Young Men's Christian Association (YMCA), Mississippi Flood Relief (1927), and Texas Christian University (TCU). Little wonder then that his name was the first inscribed in the Book of Golden Deeds by the Exchange Club, an exclusive Fort Worth men's organization.[34]

Initially, Carter funded many of his public interests and charitable gifts through the *Star-Telegram*. But with escalating debts and mounting loans, he tried "wildcatting" and struck oil in 1920. Years passed, however, without another gusher, and Carter became known as "the only big producer who never produced." Then, in 1935 after ninety dry holes, he at last struck oil again at the Mattix Pool in New Mexico and at the vast Wasson Pool in Gaines and Yoakum counties. This bonanza, along with the 1926 oil depletion allowance that allowed producers a liberal tax deduction, alleviated his financial worries and provided the seed money for his philanthropy.[35]

A self-made millionaire at age fifty-eight, Carter not only dispensed innumerable, often unpublicized gifts of varying sizes, but practiced organized philanthropy as well. On April 7, 1945, along with former wife Nenetta, he created the Amon G. Carter Foundation to support "benevolent, charitable, educational or missionary undertakings." One early grant provided funds to purchase the William Luther Lewis literary collection of rare first editions and original manuscripts housed at TCU. Carter also purposely limited the geographical scope of his benevolence to Texas recipients, especially residents of Fort Worth and Tarrant County. "I am part of the heritage of Texas," Carter proudly wrote. "I wish to share it with others who would make Texas their home and their inspiration."[36]

Following his death on June 23, 1955, Carter posthumously enlarged his philanthropic vision. He bequeathed his extensive western art collection –"paintings of great value," statuary, sculpture and other *objets d'art*—to his foundation. Possessing a strong identification with his local roots, Carter had started collecting "scenes of the West or themes relating to the life of that region." To him the pioneering spirit depicted by artists such as Charles Russell and Frederic Remington symbolized a heroic, bygone era that should be preserved. He further reasoned that the presence of an art museum might shore up the sagging image of Fort Worth as an unrefined cow town. By cultivating its aesthetic spirit, engaging its youth in "artistic imagination," and restoring its competitive edge with rival Dallas, the museum would bring the city national recognition. Carter therefore enjoined the foundation trustees to establish a museum to house the Amon Carter Collection of Western Art, which opened its doors in 1961. By employing cultural philanthropy, Carter returned a portion of his wealth to his hometown, influencing the character of an entire city and region that he loved.[37]

Other wealthy benefactors also turned to large-scale giving to better their local communities. For instance, Galveston benefited from the largesse of the Moody and Kempner families. William L. Moody amassed his initial fortune that would fund a permanent philanthropy as a successful cotton trader and banker after the Civil War. Following his death in 1920, son William L. Moody, Jr., continued to enlarge the family assets by acquiring insurance companies, printing enterprises, and hotel establishments. He also owned ranches in Texas and Oklahoma. Like other wealthy individuals, William and wife Libbie wanted a more efficient allocation of their charitable dollars. In 1942 they therefore created a private foundation "for the benefit of Texans," especially the citizens of Galveston. Afterwards, the Moody Foundation approved grants to many local projects, such as the Santa Fe railroad station renovation to house several nonprofit organizations, a residential treatment facility for head-injury patients, and an outpatient recreational program for disabled citizens of Galveston County. Harris Kempner, a Jewish immigrant and successful shopkeeper and cotton merchant, also settled in Galveston just prior to the Civil War. Along with wife Eliza, he supported public benefactions that significantly enhanced the city's standard of living. Orphanages, schools, and hospitals, as well as the Jewish temple, were major recipients of their generosity. Then, in 1946 Kempner descendants decided to institutionalize the family philanthropy, due in part to financial considerations. With an emphasis on local projects, they organized the permanent Harris and Eliza Kempner Fund to benefit Galveston, as well as "a large variety of other minority causes."[38]

Many other cities across the state benefited from wealthy philanthropists either directly or indirectly. Wildcatter Edgar B. Davis established the Luling Foundation in 1927 to build and maintain a $1 million demonstration farm for Caldwell and Guadalupe counties. In 1943 businessman and novelist Madison A. Cooper, Jr., established the Cooper Foundation to "make Waco, Texas, a better or more desirable place in which to live." Fort Worth oilman Sid W. Richardson created his permanent fund in 1947 to benefit Texas residents, but especially Fort Worth's arts, health-care, and education communities. Algur and Virginia Meadows of Dallas started their private foundation "to assist the people and institutions of Texas" in 1948 with the proceeds from the General American Oil Company of Texas. From its inception to the present, the Meadows Foundation has supported cultural, medical, and human services throughout the state and especially in Dallas County. The Brown Foundation (1951), created by Herman Brown from the profits of his worldwide engineering and construction firm, Brown and Root, assists education and the arts within the state, as well as the needs of children, especially in the Houston area. In Beaumont the mission of the Mamie McFaddin Ward Heritage Foundation, established in 1976, supports its historic property—the McFaddin-Ward House—as well as cultural and educational programs within Jefferson County. More recently, Albert and Bessie Mae Kronkosky, owners of several successful business ventures in Texas, funded a sizeable private foundation (1991) in their name to improve living conditions in San Antonio, Bexar County, and the surrounding counties of Bandera, Comal and Kendall.

During the next stage, from 1945 to 1970, Texas led the Southwest in the creation of philanthropic institutions. Texas' robust economy and expanding population of 7,711,194 by 1950 spurred an "Age of Foundations." Thousands of charitable-minded Texans practiced individual good works, as well as establishing over 2,500 additional permanent foundations. But why did so many Texans turn to large-scale, organized philanthropy after years of private giving? Was it simple altruism, estate planning, tax avoidance, or a hope of remembrance? As in the case of most human affairs, their motives were mixed. For many, a foundation served several purposes: It represented a sound business decision for their surplus income; it created a lasting vehicle to support favorite causes; it permitted a more impersonal, professional distribution of their wealth; and for some it fulfilled a desire for recognition and respectability. Whatever the cause, more Texans of varying degrees of wealth increasingly turned to organized giving, returning a portion of their earnings to benefit the public good.[39]

Despite the phenomenal growth in Texas foundations, many operated in isolation, resulting in duplication of services and the inefficient allocation of philanthropic dollars. No organization existed at the national or state levels to provide a directory of foundations, identify concerns, or coordinate grants. Consequently, in 1948 three foundation representatives—Dr. Robert Sutherland of the Hogg Foundation, Mary Elizabeth Butt of the H. E. Butt Foundation,

and Margaret Scarbrough of the Leland Scarbrough Foundation—
met in Austin and organized the Conference of Southwest Foundations (CSF). Its purpose was an informal "exchange of ideas" by
foundation donors, trustees, and professionals and included representatives from neighboring states such as Oklahoma, Arkansas,
Arizona, and New Mexico. At its annual meetings CSF members
discussed trends in philanthropy, legislative and tax issues, and the
needs of an urban society. As the first regional philanthropic community in the nation, the CSF identified social problems, offered
organizational support, and promoted foundation philanthropy as
a vehicle to serve Texas and the Southwest. From its inception until
the present day, the CSF continues to guide and define the Texas
philanthropic experience.[40]

Throughout their existence Texas foundations and their donors, like their national counterparts, attracted both praise and con-
demnation—even congressional inquiry. Initially, state, community,
and church leaders heralded generous donors as civic stewards and
"great benefactors." Others, such as sociologist Dr. Robert Sutherland, "the most knowledgeable person in the Southwest on matters relative to philanthropic foundations," lauded the generosity
of wealthy Texans who "like to make money and they also like to
give money." But the vast accumulation of private wealth in au-
tonomous grant-making institutions aroused suspicions as early as
1915. With their tax-exempt status and self-perpetuating boards of
directors, usually composed of family members, private foundations
functioned as "exclusive clubs" with little oversight. Furthermore,
many operated behind a shroud of secrecy and, before 1969, without governmental constraints. As a consequence, the U.S. Congress
undertook several investigations throughout the twentieth century
into their unparalleled financial and political influence. In particular,
in 1961 Representative Wright Patman of Texarkana conducted an
inquiry into their "undesirable concentration of economic power."
Although Texas foundations were never at the nerve center of Pat-

man's ire—he was targeting larger, national funds—he placed nine philanthropic foundations in Texas on a list of suspect institutions. His sustained attack on the foundation world resulted in the passage of the Tax Reform Act of 1969, which altered and reformed the practices of organized philanthropy, including those operating in Texas.[41]

Despite the praiseworthy efforts by many early Texas philanthropists and the commendable missions of their private foundations, wealthy donors did not always address the immediate social and racial problems facing the state. By favoring long-term solutions over immediate relief, they rarely used their wealth or position to challenge the status quo, which in Jim Crow Texas meant segregation, discrimination, even lynching. Instead, until the mid-1960s wealthy Texans used their resources to assist minorities within the prevailing class system of "separate but equal" facilities. For instance, George Brackenridge aided black colleges; Jesse Jones assisted black churches and schools; and Amon Carter financed improvements at segregated parks.

Initially, during the most recent stage of philanthropic development since 1970, start-up foundations declined in the wake of the Tax Reform Act of 1969. Weakened tax incentives and negative asset growth from the new legislation, as well as shrinking resources from the financial market collapse of 1973–1974, resulted in a decline in new Texas foundations. With the surge in oil prices in the mid-1970s, however, petroleum revenues once again encouraged institutional philanthropy. According to the 1982 *Directory of Texas Foundations*, Texas donors founded 950 additional foundations, many of them fueled by the upward oil and financial markets. After 1983, when oil rates dropped precipitously and the Texas economy stagnated, contributions to grant-making institutions fell once again. Not until a decade later, with the added stimulation of electronics and "high tech" plants, did the recession ebb, thereby creating a younger, more socially diverse class of wealthy Texans who could leverage their private wealth for the public good.[42]

During the last quarter of the twentieth century new Texas business entrepreneurs generated additional philanthropic capital. The emerging information and computer technology, the tele-communications industry, and global market expansion, such as the North American Free Trade Agreement (NAFTA), led to an increase in the number of wealthy Texans. These "modern-day Gilded Age millionaires" applied the same kind of entrepreneurial drive and public-spiritedness to their "getting" and "giving" as did the early pioneers. But there were some differences. Many created their foundations at a much earlier age and while they were still building their financial empires. For example, H. Ross Perot (EDS) was thirty-nine years old when he established the Perot Foundation (1969) to support higher education, the Salvation Army, and the Presbyterian Church. Billy Joe "Red" McCombs (Red McCombs Automotive Group, Clear Channel Communications, and several sports franchises) started the McCombs Foundation (1981) at age fifty-four to provide grants to the arts, education, and medical re-search. And Michael Dell (Dell Computers) was only thirty-four years old when he and his wife Susan created their foundation. Its mission was to enhance the quality of life in communities where Dell employees lived and worked, as well as to benefit youth "to excel in a world driven by the digital economy." In addition, a few members of this new breed of goal-oriented donors promoted "so-cial venture philanthropy"—the application of business expertise to the nonprofit sector—with expectations of tangible results from their grantees. Thus, by the end of the twentieth century the *Directory of Texas Foundations* listed an additional 1,718 private founda-tions, an increase of approximately 85 percent since the 1980s.[43]

One recent private foundation, the Summerlee Foundation, in particular has benefited the promotion and study of Texas history. Created in 1988 by Dallas philanthropist Annie Lee Roberts, the organization derived its name from Roberts' middle name and that of her late husband, Summerfield G. Roberts, a successful oil executive and business leader. The foundation championed two distinct, but different causes—animal protection and Texas history. Sensitive all her life to the pain and suffering sustained by animals, Roberts restricted foundation grants to programs that supported animal shelters, wildlife sanctuaries, and emergency care. In addition, due to her family's pioneering efforts in Texas, dating from 1825, as well as the interests of her husband, who had supported research and writing on the Republic of Texas, she also selected Texas history as an additional recipient for grants. Today, the Summerlee Foundation is one of the leading philanthropic organizations in the state that specifically promotes Texas history by funding scholarly research, historical events, restoration projects, and other endeavors such as the publication of *The New Handbook of Texas* (1996) and the recovery of La Salle's ship, the *Belle*, from Matagorda Bay in 1996–1997.[44]

During the final decades of the twentieth century, following the corrective provisions of the Tax Reform Act of 1969, a basic philosophical shift had occurred within the Texas philanthropic community. While some larger eastern foundations such as the Ford Foundation had already provided more transparency to their grant making, many Texas foundations were slower to comply. Some feared negative publicity might someday destroy the independence of family foundations, another hallmark of private philanthropy. Nevertheless, the CSF recommended that foundations and their donors become less secretive, even self-promotional, and educate the public about their good work. Increasingly, they issued annual reports, published newsletters, publicized their grant-making guidelines, and establishing partnerships with their grantees. Rather than a "top-down" management style, foundations began to emphasize a less elitist, more "bottom-up" approach, thereby hoping to forestall future congressional inquiries and foster goodwill. At the same time more women and minorities, as they gained access to power and wealth, established their own philanthropies and occupied the ranks of professional positions within public and private foundations. For example, Clarence R. "Reggie" Williams, an African American, is the president of the San Antonio Area Foundation, Mary Kay Ash founded the Mary Kay Ash Charitable Foundation (1996) using profits from her cosmetics empire, and Mary M. Jalonick heads the Dallas Foundation.[45]

That Texas and Texans have benefited from private philanthropy is undeniable. Much of the social and cultural infrastructure of the state would not exist without it, including Brackenridge Park and the Mexican American Cultural Center in San Antonio, Hogg Auditorium and the Peoples Community Clinic in Austin, Bass Performance Hall and the Amon Carter Museum in Fort Worth, the Houston Symphony and M. D. Anderson Cancer Center in Houston, the Museum of Natural History and the West Dallas Multipurpose Center in Dallas, the Rosenberg Library and John Sealy Hospital in Galveston, the Julie Rogers Theater for the Performing Arts in Beaumont, the Stark Museum in Orange, Ballet of the Americas in El Paso, Senior Citizens Services of Wichita Falls, Driscoll Children's Hospital in Corpus Christi, and the South Plains Wildlife Rehabilitation Center in Lubbock, as well as numerous other libraries, youth camps, hospitals, schools, universities, scholarships, museums, research centers, and community projects. By supporting "ladders upon which the aspiring can rise," Texas philanthropists have helped bridge the gap between the "haves" and the "havenots." Without the use of private wealth for the public good, the social and cultural landscape of Texas would look very different.

So as Texans enter the new millennium, as more citizens accumulate surplus funds, and as aging baby boomers prepare for retirement—and the projected multi-million dollar intergenerational transfer of wealth—Texans are uniquely positioned to create unprecedented philanthropic capital. Unlike earlier donors, a large portion of the assets of twenty-first century Texas philanthropists will be inherited and unearned. But many of the problems faced by earlier generations remain: legislative budgetary cuts to social programs such as the Children's Health Insurance Program (CHIP), the rising cost of public education, the under-funding of cultural and artistic endeavors, and the personal and financial devastation caused by natural disasters such as Hurricane Rita in 2005. Whether and how Texans leverage their private wealth for the public good is the major question for the twenty-first century.[46]

Selected Bibliography

Barr, Alwyn. "The Other Texas: Charities and Community in the Lone Star State." *Southwestern Historical Quarterly* 97 (July 1993): 1–10.

Carnegie, Andrew. "Wealth." *North American Review*, 148 (June 1889): 653–64.

Culler, Ralph E., III, and Wayne H. Holtzman. *The Ima Hogg Foundation: Miss Ima's Legacy to the Children of Houston*. Austin: Hogg Foundation for Mental Health, 1990.

Garrett, Judith. *A History of the Dallas Foundation, 1920–1991*. Dallas: Dallas Foundation, 1991.

Howard, James. *Foundation Philanthropy in Texas*. Austin: University of Texas Press,1963.

Hyman, Harold M. *Oleander Odyssey: The Kempners of Galveston, Texas, 1854–1980s*. College Station: Texas A&M University Press, 1990.

Kelley, Mary L. *The Foundations of Texan Philanthropy*. College Station: Texas A&M University Press, 2004.

Lagemann, Ellen Condliffe, ed., *Philanthropic Foundations: New Scholarship, New Possibilities*. Bloomington: Indiana University Press, 1999.

McCarthy, Kathleen D. *Lady Bountiful Revisited: Women, Philanthropy, and Power*. New Brunswick, N. J.: Rutgers University Press, 1990.

Nielsen, Waldemar. *Inside American Philanthropy: The Dramas of Donorship*. Norman: University of Oklahoma Press, 1996.

Peyton, Robert L. *Philanthropy: Voluntary Action for the Public Good*. New York: American Council on Education and Macmillan, 1988.

Sealander, Judith. *Private Wealth & Public Life: Foundation Philanthropy and the Reshaping of American Social Policy from the Progressive Era to the New Deal*. Baltimore: Johns Hopkins University Press, 1997.

Sibley, Marilyn McAdams. *George W. Brackenridge: Maverick Philanthro-pist*. Austin: University of Texas Press, 1973.

Endnotes

1. The word *philanthropy*, meaning love of mankind, comes from the Greeks. The American philanthropic tradition dates back to 1492 when the native inhabitants of San Salvador and Hispaniola were "ingenuous and free" with their possessions to Christopher Columbus and his men after landfall in the New World. It continued in the colonial period when Massachusetts Bay Governor John Winthrop urged each person to "afford his help to another in every want and distress." Furthermore, those of greater means should aid "the poor and inferior sort," becoming stewards of God's wealth. Frenchman Alexis de Tocqueville observed in the nine-teenth century that Americans relied on each other for their needs, such as hospitals and schools, and "spontaneously and eagerly" lent assistance to one another. British author James Bryce observed in 1888: "Nowhere is money so readily given for any public purpose" or "so many acts of private kindness done" than in the United States. And historian Arthur M. Schle-singer, Sr., asserted in 1953 that successful citizens have always "shared their money with others . . . returning at least part of their substance to channels of social usefulness through munificent gifts and bequests." Al-wyn Barr, "The Other Texas: Charities and Community in the Lone Star State," *Southwestern Historical Quarterly* 97 (July 1993): 1; Peggy Hil-dreth, "Howard Associations," *New Handbook of Texas*, ed. by Ron Tyler et al, Austin: Texas State Historical Association, 1996, vol. 3, 747–48.

2. See Andrew Carnegie, "Wealth," *North American Review* 148 (June 1889): 653–64, and Richard Hofstadter, *Social Darwinism in American Thought* (New York: Braziller, 1956).

3. F. Emerson Andrews, an early authority on organized philanthropy, defined a foundation as "a nongovernmental, nonprofit organization hav-ing a principal fund of its own, managed by its own trustees or directors, and established to maintain or aid social, educational, charitable, religious, or other activities serving the common welfare." Steel master Andrew Car-negie established his first general-purpose foundation in 1911. Statistics in 2006 confirm that more individuals (75 percent) practice charitable giving than start foundations (12 percent). See F. Emerson Andrews, *Philanthropic Foundations* (New York: Russell Sage Foundation, 1956); Carnegie, "Wealth," 660–63; Barr, "The Other Texas," 3, 6; Robert H. Bremner, *American Philanthropy*, 2nd ed. (Chicago: University of Chi-cago Press, 1988), 3.

4. See Bremner, *American Philanthropy*, and Lawrence J. Friedman and Mark D. McGarvie, eds., *Charity, Philanthropy, and Civility in Amer-*

ican History (Cambridge: Cambridge University Press, 2003).

5. See Lewis L. Gould, *Progressives and Prohibitionists: Texas Democrats in the Wilson Era* (Austin: University of Texas Press, 1973). Also, Judith N. McArthur, *Creating the New Woman: The Rise of Southern Women's Progressive Culture in Texas, 1893–1918* (Urbana: University of Illinois Press), 31–96ff.

6. See Louis J. Rodriquez and Yoshi Fukasawa, eds., *The Texas Economy* (Wichita Falls, Tex.: Midwestern State University Press, 1996).

7. See Frances Atwood, ed., *Directory of Texas Foundations,* 19th ed. (San Antonio: Nonprofit Resource Center, 2000.)

8. The Civil War divided the Brackenridge family: three brothers fought in the Confederate army while George, a Unionist, served with the U.S. Treasury Department. *San Antonio Express,* December 29, 1920, p. 1; Sibley, *George W. Brackenridge: Maverick Philanthropist* (Austin: University of Texas Press), 5–8.

9. *San Antonio Express,* January 14, 1912, p. 12A; December 29, 1921, p. 6; "Two Interesting Wills," *Alcalde* 10 (November 1922): 1519; Roy Bedichek, "The Patron Saint of the University of Texas," *Alcalde* 5 (April 1917): 481–83; Sibley, *George W. Brackenridge,* 15–16.

10. *San Antonio Express,* December 30, 1921, p. 1; December 26, 1921, p. 8; *Austin American,* January 11, 1921, p. 1A; Sibley, *George W. Brackenridge,* 254.

11. Gilbert M. Denman, Jr. (Brackenridge Foundation trustee), interview by author, October 21, 1997, San Antonio; *Austin American,* July 19, 1936; Franklin, "George W. Brackenridge," *Alcalde* 8 (March 1921): 407, 410; Sibley, *George W. Brackenridge,* 6.

12. Mary L. Kelley, *The Foundations of Texan Philanthropy* (College Station: Texas A&M University Press, 2004), 91.

13. David C. Hammack, "Community Foundation: The Delicate Question of Purpose," in *An Agile Servant: Community Leadership by Community Foundations,* Richard Magat, ed. (New York: Council on Foundations, 1989), 28–32.

14. Dallas was founded in 1841 by John Neely Bryan who parked his covered wagon on the east bank of the Trinity River. U.S. Bureau of the Census, *Fourteenth Census of the United States, 1920,* vol. 2, Washington D.C.: Government Printing Office, 1922, 133; Kenneth B. Ragsdale, *The Year America Discovered Texas: Centennial '36* (College Station: Texas A&M University Press, 1987), 82–83.

15. See Robert B. Fairbanks, *For the City as a Whole: Planning, Politics, and the Public Interest in Dallas Texas, 1900–1965* (Columbus: Ohio State University Press, 1998); Michael V. Hazel, "The Critic Club: Sixty Years of Quiet Leadership," *Legacies* 2 (Fall 1990): 9–17ff; Judith Garrett, *A History of the Dallas Foundation, 1920–1991* (Dallas: Dallas Foundation, 1991), 6–10, 30–31.

16. George B. Dealey to O. D. Montgomery, April 23, 1930; George B. Dealey to A. H. Bailey, June 11, 1930, A6667 File 44, George B. Dealey Papers (hereafter referred to as GBDP); Robert Lee Bobbitt to Dealey, Nov. 15, 1929, A6667, File 43A, GBDP; Dealey to Briggs, October 22, 1930, A6667, File 44A, GBDP; Ernest Sharpe, *G. B. Dealey of the Dallas News* (New York: Holt, 1955), 278.

17. See Ben Procter, "Texas From Depression Through World War II," in *Texas Heritage*, 4th ed., Ben Procter and Archie P. McDonald, eds. (Wheeling, Ill.: Harlan Davidson,) 162–181. Dealey to Hayes, January 5, 1931, A6667, File 46, GBDP; Briggs to McNeny, April 15, 1930, *Archive Book: Dallas Community Trust and Dallas Foundation, 1930–1961,* (Dallas: n.p., n.d.), 7; *Dallas Morning News,* June 30, 1929; Garrett, *History of The Dallas Foundation,* 3, 12–20; *Texas Business Review* (July 28, 1932): 2–3; *Dallas Foundation 2000 Annual Report,* 4–7.

18. Peter Dobkin Hall, "The Historical Overview of the Nonprofit Sector," in *The Nonprofit Sector: A Research Handbook,* Walter W. Powell, ed. (New Haven: Yale University Press, 1987), 15–18.

19. See Robert C. Cotner, ed. *Texas Cities and the Great Depression* (Austin: Texas Memorial Museum, 1973), and James Smallwood, *The Great Recovery: The New Deal in Texas* (Boston: American Press, 1983).

20. As vice president Garner once counseled his friend: "Jesse, Congress has given you powers which no man ought to have, and I know of no one but you who could get them." Walter L. Buenger, "Between Community and Corporation: The Southern Roots of Jesse H. Jones and the Reconstruction Finance Corporation," *Journal of Southern History* 46 (August 1990): 482–85.

21. *Houston Post,* April 21, 1934; June 2, 1956; *Houston Chronicle,* June 2, 1956; *Saturday Evening Post,* December 7, 1940; Bascom N. Timmons, *Jesse H. Jones: The Man and the Statesman* (New York: Holt, 1956), 72, 76–66, 117, 153–61.

22. Memorandum, pp. 1–2, Box 3M484, File: Book Files, *Jesse H. Jones: The Man and the Statesman,* Jesse H. Jones Papers (hereafter referred to as JHJP); *Saturday Evening Post,* November 30, 1940; December 7, 1940; *Houston Chronicle,* June 2, 1956; Timmons, *Jesse H. Jones,* 129–30.

23. *Houston Endowment, Inc.: A Report of the First Twenty-five Years,* Houston: Houston Endowment, 1962, 4–5; Jesse Jones to Mike Hogg and Raymond Dickson, June 13, 1924, File Quotes, Houston Endowment Archives, Houston, Texas; Timmons, *Jesse H. Jones,* 377–378.

24. Box 3M491, File Misc. Files: Houston Endowment, Info, Questionnaire answers, pp. 2, 28, JHJP; Background—Mrs. Jesse Holman Jones, p. 6, Box 3M472, File Posthumous Files, Texas Heritage Foundation release, May 27, 1958, JHJP; Timmons, *Jesse H. Jones,* 377; Andrew Carnegie, "Wealth," *North American Review* 148 (June 1889): 663.

25. Joanne Scanlan, ed., *Culture of Caring: Philanthropy in Diverse American Communities* (New York: Council on Foundations, 1999), 15–18; Emmett D. Carson, "The Evolution of Black Philanthropy: Patterns of Giving and Voluntarism" in *Philanthropic Giving: Studies in Varieties and Goals* by Richard Magat, ed. (New York: Oxford University Press, 1989), 92–102.

26. See Anne Firor Scott, *Natural Allies: Women's Associations in American History* (Chicago: University of Illinois Press, 1993). Also see McArthur, *Creating the New Woman.*

27. See Joan M. Fisher, "A Study of Six Women Philanthropists of the Early Twentieth Century," Ph.D. dissertation, Union Institute, Cincinnati, Ohio, 1992.

28. *Houston Post,* August 21, 1975, pp. 1A, 21; *Houston Chronicle,* August 21, 1975, sec 4, p. 4; philanthropic, civic, and cultural activities, Box 2.325/D31a, Ima Hogg Papers, Center for American History, University of Texas, Austin, Texas (hereafter cited as IHP); Kate S. Kirkland, "A Wholesome Life: Ima Hogg's Vision for Mental Health Care," *Southwestern Historical Quarterly* 104 (January 2001): 417–19; Kathleen McCarthy, *Noblesse Oblige: American Philanthropy and Art, 1830–1930* (Chicago: University of Chicago Press, 1991), ix.

29. Box 3F389, Hogg Family Papers, Center for American History, University of Texas, Austin, Texas. See also will of Will Hogg, p. 405, Box 2J330, Will Hogg Papers, Center for American History, University of Texas, Austin, Texas; *The Hogg Foundation for Mental Health: The First Three Decades, 1940–1970* (Austin: Hogg Foundation for Mental Health, 1970), vii-vii, 13; Louise K. Iscoe, *Ima Hogg: First Lady of Texas* (Austin: Hogg Foundation for Mental Health), 27.

30. Kirkland, "A Wholesome Life," 424–25; Iscoe, *Ima Hogg,* 7; Virginia Bernhard, *Ima Hogg: The Governor's Daughter* (Austin: Texas Monthly Press, 1984), 59.

31. Ima Hogg, Condensed Notes, Intent of Trust, p. 1, Box 4W241, File Activities: Statewide, IHP; "Hogg Foundation Inaugurated on Campus," *Alcalde* 6 (March 1941): 128.

32. Ima Hogg, interview by Robert Sutherland, November 21, 1961, p. 3, in possession of author; Condensed Notes, p. 2, IHP; Uriel E. Dutton to Ima Hogg, April 5, 1964, pp. 1–2, Box 4W241, File Activities; Statewide, IHP; *Houston Chronicle,* August 21, 1975, sec. 4, p. 4; *Houston Post,* August 22, 1975, p. 8A; Ralph E. Culler III and Wayne H. Holtzman, *The Ima Hogg Foundation: Miss Ima's Legacy to the Children of Houston* (Austin: Hogg Foundation, 1990), 5-31ff.

33. *Fort Worth Star-Telegram,* June 25, 1955, pp. 1-2; Jerry Flemmons, *Amon: The Life of Amon Carter, Sr., of Texas* (Austin: Jenkins, 1978), 57, 109–122; Oliver Knight, *Fort Worth: Outpost on the Trinity* (Fort Worth: Texas Christian University Press, 1990), 123–49ff.

34. Manuscript, pp. 1–4, Record Group H, Box 7, File Amon G. Carter, Personal, 1941, Amon G. Carter Papers, Texas Christian University, Fort Worth, Texas (hereafter cited as AGCP); John B. Brewer to the *Fort Worth Star-Telegram*, December 15, 1923, Record Group J, Box 1, AGCP; *Fort Worth Star-Telegram*, June 25, 1955, pp. 2, 8; *Fort Worth Star-Telegram, Jr.*, February 2, 1954; July 1955, p. 3; March 25, 1978, sec B, p. 1.

35. *Fort Worth Star-Telegram*, August 31, 1947, sec 3., p. 1; June 24, 1955, p. 2; June 25, 1955, p. 2; Historical Committee of the Fort Worth Petroleum Club, *Oil Legends of Fort Worth* (Dallas: Taylor, 1993), 94.

36. Chartered in 1945, the Carter Foundation began active operation in September 1947. Clipping, *Pecten* (September 1947): 3, Record Group H, Box 8, File Amon G. Carter Foundation, 1945–1947, AGCP; Disposition of Income, Dues, Contributions, etc., 1947–1951, p. 1012, AGCF; Amon Carter will, pp. 5, 14–31ff, AGCP.

37. Carter will, pp. 24–31ff, AGCP; *Fort Worth Star Telegram*, June 24, 1955, p. 1; August 18, 1963, sec 4, p. 3; Flemmons, *Amon*, 81, 309; *Amon Carter Museum of Western* Art (Fort Worth: Amon Carter Museum, 1973), 1; *Fort Worth Builds an Art Center* (Fort Worth: Fort Worth Art Association, 1952), 4–12.

38. Harold M. Hyman, *Oleander Odyssey: The Kempners of Galveston, Texas, 1854–1980s* (College Station: Texas A&M University Press, 1990), 5–16, 70–79, 422–28; Waldemar A. Nielsen, *The Big Foundations* (New York: Columbia University Press, 1972), 151–57.

39. See Francie Ostrower, *Why the Wealthy Give: The Culture of Elite Philanthropy* (Princeton, N.J.: Princeton University Press, 1995).

40. The Foundation Center in New York was not founded until 1956, eight years after the CSF. Maud Keeling, "Background of the Conference of Southwest Foundations," February 1959, p. 1, Box 2.325/V126a, File 1959, Annual Conference, Conference of Southwest Foundations, Center for American History, Austin, Tex.; Kelley, *Foundations of Texan Philanthropy*, 70–79.

41. Congressional investigations started in 1915 with the Walsh Commission, followed by the Cox Committee investigation in 1952, the Reece Committee investigation in 1953–1954, and the Patman investigation in 1961. The announced intention of the Patman investigation was to study the impact of foundations upon the economy, especially their tax-exempt status, unreasonable accumulation of income, and political activities. The Patman probe targeted the Amon G. Carter Foundation, the Houston Endowment, M. D. Anderson Foundation, Clayton Foundation for Research, the Cullen Foundation, the Gulf Oil Foundation, the Hoblitzelle Foundation, the Moody Foundation, and the Robert A. Welch Foundation. The provisions of the Tax Reform Act of 1969 included a 4 percent annual excise tax on net investment income, prohibitions against self deal-

ing, a 6 percent annual pay out of assets (later lowered to 5 percent), a 20 percent limitation on ownership of any corporation, restrictions on political activities, and various disclosure requirements. See Joseph C. Kiger, *Philanthropic Foundations in the Twentieth Century* (Westport, Conn.: Greenwood Press, 2000), 21–38; and Thomas C. Reeves, ed. *Foundations Under Fire* (Ithaca: Cornell University Press, 1970). Also see House, *Chairman's (Patman) Report to the Select Committee on Small Business, Tax-Exempt Foundations and Charitable Trusts: Their Impact on Our Economy*, 87th Cong., 2nd sess., 1962; Robert Sutherland, interview by Graham Blackstock, October 30, 1971, Box 3M361, File: Talk Notes: Austin, Texas, Robert Sutherland Papers, Center for American History, Austin, Texas; *San Antonio Express*, December 29, 1920, pp. 2, 6; December 30, 1920, pp. 1–2.

42. See Atwood, ed., *Directory of Texas Foundations*, 1982.

43. Carnegie was sixty-six and John D. Rockefeller was seventy-four years old when they turned to organized philanthropy. See Atwood, ed., *Directory of Texas Foundations*, 2000.

44. "Summerlee Foundation," *New Handbook of Texas*, vol. 6, 148–49; "Summerfield G. Roberts," *New Handbook of Texas*, vol. 5, 612–13.

45. Lucy Bernholz, "The Future of Foundation History," in *Philanthropic Foundations: New Scholarship, New Possibilities*, edited by Ellen Condliffe Lagemann (Bloomington: Indiana University Press, 1999), 359–64.

46. Mark Dowie, *American Foundations: An Investigative History* (Cambridge: MIT Press, 2001), 266.

Public Education Comes of Age

Gene B. Preuss

ON JANUARY 24, 2001, PRESIDENT George W. Bush swore in former Houston Independent School District superintendent Roderick Paige as secretary of education. In extolling the qualifications of the new secretary, Bush told the audience that they were about "to witness the swearing-in of a man who will help us see important reforms for education become reality." Paige was an ideal choice as the nation's new education czar because, Bush continued, "Every problem now facing our nation's public schools Dr. Paige faced as superintendent of the Houston Independent School District — children unable to read at basic levels; falling scores in science and math; problems with discipline and order." Bush announced at the beginning of his administration that he wanted to be known as the "education president." He claimed that education reform was "the hallmark of my time as governor of Texas," and, likewise, he would make education his "first priority as president, first in time, and first in importance."[1]

How did Texas public schools become the prototype for national public school reform? It seems that Texas spent much of the last half of the twentieth century in the public education spotlight. Texans first came to national prominence in education during the 1950s when President Dwight Eisenhower named Houston newspaper publisher Oveta Culp Hobby as the first secretary of Health,

Education and Welfare. Texan Lyndon Johnson became the first president to earn the moniker "education president" by signing over 60 major legislative initiatives to restructure the nation's education system. Later Texas Tech President Dr. Lauro Cavazos, who grew up on the King Ranch, was secretary of education during the Ronald Reagan and George H. W. Bush administrations. Few, however, would have predicted at the beginning of the twentieth century that the state could claim a role in the leadership of a national educational initiative.

The history of Texas education during the twentieth century is one of tremendous change affecting the majority of the state's population. Educational history is tied to almost every historical topic in twentieth-century Texas, from politics and the state's economic development and infrastructure to social and cultural topics, including race relations, women's rights, family history, the history of childhood, the growth of professions, and labor movements. Despite the importance of public education in Texas, few historians have written at length about the development of the state's public education system. Historians published only two books focusing upon the development of education in the state during the twentieth century. In 1925, Frederick Eby wrote *The Development of Education in Texas*, and thirty years later, former Southwest Texas State Teacher's College president Cecil Evans wrote the *Story of Texas Schools*. Despite the absence of more recent surveys, there are several identifiable themes in the history of Texas public education. Educational analyst Louann Bierlein Palmer identified "four underlying societal values [that] drive debates within the educational policy arena" at the national level: equity, efficiency, liberty, and excellence. These same themes are reflected in the development of Texas education, a story that involves transportation issues, civil rights, taxation, centralization at the state and national levels, federal funding, social services, school choice, free lunches, mandatory attendance, and home schooling. During the first two decades of the twentieth century, rural schools became the focus of reformers interested in providing rural children with equitable educational opportunities. During the next few decades, Progressive-Era reformers stressed the need for better efficiency in public school administration, at both the local and state levels. Prior to American involvement in World War II and for the next two decades, politicians and reformers stressed the importance of education in the struggle to preserve democracy. Since the 1960s, the discussion about public education has focused on the results of our educational system. Fearing that American public schooling underprepared students for the competitive world economy, Americans wanted their children to attend the best schools, and they raised questions about the quality the public education system provided. This essay touches briefly on these issues, primarily addressing the evolution of the state-supported public education system at the grade school level (1–12).[2]

At the dawn of the twentieth century the school system was rudimentary, without any standard of pedagogical or curriculum expectations. Only two decades earlier, in 1880, Governor O. M. Roberts vetoed an education appropriations bill, threatening to bring a halt to the state's public schools. Four factors, however, assisted in improving Texas schools. First, the state legislature reestablished the office of state superintendent in the mid-1880s as a two-year elected position. Many of the men and women who served as superintendent made recommendations to strengthen the state's public education system, especially suggesting investment initiatives to encourage public school buildings. The University of Texas was a second factor. When the university opened in the early 1880s, it faced the dilemma of recruiting enough qualified students to fill the new classrooms. The state had few high schools, and unless the university included a remedial program, it needed some way of ensuring a curriculum at the state's high schools to develop an adequately prepared student body. In 1885 the university began to accredit high schools on a voluntary basis. Third, late in the nineteenth century the Sam Houston Normal School in Huntsville admitted state-supported students who would learn teaching methods, then return as professionally trained teachers to their home areas in exchange for their education. The legislature expanded its effort to train more teachers with the establishment of two normal schools in 1899, the North Texas State Normal School in Denton and the Southwest Texas State Normal School in San Marcos, to supplement the work of the Sam Houston Normal School. Finally, educational associations such as the Texas State Teachers Association and the Teachers State Association of Texas provided organized voices beginning in the 1880s for white and African-American educators, respectively, and called attention to the needs of the state's public schools.[3]

These four factors were part of the Progressive education reforms that called for increased professionalization and efficiency in public education, while adhering to the policy of Jim Crow segregation. In the first two decades of the twentieth century, Progressive reformers encouraged legislation to improve public education, including free textbooks and mandatory attendance laws. They supported organization-building efforts, such as the development of the University Interscholastic League as part of the extension service at the University of Texas (and soon thereafter the segregated Prairie View Interscholastic League) and the Texas Congress of Mothers and Parent-Teacher Associations (soon followed by the Texas Congress of Colored Parents and Teachers, later renamed the Texas Congress of Parents and Teachers). Texas educational Progressives especially identified funding inequality and economic waste in rural schools. Rural areas operated under the common school system. If enough parents made a request to the county school board, communities could operate schools wherever a parent or group of parents could find accommodations. The legislature, on the other hand, mandated that cities establish independent school districts that operated on a more permanent basis in dedicated buildings.

Because of higher tax bases, urban schools usually paid better salaries, attracted better qualified teachers, provided better buildings that included libraries, and offered a wider curriculum. This created a disparity between rural and urban areas.

No better window into the troubles of rural farm life and deficiencies of rural Texas public education at the turn of the century exists than William A. Owens' autobiographical account of his childhood in northeast Texas, *This Stubborn Soil* (1966). In the book, Owens describes his attempt to get an education despite the inadequacies of his local rural public schools. There have been several oral histories of early twentieth-century one-room schools, but they are suspect because of a tendency to romanticize the past. It is useful to remember that many who have fond memories of one-room schools were children at the time. The memoirs of rural schoolteachers, on the other hand, often recall the problems associated with teaching in makeshift classrooms, trying to establish discipline, and having few, if any, supplies.[4]

Texas educational historian Frederick Eby blamed poorly equipped schools on voters. The public had been led to believe that the schools were well-funded by the permanent school fund—income projected by the sale of land set aside to fund public schools. Eby wrote that the voters believed that with the vast amount of land available to fund schools, extra taxation to support public education was unnecessary. Moreover, "the majority of the people had no knowledge whatever of genuine standards of educational achievement. Having attended only the makeshift schools of the rural districts and never having seen any progressive methods, it was quite impossible for them to visualize the new spirit and the techniques of up-to-date instruction."[5]

In early 1907 a group of education professionals and interested laypeople formed the Conference for Education in Texas (CET). The CET modeled itself after the Conference for Education in the South, a reform group that sought to publicize the need to improve southern education in order to attract increased business opportunities and provide a general uplift for southern rural children. The southern conference also received additional funding and support from the Rockefeller Foundation's General Education Board. Texas, however, was not included in the philanthropy because of the state's abundant natural resources, namely oil and natural gas, which were becoming apparent at the turn of the century. Finally, with the prodding of educational leaders, the CET was formed. It included among its members University of Texas education professor William Seneca Sutton, State Superintendent Robert Bartow Cousins, former state superintendent and then-president of Sam Houston Normal Institute Henry Carr Pritchett, and newspaper editor and educational promoter Clarence N. Ousley, who had also been a school teacher in Waxahachie. The conference received financial assistance from the George Peabody Educational Fund and some $10,000 donated by Texas teachers. Although the CET dissolved after five years, efforts to improve the state's public school system attracted the attention of many groups.[6]

One of the goals of the CET was to expand educational opportunities for rural school children. Writing in 1925, Eby again reflected the common attitude school reformers held about the plight of rural education:

> It is well-nigh incredible that such gross inequalities should be permitted to grow up among a people who claimed to be democratic. But still more astonishing is the fact that these unjust discriminations against the country children had their foundations in the laws and constitution of the state; they were not accidental, or due merely to the unfavorable circumstances of a pioneer people. The country people were not allowed the same freedom of judgment and action in the management of their schools that was granted to the parents and citizens of the towns.[7]

Efforts to improve rural schools coincided with a nationwide interest in farm problems. As a result, advocates established the Country Life Movement, an interest group supporting a back-to the-farm lifestyle. With increased industrialization and urbanization in the late nineteenth and early twentieth centuries there was a fear that the nation's farmers would leave the farms for jobs in the cities. In 1915 the president of the Texas Farmers' Congress, H. E. Singleton, echoed this concern. "The country man is fast recognizing that the towns are drawing the best and strongest character from the country to the town." Furthermore, he observed that "the towns have noted an increase in their population of retired farmers." This led Eby to conclude that "the country has lost much, and the towns gain but little by the change." In 1907 the movement drew presidential support when President Theodore Roosevelt assigned a Country Life Commission to look into improving rural life. The commission devoted special attention to the nation's rural schools. Education for farm families was no longer a luxury; it was imperative if the farms were to survive.[8]

Texas Governor James "Farmer Jim" Ferguson was also a strong supporter of rural school reform. He advocated and won legislative support for the "Million Dollar Appropriation for Rural Schools." Ferguson's efforts were stymied, however, when he became embroiled in a battle with the University of Texas Board of Regents that culminated in his impeachment. As World War I ended Texas voters elected William P. Hobby to replace Ferguson.

Hobby earned the support of Texas suffragettes and enlisted Annie Webb Blanton, a member of the English faculty at North Texas State Normal College, to run for the post of state superintendent. Blanton had been the first woman elected president of the Texas State Teachers Association. She then became the first Texas woman elected to public office, serving two terms as state superintendent. During her first term Blanton organized the Better Schools Campaign to persuade voters to approve a constitutional amendment that would allow local districts to increase the property tax to support public schools. After the war, however, the state's economic problems made it more difficult to finance the school system's costs.[9]

The Better Schools Campaign became a grassroots movement with a massive distribution of literature, public speeches, songs, slogans, and press support. One flyer informed voters that despite the state's tremendous wealth, public schools in Texas ranked far behind that of other states:

TEXAS

First in Size.
First in Agricultural Products.
First in Production of Cotton.
Third in Production of Oil.
Seventh in Wealth.
Thirty-Ninth in Education.

Shall Texas keep this rank?[10]

The Better Schools Campaign was successful, and the amendment passed by a margin of almost two to one.[11]

Debbie Cottrell's biography of Annie Webb Blanton remains the only published study of this remarkable woman. Cottrell's monograph also describes the Progressive Era in Texas and the political, cultural, and social events in which Blanton participated, including the groundswell of opposition to Governor Ferguson after he declared a funding war on the University of Texas. Cottrell also notes that Blanton's opportunities came because of increased educational opportunities for women in higher education, such as the creation in 1903 of the first state-supported college for women—the Girls Industrial College (now Texas Woman's University). "Blanton herself," Cottrell writes, "would not have risen to face the challenges of reforming Texas schools in the twentieth century without . . . the broadening of higher educational opportunities, including the increasing place for women in such facilities." Blanton's life and work also displayed racism against ethnic and racial minorities, reflective of one of the negative aspects of the Progressive movement. Cottrell considers Blanton a product of her time, stating that she "shared the prevalent attitude of her time that racially segregated schools were socially and educationally appropriate." Although Blanton believed education for African Americans needed improvement, she never made it a high priority. Cottrell concludes that "indifference more than outright opposition characterized [Blanton's] attitude toward improving education for black students."[12]

Historian Carlos Blanton, however, views the Progressive educational reformer much more critically. He notes that the Progressive Era coincided with an Americanization movement in the United States. Increased immigration nationwide occurred about the same time that Mexican immigration to Texas increased, fueled by the Mexican Revolution and greater economic opportunities north of the Rio Grande. Carlos Blanton places Annie Webb Blanton's administration at the heart of the "institutionalization of Americanization in Texas," arguing that Annie Webb Blanton supported a nativist campaign that "intermingled education policy with the potent issues of prohibition, wartime loyalty, anti-Germanism, and anticommunism." The legislature passed the state's first effective English-only law during World War I, but afterwards, with the anti-German campaign fading, Superintendent Blanton shifted from enforcing Americanization for German Americans toward Americanization for Mexican and Mexican-American students. Annie Webb Blanton's life and career clearly illustrate the many paradoxes of the Progressive movement and educational reformers of the period. Despite her concern for rural school reform and stronger financial support for public education in general, she exhibited the racial attitudes of her era. At the same time, Blanton believed in a meritocracy, that talent and experience should play a more important role than other considerations such as gender and race. She incorporated this concept into the professional educators' sorority she founded in 1929, Delta Kappa Gamma.[13]

School reformers during the inter-war period also took advantage of school surveys, a tool that was growing in popularity in school systems around the nation. In 1923 George A. Works led the first major survey under the auspices of the Texas Educational Survey Commission. The Commission published its findings in 1925 in eight volumes entitled the *Texas Educational Survey Report*. The *Report* proposed sweeping changes in every aspect of the state's public schools and higher education system, including calling for greater efficiency and consolidation of smaller community schools, better teacher salaries, and an appointed state superintendent. In 1937 the State Board of Education released the results of a survey completed by the Works Project Administration (WPA), *Report of the Results of the Texas Statewide School Adequacy Survey*. The 1,800-page report emphasized the importance of rural school consolidation, the need to restructure the state educational system, and the significance of equalizing funding. Both surveys blamed the continued maintenance of small community schools for wasting limited school funds. In the words of the WPA survey, "The facts and findings show rather convincingly that satisfactory educational opportunities are not being provided in all of the present school organizations," and the primary reason for the inequity was "the continued support and sponsorship of small local school units." The judicious application of limited school funds was important to Texans, but with attention focused on the economic crisis of the 1930s, and later the war effort in Europe and Asia, public school reform was not a primary concern for Texas voters or lawmakers. In fact, the Great Depression and World War II may have sped the process of consolidation, as smaller agricultural communities dwindled and families either left small farms for jobs and other opportunities in urban areas or saw their farms sold at auction.[14]

In the midst of all this, two tragic events affected the state's schools. On March 18, 1937, one of the worst public school disasters happened in the east Texas town of New London, twelve miles southwest of Kilgore, in the east Texas oilfields. Almost 300 students and teachers died following an explosion when a manual trades instructor turned on an electric sander in the school's basement. Unbeknownst to him, a faulty natural gas connection leaked the odorless gas into the building. A decade later, in April 1947, Texas City schoolchildren went to the port to watch firefighters battling flames aboard a cargo ship carrying ammonium nitrate when the ship exploded. These children were among the estimated 600 killed in the Texas City disaster, while others watching from a distance suffered injuries from debris. In both cases state and local officials implemented new regulations and safety procedures. The New London explosion led state lawmakers to require the infusion of a warning odor into natural gas as a precaution, and evacuation and safety procedures in industrial areas resulted from the Texas City explosion. Despite the tremendous loss of lives, it appears lawmakers realized that these industrial accidents were not isolated to schools and did not enact legislation specifically aimed at protecting schoolchildren following the disasters.

The end of World War II brought significant changes to Texas public education, especially with the educational benefits of the Servicemen's Readjustment Act, commonly known as the G. I. Bill of Rights. The G. I. Bill helped expand enrollment in the state's colleges and universities, and many returning veterans pursued teaching certificates. Moreover, the end of the war resulted in a baby boom that forecast a wave of increased enrollment beginning in the elementary schools. Schools had a difficult time, however, anticipating enough funds to accommodate the projected increases because wages were so low in rural areas that many teachers sought jobs in urban areas. Even if many of the rural and poorer urban districts wanted to raise salaries to make their schools more attractive, or simply to upgrade buildings, libraries, and physical plants, limitations on funding made it difficult.

In 1947 the Texas legislature commissioned a study of teachers' salaries that resulted in a series of recommendations to overhaul the state school system. The legislature restructured the public school administration in 1949 with the passage of the three Gilmer-Aikin laws, which replaced the biannually elected state superintendent and the appointed state board with a State Commissioner of Education who was appointed by an elected state board of education. The laws

Rae Files Still of Waxahachie *(center)*, a former high school history teacher, served in the 47th–51st Texas legislatures, and guided the controversial Gilmer-Aikin laws through the House as chair of the Education Committee. She is with Mrs. Merle O'Daniel and Governor W. Lee O'Daniel, who unsuccessfully encouraged public school reorganization as governor (1939–41). Courtesy Texas State Library and Archives Commission.

also mandated a minimum foundation program to set a funding baseline for school districts based upon their students' average daily attendance. Previously the state had funded schools on the basis of the number of students living in the districts whether they attended or not. The changes also hastened the pattern of school consolidations, established that children should attend school through the twelfth grade, and set a statewide minimum annual salary for teachers at $2,000.

The Gilmer-Aikin legislation affected almost all aspects of the state's school system, but the matter of replacing then-current superintendent Littleton A. Woods with an appointed school superintendent aroused concerns from many areas. A. M. Aikin, Jr., the state senator who supported the legislation, likewise opposed the move from an elected to an appointed office. Some charged that the purpose of the legislation was to oust Woods, who supported University of Texas president Homer Rainey in a recent political struggle with the university Board of Regents. Rainey took a liberal position supporting academic freedom when he refused to fire UT professors who had suspicious books on their reading lists. The board eventually removed Rainey, but Woods remained a supporter of the beleaguered university president. Some observers believe segregationist motives were a factor, inasmuch as Woods was receptive to integrationist policies. Nevertheless, the administrative restructuring also reflected an organizational trend sweeping school systems in other states after World War II. By improving educators' salaries and encouraging rural school consolidation, the Gilmer-Aikin laws were in harmony with many of the objectives of public school advocates, the various educational surveys, and lawmakers themselves. Essentially, the laws modernized the public school administration and remained the basic structure of the state's educational system throughout the rest of the century. While consolidation, school funding, and administrative organization were important, they were not the only issues facing public education. In the latter twentieth century Texans increasingly had to react to national events, especially civil rights, the Cold War, and growing federal oversight.

The civil rights movement had a tremendous effect on Texas education at all levels. In 1948 State District Judge Ben Rice issued a decision that marked the beginning of the campaign against school segregation in Texas. The American G. I. Forum brought the case on behalf of Minerva Delgado, who attended schools in the Bastrop Independent School District. The decision came on the heels of a similar California case, *Mendez v. Westminster* (1946), which determined that the state could not discriminate against Mexican-American children by segregating them in separate schools. Earlier in the 1930s, in the *Salvatierra v. Del Rio* decision, the U.S. Supreme Court had prohibited school segregation for Mexican-American students except to allow separate classes for students with limited English proficiency. This exception effectively allowed school districts to segregate based upon the assumption that all Mexican-American students had a limited command of English. Judge Rice's ruling prompted Texas Superintendent of Public Instruction Woods to prohibit the arbitrary separation of Mexican-American children in schools. The ruling did not end the problems Spanish-speaking children faced in school, which resulted in a high dropout rate. In the late 1950s, the national president of the League of United Mexican American Citizens (LULAC), Houston restaurateur Felix Tijerina, proposed teaching Spanish-speaking children a basic vocabulary of 400 English words to help prepare them for school. The Little Schools of the 400 opened in 1958 with private support. Tijerina, with the support of Governor Price Daniel and State Senator A. M. Aikin, Jr., lobbied for state support of his initiative. The next year, the legislature funded the Preschool Instructional Classes for Non-English Speaking Children program. Although Tijerina's Little Schools could only reach about 1,000 students, with the adoption of the state program over 18,000 children participated in the preschool classes. The program ended when the federal government sponsored Project Head Start, which many believe was inspired in part by the Little Schools initiative.

African Americans were also battling racial segregation, but their situation was different from that of Mexican Americans. While school administrators could treat Mexican Americans as legally white because of the *Del Rio* decision, African Americans were considered a race apart. This distinction presented problems in the 1960s as court-ordered integration began in Texas, but in the 1940s it meant that schools could not segregate Mexican-American students based solely upon race. For African Americans, however, state law adhered to the Jim Crow system in the public schools. Attorneys for the National Association for the Advancement of Colored People (NAACP) encouraged strategies to contest the dual-school systems throughout the South. Their efforts produced two major successes in the 1940s: first, in 1943 lawsuits filed in Dallas and Houston challenged the practice of paying African-American teachers lower salaries than their white counterparts. The Gilmer-Aikin laws addressed this concern by calling for standardized pay for teachers regardless of race. Second, in 1950 the U.S. Supreme Court ruled in favor of Heman Sweatt's application to the University of Texas Law School. The Texas legislature had sought to circumvent this by, first, attempting to create an ad-hoc law school for blacks and, second, taking control of the Houston Independent School District's College for Negroes in 1947 and renaming it the Texas State University for Negroes. The university later changed its name to Texas Southern University (TSU).[15]

While the *Sweatt v. Painter* case applied to graduate and professional schools, it was not long before Jim Crow education legally ended due to the ceaseless efforts of the NAACP's legal team led by Thurgood Marshall. In 1954 the U.S. Supreme Court in *Brown v. Topeka Board of Education* finally overturned the 1896 *Plessy v. Ferguson* decision, which had sanctioned the "separate but equal" rule in the South's schools. Civil rights supporters had hoped that Jim Crow schools would soon end as a result of federal judicial decisions and the support of the executive branch of government, but *de facto* segregation remained a common practice. The 1954 decision is often called *Brown I*, while the Court mandated the next year, in *Brown II*, that schools begin integrating "with all deliberate speed."

One of the earliest challenges to the Supreme Court's *Brown* decisions occurred in Texas. Most American history texts recount the confrontation between the Arkansas Governor Orval Faubus and President Dwight D. Eisenhower during the Little Rock crisis, but historian Robyn Duff Ladino contends that the first serious challenge to the two *Brown* decisions erupted in Mansfield, a small community just southeast of Fort Worth. Governor Allan Shivers, who broke with his fellow Democrats and endorsed the Republican Eisenhower, and State Commissioner of Education J. W. Edgar encouraged schools to maintain segregated facilities. According to Ladino, by 1956 hundreds of school districts had announced that integration plans were in place affecting hundreds of thousands of Texas school children, but the numbers were misleading. Since many schools had plans for gradual integration, the actual number of students in racially mixed classes was smaller than reported. Additionally, many school districts effectively maintained segregation throughout the twentieth century due to the ethnic composition of neighborhoods, white flight to the suburbs, and school district gerrymandering.

In Mansfield the obvious troublemakers were the segregationists who mobbed the high school for several days, hung effigies of African Americans from the school building and flagpole, and intimidated African-American students who attempted to register. But Governor Shivers, who ordered Texas Rangers to arrest anyone creating a disturbance, implied that the source of the problem was the African-American students who wanted to enroll in the high school. He also authorized the Mansfield school board to transfer any African-American students to Fort Worth schools to avoid integration. Although President Eisenhower surely was aware of the situation, his reticence on school desegregation encouraged segregationists, many of whom assumed the president condoned their defiance.[16]

While Mansfield's resistance certainly mirrored segregationist opposition to school integration and the civil rights movement in other southern cities, it was a town of less than 1,500 residents. The largest segregated school system in the South, however, was in Houston. In mid-June 1955 the Houston Independent School District board convened a Biracial Committee to study integration and make recommendations for an orderly process. William Henry Keller, who has studied the Houston school district's response to integration, explained that conservative board and committee members, inspired by recent Red Scare activities, considered integration unconstitutional and even un-American. As Keller stated, "Race-mixing had replaced Communism as the new demon, and, in a very real sense, the 'Red Scare' had become the 'Black Scare.'" In 1957 Houston voters elected a more conservative school board that quickly replaced the Biracial Committee with an all-white Committee to Study Integration. Belatedly, two African Americans were added to the committee. The conservative-led school board managed to delay desegregation of Houston schools until forced by a court order to implement a plan at the start of the 1960–61 school year. Keller pointed out, however, that the district imposed strict requirements that effectively prohibited most African-American students from attending white schools.[17]

School districts successfully delayed the spirit, if not the letter, of the *Brown* decision by integrating African-American and Mexican-American students without blending Anglo-American students into desegregated schools. After a 1970 federal district court ruling allowed Houston schools to integrate Mexican-American children, who were legally considered "white," with African-American children on the city's north and east sides, activists began arguing that Mexican Americans formed a distinct ethnic group. This growing awareness of a sense of "otherness" among Mexican-American young people coincided with the emerging Chicano movement. Students began protests against the high school's unofficial "whites only" policy for cheerleaders in the south Texas town of Crystal City, about 110 miles southwest of San Antonio and 40 miles east of the Texas border town of Eagle Pass. The student strikes spilled over into a general outcry about the control the Anglo minority held over the school board and city politics. These protests led to the formation of the Mexican American Youth Organization (MAYO) and the *Raza Unida* political party. In Houston, the struggle to prevent the school district from obfuscating attempts at actual desegregation by integrating two ethnic minority groups together lasted two years.[18]

In the mid-1960s the assassination of President John F. Kennedy in Dallas led to the ascension of central Texas political juggernaut Lyndon Baines Johnson to the nation's highest elected office. Johnson was educated as a public school teacher at Southwest Texas State Normal College in San Marcos. He spent his training year serving as the principal of an elementary school in Cotulla where he came face-to-face with the stifling poverty and discrimination experienced by children in a Mexican-American ward near the border. Upon graduation from Southwest Texas, Johnson taught briefly at Sam Houston High School in Houston. Although his teaching career was brief, as president he referred to his experiences at Cotulla repeatedly as inspiration, or perhaps justification, for his support of civil rights legislation. Whether or not teaching influenced Johnson's civil rights legacy, it certainly influenced his support for national educational initiatives. As president, LBJ signed over sixty pieces of legislation relating to education, including the landmark Elementary and Secondary Education Act of 1965, which denied federal funding to schools that refused to integrate. In 1970 one of Johnson's appointments to the federal bench, District Court Judge William Wayne Justice, mandated the state integrate its public schools in *United States v. Texas*, Civil Order 5281.[19]

Governor John Connally commissioned a study in 1965 led by Houston attorney Leon Jaworski to evaluate the state school system. Published in 1968, the Jaworski committee's report, *The Challenge and the Chance*, proposed updating the Gilmer-Aikin reforms so that Texas schools could meet the challenges of the latter twentieth century by staying abreast of new technology, providing opportunities for undereducated adults, and improving profes-

Lyndon Johnson signed the landmark 1965 Elementary and Secondary Education Bill in front of the Junction Elementary School in his hometown of Johnson City, Texas. LBJ invited friends from Southwest Texas State Teachers College and former students from Cotulla and Houston. Kate Deadrich Loney, his teacher at Junction Elementary, was present at the ceremony. Courtesy Lyndon Baines Johnson Library and Museum, National Archives and Records Administration.

sional opportunities for teachers. It further noted that "Texas must eliminate inefficiencies and financial favoritism among local school districts," an issue the legislature had failed to address. In mid-May 1968 some 400 students walked out of San Antonio's Edgewood High School. Located in a predominately poor Mexican-American area of San Antonio, the school was underfunded, despite a high tax-rate, because the property values were so low. Edgewood parents filed a class-action suit, *Rodríguez v. San Antonio ISD*, claiming that the Fourteenth Amendment to the U.S. Constitution guaranteed education, and that Texas' tax policy discriminated against minorities and the poor in general. Although the Supreme Court struck down the plaintiff's claims in 1973, the matter was raised again a decade later in *Edgewood ISD v. Kirby*. This 1984 case, eventually representing over 70 poor school districts across the state, challenged the state's method of funding schools via property taxes as inherently unequal and ultimately in violation of the state constitution's education clause. The state Supreme Court agreed, and the legislature created an ad-hoc method of equalizing funds known as the "Robin Hood Plan" because it drew money from property-wealthy districts and redistributed it to poorer ones. This plan satisfied neither the court nor the wealthy districts. The court therefore mandated that the legislature devise a plan both constitutional and equitable, a requirement that remained unfulfilled through the end of the century.[20]

By the end of the century Texans could no longer expect that they could exercise complete control over their public school system. Curriculum reform and accountability became the subject of increased scrutiny in the 1980s. As more and more monies went toward public education, lawmakers at the state and national levels began demanding increased results based upon a growing national standards movement. While federal interest in public education dates back to the Articles of Confederation (1781–1789), it remained limited until the twentieth century. Through the

1930s and World War II the government supported little more than school lunch programs, but that changed as a result of the large number of draft-board rejections during the war. Local draft boards rejected some 40 percent of enlistees, and the army dismissed another 15 percent for educational and physical disabilities. The army turned down over 100,000 men the first summer of the war because they could not read at a fourth-grade level. This brought public schools to the nation's attention, as did the civil rights movement. However, it was Russia's successful launch of Sputnik I that led to significant increases in federal funding. When the Russians beat the Americans into space, federal officials and others sought explanations. A frequent target of blame was the public school curriculum, particularly for a lack of emphasis on mathematics and sciences. This prompted a national effort to improve the nation's schools and led to passage of many of the bills President Johnson signed affecting the relationship between the federal government and the public schools.[21]

Despite earlier support for reforms, by the late 1960s many people no longer shared the popular conception of education as a panacea for society's ills, a perception that originated at the beginning of the century. Indeed, once the attack on the public school curriculum began in the 1950s, it persisted through the remainder of the century. One historian's recent analysis of suburban growth north of the Dallas-Fort Worth metroplex suggested that suburbs offered better schools, "or at least schools free of perceived city problems." Better education was one of the enticements of suburban living, but it appeared that schools in the state's urban and suburban areas were experiencing problems. In 1965, the Texas legislature approved public funding of public school kindergartens and other preschool initiatives aimed at better preparing students earlier in their educational careers. The Jaworski committee's report, *The Challenge and the Chance*, stated that most people saw education as an agent of "change and stability" that would be one of the agents to assist in the growing inner-city problems such as those that became apparent in the 1960s, especially "delinquency, unemployment, and soaring welfare costs." Unfortunately, the committee stated, "traditional forms and methods have failed to equip the disadvantaged for constructive citizenship in modern complex society." The report detailed a ten-year plan to expand the Minimum Foundation Program, to address the rapid advances in technology in the late-twentieth century and increases in Texas property wealth. It proposed more flexibility in educational strategies to tackle the dropout rate, improve teacher and support staff training and salaries, and expand consolidation of smaller schools. "Texas must eliminate structural inefficiencies and financial favoritism among local school districts," the report warned. "Failure to meet these challenges will plunge Texas further into the depths of educational mediocrity."[22]

In April 1983 the National Commission on Excellence in Education delivered its report, *A Nation at Risk*, to U.S. Secretary of Education Terrell H. Bell. The opening page read like a Cold War invective aimed at the nation's school systems. "If an unfriendly foreign power had attempted to impose on America the mediocre educational performance that exists today, we might well have viewed it as an act of war." The paragraph concluded: "We have, in effect, been committing an act of unthinking, unilateral educational disarmament." The report recognized that the United States in the 1980s was a nation in search of itself, a nation whose role as a superpower was threatened. It also recognized the importance of equal educational opportunity, especially if the nation was to maintain its economic prowess. "Regardless of race or class or economic status," declared the report, all children "are entitled to a fair chance and to the tools for developing their individual powers of mind and spirit to the utmost." An educational system blind to the considerations of race and class would mean that all students "by virtue of their own efforts, competently guided, can hope to attain the mature and informed judgment needed to secure gainful employment and to manage their own lives, thereby serving not only their own interests but also the progress of society itself."[23]

Soon after the release of the report Texas Governor Mark White commissioned a study of the state's public schools. He named business magnate H. Ross Perot to head the Select Committee on Public Education. The commission, widely known as the "Blue-Ribbon Commission" or the "Perot Commission," released its report in mid-April 1984. Among its recommendations, the committee suggested that the state board of education establish measurable "minimum statewide standards" for all subjects, reorganize the Texas Education Agency, develop accreditation and performance standards, and standardize teachers' training and performance evaluation. The goal was to place "Texas at the top of the academic charts," an achievement that would entail making school finances the first priority. "A key ingredient in accomplishing this objective is to simplify and improve the State school finance system and to fairly address the long-standing problem of equalization of our educational resources," explained the commission. "At the same time, we must restructure and improve the management and accountability of the public school system for the results achieved." These changes, the report promised, would "bring tremendous benefits to us in the coming years in increased educational effectiveness and cost containment."[24]

The Perot Commission's recommendations also emphasized increased professional training for schoolteachers, including salary levels based on a teacher's location on a "career ladder" instead of solely upon tenure and degree. While the Texas Teacher Career Ladder took experience and education into consideration, the plan also rewarded instructors who participated in professional development and performance evaluations. In the 1992–1993 school year the legislature abolished the career ladder before Texas educators could reach the highest rung.[25]

The most controversial provision of the commission's report was House Bill 72, the "No Pass, No Play" bill. In reality, the bill implemented many of the provisions of the Perot report, but the rule that students who earned a grade below a 70 could not participate in extracurricular activities caused the most public concern. In 1986 the U.S. Supreme Court refused to rule on the constitutionality of the "No Pass, No Play" provision, which students had claimed violated their rights. Texas already had a reputation for focusing too much energy on sports, especially football, and the outcry against the "No Pass, No Play" law seemed to validate it, and the publication of *Friday Night Lights* by journalist H. G. Bissinger confirmed it in the mind of the nation. Bissinger spent 1988 with the Odessa high school team and wrote that the town's very existence seemed tied to the success or failure of the football team. Little else mattered to most of the parents and townsfolk. The initial reaction of some Texans to the book was anger, accompanied by death threats toward Bissinger should he ever return to Odessa. Even so, in 2004 a feature film based upon the book encouraged the development of a television series of the same title that premiered at the beginning of the fall 2006 football season.[26]

The major themes in the history of twentieth-century Texas pubic schools have been equity, efficiency, liberty, and excellence. Although the belief in the curative properties of education has changed significantly since the 1970s, Texans remain strongly confident that educational opportunity should be open to everyone. This commitment reflects a democratization of education in which all students receive equitable schooling and have opportunities to advance and excel. Looking back over all the changes of the twentieth century, none was more far-reaching for Texas education than World War II. At the beginning of the century even graduating from high school, much less college, was more than most Texans could expect, but by 2000 Texans had more educational opportunities, at a lower cost, than their grandparents could have ever anticipated. At the end of World War II, and continuing through the rest of the century, Texas was finally able to fund a comprehensive, standardized curriculum of public education and to embark upon rapid and phenomenal growth in post-secondary enrollment. At a deeper level, the increased emphasis on the potentials of public education during and after World War II evolved into a growing belief that education not only preserved and transmitted democracy, but could also transform society.

For scholars, the field of Texas educational history is ripe for the harvest. Historians and students interested in researching the topic further will have a variety of sources. Many of the topics related to colleges and universities, state supported and private, including civil rights and integration, academic freedom, access for women and minorities, history of teacher training, student protests, the youth movement, and the Chicano and Black Panther movements, have been addressed in monographs, articles, theses, and dissertations. But no synthesis has been attempted since mid-century. Local heritage societies and public library archives often preserve the records of local school boards. Oral histories of teachers, administrators, and board members are also invaluable resources, and numerous retired teachers' associations hold meetings and conferences where oral historians might seek interviews. College and university trustee records are available to enterprising researchers working in university archives. Document repositories across the state house papers of individuals active on local school boards, various trustees, superintendents, principals, and teachers. Most of the larger Texas newspapers run columns on education. One little-utilized resource is the magazine of the Texas State Teachers' Association. Although the title has changed over the years, the monthly publication possesses information about current trends and important events in Texas education. The Texas Education Agency (previously the State Department of Education) has long published empirical data about the status of the state's schools, reports and information important to teachers and administrators, and the state superintendent's biannual reports.

Selected Bibliography

Blanton, Carlos Kevin. *The Strange Career of Bilingual Education in Texas, 1836–1981.* College Station: Texas A&M University Press, 2004.

Cashion, Robert Ty. *Pigskin Pulpit: A Social History of Texas High School Football Coaches.* Austin: Texas State Historical Association, 1998.

Cavazos, Lauro F. *A Kineño Remembers: From the King Ranch to the White House.* College Station: Texas A&M University Press, 2006.

Clegg, Luther Bryan. *The Empty Schoolhouse: Memories of One-Room Texas Schools.* College Station: Texas A&M University Press, 1997.

Cottrell, Debbie Mauldin. *Pioneer Woman Educator: The Progressive Spirit of Annie Webb Blanton.* College Station: Texas A&M University Press, 1993.

Eby, Frederick. *The Development of Education in Texas.* New York: Macmillan, 1925.

Evans, Cecil Eugene. *The Story of Texas Schools.* Austin: Steck, 1955.

Kellar, William Henry. *Make Haste Slowly: Moderates, Conservatives, and School Desegregation in Houston.* College Station: Texas A&M University Press, 1999.

Ladino, Robyn Duff. *Desegregating Texas Schools: Eisenhower, Shivers, and the Crisis at Mansfield High.* Austin: University of Texas Press, 1996.

Owen, William A. *This Stubborn Soil.* 1966. New York: Lyons Press, 1986.

San Miguel, Guadalupe. *"Let All of Them Take Heed": Mexican Americans and the Campaign for Equality in Texas, 1910–1981.* College Station: Texas A&M University Press, 2001.

———. *Brown, Not White: School Integration and the Chicano Movement in Texas.* College Station: Texas A&M University Press, 2001.

Shabazz, Amilcar. *Advancing Democracy: African Americans and the Struggle for Access and Equity in Higher Education in Texas.* Chapel Hill: University of North Carolina Press, 2004.

Sitton, Thad, and Milam C. Rowold. *Ringing the Children In: Texas Country Children.* College Station: Texas A&M University Press, 1987.

Endnotes

1. George W. Bush, "Remarks by the President at Swearing-In Ceremony for Dr. Roderick Paige as Secretary of Education," January 24, 2001, http://www.whitehouse.gov/news/releases/20010124-3.html; George W. Bush and Roderick

Paige, "Press Conference with President George W. Bush and Education Secretary Rod Paige to Introduce the President's Education Program," January 23, 2001, http://www.whitehouse.gov/news/releases/2001/01/20010123-2.html.

2. Louann A. Bierlein, *Controversial Issues in Educational Policy*, Controversial Issues in Public Policy, eds. Dennis Palumbo and Rita Mae Kelly, no. 4 (Newbury Park, Calif.: Sage Publications, 1993), 3; Frederick Eby, *The Development of Education in Texas* (New York: Macmillan, 1925); Cecil E. Evans, *The Story of Texas Schools* (Austin: Steck, 1955).

3. Eby, *Development of Education in Texas*, 250–51; Evans, *Story of Texas Schools*, 109.

4. Mary Ley and Mike Bryan, eds., *Journey from Ignorant Ridge: Stories and Pictures of Texas Schools in the 1800s* (Austin: Texas Congress of Parents and Teachers, 1976) deals with late-nineteenth century schools, but is useful for comparison with later works, especially Thad Sitton and Milam C. Rowold's *Ringing the Children In: Texas Country Children* (College Station: Texas A&M University Press, 1987) and Luther Bryan Clegg's *The Empty Schoolhouse: Memories of One-Room Texas Schools* (College Station: Texas A&M University Press, 1997). Dorothy Redus Robinson provides an honest account of an African-American schoolteacher's experiences in segregated rural schools in *The Bell Rings at Four: A Black Teacher's Chronicle of Change* (Seattle: Madrona Press, 1978) while a different perspective can be found in the very brief collection of memories by the sister of *Old Yeller* author Fred Gipson, Stella Gipson Polk, in *For All Those Pupils Whose Lives Touched Mine* (College Station: Texas A&M University Press, 1989). Another collection of teachers' stories can be found in Diane Manning, *Hill Country Teacher: Oral Histories from the One-Room School and Beyond* (Boston: Twayne, 1990), and descriptions of early public schools from the perspective of one of the state's leading reformers are found in Debbie Mauldin Cottrell, *Pioneer Woman Educator: The Progressive Spirit of Annie Webb Blanton* (College Station: Texas A&M University Press, 1993). Other accounts by Thad Sitton expose the difficulties rural communities had in sustaining local schools and the lengths they went to do so because of the importance of schools to communities. See chapters in his *Harder than Hardscrabble: Oral Recollections of the Farming Life from the Edge of the Texas Hill Country* (Austin: University of Texas Press, 2003) and in his work with James H. Conrad, *Nameless Towns: Texas Sawmill Communities, 1880–1942* (Austin: University of Texas Press, 1998) and *Freedom Colonies: Independent Black Texans in the Time of Jim Crow* (Austin: University of Texas Press, 2005). See also Carlos Kevin Blanton, *The Strange Career of Bilingual Education in Texas, 1836–1981* (College Station: Texas A&M University Press, 2004) for an account of early twentieth-century schools.

5. Eby, *Development of Education in Texas*, 218.

6. Ibid., 214, 220–21; Evans, *Story of Texas Schools*, 115; *Handbook of Texas Online*, s.v. "Ousley Clarence N.," http://www.tsha.utexas.edu/handbook/online/articles/OO/fou2.html.

7. Eby, *Development of Education in Texas*, 217.

8. H. E. Singleton, "Annual Address of the President," in *Proceedings of the Eighteenth Annual Session of the Texas Farmers' Congress in College Station, Texas, August 2–4, 1915* (Austin: Von Boeckmann-Jones, 1916), 12; Richard Hofstadter, *The Age of Reform: From Bryan to F.D.R.* (New York: Knopf, 1955; Vintage Books, 1960), chapter 1; Lawrence A. Cremin, *The Transformation of the School: Progressivism in American Education, 1876–1957* (New York: Knopf, 1961), 41–50, 75–85; David B. Tyack, *The One Best System: A History of American Urban Education* (Cambridge, Mass.: Harvard University Press, 1974), 23; David B. Danbom, *Born in the Country: A History of Rural America* (Baltimore: Johns Hopkins University Press, 1995), 167–75.

9. Cottrell, *Pioneer Woman Educator*, 67–8.

10. Evans, *Story of Texas Schools*, 125.

11. *Handbook of Texas Online*, s.v. "Better Schools Campaign," http://www.tsha.utexas.edu/handbook/online/articles/BB/kgb1.html.

12. Cottrell, *Pioneer Woman Educator*, 5, 67.

13. Blanton, *Strange Career of Bilingual Education*, 59. Educational historian Guadalupe San Miguel, Jr., explains the growing Mexican and Mexican-American community in Texas in *"Let All of Them Take Heed": Mexican Americans and the Campaign for Educational Equality in Texas, 1910–1981* (Austin: University of Texas Press, 1987), 13, but the topic is also elaborated in Arnoldo de León's *Ethnicity in the Sunbelt* and David Montejano's *Anglos and Mexicans in the Making of Texas*, among others; Blanton, *Strange Career of Bilingual Education*, 63–73.

14. Texas Education Survey Commission, *Texas Educational Survey Report*, 8 vols. (Austin: Texas Educational Survey Commission, 1924–25); Texas State Board of Education, *Report of the Results of the Texas Statewide School Adequacy Survey* (Austin: Texas State Board of Education, 1937), 92.

15. William Henry Kellar, *Make Haste Slowly: Moderates, Conservatives, and School Desegregation in Houston* (College Station: Texas A&M University Press, 1999), 35–41.

16. Robyn Duff Ladino, *Desegregating Texas Schools: Eisenhower, Shivers, and the Crisis at Mansfield High* (Austin: University of Texas Press, 1996), 47, 51–55.

17. Kellar, *Make Haste Slowly*, 85.

18. Guadalupe San Miguel, *Brown, Not White: School Integration and the Chicano Movement in Houston* (College Station: Texas A&M University Press, 2001), 87. See John S. Shockley, *Chicano Revolt in a Texas Town* (Notre Dame, Ind.: University of Notre Dame Press, 1974). Elementary and secondary schools were not the only ones to experience violence and resistance to integration. Historian Amilcar Shabazz details opposition to integration at Texas colleges and universities in *Advancing Democracy: African Americans and the Struggle for Access and Equity in Higher Education in Texas* (2004). In 1967 racial tensions in Houston spilled over onto the Texas Southern University campus when in the early morning hours of May 17 police stormed the men's dormitories and arrested nearly 500 students. The police had been under siege for several hours from snipers shooting from somewhere in the men's dormitories. The TSU riot resulted in the death of

one police officer and the wounding of two officers and two students. *Handbook of Texas Online*, s.v. "Riots," http://www.tsha.utexas.edu/handbook/online/articles/RR/jcr2.html.

19. Ibid., s.v. "*United States v. Texas*," http://www.tsha.utexas.edu/handbook/online/articles/UU/jru2.html.

20. Ibid., s.v. "*Rodríguez v. San Antonio ISD*," http://www.tsha.utexas.edu/handbook/online/articles/RR/jrrht.html; Governor's Committee on Public School Education, *The Challenge and the Chance*, Digest of Recommendations (Austin: Governor's Committee on Public School Education, 1968), 32; *Handbook of Texas Online*, s.v. "*Edgewood ISD v. Kirby*," http://www.tsha.utexas.edu/handbook/online/articles/EE/jre2.html.

21. George Q. Flynn, *The Draft, 1940–1973* (Lawrence: University of Kansas Press, 1993), 31–32.

22. Mark Friedberger, "Development, Politics, and the Rural-Urban Fringe in North Texas," *Southwest Historical Quarterly* 109 (January 2006): 374; Governor's Committee, *Challenge and the Chance*, i, 8, 76.

23. National Commission on Excellence in Education, *A Nation at Risk: The Imperative for Educational Reform: A Report to the Nation and the Secretary of Education,* U.S. Department of Education (Washington, D.C.: U.S. Government Printing Office, 1983), 5, 8.

24. Select Joint Committee on Public Education, "Recommendations," 68th leg. sess., 1983, Interim Report, Legislative Reference Library of Texas, Legislative Reports, Public Education, Select - 68th Session (1983), 43, http://www.lrl.state.tx.us/research/interim/reportDisplay.cfm?cmteID=8530&isSupport=0.

25. Carole Keeton Strayhorn, *Special Report: The Cost of Underpaying Texas Teachers* (Austin: Texas Comptroller of Public Accounts, 2004), 16, http://www.window.state.tx.us/specialrpt/teachersalary04/.

26. "Court Lets Stand No Pass, No Play," *New York Times*, February 25, 1986, *New York Times* Archives, http://query.nytimes.com/gst/fullpage.html?res=9A0DE4DC123CF936A15751C0A960948260.

Lone Star Landscape

Texans and Their Environment

Tai Kreidler

GLISTENING WITH RAINBOW COLORS against the setting sun, the ocean swells roiled past the ship's wooden hull and swirled smoothly into a wake that trailed like furrows behind a plow. The experienced lookout in the crow's nest was mesmerized by the view. For as far as the eye could see the rough edges of breaking waves, gentle swells, and windblown eddies were seemingly smoothed by an invisible blanket overlaid on the scene. The surface had a glistening sheen that was complemented by a translucent swirl of color. Alarmed and curious, the crew scampered aloft in the rigging for a better view. What magic was this? Was it some sort of miracle? Was it an omen? No one had an answer, at least not for another 400 years. What the ship reported was the first sighting of an oil slick glistening on the surface of the Gulf waters. While it would be commonplace many years later, it is not something one would expect during the so-called pristine pre-history period of the New World story. But it is an example of how "pollution," or environmental degradation, as it would come to be called, is an entirely subjective manifestation, taking on a negative connotation only when human action or malfeasance is involved. In fact, natural environmental degradation has occurred from time immemorial, but only now, with the rapid movement of the human hand and the inability of nature to respond quickly enough, has it become a serious problem for humanity.[1]

The Texas environment has been exposed to human contact, interaction, and impact for over half a millennium and, iconic romantic ideals notwithstanding, it has been among the most severely affected environments in the world. Texas has been blessed with vast amounts of available space out of which it has carved for itself a legendary place in national and world history. Thoughts of Texas, at least in popular culture, bring to mind Indians, cattle barons, timber tycoons, and oil kings, and there certainly is some basis for such a perception. Texas was in fact a vast frontier of open space populated by Indians and buffaloes, and later cowboys and longhorns. While this mythic image persisted in popular lore, song, and literature, by the early twentieth century Texas had become something quite different. Through the discovery of oil and the attendant production and refining activities, it had become one of the more industrialized states in the union, even comparable to Pennsylvania. Just as the Homestead steel mills near Pittsburgh were described as "hell with the lid off," various parts of Texas, through the pell-mell oil-well drilling and resultant pollution, looked otherworldly—like the surface of the moon.[2]

As industrialization followed, predicated upon the distribution of lands to individual or corporate ownership, the "hothouse" environment created a positive climate for exploitation of natural resources by corporations at an unprecedented level. While progressive reformers of the early twentieth century managed to rein in business to some extent and thereby preserve in other parts of the nation the landed legacy of the frontier and the public domain, they had little success in Texas, where land was quickly gobbled up. To escape efforts at federal regulation, corporations in Texas divorced themselves from their larger national affiliates and became independently chartered in the state. As a consequence, the regulatory reform spirit had little impact in Texas, and companies continued to exploit the state's resources at will. Within such a *laissez-faire* climate, there was less government oversight. Regulation, if it existed at all, only occurred to ensure that companies did not destroy themselves in the competitive fray.

So, in that spirit, twentieth-century Texas allowed for minimal oversight over the use of its land and resources. There were efforts to address immediate issues when they arose, but there was no effort at long-range planning to forestall problems before they occurred. Hunting game to extinction occurred frequently. The east Texas black bear, the passenger pigeon, deer, elk, and others vanished from the landscape. The eradication of "nuisance" wildlife was a foregone conclusion. Poisoning, hunting, and mass drives to eradicate various wild species such as the jack rabbit were common.

The first state law reining in unrestricted hunting of game was not passed until 1860. It restricted the hunting of quail on Galveston Island for two years. Unfortunately, these early measures had little impact since many counties held the power of passing and enforcing game laws. When early settlers encountered the forests of east Texas, they were teeming with wildlife— a veritable treasure trove of game. But lumbering and farming quickly destroyed the natural habitat, and recreational and subsistence hunting eliminated many species entirely. Allegedly, one hunter killed over 200 bears during his life, and as many as four a day. Another claimed to have bagged a record 305 bears. The human predisposition to overhunt eradicated black bears, as well as other species, including birds. For example, at the turn of the century the hat-making industry put great pressure on herons, sea gulls, and egrets, the most prized species. By 1890 herons and snowy egrets were nearly wiped out. By 1900 the passenger pigeon that had swarmed by the millions at "pigeon roost prairie" south of Hardin had disappeared from Texas skies.[3]

Conservation efforts began in the later part of the nineteenth century. Unfortunately, they achieved little initial success. Texans lulled themselves into complacency by arguing that wildlife species could always be found farther west. And it was true for a time when west Texas settlers in 1907 chased and bagged the plentiful pronghorn antelope from the seats of the new fangled automobile. Only when eradication seemed probable did citizens take action. Ironically, in many cases it was too late. Moreover, state conservation laws and policies failed to have any effect upon counties that either refused to follow state laws or claimed that county law overrode any state dictates. In 1883, 130 counties claimed exemption from state game laws. Not until after the passage of constitutional amendments giving overriding authority to the state was there any substantive impact of state game regulations over counties.

The initial steps toward protecting and assisting the propagation of state game came in the early decades of the twentieth century. The first was the passage of the Model Game Law in 1903. It required the licensing of all hunters, both residents and non-residents, and that fees and fines be used solely to help with game protection. By the 1920s sport hunting groups successfully lobbied to limit the hunting season in order to sustain hunting yields. Called conservation, it was a move by hunting groups to preserve wildlife so it could be hunted again. It was predicated upon the progressive reformist notion of efficiency and usefulness. In 1925 Texas implemented the State Game Preserve system that allowed landowners to sell hunting privileges as a means of managing game populations. What started as an individual method of managing game became an important comprehensive game-management program in a state where most of the lands were already in private hands. In the 1920s the old Fish and Oyster Commission that was created in 1907 was reorganized and revitalized into the Game, Fish and Oyster Commission. Properly funded for the first time, the commission enforced the use of hunting and fishing licenses and in turn used the revenue to hire more game wardens. For the first time game laws were effectively enforced. In 1937 the passage of the Pittman-Robertson Act imposed a federal firearms tax that would benefit various state wildlife conservation programs. Since Texas claimed more game than any other state, it garnered $40,000 annually.[4]

Today there is a broad range of national wildlife refuges throughout the state that serves these interests and work toward not only conservation, but also preservation of species that would otherwise be extinct. In 1935 the Texas legislature established the Muleshoe Wildlife Refuge as a wintering area for migratory waterfowl and sandhill cranes, and in 1937 it founded the Aransas Pass Wildlife Refuge to preserve the fast-disappearing flamingos, egrets, terns, and other species that the Audubon Society sought to save. In the celebratory activity revolving around the Texas Centennial in 1936 the initial steps were taken to create the first national parks and preserves. Leading up to the event in 1935, Congress authorized the creation of Big Bend National Park that opened in 1944. The next year the biological survey of the Big Thicket was completed; however, it was not until 1974 that the first preserve in the national park system was formally created. But for all of the "Big as Texas" bluster ascribed to the names, Texas continues to rank lowest among the states in terms of lands assigned to parks and wilderness areas. When compared against its total size, Texas is twenty-eighth in state park acreage. In terms of land designated as wilderness, it has only 85,333 acres, which ranks it twenty-fourth of all the states and fortieth in terms of percentage of state lands designated as wilderness.[5]

The cattle industry has been one of the more symbolic and romantic icons in Texas history, but in many ways it has been among the most intrusive agents upon the environment. The image of the cowboy on horseback working cattle is universally identified as something distinctively Texan, and the cattle industry was definitely a factor in the economic recovery of Texas after the Civil

War. Drawing upon the monetary benefit of the cattle drives, the cattle industry grub staked the expansion of free-range ranching and eventually paved the way for its transition to fenced range operations. While ranching appears to work cooperatively with the natural environment, its proliferation and success actually brought about the wholesale transformation of the land.

Fencing compartmentalized the land, preventing or at least hindering the natural migration cycles, and thereby placing further stress upon wildlife stocks that were already being hunted aggressively. The buffalo were hunted nearly to extinction and eventually removed entirely. In order to free up the land, even the indigenous population of Native Americans was ushered out of the state. Exotic cattle species replaced them, in some cases ill-suited to the climate, but brought in only because they produced maximum profits per unit weight. The fencing of land also made it possible for cattle to overgraze the range, unless proper attention and management ensued. With overgrazing came the proliferation of mesquite trees and salt cedar wherever the natural ground cover had been disturbed.

Place names like Lumberton, Woodville, Pineland, and Village Mills, as well as mascot names such as the Lumberjacks of Stephen F. Austin University in Nacogdoches point to a timbering legacy on a par with anything that existed in the so-called great forests of the American Southeast and in the mountain West. When the first settlers entered Texas, journal entries told about the towering pine and hardwood forests and the cathedral-like canopy that was provided. Like settlers elsewhere, Texas settlers made use of the timber for fuel and housing. Clearings were used to build a house and to graze cattle. The massive influx of settlers placed exponential pressure upon the environment as more settlement led to more land cleared and placed under cultivation and more hunting of the local wildlife.

Following closely behind the settlers was the timber industry. At the turn of the century the lumber crews swept through the region, selectively cutting the larger southern magnolias, black cherries, and white ash for use as "furniture, boxes, bats, and even railroad ties." Initially, the smaller trees and the undergrowth were not cleared out, thus allowing forest regeneration. In the 1950s, however, "indiscriminate clear cutting" began. This signaled the radical and almost irrevocable transformation of the southeast Texas and east Texas forest system into a monoculture. After cutting the larger trees, lumber crews bulldozed the remainder, eliminating any possibility for old forest regrowth. Instead, the foresters "regenerated" the land with loblolly pine or similar varieties. Essentially, it converted the "Big Thicket" into a "tree farm."[6]

In the 1960s lumber companies sprayed the Thicket from airplanes killing the less profitable hardwoods interspersed amidst the pine. The industry sought to clear out the hardwoods that would sap important water and nutrients from the pine. As one observer described it, "pine grows faster and makes more money for the lumber companies." Pine brought ten times the price of hardwoods. So the oaks, hickories, and magnolias were sacrificed for the more lucrative loblolly. The larger ones were girdled or poisoned, the sproutlings torched, and the rest were clear-cut and then bulldozed. Even the majestic longleaf pines were cut out because of their slow-growing characteristics. As a result, the lumber industry transformed the southeast Texas forest into a highly productive commercial forestry system without the biological diversity that is usually required for a healthy and sustainable ecosystem.[7]

Another economic engine that further vaulted Texas beyond the other southern states was the discovery of oil at an unprecedented level. Ushered in by the famed Spindletop discovery in 1901, Texas oil dominated the first half of the twentieth century. Fields in Caddo, Ranger, Mexia, Burkburnett, Electra, Breckenridge, east Texas, and elsewhere led the state, America, and the world in terms of discovery wells and production capacity. Unregulated in the beginning, it was America's prime example of pure unfettered capitalism. Driven by the "rule of capture," crews drilled as fast as possible in order to pull the oil out of the ground first. Gushers were allowed to flow in the early days and earthen tanks caught only some of the spillage.

In the 1910s and 1920s Texas' Gulf Coast shipping points, including the Houston Ship Channel, were literally covered in oil, and the inundation was so extensive that it drove away other industry. Lumber companies shut down because of the damage to timber and lumber. Local wildlife left or were reduced in number. In addition, the fishing industry declined. East Texas cities even experienced problems with their drinking water as a direct result. In 1939 the city of Beaumont saw saltwater runoff from the east Texas oil field pollute the Neches River to the point that it could not be used. One scholar speculated that as much oil splattered on the Gulf Coast soil as found its way to market.[8]

The Texas Railroad Commission eventually assumed responsibility for monitoring spillage, along with its more visible responsibility of regulating production, field unitization, and other important regulatory tasks. Using fines and other reprimands, the flagrant and willful spillage that had been part of a colorful past was reduced. But without a doubt Texans and Texas were most forgiving of industry, inasmuch as it provided jobs and pumped money into the economy. As long as it did not visibly or visually impinge on Texans or directly impair another business, nothing was done to hinder or sanction the industry. As one insider said about the public attitude toward the industry and oil accidents along the Gulf Coast: "This pollution thing has been over-played and has undoubtedly hurt us somewhat, but fortunately people have short memories." Also, while some government oversight did exist, it was "never . . . directly active or effective." Such attitudes meshed well with the industry attitude that oil like public concern would eventually dissipate.[9]

Texans accepted pollution as a part of doing business. First, it was always recognized that some level of sacrifice came with progress. The expedient way in which the natural environment was used seemed to indicate that Texans believed the land and resources were inexhaustible. The mythic and visionary consciousness of what Texas was always combined with the bottom-line expectation that Texans could rebuild themselves financially. It was the place where dreams were made manifest, but natural resources were sacrificed to realize that vision. As a result, oil spills were the natural course of such business. While spills were avoided whenever possible, Texans held a "live and let live" outlook about nature.

Industrial pollution has been a continuing problem since the turn of the century. Considering the heavy concentration of refineries and other oil-service manufacturing activities, air, water, and land pollution have been a constant. Immediately after Spindletop numerous refineries were built along the Gulf Coast in 1902 and 1903. As Texas became the leading oil producer in the United States, refinery construction escalated, and the area from Houston to Baton Rouge, Louisiana, became one of the larger concentrations of refineries in the world. Texas in the 1990s was home to 45 percent of America's petrochemical industry, and 50 percent of the nation's total refining capacity lies in the area from Freeport, Texas, to Pascagoula, Louisiana. In the 1950s and 1960s the region actively courted the construction of additional refining infrastructure, service industries, and manufacturing plants. Because of the economic benefit, local communities gave away tax exemptions to entice new plants and facility expansion. Beaumont, Port Arthur, Houston, Baytown, Texas City, and Galveston experienced a booming economy from the 1950s through the 1970s.[10]

State oversight on air and water had been fairly relaxed. Not until after World War II would there be any steps taken to prohibit pollution, and even then they would come only on the heels of federal clean air and water measures. The state did not take any action on water quality until 1945 when it put into place standards for municipal water systems. Later, in 1953 the state created the Texas

Water Pollution Advisory Council, the first state agency charged with the responsibility of dealing directly with pollution. But it would not be until 1961 when the state created the Texas Water Pollution Control Board that it would have a true pollution oversight. In 1951 concerns over air quality prompted the Department of Health to perform the first air study. In 1965 the state created the Air Control Board, and for the next thirty years it carried out federal mandates for clean air that included monitoring, setting up sampling stations, and submitting reports.

Regardless, state attempts to provide pollution oversight left much undone, and reports began to surface indicating problems. Information in the 1990s revealed flaws in Texas' pollution control program. Independent and federal findings showed that Texas, far from being the last rustic frontier, was home to some of the highest industrial pollution levels of any state. Of the 500 most polluted counties in America, Texas claimed four of the top ten. Moreover, Texas led the nation in total pollution volume—1.6 billion pounds a year—and had 1,000 hazardous waste superfund sites of the 25,000 listed nationally. What had gone wrong? Critics suggested that there were too many agencies often working at cross-purposes. Perhaps consolidating some of the entities and streamlining others could solve part of the problem. To that end in 1993 the state created the Texas Natural Resources Conservation Commission, combining all of the air, water, and waste programs under one banner. In 2002 it changed its name to the Texas Commission on Environmental Quality.[11]

Catastrophic pollution has been an ongoing problem since the beginning of the twentieth century. Oil spills in particular have been a nagging problem since the dawn of the modern petroleum age. World War I and World War II were won literally on a river of oil. As a consequence, the earliest major oil spills were related to destruction caused by war, and World War II represents a watershed period. The destruction imposed on the Port of Dunkirk during the

British evacuation in 1940 and on Pearl Harbor from the Japanese attack in 1941 precipitated some of the biggest oil spills on record. Pearl Harbor had a six-inch oil slick that overlay the entire harbor. The cleanup was long and arduous and in some cases solutions were never found. Today, the wreck of the *USS Arizona* still has 500,000 gallons of fuel in its fuel bunkers, and the National Park Service is concerned about the possibility of a future spill when the tanks collapse completely from rust.[12]

Public awareness and concern for oil inundation ebbed and receded after each spill. With each new accident a new furor ensued and public attention was whipped into a frenzy. In the 1960s the issue roared back when a series of shipwrecks occurred that included the *Torrey Canyon* and other oil tankers. Public consciousness peaked with the 1969 Santa Barbara oil spill in California's offshore waters. Each accident prompted a large and unprecedented cleanup effort, but with the high-profile Santa Barbara spill public environmental awareness was heightened and it fueled support for the passage of the National Environmental Policy Act (NEPA) in 1969. In 1989 another high-profile accident, the *Exxon Valdez* oil spill, captured international attention because it occurred in the so-called pristine waters off the shore of Alaska. As a result, it generated renewed public outrage about oil industry transgressions upon the environment. For the first time in a generation, the American public came face-to-face with the sad and tragic impact of crude oil inundation.

In Texas the earliest oil spills in the twentieth century probably can be linked back to Spindletop and Caddo Lake at the turn of the century. In the years after World War II the offshore oil exploration and production boom in the Gulf of Mexico on the Texas coast had mushroomed into a hugely successful venture. While the fishing industry and citizens periodically accused oil companies of polluting the water and hurting fishing yields with seismic explosions, nothing was done to restrict industry operations. Even the Santa

Barbara spill garnered slight reaction in Texas. This all changed in 1970 with a huge blowout and fire that erupted at a Chevron well in federal waters off the shore of Louisiana. Six of the platform's twelve wells caught fire, and for several weeks the wells spewed 50,000 gallons of oil a day into the Gulf. U.S. Interior Secretary Walter Hickel visited the site and held Chevron accountable for the accident. He commented publicly that "If Santa Barbara was an accident, this is a disaster."[13]

Allegations circulated that appropriate safety valves were missing, and both Chevron and the federal government blamed each other for the situation. Meanwhile, oyster and shrimp fishermen blamed Chevron and filed suit. Others voiced protests on the clean-up effort that was using a myriad of new methods and technology developed in the aftermath of the Santa Barbara accident. One group charged that too much oil dispersant was being used. Meanwhile, the federal government began to feel that the technology did not exist to guarantee a 100 percent pollution-free operation. Frustrated and embarrassed, the Interior Department temporarily halted all federal offshore leasing and began a comprehensive review of offshore operations.[14]

While the impact of these two events prompted the passage of NEPA in 1969, it also resulted in the enactment of other measures, including the extension of the Clean Air Act in 1970, which regulates the emission of air pollutants from industrial activities, the Coastal Zone Management Act in 1972, and the Clean Water Act in 1977, which regulates the discharge of pollutants into surface waters. However, even with such legislative measures on the books, accidents continued, and in Texas such events were just part of doing business. In fact, Texas had more frequent and in some cases larger oil spills than anything served up by Santa Barbara or the *Exxon Valdez*. In June 1979 the Ixtoc I blowout occurred offshore the Yucatan Peninsula in Mexico. By August 1979 the Gulf current brought the oil northward and it coated the entire Texas coast. As the largest oil spill that had any impact on U.S. history, the Ixtoc oil disaster spewed 4.2 million barrels of crude before it was brought under control. (Persian Gulf spill after Operation Desert Storm is estimated at 3.95 million barrels). In November 1979 the oil tanker *Burmah Agate* collided with another ship in Galveston Bay, dumping 254,761 barrels of crude into the water. By volume it was comparable to the *Exxon Valdez* spill, but ironically it gained little public attention or protest. Aside from the Gulf Coast community, hardly anyone else in the state knew anything about it.[15]

While farming and farmers may be less iconic when compared to gushing oil wells splattering "black gold" on Jett Rink and John Wayne driving cattle to the "Red River," they are nonetheless an extremely important aspect of the Texas economy. Texas has always had land as a resource that helped fuel its various economic miracles. Land hunger ignited nineteenth-century immigration into Texas where land was given free to any settler willing to come. By the eve of the twentieth century land was still available, but only through purchase. In the 1920s ranches, timber companies, and railroads were selling off acreage as farmsteads. The open country that had been Texas was parceled and distributed into increasingly smaller units. The process of farmland conversion also introduced an agricultural activity that relied heavily on regular rainfall and fertile soil. In some cases the land was plowed up where there was not enough rainfall, such as portions of west Texas, or where the soil was not fertile enough, such as areas of east Texas. After clearcutting the timber, the land in east Texas often was not capable of sustaining agriculture for very long and reverted to grazing land or second growth "tree farms." In western areas, when drought came, the region experienced "dust bowl" conditions.

In the late 1920s and early 1930s west Texas was suffering through a drought of seemingly unprecedented proportions. By the spring of 1930 crop damage was widespread and farmers were already receiving considerable state and federal emergency relief funding. Two years later portions of the southern Great Plains of Texas, New Mexico, Oklahoma, and Kansas, had become home to the worst agricultural disaster of the modern era—the Dust Bowl.

"Black blizzards" and southwesterly dusters of immense size rolled across the region choking the farmers and livestock and sweeping away crops. Scorched by the searing summer heat and frozen by frigid "blue northers," the unrelenting wind blew untold quantities of topsoil eastward. Many thought that the end of the world had come. Some farmers began to exit the region, while others remained behind. As the wind and erosion continued, it became clear that emergency farm relief measures would have to give way to more permanent programs predicated upon farmer acceptance of revised cultivation practices.

An approaching dust storm in the Texas Panhandle, March 1936. Note the border of sand on either side of the road. Courtesy Library of Congress, Prints and Photographs Division, FSA-OWI Collection, LC-USF346-002486-C DLC.

One of the emergency measures President Franklin Roosevelt recommended to the Forestry Service was the shelterbelt tree-planting program. Fearful that wind erosion would unhinge the entire Great Plains and roll it eastward, the federal government dug in with a tree-line defensive wall that ran in zigzag fashion from Texas to Minnesota. The Forestry Service learned that a variety of trees planted in multiple rows would slow down the wind and protect the land. In fact, for winds below 20 miles per hour, the velocity was reduced by half for a distance from four to eight times the height of the trees. As a testament to the severity of conditions in the southern region, the first shelterbelt was planted in 1935 just outside of Granite City, Oklahoma. Two years later a whole series of shelterbelts were planted just across the state line into Texas, just south of Vernon. Nearly seventy-five miles of trees were planted the first year alone. To the west in the area around Childress another program was started. As a voluntary effort, the agents encountered initial resistance from the farmers, but eventually there was general acceptance, especially when it seemed to be working.[16]

By the late 1930s and early 1940s the drought eased and then disappeared completely. The rains returned and World War II pushed demand and prices to new highs. While everyone agreed that the conservation ethos and protocols had helped farmers survive, bad memories faded and old habits returned. In the 1950s dust bowl conditions returned, and for Texas it was much worse than the notorious "dirty thirties." Rainfall levels had dropped off on average 40 percent from standard years. In a few isolated cases it was much worse. Lubbock in 1952 did not record a trace of rain. On February 19, 1954, a monstrous dust storm comparable to anything seen in the 1930s blew through the southern plains. Three weeks later, on March 11–13, Lubbock recorded a dust storm lasting 55 hours, and visibility dropped to 600 feet. Even Eleanor Roosevelt, writing from the relative security of her East Coast home, was worried and moved by what she heard and read about the new emergency.

She noted that "there was a horrible picture in the papers recently showing the ravages brought about by the dust storm." Before it was over all but ten of Texas' counties were declared federal disaster areas.[17]

Observers began to realize that the 1950s was setting its own benchmark for destruction. In Texas wind erosion had not only hit the areas destroyed in the 1930s, but it also spread to land that had been plowed up since 1941. Throughout the region farmers had added five million acres to production, of which three million came from marginal lands. With the return of drought conditions, farmers and conservation experts began to realize that dry spells were not an anomaly, but actually part of a recurring twenty-year climatological cycle. The ebb and flow of drought and wet conditions had gone on for centuries, but gained notice only because West Texas was now home to so many people. Easterners remarked that "measures should have been taken to plant trees and the kind of grass which holds the soil and brings the water back." Ironically, it had already been tried in the 1930s, but the program had been allowed to lapse.[18]

In Texas a highly practical and utilitarian land-use attitude held sway, and it was hard to convince a culture that took immense pride in its pioneer heritage to ease its grip on the natural world. While on a writing retreat at the King Ranch in the 1950s, western writer Francis Fugate, who was working on Tom Lea's history of the ranch, remembered Dick Kleberg taking a rifle shot at a low-flying hawk. It was a spur-of-the-moment thing and no one expected him to have a chance of hitting the target. To everyone's surprise the dead hawk tumbled to the ground and everyone congratulated Kleberg, who was as surprised as everyone else. The story is representative of accepted attitudes that Texans had toward nature, but ironically, while Kleberg was receiving congratulations winds of change were already blowing across the landscape. In what may be described as a backlash against the horrors of war, post-World War II attitudes showed an easing of hard-line utilitarian environmental notions and an embrace of something called a "land ethic." Proposed by Aldo Leopold in the prewar years, the idea became a compelling force in 1948, providing an alternative approach to how humans might interact with the natural world. It held that despoiling the land was both inexpedient and wrong, and that humans, rather than "conquerors," were simply members of the natural community. Such simple thoughts spread widely and underpinned the future thinking about preservation and wilderness consciousness. It also became an important point of discussion in agricultural schools throughout the country.[19]

The new philosophy became not only the "sharp point of the spear" for conservationists, but also incorporated farming practices field-tested in the 1930s into postwar college and university curriculum. Such immediate conservation remedies were combined with the creation of the Soil Bank, which paid farmers to take marginal land out of production. Even more far-reaching was the 1956 creation of the Great Plains Conservation Program (GPCP), a voluntary and comprehensive conservation system helping farmers and ranchers in changing crop types and land uses so as to conserve soil and water resources and preserve and enhance the agricultural stability of an area. Such practices included contour strip-cropping, terracing, grassed waterways, land leveling, reorganizing irrigation systems, and windbreaks. It also encouraged crop diversification.

Working out of Lubbock County, James D. Abbott spearheaded the GPCP's implementation on the Southern Great Plains—one of the hardest hit areas. Abbott was representative of the new cadre of college-educated field conservationists that stepped forward after the war to join the ranks of the Soil Conservation Service. He was a 1948 graduate of Texas Tech University. During the course of a 46-year career he effectively implemented the GPCP on the south plains, and as a result much of his own operational template became the model for the rest of the region. For his contributions Abbott is generally recognized as one of the key figures in the success of the program not only in Texas, but also throughout the Great Plains. By the time he retired in the early 1990s, Texas agriculture was on firm footing. While the GPCP and the Soil Bank had been phased out, its vision was carried forward by the Conservation Reserve Program.[20]

Part of the solution for droughts came from the miracle of finding enough water. The Ogallala Aquifer, a seemingly endless reservoir of underground water, stimulated a transformation of farming on the western plains. In the 1950s high-speed gasoline pumps replaced the underpowered windmills and pulled water from deep underground. In 1965 the Internal Revenue Service, acceding to the federal and circuit court decisions in *U.S. v. Shurbet et ux*, granted a tax depletion allowance for water pumped from the aquifer. The decision was a clear-cut acknowledgement that water from the Ogallala was as important as oil, which had its own and much more famous depletion tax break. But more importantly, it symbolized a growing realization that water was a finite and non-renewable commodity.

Throughout the twentieth century towns and cities spent much of their time drilling wells and building reservoirs to ensure that enough water was available. The droughts of the 1910s, 1930s, and 1950s ignited a drive to find and hold water so that by the end of the century Texas had the most lakes of any state outside of Minnesota. City leaders and irrigation pioneers such as J. A. Kemp of Wichita Falls pushed for reservoir construction that guaranteed enough water for farmers and city dwellers even during droughts. Reacting to his own experience with the ill-famed 1886 drought that pushed back the Texas farming frontier nearly 100 miles and delayed westward settlement for nearly a generation, Kemp built Lake Wichita in 1901. This lake led to the formulation and implementation of an entire system of reservoirs and irrigation canals that would sustain north central Texas for much of the twentieth century. It also sparked some innovative discussions on how to change rainfall patterns. Weather modification methods had been around since 1910–1914 when C. W. Post, the cereal magnate and west Texas town builder, carried out experiments with dynamite explosions. While his results were inconclusive, that did not prevent others from trying. Not until the postwar period did scientists discover that dry ice under the proper conditions could help make rain. The discovery led to a period of renewed experimentation in weather modifications with promising results. Meanwhile, others wanting a more reliable way to bring water to the state suggested piping it in from the Mississippi River. Water, Inc., which was founded during the unfettered optimism of the 1960s when the "space race" brought the moon within reach of humanity, worked during the

Dam construction on White River in west Texas, ca. 1919, representative of the statewide push to ensure water stocks. This dam was made of concrete, but many earthen dams were used. Courtesy Southwest Collection/Special Collections Library, Texas Tech University, Lubbock, Texas, Museum Photograph Collection.

early 1970s to gain enough support for the project. But the high price tag and the lack of sufficient political support doomed the project.[21]

By the end of the twentieth century increasing demand upon water resources by both rural and urban sectors prompted an aggressive search for new or unclaimed resources. North central Texas and the Dallas-Fort Worth metroplex, for example, have been tapping into surplus water from southern Oklahoma. Houston is seeking additional water reservoirs in east Texas. Meanwhile, San Antonio is working to augment underground water stocks from the Edwards Plateau. Water brokers are seeking to separate water rights from the land and dealmakers like T. Boone Pickens are peddling water to the highest bidder. Water as a marketable commodity has everyone's attention and it has become big business. As many environmental observers have commented, with finite reserves and growing demand, water will follow the money.

In the postwar period wildlife conservation, particularly in the areas of game management, took great strides. As the economy improved and Texas returned to a peacetime cycle, interest in sport hunting returned, bringing an increase in revenue from licensing. As a result, the Fish, Game and Oyster Commission had sufficient funding to hire more wardens and game-management specialists. Also, the Dingell-Johnson Act, which placed a tax on fishing equipment, helped subsidize the hiring of new game employees who worked to promote fishing stocks. It was also a time when a whole new cadre of college-trained professional game regulators and wardens joined the commission. With such resources the commission in the 1950s was able to finally limit subsistence poaching, particularly in the heavily forested east Texas region.

Also emerging out of the postwar period, Texans became increasingly interested in the patterns of migratory birds. The state has always boasted that it had some of the largest numbers of wild birds in the nation. The work of Harry Oberholser and the United

States Bureau of Biological Survey in the early 1900s did much of the work that provided the basis of that knowledge. Complementing his efforts were the individual volunteers throughout the twentieth century, often working alone, who collected some of the earliest data delineating what would become known as the Central Flyway corridor for the migratory birds of North America. In 1938 Conger "Connie" Hagar of Rockport began collecting information about birds and in the process would become one of the first to document bird sightings. From 1943–1945 Art Hawkins, who had been Aldo Leopold's first graduate student at the University of Wisconsin, performed some of the first scientific observations and documentation of migratory bird activity in Texas. His work eventually helped delineate the migratory bird routes through Texas and paved the way for the eventual founding of the Central Flyways Council in 1947.[22]

The emergence of the land ethic and the belief that human beings have an ethical responsibility to care for the natural world has done much to sponsor the important conservation and preservation work done by individuals or by state and federal agencies. Finding ways to ease human demand on the ecosystem is increasingly a part of the environmental vision of the early twenty-first century. A high priority is discovering a clean-burning fuel for automobiles and power plants. While hydrogen fuel cells and batteries are possible alternatives for cars, wind power initiatives have become a popular way for Texans to articulate environmental concern and at the same time enhance the state's energy self-sufficiency, not to mention garnering some federal tax incentives in the process. The growing popularity of wind power notwithstanding, Texas continues to give serious consideration to the building of more coal-fired plants to offset the possibility of an energy shortfall in the face of ongoing industrial and urban expansion. From some nine million in the 1960s, the state's population had swelled to approximately twenty-four million by 2006. Even with modern "scrubbers" to clean the exhaust, coal-fired plants are seen by many Texans as environmentally risky. As a result, toward the end of the twentieth century Texans embraced the nuclear age, completing in 1988 and 1990 two nuclear power plants. While such activity stands in stark contrast to the state's mythic persona characterized by the cowboy, oil well drillers, and ranchers, Texans are committed to using nuclear power and have built disposal repositories to store radioactive waste.

Texas is no stranger to radioactive industries. Since 1951 Amarillo has been home to Pantex, the assembly facility for most of the nuclear warheads produced during the Cold War. Since the end of the arms race, the plant has become an important disassembly site. In recent years Texas has also attracted attention as a prime location for potential waste repositories. In the 1980s the United States Department of Energy (DOE) tried to locate a high-level radioactive waste disposal site in Texas. Faced with increasing accumulation of spent fuel from power plants and nuclear weapons processing facilities from across the country, the DOE targeted a possible site in Deaf Smith County. However, citizen opposition in 1987 forced the DOE to cancel the project and move the project to Yucca Mountain, Nevada.[23]

In the meantime, Texas and other land-rich states were targeted for so-called low-level disposal projects. With soaring population and industrial growth in the rest of the country, the wide-open spaces of Texas became a perfect place for waste disposal of all kinds. As one observer commented, "people think of West Texas as an empty wasteland, a place of little or no value or importance— a 'backyard'." To that end, an Oklahoma company in 1992 purchased 90,000 acres outside Sierra Blanca and began dumping treated New York sewage. That same year the state of Texas selected Sierra Blanca also as a dumpsite for low-level radioactive waste from hospitals and research faciltiies.[24]

In 1998 the plan for a high-level radioactive waste disposal site in Texas was revived. It was announced that a high-level radioactive dump west of Andrews would be built. Unlike the previous proposal that had been blocked by grassroots opposition to the plan, the city of Andrews and its people supported the proposal. Planned in conjunction with a plutonium enrichment plant slated for construction just across the state line in Eunice, New Mexico, the disposal site opened for business in 2005. The first shipment of nuclear waste arrived from the defunct Fernald uranium processing plant near Cincinnati. With the nation's only high-level nuclear waste disposal site in operation, Andrews County became the only location approved for high-level radioactive waste. While the merits of the DOE high-level disposal site at Yucca Mountain were still being debated, Andrews, Texas, became the primary destination for radioactive waste for the entire nuclear power industry. In 2006 a nuclear power consortium of private industry, educational groups, and the state of Texas, attracted by the convenience of having a waste dump site immediately at hand, announced plans to build a high-temperature nuclear power reactor in Andrews County.[25]

The decision to pursue nuclear energy and build waste repositories in Texas is an important one. The special hazards of radioactive materials beg answers to storage questions that scientists and engineers have yet to answer. The most significant question is how do you build a safe repository that can last 20,000 years, which is seven times longer than the span of recorded human history. Regardless of the lingering questions and apprehension, Texans have moved toward nuclear energy production and have shouldered the responsibility for handling radioactive waste disposal confident that the answers will be found.

The collective personality of Texans as self-reliant, born of plenty and not of scarcity, and beholden to no one has shaped attitudes regarding environmental issues. Frank Ford, who founded Arrowhead Mills, the organic food company, did it alone and according to his own firmly held ethics and beliefs about how the land should be treated. As a freethinking force of nature, he was both "book smart" and "street savvy" and emblematic of the strong and independent Texan. In high school he was the top debater and the valedictorian of his graduating class. He graduated at the top of his class at Texas A&M University with a degree in agronomy and was commissioned an officer in the U.S. Army's first nuclear artillery unit. Following a desire to return home and farm he got out of the army after one tour.

Ford's vision to farm without pesticides and herbicides was based on his informed perception that chemicals weakened crop varieties, broke down resistance to disease and pests, and ultimately polluted the food chain. In 1960, as a one-man organic-food operation, he created Arrowhead Mills in Hereford. He spent his life savings on a used tractor, a second-hand pickup, and a stone-grinder. He worked 18-hour days and transformed his farm and mill into one of the first organic-food production facilities in the country. At first he sold locally, literally off the tailgate of his pickup. "Locally" in Texas meant in some cases driving 150 miles.

Eventually, in the late 1960s word of mouth reached national markets, and Ford was sending his ground meal to places such as Boston and San Francisco. It tickled him to think that a "redneck" Texas farmer like himself was doing business with "longhair hippies" in California. Ironically, he and the hippies were brought together because they wanted the same thing—food without chemicals. During his 36-year career he not only nurtured his company to success, but he was a tireless advocate for organic foods. Through his pioneering efforts he helped start a grassroots network of farmers, distributors, and retailers that evolved into the organic food industry. In 1999 the Organic Trade Association with its Leadership Award honored him for his work in founding the natural and organic food movement.[26]

However, his interest in natural foods went far deeper than having good food to eat. Ford wanted to find a way of working with the land in ways that would not permanently disable the cycle of

life—its sustainability. His concern about using chemicals as fertil-
izer, herbicide, and pesticide was the permanent transformation of
the soil. "You should base your judgment of natural farming methods on whether or not they maintain and improve—or deplete—
the soil. If the improvement shows up as a plus in the food, that's
an additional benefit."[27]

All the awards and recognition notwithstanding, Ford's vision
was based on being a good custodian of the land. Within the larger
context of environmental awareness, he firmly held to the belief
that individuals should take responsibility for the impact they have
on the natural world. Being a steward was serious business. "I favor
anything that creates a sense of responsibility for the proper use of
the land."[28]

The fence posts whipped past quickly as the car cut through the
countryside and the occupants made their way through the stream
valleys and over the ridge tops. The two companions shared a pleasant afternoon with each other as they rode and talked. Each crest
line traversed unfolded a new landscape and their eyes took in the
trees, grass, cattle, planted fields, and the range land. The older
man, Robert "Bob" Fee, a retired rancher from the Roscoe-Snyder,
Texas, area, commented frequently on each farm and ranch they
passed, giving out information about who lived where and when,
and who was living there now. It was as if he were walking down a
neighborhood lane pointing out the homes of all who lived there,
how long they had been there, and when they had moved in. He
knew them all and on the three-hour trip he continued calling out
the family names. He remembered their trials and successes. More
importantly, he chronicled their connection to the land, describing
what crops they planted and the variety of cattle they raised. Occasionally, the guided-tour patter would stop for a moment and he
would say, "Look at that. They sure let that land go." His companion would look, but didn't see anything out of the ordinary. With a
trained eye he commented on the overuse, misuse, or abuse of the

land and at the end of the commentary he usually concluded by saying, "That's unfortunate."

Implied in Fee's statement is the philosophy that people should know better than to forsake a responsibility and ignore the greater good for the short-term gain. They should have the maturity to understand that they are responsible for the way the world is and only they can make change for the better. Such beliefs are all the more important as Texas moves into the twentieth-first century—an age where horizons are no longer limitless and neither are the resources. The boundless Texas frontier must forever more be a vision and a mindset, for it no longer exists in reality. Water, air, land, and even open space are under increasing pressure from more people needing more of it.

Texas braggadocio underpinned by confidence and a unique sense of self has always been an illusory and ephemeral thing. Nevertheless, it has had a profound impact on how Texans act and react, and the optimism to find answers to difficult environmental questions may be what sustains them in the twenty-first century. While large enough to have four or five culturally and economically diverse regions, Texas is linked and held together by an indelible sense of community that transcends the regional divides and helps each of its citizens know its neighbors who live beyond each crest line and in each valley. However diffuse and individualistic the Texas environmental persona may be, it is forged and held together by a unique identity—a common legacy that all Texans share. It will be through this shared identity—this sense of community—that Texas will forge for itself a new history and embrace an environmental ethic that it deserves.

Selected Bibliography

Bartlett, Dick. *Saving the Best of Texas: A Partnership Approach to Conservation.* Austin: University of Texas Press, 1995.

Bedichek, Roy. *Adventures with a Texas Naturalist.* Austin: University of Texas Press, 1961.

Cozine, James. *Saving the Big Thicket: From Exploration to Preservation, 1685–2003.* Denton: Big Thicket Association, University of North Texas Press, 2004.

• Doubty, Robin W. *Wildlife and Man in Texas: Environmental Change and Conservation.* College Station: Texas A&M University Press, 1983.

Flores, Dan. *Caprock Canyonlands: Journeys into the Heart of the Southern Plains.* Austin: University of Texas Press, 1990.

Francaviglia, Richard V. *The Cast Iron Forest: A Natural and Cultural History of the North American Cross Timbers.* Austin: University of Texas Press, 2000.

Goldsteen, Joel B. *Danger All Around: Waste Storage Crisis on the Texas and Louisiana Gulf Coast.* Austin: University of Texas Press, 1993.

Jameson, John. *Big Bend on the Rio Grande: Biography of a National Park.* New York: Lang, 1987.

Miller, Char, ed. *On the Border: An Environmental History of San Antonio.* Pittsburgh: University of Pittsburgh Press, 2001.

Schmidly, David J. *Texas Natural History: A Century of Change.* Lubbock: Texas Tech University Press, 2002.

Steely, James Wright. *Parks for Texas: Enduring Landscapes of the New Deal.* Austin: University of Texas Press, 1999.

White, Matt. *Prairie Time: A Blackland Portrait.* College Station: Texas A&M University Press, 2006.

Endnotes

1. Spanish records of floating oil date from the sixteenth century. Ian MacDonald, "Natural Oil Spills," *Scientific American* 279, no. 5 (November 1998): 56. John P. Hogan, in a presentation to the board of directors of the West Penn Oil and Gas Company in Buffalo, New York, referred to an article written by Navy Lt. John C. Soley entitled "The Oil Fields of the Gulf of Mexico[1910] ." It listed a number of the oil slicks found in the Gulf. He commented on one reported by *S S Comedian* that bubbled to the surface in three jets. Soley speculated that the water depth reached 600 fathoms. John P. Hogan, "Supplementary Discussion of the Saline Domes of the Gulf Coastal Plain Submitted to the Board of Directors of the West Penn Oil and Gas Co.," January 16, 1919, pp. 2–3, box 127, folder 5554, Everette Lee DeGolyer Papers, DeGolyer Library, Fikes Hall of Special Collections, Southern Methodist University, Dallas.

2. "... dotted by drill cores, archeological debris piles, and blue-green translucent runoff pools that have accumulated in depressions caused from the long-term extraction of crude and sulphur. Yellowish-orange mounds of sulphur lay everywhere, giving off that distinctive smell of rotten eggs and causing the immediate vegetation to be a little "sparser and lighter." Field notes of the McFadden Lease, June 21, 1989, Beaumont, Texas. Notes in the possession of the author.

3. William O. Douglas, *Farewell to Texas: A Vanishing Wilderness* (New York: McGraw-Hill, 1966), 34; Robin W. Doubty, *Wildlife and Man in Texas: Environmental Change and Conservation* (College Station: Texas A&M Press, 1983) 33, 101–2, 105–7.

4. Ibid.,164, 175–79.

5. U.S. Department of Agriculture, Economic Research Service, *Major Uses of Land in the United States,* Statistical Bulletin no. 973, appendix table 1, pp. 32, 33; Texas Comptroller of Public Accounts, *Forces of Change*, vol. 2, part 1, 1994, 399; from National Association of State Park Directors, Annual Information Exchange, April 1990.

6. Edward C. Fritz, *Realms of Beauty: The Wilderness Areas of East Texas* (Austin: University of Texas Press, 1986), 4.

7. Fritz, *Realms of Beauty*, 4–5, 59, 71.

8. Joseph A. Pratt, *The Growth of A Refining Region* (Greenwich, Conn.: JAI Press, 1980), 227, 234, 239.

9. Alden J. Laborde to John T. Hayward, April 14, 1969. John T. Hayward Papers, ODECO 2 folder, Howard-Tilton Library, Tulane University; George B. Field to John McKee, April 18, 1969. New Orleans Chamber of Commerce Records, Air and Water Pollution folder, 370:13, Archives and Manuscripts Department, Earl K. Long Library, University of New Orleans; Joel B. Goldsteen, *Danger All Around: Waste Storage Crisis on the Texas and Louisiana Gulf Coast* (Austin: University of Texas Press, 1993), 61.

10. *Dallas Morning News*, [no date]; Pratt, *Growth of A Refining Region*, 267–72. Goldsteen, *Danger All Around*, 195; W. F. Riggs, Jr. (executive vice president of the New Orleans Area Chamber of Commerce) to senators and U. S. representatives, telegram, July 25, 1956; Attachment to Minutes of the Executive Committee, Chamber of Commerce of the New Orleans Area, July 30, 1956, p. 6; Minutes of the Board of Directors/Executive Committee, 1956, vol. 2 (of two); George B. Field (mgr. of state legislation committee) to W. O. Turner (president of New Orleans C of C), attachment to letter, May 25, 1961; Minutes of Meeting of the Board of Directors, New Orleans Area Chamber of Commerce; Minutes of Board of Directors/Executive Committee 1961, vol. 1, Archives and Manuscripts Department, Earl K. Long Library, University of New Orleans.

11. *USA Today*, August 1, 1989.

12. Charles C. Bates and Alfred H. Glenn, "Oceanography in the Off-shore Drilling Campaign," *World Oil* 127, no. 13 (April, 1948): 114–26.

13. S. H. Hopkins to Thurlow C. Nelson, March 7, 1947, folder 3-1, Hopkins Collection, Oyster Mortality Reports, Special Collections Library, Texas A&M University; "Huge Cleanup Force Works on Spill in Gulf," *Offshore* 30, no. 4 (April 1970): [33–37], p. 33.

14. "Huge Cleanup Force Works on Spill in Gulf," *Offshore* 30, no. 4 (April 1970): [33–37], p. 36–37; Anne Worcester Coleman, "Observations About the Leasing of the Outer Continental Shelf for Petroleum Exploration—The Case of Texas" (master's thesis, University of Texas, 1981), 106; Offshore Newsletter, *Offshore* 20, no. 13 (December 1970): 6.

15. R. Ditton, C. Gunn, F. Lamphear, J. Nichols, C. Restrepo, L. Restrepo, *Economic Impact of Oil Spills on the Texas Coast, FY 1980—IXTOC I Oil Spill Economic Impact Study* (U.S. Minerals Management Service, 1982), p. 1.

16. Tai Kreidler, field notes, June 22, 1989. Notes in possession of the author; Lake States Forest Experiment Station, U.S. Forest Service, *Possibilities of Shelterbelt Planting in the Plains Region.* (Washington, D.C.: U.S. Government Printing Office, 1935), 2, 8, 57; Tom Croker, *The Great Plains Shelterbelt* (Greenville, Tenn.: Artistic Printers, April 1991).

17. Jeffrey A. Lee and Vatche P. Tchakerian, "Magnitude and Frequency of Blowing Dust on the Southern High Plains of the United States, 1947–1989," *Annals of the Association of American Geographers* 85, no. 4, pp. 684–93, p. 690; Eleanor Roosevelt, "My Day February 27, 1954," (newspaper column) Eleanor Roosevelt Papers, George Washington University Archives., Washington, D.C.

18. Eleanor Roosevelt, "My Day February 27, 1954."

19. Francis Fugate, in conversation with author, November 1992.

20. James D. Abbott, in conversation with author, c. 1992; Douglas Helms, "Great Plains Conservation Program: 25 Years of Accomplishment," SCS National Bulletin Number 300-2-7. November 24, 1981, p. 10.

21. Water, Inc., records; Wichita County Water Improvement District No. 1 and 2 records, Southwest Collection, Texas Tech University, Lubbock.

22. Art Hawkins, interview, June 16, 1993, and May 21, 1999. In possession of author.

23. Final Report: Castro, Parmer, Swisher Counties Repository Assessment Commissions Texas Governor's Nuclear Waste Program Office, 1988, microfilm, i, iv, Southwest Collection, Texas Tech University.

24. E. A. Addington to Delbert Devin, July 4, 1986, Nuclear Waste Task Force records, Southwest Collection, Texas Tech University.

25. "Novastar Resources Joins Consortium for Pre-Conceptual Design Phase to Build Next Generation High-Temperature Reactor in Texas," *Business Wire*, February 22, 2006,

26. Frank Ford, in conversation with author, c. 1992. Notes in possession of author.

27. Frank Ford, interview, *Mother Earth News*, no. 29, September/October 1974.

28. Ibid.

The Second Texas Revolution

From Cotton to Genetics and the Information Age

Kenneth E. Hendrickson and Glenn M. Sanford

AT THE DAWN OF the twentieth century Texas science and technology offered poor prospects indeed. Higher education had made only the most modest progress since the foundation of the two main state colleges less than thirty years before. Texas could boast of very little manufacturing, very little electrification, very little mechanization or mass transit, and only a tiny professional class possessing the skills and credentials to make change more than a wish. While growing, the population necessary to support growth was barely over three million and was overwhelmingly poor and rural. The urban base was practically nonexistent. Yet, by the close of the twentieth century, Texas had experienced remarkable scientific, medical, and technological progress, putting it alongside states like California, Florida, Massachusetts, and North Carolina at the forefront of the American economy.

Several developments help explain this transformation. The development of an infrastructure of higher education proved vital to these changes. By the 1990s the state claimed no fewer than nine major medical schools with multiple campuses and research facilities. Texas universities ranked among the best in the nation, with Texas A&M exhibiting phenomenal growth both in size and re-

search capacity. The University of Texas system oversaw the largest
and the best of the state's medical training facilities, while hosting
several Nobel laureates among its faculty in other programs. Alongside education, and in tandem with constant population growth
and urbanization, federally sponsored programs and indigenous
industry also transformed the economy. By 2006 the Texas population stood at over 23 million. Only in the decade of the Great Depression had the state failed to achieve at least 15 percent growth.
The expanded workforce, increased economic diversity, and investment generated by this general growth all contributed to a profoundly new economic environment by the latter 1960s and the
1970s. Additionally, technological innovation spurred increasing
change. After invention of the integrated circuit, Texas electronics rivaled the traditional hegemony of California's Silicon Valley.
From the 1960s Houston served as a major center of operations for
NASA. Throughout the century Texas agriculture and agricultural
science ranked among the most productive in the United States. Finally, the vital petrochemical industry, from its explosive start in the
1920s, continued to dominate both the economics and the politics
of the state through the year 2000. None of these changes would
have been readily apparent even to the keenest forecaster surveying
the Texas economy circa 1900.[1]

Periodizing the development of Texas over the course of the
century is a difficult and tendentious task. Nonetheless, some thematic trends and their chronologies stand out clearly. This essay
adopts a tripartite approach to the state's advancement, highlighting the most significant developmental impulses of the era and linking them to internal state events. First, technological development
constantly responded to the changing role of agriculture. Some of
the first notable scientific progress in the state stemmed from the
basic need to rationalize and commercialize the state's main economic function in the era after the Civil War. This was the man-
date for the founding of Texas A&M in 1876. Around the turn of

the century the Texas economy was essentially agricultural, but not well diversified. Cotton completely outclassed all other agricultural pursuits, and revenues from that crop dwarfed all others, including beef. Not until 1921 did Texas exports and values from manufacturing surpass that of cotton and other agricultural crops. This basic change proved to be a necessary prerequisite for the development of medicine and higher science in later decades.[2]

Because of the rapid and surprising growth of the state's petroleum industry, the early 1920s also work well as a period marker. Despite the famous Spindletop gusher of 1901, the real wealth and potential of Texas petroleum did not become fully apparent until after World War I. While industrial science and applied technologies do not constitute the main thrust of this chapter, the wealth and investment generated by the Texas oil boom played a vital role in the expansion of higher education and Texas industry, including the company that became Texas Instruments. Texas petroleum wedded Texas education to the Permanent University Fund (PUF), first established during the Republic. Marginal for decades, the Fund became a decisive education catalyst when oil was found on university land in Reagan County. As a result of the strike on May 28, 1923, oil revenue poured into the Fund, stimulating exponential growth. In 1925 oil revenues totaled over $4 million. At mid-century the Fund had increased to nearly $285 million, providing more than $8.5 million annually to the University of Texas and Texas A&M. The legislature expanded the list of recipient universities in 1984. As of 2000 the PUF had increased to over $10 billion, subsidizing university faculty salaries, library and equipment purchases, and student support.[3]

The second major period in Texas development runs from the oil boom era to the close of the Apollo manned moon missions in the early 1970s. Though education suffered with the onset of the Great Depression, federal money, especially subsidies through the National Youth Administration, bolstered enrollment after 1935, helping both students and institutions continue their work. Particularly, the University of Texas and Rice University created programs and attracted faculty to enhance their institutional research pretensions. This era witnessed the creation and expansion of the medical training facilities that were so successful by the end of the century. Lastly, the period encompassed the beginnings of the electronics industry. The creation and commercialization of the integrated circuit chip formed the basis for the late century computer revolution. [4]

The last period of significant growth runs from 1972 through the turn of the century. During that period NASA underwent, first, retrenchment and, then, renaissance in its missions of space exploration and manned space flight. Not until the turn of the new century did poor performance of the International Space Station and the tragic loss of the Columbia in 2003, the second catastrophic shuttle accident to mar the program, cast a shadow on NASA and its future. In the last third of the century as well, new developments in education once again recast the scientific landscape of the state. Already well-established as important centers for pure science and research, Rice and the University of Texas found themselves challenged by the rapid growth of Texas A&M. From the early 1970s the school roughly quintupled its enrollment, shifted away from its military academy and vocation education roots, and plunged headlong into research, developmental, and pure science programs. In engineering, materials science, construction-related applied sciences, physics, as well as several fields of biological science, A&M emerged as a major educational and research center. Other universities also showed remarkable growth, notably Texas Tech and the University of North Texas. This final period revealed continued development of an extensive and highly successful medical research and educational infrastructure. The University of Texas Health Science Centers, M. D. Anderson Cancer Research Center, the Baylor School of Medicine, and additional programs of other public universities all competed with each other and constituted an overall medical education and research network on a par with those in states like New York, Illinois, and California. [5]

Creation of a medical education system began early in the century. The Baylor University Medical Center commenced operations in 1903 as the Texas Baptist Memorial Sanitarium. It was the product of the combined forces of early Progressive-era professionalism and traditional religious philanthropy. Dr. Charles Rosser, founder and head of the Baylor College of Medicine, worked to combine his professional vision with the progressive reform of Dallas. Area Baptist clergy supported the creation of a flagship humanitarian institution and moneyed oil and cattlemen contributed funds to begin the project. Later, the Baptist General Convention of Texas also undertook to oversee administration and continued financial support. After years of concentrating on nursing and running a sanitarium, administrators in 1921 integrated the facility into the Baylor University medical education complex. The hospital prospered for the next several years, but was sorely tested by the trials of the Great Depression. While commendable, the hospital's emphasis on charity health care during the Depression almost destroyed the institution. By 1943, facing severe financial crisis, the Baylor College of Medicine opted to follow grant money from the M. D. Anderson Foundation and relocate to Houston. Despite the loss of the medical school, the hospital remained and continued to redefine its mission. Hospital administrators led by Lawrence Payne realized the necessity of increasing the hospital's flow of private, paying patients. [6]

Boone Powell, Sr., became the business manager in 1945 and CEO in 1948. His aggressive management style brought Baylor almost thirty years of growth. Payne, who first made the case of recasting Baylor's revenue profile, moved to overseeing fundraising and expansion of facilities. In the next twenty years Baylor modernized and dramatically improved services. The Truett Memorial

Hospital began operations as part of the Baylor University Hospital in 1950. The nearly 500 beds and modern amenities in Truett helped Baylor become the fifth largest general hospital in America. Along with the growth in facilities, Baylor concentrated on recruiting and developing medical talent. The hospital expanded cancer radiation therapy. Baylor surgeons began doing open-heart operations in 1958. Women's and children's health services expanded with new facilities. The increasing size and complexity of the physical plant prompted directors to rename the facility the Baylor University Medical Center. In the 1960s and early 1970s cardiac care and cardiac surgery constituted some of the best achievements of the Center. By the 1980s BUMC commanded an extensive Dallas complex as well as peripheral facilities in surrounding communities. All along, BUMC remained a teaching hospital, hosting residents, fellows, and nursing students as well as students in allied health sciences. From 1993 until the early twenty-first century, BUMC ranked among America's top ten hospitals chosen by *U.S. News and World Report*.[7]

Though Dallas was the original flagship city of Texas medicine, from World War II on Houston hosted a burgeoning medical complex of its own. The Texas Medical Center in Houston originated in a twofold development.[8] In 1941 the Texas legislature passed legislation calling for a Texas State Cancer Hospital and Division of Cancer Research. The 1941 bill revived legislation from 1929, passed for similar purposes but never funded. The renewed effort now boasted a $500,000 allocation to begin construction. Immediately, arguments over the location of the new facility ensued. In 1929 with Baylor Hospital the state's most important teaching hospital, advocates had assumed that the new facility would be in Dallas. The Depression intervened and stalled funding of the new project, and by 1941 several factors had changed. Baylor, close to dissolution during the 1930s, was still in the process of shedding its charity hospital identity. Moreover, in the years after World War I,

Houston had become the focus of population growth and business power in Texas. [9]

For some years Dr. Ernst Bertner, Houston gynecologist and associate of developer Jesse Jones, had promoted the idea of a comprehensive medical center in the Bayou City. Bertner believed that American medicine stood on the precipice of a technological and therapeutic revolution that promised to render existing medical facilities obsolete. The future demanded a wave of new hospitals and treatment infrastructure that would organize different medical specialties in close proximity to each other. They should possess a physical plant with sufficient electrical power to operate the new generation of diagnostic and therapeutic machinery. Lastly, a comprehensive medical center should have a medical school and allied health-services training, closely linking research, teaching, and clinical practice.

Just two years before the passage of the Cancer Hospital Bill, millionaire cotton tycoon Monroe Dunaway Anderson died a childless bachelor. In 1935 the administration of President Franklin D. Roosevelt had secured passage of comprehensive tax reform legislation to pay for the burgeoning costs of the New Deal. Anderson, as one of the surviving partners of the giant cotton firm Anderson, Clayton & Co., held over half the corporate stock in 1936. Under the new law, if he or the other surviving partner and major stockholder were to die, the resulting estate taxes would destroy the company. Anderson and his attorneys opted to create the M. D. Anderson Foundation. In the remaining two and a half years of his life, Anderson transferred millions from his fortune into the foundation. At his death, the foundation capital exceeded $20 million, but the charter did not direct the trustees to any specific work.

Entrepreneur and longtime Houston developer Jones, a friend and supporter of Bertner, helped create a solution. According to Jones' proposal, Houston should receive the new cancer hospital. The Anderson Foundation would supply a matching grant, doubling the state money, if the center located to Houston and bore Anderson's name. Jones' proposal envisioned the cancer hospital becoming the centerpiece of a medical complex replete with the necessary physical plant, consolidated to link research and the various medical specialties, and centrally located in downtown Houston. In 1943 a Houston referendum approved the sale of city lands to the Anderson Foundation: 134 acres near Hermann Park became Anderson property. The Foundation then donated the land to the proposed center, which attracted the Baylor Medical School as one of its first components. The board of directors of the newly created Texas Medical Center appointed Bertner the first president, a post he held until Dr. R. Lee Clark began a thirty-two-year tenure in 1946.[10]

Over the course of the 1950s the various programs and the physical facilities surrounding the Anderson Cancer Hospital increased substantially. By the early 1960s the medical center consisted of Anderson and the medical school, but also other important hospitals like Methodist, Shriners Texas Children's, and the Dental Branch of the UT System. In 1972 the University of Texas opened its Houston Health Science Center (UTHSCH) as part of the Texas Medical Center. The UTHSCH, operating in part on money accumulated from the Permanent University Fund, had a profound effect on both the regional economy and the medical sciences beyond Texas. At century's end M. D. Anderson alone piped over $700 million in operating expenditures into the Houston-area economy, supplied over 14,000 jobs, and accounted for millions of additional dollars and thousands of jobs in contracted construction. Anderson cancer therapies had expanded from early surgery and radiological treatments to hyper-advanced techniques, gene therapies, and radical manipulations of patients' immune systems. Another field of tremendous research potential would be biological therapy such as the design and application of new cancer therapeutic drugs.[11]

Just as Texas education had once benefited from the political career of young Lyndon B. Johnson at the National Youth Administration, in later years Texas science and technology reaped rewards from his rise through the Senate to the White House. Assessing the impact of the Russian Sputnik launch, then-Senator Johnson, in his opening remarks for the Preparedness Subcommittee Hearings on November 25, 1957, expressed the sense of urgency that gripped many Americans. Comparing the launch to the Japanese attack on Pearl Harbor, he added: "In my opinion we do not have as much time as we had after Pearl Harbor." By February 1958, as chair of the Senate's Special Committee on Space and Astronautics, Johnson helped shepherd the legislation to create the National Aeronautics and Space Administration (NASA), which officially commenced operations on October 1, 1958. Manned space flight quickly became the principal focus of NASA planning, and a "space race" with the Soviet Union ensued. [12]

In the summer of 1961 President John F. Kennedy issued his famous challenge to send astronauts safely to the moon and back before 1970. Though the agency already operated launch facilities in Florida, control and rocket development facilities in Alabama and Mississippi, and headquarters in Virginia, new planning called for the creation of a new mission control and crew-training center. In the fall of 1961 administration officials announced the decision to build the new facility just south of Houston on 1,000 acres of land made available by Rice University. Johnson, now vice-president, served as the chair of the National Aeronautics and Space Council. Houston congressman Albert Thomas, an important member of the House Appropriations Committee, worked with Johnson to secure the selection of the Houston site. Critics balked at the insider arrangements, but NASA nevertheless quickly proceeded to create the Manned Spacecraft Center (MSC). Though not yet in its permanent buildings, the MSC directed the ongoing Mercury, Gemini, and Apollo projects by the end of 1962. Since the summer of 1964, with preparations for the Gemini IV launch, the MSC has been responsible for command and control of every manned space mission operated by NASA. The famed lunar preparatory missions and subsequent landings were all directed from Houston, which was renamed the Lyndon B. Johnson Space Center upon Johnson's death in 1973.

Following several successful unmanned Mercury flights, the Russians drastically raised the stakes on April 12, 1961, when Yuri Gagarin became the first human to orbit the earth. Eight days later President Kennedy sent a memo to Vice President Johnson demanding to know, "Do we have a chance of beating the Soviets by putting a laboratory in space, or by a trip around the moon, or by a rocket to land on the moon, or by a rocket to go to the moon and back with a man? Is there any other space program which promises dramatic results in which we could win?" Within weeks of the Gagarin flight, Alan Shepard, Jr., piloted the first of the Project Mercury's six manned space missions. Houston was the center of an all-out space race in which the Americans staked all on the Apollo lunar exploration program. [13]

Announced in July 1960 with the goal of orbiting the moon, the initial launches of the Apollo program were unmanned flights to test the multistage Saturn boosters in conjunction with the command module. The first manned mission, Apollo 1, resulted in a tragic failure during preflight tests on January 27, 1967. A fire, exacerbated by the 100 percent oxygen environment of the command module, claimed the lives of three astronauts: Virgil "Gus" Grissom, Eddie Walker, and Roger Chaffee. The horrible loss notwithstanding, success was not long deferred. Launched on July 16, 1969, Apollo 11 carried the Eagle Lunar Module into lunar orbit. Neil Armstrong and Edwin "Buzz" Aldrin, Jr., landed the Eagle in the Sea of Tranquility. After nearly twenty-two hours on the moon, they returned to debriefing and quarantine at NASA's Houston facilities. They brought back approximately forty-five pounds of lunar

rocks for further study. Among other items, they had left a retrore-
flector array on the moon, allowing UT's McDonald Observatory,
in conjunction with three other labs, to perform laser ranging of
the moon-earth separation. There would be five more manned missions to the moon, but none captured public attention or put the
Houston MSC back on the map like the ill-fated 1970 Apollo 13
mission. After a devastating oxygen tank explosion, Commander
James Lovell, Jr., confirmed the damage with his famous cryptic
message, "Houston, we've had a problem." Over the next days and
under intense world media scrutiny, engineers at the MSC worked
out the details of returning their crippled craft to earth. Their success transformed a fiasco into a public relations coup and elevated
the already lionized role of the MSC to near mythological levels. In
the public mind, Houston was now synonymous with "high-tech"
and America's "can-do" attitude. [14]

Houston Space
Center rocket.
Courtesy NASA.

After the spectacular moon shots, NASA struggled to establish another program with such popular appeal. Several missions of the Skylab space-station project returned important scientific and engineering data, but failed to dominate the American imagination. Additionally, in 1977 it was determined that increased solar activity had degraded Skylab's orbit. On July 11, 1979, years short of the promised lifetime, Skylab fell to earth, spreading debris across the Indian Ocean and uninhabited areas of Australia. Beginning in 1981 the shuttle program aimed to deliver frequent orbital transport missions for a wide array of proposed schemes, eventually including a new space station project. Despite early success, the program struggled when, on January 28, 1986, the space shuttle Challenger exploded seventy-three seconds after launch. The shuttle fleet resumed service some two years later, supporting joint Russo-American missions and construction of the hotly debated International Space Station. Early in the new century tragedy once again marred the program. During re-entry on February 1, 2003, the shuttle Columbia disintegrated over northeast Texas with the loss of all its crew. [15]

The large federal budgets assigned to NASA were not the only federal monies coming to big-scale Texas science. Entrenched pork-barrel politics relating to Texas science and technology through the NASA experience verged on boondoggling near the end of the century. Texas was the winner of one the largest scientific sweepstakes since the Manhattan Project. In 1987 twenty-five states submitted a total of forty-three bids (Texas had seven) to the Department of Energy (DOE) in the competition to construct the Superconducting Super Collider (SSC). When finished, the SSC would be the largest scientific instrument ever constructed. From 1984 through 1989 Congress appropriated $205 million for the DOE to research the feasibility of building the colliding-beam accelerator, which centered on a fifty-three-mile main ring designed to "smash" two 20-trillion electron volt (TeV) beams into each other. The SSC would provide a tenfold increase in power output over the collider at Fermi National Accelerator Laboratory in Illinois, then the most powerful accelerator in the world. The 40-TeV collisions, initially targeted to begin in 1996, would have nearly tripled the output of the 14-TeV proton collisions projected for the new world leader, the European Organization for Nuclear Research's Large Hadron Collider, scheduled for completion in 2007. The SSC was expected to provide researchers the ability to investigate conditions thought likely one-ten-trillionth of a second after the Big Bang. [16]

Unfortunately, Texas' winning entry went bust when Congress cancelled the project's funding in 1993 amid increasing pressure to balance the federal budget. Officials had already spent just over $2 billion on research and development, digging fourteen miles of tunnels and constructing a clutch of buildings in Waxahachie, Texas. The program is now better known scientifically for what might have been and politically for epitomizing the dangers of special-interest funding. Despite its scientific promise and support from the Ronald Reagan, George H. W. Bush, and Bill Clinton administrations, the SSC's expense eventually became a target for fiscal conservatives outside Texas. The DOE's 1988 budget had called for $3.9–$4.8 billion for construction; however, that same year the Congressional Budget Office projected total costs of $4.5–6.4 billion. By the time of its cancellation, planners had already awarded more than 45,000 contracts to contractors from at least forty-five states for a project whose estimated costs had grown to $8 billion. [17]

As part of the cancellation negotiations, the federal government gave Texas $68 million to help offset the $1 billion Texas had invested in the project. Initially, this money was offered as an incentive to support redevelopment of the site, but that plan failed when Governor George W. Bush decided to use the money to retire bonds associated with the state's initial investment.[18]

While the story of the SSC demonstrates the dangers of politically driven big-money science projects, the story of Texas electronics shows the potential of market-driven industrial innovation. In 1930 investors founded Geophysical Service, Inc. (GSI) to exploit the new process of reflection seismography. In this technique investigators set off small charges of dynamite and measured the properties of the reflected sound waves to determine the characteristics of the substrata. By 1939, under the name Coronado Corporation, the company had incorporated a subsidiary, Geophysical Services, Inc., to operate its own oil fields. On Saturday, December 6, 1941, Coronado sold GSI to a group of four investors. Events the next day wrecked their plans to pursue Indonesian oil development. However, in the subsequent years GSI parlayed its seismic and electronic technologies into lucrative war production contracts, including the first U.S. Navy submarine detection devices. [19]

In 1951 the company reorganized as Texas Instruments Incorporated (TI). GSI became a wholly owned subsidiary of the new firm, whose contracts eventually included the usage of its seismic technologies to monitor underground nuclear testing by the Soviet Union. In 1954 TI introduced the silicon transistor and produced the first transistor radio. The real revolution began four years later. Jack Kilby demonstrated the first integrated circuit on September 12, 1958. Less than three months later a TI team had sketched the first integrated circuit as an alternative to conventional circuit-miniaturization methods. Reflecting on this historic event, Kilby quipped, "What we didn't realize then was that the integrated circuit would reduce the cost of electronic functions by a factor of a million to one. Nothing had ever done that for anything before." Integrated circuits soon dominated U.S. high technology, appearing in devices like guidance systems of the Minuteman II intercontinental ballistic missiles. By the end of the century integrated circuits were ubiquitous and had ushered in a digital revolution that provided unprecedented access to information and communication technologies. [20]

In addition to numerous other honors, including winning the National Medal of Science in 1969, Kilby earned half of the 2000

The first integrated circuit. Courtesy Texas Instruments.

Nobel Prize in Physics "for his part in the invention of the integrated circuit." In his Nobel acceptance speech Kilby recognized Robert Noyce of Fairchild Semiconductor for his work leading to the introduction of the first commercially viable silicon integrated circuit in 1959.[21] Kilby's circuit had used the then-common germanium as his semiconductor of choice. Kilby's extraordinary career also included heading the teams that built the first military systems to include integrated circuits and the first computer to include integrated circuits. In addition, he helped develop the handheld calculator and the thermal printer. From 1978–1984 Kilby served as Distinguished Professor of Electrical Engineering at Texas A&M University. Finally shedding its oil field roots in 1988, Texas Instruments sold GSI to Halliburton as part of a restructuring effort aimed at focusing the company entirely on electronics. The close of the twentieth century saw TI as an industry leader in electronics design and application with the invention and subsequent commercialization of Digital Signal Processing and Digital Light Processing technologies, as well as a continuous record of incorporating an increasing number of functions into single-chip solutions. In 2000 *Fortune* magazine ranked TI as the 180th largest company in the world with annual revenues of $9.4 billion generating profits exceeding $1.4 billion. [22]

Of all the fields discussed so far, none could outweigh developments in biology and genetics. It is no overstatement to claim that innovations in these fields represented a brand new scientific and industrial revolution at the close of the twentieth century. The state's contribution to biology and genetics has been so vast that it cannot be done justice in such limited space. Consequently, just a few representative figures and projects from the twentieth century have been selected for review. These episodes include "the other fly room," "two women above the glass ceiling," the rise of scientific agriculture, animal cloning, and the Human Genome Project.

The Rice Institute opened as a private, co-educational college on September 23, 1912. The following year Julian Huxley, brother of famed author Aldous Huxley and grandson of Darwin's bulldog, Thomas Henry Huxley, assumed the chair of biology. Huxley recruited Hermann Muller to a position in his department, thus creating the first link to Texas for the future Nobel Laureate. Over the next five years Muller shared time between the Rice Institute and Columbia. He had done graduate study with Thomas Hunt Morgan at Columbia University when Morgan conducted his Nobel-winning research on fruit fly genetics. At the start of the 1920s Columbia University's "fly room," with Thomas Hunt Morgan, Alfred Sturtevant, and Calvin Bridges, was the hub of U.S. genetic research. Over the latter half of the decade, by developing associations with investigators like Muller, the University of Texas became one of the primary U.S. centers for genetic research. Success at Austin's zoology department stemmed from the hiring of three men. Embryologist John T. Patterson joined the university's zoology department in 1908. In 1916 Theophilus S. Painter, a cytologist, began his tenure there. Lastly, Hermann Muller signed on in 1920.

Building on his work at Columbia, Muller was able to show that mutations were the result of errors in the gene-copying process and that the error rate could be influenced by temperature change or via exposure to x-rays. Following Muller's 1927 publication concerning the effects of x-rays on mutation rates, the Rockefeller Foundation provided a grant for Muller, Patterson, and Painter to continue their studies. Additionally, Muller discovered that x-rays not only caused mutations, but also broke chromosomes and caused rearrangements. Muller and Painter used cytological techniques to study the chromosomal rearrangements. In 1931 Painter published an article in *Science* that drew on cytological evidence to provide the locations of specific genes on the X-chromosome of the fruit fly (*Drosophila melanogaster*). That same year, through cytological study, Patterson and Painter demonstrated that "mosaic eyes," partial white facets covering a portion of a fruit fly's eyes, and notched wings were the result of an extra segment of X-chromosome attached to the fourth chromosome. Patterson earned the Elliot Medal from the National Academy of Sciences in 1947 for his work in genetics. In 1965 the UT System Board of Regents dedicated a building in his honor. Completed in 1968, the Patterson Laboratories Building currently houses faculty in cell and developmental biology, integrative biology and neurobiology. In 1934 Painter won the Elliott Medal for his work on *Drosophila* chromosomes. He served as UT president from 1946–1952. In 1969 he received the first M. D. Anderson Award for Scientific Creativity and Teaching. Despite publishing the work that would later win him the Nobel Prize, by 1932 Muller found himself unwelcome at the University of Texas and under surveillance by the FBI for his support of a communist student newspaper and for his Soviet sympathies. Muller subsequently departed for the Soviet Institute of Genetics, where he served as senior geneticist from 1933–1937. Barely escaping a Stalinist purge, he returned to

America, finally joining the faculty at Indiana University. However, the construction of the UT zoology department set the precedent for Nobel-quality genetics and science research in Texas. Since the 1930s Texas research institutions have boasted pioneers in several fields, eventually including the Human Genome Project, cloning, and genetic engineering. [23]

It is also significant that Texas provided a setting for the careers of important women in science. Traditionally, Texas higher education was not a friendly environment for women scholars. Despite the obstacles, Marie Betzeer Morrow and Hilda Florence Rosene both built careers during the critical transition period of the 1920s and 1930s. Morrow received her B.A., M.A., and Ph.D. from the UT Department of Botany and Bacteriology in 1926, 1927, and 1932, respectively. She joined the faculty and became a full professor by 1957. Working with Dr. Charles Tom, chief of the Bureau of Chemistry and Soils of the United States Department of Agriculture (USDA), her early work resulted in methods for studying microorganisms in the soil and pioneered the inoculation of seeds to prevent root rot in cotton. Following the completion of a Ph.D., she turned her attention to a collaborative project with Homer E. Price, M.D. Over the next thirty years she developed maps showing the geographical distribution of molds. She also perfected techniques for producing extracts used in allergy testing and mold allergy desensitization treatments. She continued her research and teaching until her retirement from the Department of Microbiology at age seventy in 1966.[24]

Rosene earned her B.S. (1922) and M.S. (1924) degrees from the University of Washington before entering UT to study physiology and zoology in 1929. She received her Ph.D. in 1933 while studying with E. J. Lund. She taught as an instructor (1933–1937), assistant professor (1937–1943), and associate professor (1943–1958) in the Department of Zoology. While holding a Guggenheim Fellowship (1939–1940), she began work on the research program that produced a technique that allowed research-ers to measure the amount of water absorbed by a single root hair. Morrow and Rosene were the only two women to hold tenured positions in the natural sciences at UT into the 1950s.[25]

Texas agriculture not only remained an important sector of the state economy, it also provided an arena for important scientific advances. Examples include Morrow's pioneering work on cotton root rot, establishing the National Clonal Germplasm Repository for Pecans, Hickories, and Chestnuts, creation of the Vidalia onion, and the eradication of the screwworm. In 1932 the USDA estab-lished the world's only pecan-breeding facility, planting 35 acres of native trees near Brownwood. Though the facility nearly lost funding during World War II, the program survived to produce multiple hybridization combinations that improved yields and were stress and insect resistant. At present, the expanded collection sup-ports over 250 cultivars. It is the most complete collection in the world, developing three-fourths of all the cultivars recommended for planting in Texas.[26]

During the 1920s the agricultural economy began to diversify as Texas farmers sought to offset the problems of the agricultural slump. Vegetable crops became a potentially lucrative component of the new production. For example, into the mid-1920s Texas farmers planted Bermuda onions in ever-increasing quantities, but decreas-ing seed quality and poor yields undermined profits. By the latter 1940s the Texas Agricultural Extension Service and Texas A&M had produced new varieties like Excel (986) or Texas Early Grano 052.[27] Subsequent hybridization and breeding created the modern Vidalia onions. In the early 1980s Leonard Pike, Paul Leeper, and Marvin Miller of Texas A&M University, College Station, and its Agricultural Research and Extension Center at Weslaco introduced the Texas Grano 1015Y variety ("1015Y" designates a yellow onion that should be planted on October 15), marketed under the brand name SuperSweet. In addition to its much sought-after taste, this new variety produced up to four times the yield of older standard varieties. From 1983–1998 the SuperSweet by itself accounted for $350 million in farm-level and $1.2 billion in total impact on the Texas economy. In 1992 Pike helped found the Vegetable and Fruit Improvement Center in College Station.[28]

In 1946 the Agricultural Research Service (ARS) established the United States Livestock Insects Laboratory in Kerrville, Texas. From this outpost, Edward Knipling and Raymond Bushland pioneered the release of sterile male insects as a non-toxic means of controlling pest populations. Prompted by Herman Muller's 1950 discovery that otherwise healthy fruit flies could be rendered sterile, Knipling and Bushland smuggled screwworms (the larvae of the parasitic fly *Cochliomyia hominivorax*) into a San Antonio army hospital where they secretly used the x-ray machine. Having thus produced healthy but sterile flies, Bushland tackled the practical problems of raising the massive quantities of males needed for biological control. Meanwhile, Knipling developed a population model to determine the specific numbers needed. In 1954 Dutch officials facing an epidemic of screwworms on the island of Curacao sought help from the USDA. The agency picked Knipling and Bushland to test their strategy. Within approximately three generations the flies had been eradicated. The last case of screwworm infestation in the United States was in 1966, a fact that represents billions of dollars saved from potential crop-damage costs. The technique has since been applied to control Mediterranean fruit flies, tsetse flies, and others. In 1992 Knipling and Bushland shared the World Food Prize. Knipling was awarded the National Medal of Science in 1966. Texas A&M's Knipling-Bushland Southwest Animal Research Foundation, established in 1999, aims to honor and continue their legacy.[29]

Excitement and ethical questions swirled following the 1996 announcement that Dolly, the first mammal successfully cloned using the genetic material from an adult cell, had been born. In July

1997 Texas A&M University established the Missyplicity Project—a privately funded $3.7 million research program aimed at cloning "Missy," a mixed-breed border collie. As of 2006 the project had not reached its stated goal but had by 2001 resulted in the first cloned companion animal, a cat named "cc." In 1999 Jonathan Hill and Mark Westhusin of Texas A&M University successfully cloned a 21-year-old bull. Using the DNA from "Chance," the scientists performed 189 nuclear transfers before achieving the successful pregnancy that resulted in "Second Chance." As of June 2005 Texas A&M researchers have also been responsible for numerous clones, including multiple litters of piglets, a Boer goat, and an Angus bull. [30]

In 1990 a consortium of the Department of Energy, many government laboratories, and non-governmental institutions launched the Human Genome Project (HGP). Baylor College of Medicine (BCM) played an important role in this massive program, establishing the Human Genome Sequencing Center (HGSC). In 1999 the center garnered the largest grant ever awarded to the BCM, $80 million from the National Human Genome Research Institute. By the close of phase sequencing in 2003, Baylor's HGSC had climbed into the top five most prolific sequencing centers. By sequencing chromosomes 3, 12, and X, it contributed approximately 10 percent of the overall genome sequence. Ongoing sequencing in Phase III currently emphasizes the effect of individual DNA on human phenotypes and sequencing the genomes of various animals. [31]

Given the incredible diversity, creativity, and economic impact of Texas science development in the twentieth century, a simple summation of that history is impossible. This essay highlights only major aspects of the complicated story. The most obvious conclusion at the dawn of the twenty-first century is that Texas, across a spectrum of fields, possessed a scientific, medical, and research industrial infrastructure equal to top-tier institutions in other states like Florida, California, and New York. Indeed, in terms of its scientific achievement, Texas had emerged as a distinct member of the world scientific community, integrally connected to the ongoing globalization of technology and scientific development.

Selected Bibliography

Berry, Margaret Catherine. *The University of Texas: A Pictorial Account of its First Century.* Austin: University of Texas Press, 1980.

Dethloff, Henry. *Suddenly Tomorrow Came: A History of the Johnson Space Center.* NASA History Series SP-4307. Houston: NASA, 1993.

Elliott, Frederick C. *The Birth of the Texas Medical Center: A Personal Account.* College Station: Texas A&M University Press, 2004.

Haigh, Berte R. *Land, Oil, and Education.* El Paso: Texas Western Press / University of Texas, 1986.

Kay, W. D. *Defining NASA: The Historical Debate Over the Agency's Mission.* Albany: State University of New York Press, 2005.

Meiners, Fredericka. *A History of Rice University: The Institute Years, 1907–1963.* Houston: Rice University Studies, 1982.

Pirtle, Caleb, III. *Engineering the World: Stories from the First 75 Years of Texas Instruments.* Dallas: Southern Methodist University Press, 2005.

Portee, David S. F. *NASA's Origins and the Dawn of the Space Age* [electronic resource]. NASA History Division, Office of Policy and Plans, NASA Headquarters, 1998.

Riordan, Michael, and Lillian Hoddeson, *Crystal Fire: The Birth of the Information Age.* New York: Norton, 1997.

Shayler, David. *Skylab: America's Space Station.* London: Springer, 2001.

Endnotes

1. Texas State Data Center and Office of the State Demographer, *Total Resident Population and Percent Population Change in Texas: 1850 to 2000,* http://txsdc.utsa.edu/txdata/apport/hist_b.php (accessed July 16, 2007).

2. Rupert N. Richardson et al., *Texas: The Lone Star State* (Upper Saddle River, N. J.: Prentice Hall, 2005), 348–51.

3. Berte R. Haigh, *Land, Oil, and Education* (El Paso: Texas Western Press/University of Texas: 1986), passim.

4. Richard A. Reiman, *The New Deal & American Youth: Ideas & Ideals in a Depression Decade* (Athens: University of Georgia Press, 1992); Fredericka Meiners, *A History of Rice University: The Institute Years,*

1907–1963 (Houston: Rice University Studies, 1982), 147–57, 169–78; Margaret Catherine Berry, *The University of Texas: A Pictorial Account of its First Century* (Austin: University of Texas Press, 1980), 113–93.

5. W. D. Kay, *Defining NASA: The Historical Debate over the Agency's Mission*, (Albany: State University of New York Press, 2005), 151–78; *Handbook of Texas Online*, s.v. "Texas A&M," http://www.tsha.utexas.edu/handbook/online/articles/TT/kct8.html (accessed October 25, 2006).

6. *Handbook of Texas Online*, s.v. "Baylor University Medical Center," http://www.tsha.utexas.edu/handbook/online/articles/BB/sbb3.html (accessed October 25, 2006); R. D. Dignan, M.D., "History of Colon and Rectal Surgery at Baylor University Medical Center," *Baylor University Medical Center Proceedings* 17, no. 3 (July 2004): 289–91.

7. Baylor Health Care System, s.v. " History 1903–2005," http://www.baylorhealth.com/aboutus/newsroom/pdf/BHCSHistoryand-2006FactSheet.pdf (accessed October 25, 2006).

8. Texas Medical Center, s.v. "A Historical Journey," http://www.tmc.edu/tmc-history.html (accessed October 25, 2006).

9. Frederick C. Elliott, *The Birth of the Texas Medical Center: A Personal Account*, (College Station: Texas A&M Press, 2004), 61–89; N. Don Macon, *Mr. John H. Freeman and Friends: A Story of the Texas Medical Center and How it Began* (Houston: Texas Medical Center, 1973), passim.

10. N. Don Macon, *Clark and the Anderson: A Personal Profile* (Houston: Texas Medical Center, 1976), 137–39, 156–62; *Handbook of Texas Online*, s.v. "Dr. Ernst Bertner," http://www.tsha.utexas.edu/handbook/online/articles/BB/fbe86.html (accessed October 25, 2006).

11. *Handbook of Texas Online*, s.v. "M. D. Anderson Foundation," http://www.tsha.utexas.edu/handbook/online/articles/MM/vrm1.html (accessed October 25, 2006); M. D. Anderson Cancer Center Web site, s.v. "Economic Impact," http://www.mdanderson.org/about_mda/who_we_are/display.cfm?id=54461b27-ea49-41d9-9211a17865b7cf08&method=displayfull (accessed October 26, 2006);

M. D. Anderson Cancer Center Web site, s.v. "Research Milestones," http://www.mdanderson.org/about_mda/who_we_are/display.cfm?id=720f1302-22b5-11d5-811000508b603a14&method=displayfull (accessed October 26, 2006);

Dr. James S. Olson (author of forthcoming authoritative history of M. D. Anderson), interview with author, August 23, 2006.

12. Henry Dethloff, *Suddenly Tomorrow Came: A History of the Johnson Space Center*, NASA History Series SP-4307 (Houston: NASA, 1993), 4; David S. F. Portee, *NASA's Origins and the Dawn of the Space Age* [electronic resource], NASA History Division, Office of Policy and Plans, NASA Headquarters, 1998.

13. John F. Kennedy to Lyndon Johnson, memorandum, April 20, 1961, Presidential Files, John F. Kennedy Presidential Library, Boston.

14. NASA, *Apollo Program Summary Report* , NASA-TM-X-68725; Donald A. Beattie, *Taking Science to the Moon: Lunar Experiments and the Apollo Program* (Baltimore: Johns Hopkins University Press, 2001), 135–38; Jim Lovell, *Lost Moon: The Perilous Voyage of Apollo 13* (New York: Houghton Mifflin, 1994), 94–95; NASA Apollo Missions Web site, s.v. "Chronology of Events Surrounding the Apollo 13 Accident," http://www.hq.nasa.gov/office/pao/History/apollo/problem.html   (accessed October 9, 2006).

15. David Shayler, *Skylab: America's Space Station* (London: Springer Praxis, 2001), 298–315; NASA History Division, Office of Policy and Plans, NASA Headquarters, *Chronology of Space Shuttle Flights, 1981–2000,* 2000.

16. Eliot Marshal, "The Supercollider Sweepstakes," *Science* 237, no. 4820 (1987): 1288;

U.S. Congress, Congressional Budget Office, "Risks and Benefits of Building the Superconducting Super Collider: A Special Study," October 1988; CERN Web site, s.v. "What is LHC?" http://public.web.cern.ch/Public/Content/Chapters/AboutCERN/CERNFuture/WhatLHC/WhatLHC-en.html (accessed October 9, 2006).

17. Information in this paragraph comes from: Ellis County Museum Web site, s.v. "Superconducting Super Collider (SSC)," http://www.rootsweb.com/~txecm/super_collider.htm (accessed October 6, 2006); and U.S. Congress, Congressional Budget Office, "Risks and Benefits of Building the Superconducting Super Collider: A Special Study," October 1988.

18. Jeffrey Mervis, "The Scientists are Long Gone, But Bitter Memories Remain," *Science* 302, no. 5642 (2003): 40–41.

19. Texas Instruments Web site, s.v. "TI Interactive Timeline," http://www.ti.com/corp/docs/company/history/timeline/popup.htm (accessed October 19, 2006).

20. Texas Instruments Web site, s.v. "1958 Integrated Circuit Invented by Jack Kilby," http://www.ti.com/corp/docs/company/history/timeline/semicon/1950/docs/58ic_kilby.htm (accessed October 19, 2006).

21. J. S. Kilby. "Turning Potential into Realities: The Invention of the Integrated Circuit" (Nobel lecture, Aula Magna, Stockholm University, Stockholm, Sweden, December 8, 2000).

22. Nobel Foundation Web site, s.v. "The Nobel Prize in Physics 2000," http://nobelprize.org/nobel_prizes/physics/laureates/2000/ (accessed October 19, 2006); Michael Riordan and Lillian Hoddeson, *Crystal Fire: The Birth of the Information Age* (New York: Norton, 1997), 256–60; CNNMoney.com Web site, s.v. "Fortune 500: 2000 Archive

Full List 101–200," http://money.cnn.com/magazines/fortune/fortune500_archive/full/2000/101.html (accessed October 27, 2006).

23. R. P. Wagner and J. F. Crow. "The Other Fly Room: J. T. Patterson and Texas Genetics," *Genetics* 157 (2001): 1–5; T. S. Painter. "A Cytological Map of the X-Chromo-Some of Drosophila Melano-Gaster" *Science* 73, no. 1902 (1931): 647–48.

T. J. Patterson and T. S. Painter. "A Mottled-Eyed Drosophila," *Science* 73, no. 1898 (1931): 530–31; University of Texas at Austin Web site, s.v. "Biographical Sketch – John T. Patterson," http://www.utexas.edu/faculty/council/2000-2001/memorials/AMR/Patterson/patterson.html (accessed October 14, 2006);

Theophilus Shickel Painter [electronic resource], http://www.utexas.edu/faculty/council/2000-2001/memorials/SCANNED/painter.pdf (accessed October 14, 2006).

Kenneth E. Hendrickson and Glenn M. Sanford, eds., *An Historical Dictionary of the Darwin Controversy* (Athens: Atiner, 2005), 212–13.

24. In Memoriam: Marie Betzner Morrow (1895–1971) [electronic resource], http://www.utexas.edu/faculty/council/2000-2001/memorials/SCANNED/morrow.pdf (accessed October 14, 2006).

25. In Memoriam: Hilda Florence Rosene [electronic resource], http://www.utexas.edu/faculty/council/2000-2001/memorials/SCANNED/rosene.pdf (accessed October 14, 2006).

26. Texas A&M University Web site, s.v. "Pecan Breeding & Genetics-History," http://aggiehorticulture.tamu.edu/carya/history.htm (accessed October 10, 2006).

27. Texas A&M University Web site, s.v. "The History of Sweet Texas Onions," http://plantanswers.tamu.edu/publications/onions/onionhis.html (accessed October 22, 2006).

28. *Monitor* Web site, s.v. "Pike Recalls Early Onion Days While Accepting Potts Award," http://themonitor.com/PrintIt.cfm?Template=/GlobalTemplates/Details.cfm&StoryID=377&Section=Rod%20Santa%20Ana (accessed October 23, 2006).

29. Perry Adkisson and James Tumlinson, *Edward F. Knipling (1909–2000): A Biographical Memoir* (Washington, D.C.: National Academies Press, 2003).

30. Science Daily Web site, s.v. "Texas A&M Clones First Cat," http://www.sciencedaily.com/releases/2002/02/020215070841.htm (accessed October 20, 2006); Texas A&M University Web site, s.v. "Texas A&M Scientists Clone First-Ever Bull," http://agnews.tamu.edu/stories/VETM/Sep0299a.htm (accessed October 20, 2006);

MyWestTexas.com Web site, s.v. "A&M Leads the World in Cloning," http://www.mywesttexas.com/site/printerFriendly.cfm?brd=2288&dept_id=475621&newsid=14763062 (accessed October 23, 2006).

31. Texas Medical Center Web site, s.v. "Baylor Among Sites Selected to Finish Genetic Map," http://www.tmc.edu/tmcnews/04_01_99/page_01.html (accessed October 16, 2006); National Human Genome Research Institute Web site, s.v. "2003 Release: International Consortium Completed Human Genome Project," http://genome.gov/11006929 (accessed October 15, 2006); Eurekalert! Web site, s.v. "Baylor Human Genome Sequencing Center marks End of Sequencing Effort with Chromosome 3," http://www.eurekalert.org/pub_releases/2006-04/bcom-bhg042506.php (accessed October 14, 2006); Human Genome Sequencing Center at Baylor College of Medicine Web site, s.v. "HGSC Sequencing Projects," http://www.hgsc.bcm.tmc.edu/projects/ (accessed October 16, 2006).

Contributors

Gerald Betty—Dr. Betty is an adjunct professor of history at Texas A&M University, College Station. His book, *Comanche Society* (2002), focuses on the relationship between a society's social institutions and its history.

Angela Boswell—Dr. Boswell is an associate professor of history at Henderson State University in Arkansas. She is the author of *Her Act and Deed: Women's Lives in a Rural Southern County, 1837–1873* (2001) and co-editor of *Searching for Their Places: Women in the South across Four Centuries* (2003) and *Women Shaping the South: Creating and Confronting Change* (2006). Currently, she is working on a manuscript entitled *The Women's History of Texas*.

Mark Busby—Director of the Southwest Regional Humanities Center and Center for the Study of the Southwest at Texas State University in San Marcos, Dr. Busby is the author of *Larry McMurtry and the West: An Ambivalent Relationship* (1995), *Ralph Ellison* (1991), *Lanford Wilson* (1987), *Preston Jones* (1983), and *Fort Benning Blues* (2001), a novel.

Don Graham—Dr. Graham is the J. Frank Dobie Regents Professor of American and English Literature at the University of Texas at Austin. He is the author of numerous books and articles, including *Kings of Texas: The 150-Year Saga of an American Ranching Empire* (2003), which won the Carr P. Collins Prize for best nonfiction book of the year, and editor of *Lone Star Literature: A Texas Anthology* (2006). His newest book is *Literary Austin* (2007). Graham is also a past president of the Texas Institute of Letters and a writer-at-large for *Texas Monthly*.

Michael R. Grauer—Mr. Grauer is the curator of art at the Panhandle-Plains Historical Museum in Canyon, Texas. He has worked previously at the Smithsonian American Art Museum, the Meadows Museum at Southern Methodist University, and the Dallas Museum of Art. He has lectured nationally and curated numerous exhibitions on historic southwestern art. He is the author of *W. Herbert Dunton: A Retrospective* (1991) and co-authored the *Dictionary of Texas Artists, 1800–1945* (1999) and *Frank Paul Sauerwein: An Early Master Painter of the American Southwest* (2002).

Gary Hartman—Dr. Hartman is the director of the Center for Texas Music History at Texas State University in San Marcos. His recent works include an introductory chapter in *The Roots of Texas Music* (2003) and two articles in the *Journal of Texas Music History*.

Kenneth E. Hendrickson—Dr. Hendrickson is an associate professor of history at Sam Houston State University. He has published on Victorian social and religious history subjects and is a co-editor of *An Historical Dictionary of the Darwin Controversy* (2005). Two forthcoming articles will critique the intelligent design movement.

Mary L. Kelley—Dr. Kelley is an associate professor of history at Lamar University in Beaumont. She was a Fulbright Scholar in Germany and has published *The Foundations of Texan Philanthropy* (2004), as well as numerous scholarly articles. She is a co-editor of this volume and is currently working on a manuscript about Texas women in the twentieth century.

Tai Kreidler—Dr. Kreidler is the co-director of the Southwest Collection/Special Collections Library at Texas Tech University in Lubbock and executive director of the West Texas Historical Association. He is also currently serving as the book review editor of the Texas Oral History Association and as an adjunct professor of history at Texas Tech University.

Bill O'Neal—Dr. O'Neal is a nationally recognized authority on sports in America who has been consulted for television documentaries for the A&E Channel, the History Channel, PBS, the Discovery Channel, and TNN. For thirty-five years he announced Panola Pony baseball games over KGAS radio in Carthage, Texas. A Piper Professor and former president of the East Texas Historical Association, O'Neal has authored numerous books, including five on baseball.

Gene B. Preuss—Dr. Preuss is an assistant professor of history at the University of Houston-Downtown. His dissertation concerned World War II and the Gilmer-Aiken laws. His research interests include reform movements, the American South, Texas, and oral history.

Anthony Quiroz—Dr. Quiroz is an associate professor of history at Texas A&M University-Corpus Christi. His recent book, *Claiming Citizenship: Mexican Americans in Victoria, Texas* (2005), was published by Texas A&M University Press. He has also published several scholarly articles.

Glenn M. Sanford—Dr. Sanford is an associate professor in psychology and philosophy at Sam Houston State University. He has written on numerous intellectual and scientific topics and is a co-editor of *An Historical Dictionary of the Darwin Controversy* (2005).

John W. Storey—Co-editor of this anthology, Dr. Storey is a Regents Professor of history at Lamar University in Beaumont. He has written extensively on religious subjects, including *Texas Baptist Leadership and Social Christianity* (1987), *Southern Baptists of Southeast Texas: A Centennial History, 1888–1988* (1988), *The Religious Right* (1995, 2nd ed., 2001, 3rd ed., 2007), *Teaching Them: A Sesquicentennial Celebration of Texas Baptist Education* (1996), and *Religion and Politics* (2002).

Cary D. Wintz—Dr. Wintz is a professor of history at Texas Southern University in Houston. As author, co-author, or editor, he has written extensively on African Americans. His works include *Black Culture and the Harlem Renaissance* (1998), *African American Political Thought, 1890–1930: Washington, Du Bois, Garvey, and Randolph* (1996), and *The Harlem Renaissance, 1920–1940: Interpretation of an African American Literary Movement* (1996).

Ralph A. Wooster—Dr. Wooster is a distinguished professor of history emeritus at Lamar University in Beaumont. He is also past president of the Texas State Historical Association and the East Texas Historical Association. His books include *Secession Conventions of the South* (1962), *The People in Power* (1969), *Politicians, Planters, and Plain Folk* (1975), *Texas and Texans in the Civil War* (1995), *Lone Star Regiments in Gray* (2001), and *Texas and Texans in World War II* (2005).

Index

19th Street Baptist Church (Austin), 153

9/11 attack, 142, 145

1918, 239

A Case of Lone Star, 240

A Clean Well Lighted Place Art Gallery, 284–85

A Cloud of Witnesses, 230

A Cold Mind, 241

A Corner in Wheat, 246

A Cowtown Chronicle, 236

A Daughter of France, 173

A History of Texas Artists and Sculptors, 268,

A Journey Through Texas, 221

A Knife in the Back, 241

A Nation at Risk, 379,

A Perfect World, 263

A Texas Steer, 248, 260

A Texian Trilogy, 230

A Vaquero of the Brush Country, 225, 250

A Walk on the Wild Side, 259

Abbott, James D., 403

Abilene, Tx., 307

Abilene Christian College, 316

academic freedom, 370, 382

Adair, Christia, 75

Adams, Andy, 225

Adams, Bud, 311

Adcock, Betty, 237

Adler, "Lefty," 283

Adventures with a Texas Naturalist, 221, 226

aerospace industries, 327

African Americans, 105

as a percentage of the population, 70, 84–85, 100–01

discrimination against, 70–71

women, 71, 75, 112, 113, 120–21, 124

women and prohibition, 116

education, 71, 88, 90–94

racial violence, 72, 76, 81–84, 96–97

newspapers, importance of, 73

religion, 74, 136, 152–53

fraternal organizations, 74–75

segregation, 75–76, 78–81

the Galveston storm of 1900, 76–77

voting rights, 80–81, 88–90, 93

Jesse Washington atrocity, 81–82

race riots, 82–83

Brownsville, Tx., incident, 82–83, 103n

Ku Klux Klan, 83–84, 87, 88

the Great Migration, 85

Black Power, 96, 98

Texas Southern University, violence at, 96

music, 97–98

Brown v Board of Education
    (1954), 93–94
desegregation, public education,
    93–95, 98–99
desegregation, public facilities,
    95–96, 99
student "sit-ins," 95
political successes of, 98–99
as farm laborers, 105–06
*After Aztlan: Latino Poetry of the
    Nineties*, 237
Agatite, 241
Age of Foundations, 345 (See
    philanthropy)
Agricultural Research and Extension
    Center at Weslaco, 435
Agricultural Research Service, 436
Agriculture, 18, 51, 105, 175, 399,
    418, 424, 432, 435
Aguilar, Pedro, 49
Ai (Anthony, Florence), 238
Aikin, A. M. Jr., 370, 371
Aikman, Troy, 312
Air Control Board, 396
Air Force (U.S), 122–23, 184, 187,
    236, 316
Al Quaran-Was-Sunnah Society, 142
Alabama and Coushatta Indian Tribes
    of Texas Restoration Act (1987),
    30
Alabama-Coushatta Indians, 5, 9,
    10–11
    and religion, 11, 20, 22
    and basketball, 13
    assimilation of, 13, 20
    government recognition of,
        14–15
    education of, 16–17,
    impact of WW II, 17–18, 20
    relations with state and federal
        authorities, 18–20, 22, 26, 27
    and tourism, 21–22, 26
    preservation of tradition, 22–23,
        25–26, 31, 32

dispute with Big Sandy High
    School, 28
casino gambling, 28–29
claim to east Texas land, 31
symbol of Texas' heritage, 32
Alamo, 1, 204, 319
    in literature, 235
    heroes of, 252, 271
    in films, 253–54, 262
    in art, 270–71
Alamo City, 270 (See San Antonio)
Albert, Susan Wittig, 240
Albright, Lloyd, 273
Aldrin, Edwin Jr. "Buzz", 426
Alexander, John, 426
Ali, Muhammad, 321
All the Dead Lie Down, 240
All the Pretty Horses, 233
Allee, A. Y., 60
Allen, Dalis, 201
Allen, Fred, 180
Allen, Larry, 312
Alley Theatre, 238
Allred, James V., 48
Amarillo, Tx., 32, 137, 267, 273,
    275–76, 283, 287, 307, 408
Amateur Athletic Union (AAU), 317
American Association of University
    Professors (AAUP), 182
American Baptist Convention of
    Texas, 152
American Basketball Association
    (ABA), 315
American Board of Catholic Missions,
    139
American Empire, 259
American Federation of Arts, 272
American Football League (AFL),
    311
American G. I. Forum Women's
    Auxiliary, 126
American GI Forum (AGIF), 51, 53,
    54, 56, 58
American Indian Center (Dallas), 25

American Indian Law Project of Legal Services of North Texas, 32
American League, 301, 303, 304
Americanization movement, 366
Paredes, Américo, 319, 235, 243, 261
Ames, Jessie Daniel, 118
Amish, 147
Amon Carter Collection of Western Art, 343
Amon G. Carter Foundation, 342
Anderson Cancer Hospital, 424
Anderson, Adrian, 2
Anderson, Broncho Billy, 249
Anderson, Clayton & Co., 423
Anderson, Frank, 316
Anderson, Monroe Dunaway, 423
Anderson, Sen. Clinton, 24
Andrews County, 409
Angel of Death, 241
Anglos, 1, 3, 42, 45, 48–50, 52–54, 59, 66n,120–21, 138–39, 141, 150–51, 153, 178–79, 210, 212, 222–23, 254, 330, 341, 375
Annual Texas Exhibition of Painting and Sculpture, 272, 293
Antone, Susan, 201
Anzaldua, Gloria, 224
apocalyptic literature (see religion)
Appleton, Scott, 308, 311
Aransas, 234, 284
Aransas Pass Wildlife Refuge, 391
Archdiocese of New Orleans, 137
Archdiocese of Santa Fe (NM), 137
Archer City, Tx., 231, 257
Arlington National Cemetery, 53
Armstrong, Lance, 321
Armstrong, Neil, 426
Army and Navy Nurse Corps, 123
Arpa, Jose, 277
Arrowhead Mills, 409–10
Art
    early artists, sculptors, 268–71, 280–81, 292–93n

the New Deal, impact of, 274–76, 294–97n
teaching schools, 277
WW II, impact of, 279–80
Cold War, impact of, 281
artistic themes, expressions:
    the bluebonnet school, 271–72, 286–87
    regionalism, 273–78, 298n
    social realism, 278, 298n
    "magic" realism, 278–79
    surrealism, 278
    abstract expressionism, 278
    European modernism, 281
    Texas Funk, 285
    the cowboy school, 286
    Latino artists, 289–90
Art Digest, 272, 274
Art Institute of Chicago, 292
Art Institute of Dallas (AID), 277
Art Students League, 279
Ash, Mary Kay, 128, 350
Ask a Policeman, 241
Association of Southern Women for the Prevention of Lynching, 118
Astrodome, 304
Athens High School, 313
Audubon Society, 391
Aunspaugh, Vivian, 277
Austin, 328, 339, 432
    art, 277–79, 280, 287
    sports, 301, 306, 319
Austin Baptist Association, 153
Austin, Dorothy, 280
Austin, Stephen F., 271, 278, 392
Autry, Gene, 201, 249, 260
Avenger Field, 123
Azteca America, 65

B'nai Israel (Galveston), 146
Baha'is, 142
Bailey, Carden, 281
Bainbridge, John, 254

Baker, Paul, 230, 238
Bakker, Jim, 154
Ball and Chain, 198
Ballet of the Americas, 350
Bandera, Tx., 280
Bandera County, 345
Banks, Ernie, 303
Bannon, Homer, 257
Baptists, 135,
    diversity of, 148
Baptist General Convention of Texas
    (BGCT), 148, 421
    internal tension, 148–50
    and Mexican Americans, 150–52
    and African Americans, 152–53
    Rio Grande River Ministry, 150
    women ministers, 157
Baptist Standard, 174
Barbarosa, 261
Barela, Patrocino, 288
Barkley, Roy, R., 2, 216n
Barney, William, 236
Bartscht, Hari, 280
Base Readjustment and Closure
    (Defense Base Closure and
    Realignment), 187
Basinger, Kim, 260
Bass Performance Hall, 350
Bass, Rick, 234
Bastrop Independent School District,
    371
Bates, David, 288
Battle of San Jacinto, 205, 270
Baugh, Sammy "Slingin'," 307
Bayles, China, 240
Baylor School of Medicine, 420
Baylor University, 150, 421
Baylor University Hospital, 422
Baylor University Medical Center,
    421–22
Bayou City, 97, 282, 423 (See
    Houston)
Bean, Judge Roy, 320
Bear, Roggie, 201

Bearing & Distance, 237
Beatty, Warren, 258
Beaumont, Tx., 234–35, 237, 259,
    302, 315, 317–18, 344–46, 350,
    394–95
Beckmann, Max, 288
Bedichek, Roy, 7, 220–21, 226–27,
    233
Beholdings, 237
Behrens, Ella, 168
Bell, Michael, 153
Bell, Terrell H., 379
Belle, 349
benevolent associations, 324
Benno, Gigi, 201
Benny, Jack, 180
Bentsen, Lloyd Jr., 186
Bermuda onions, 435
Bernson, Maurice, 273
Bertner, Dr. Ernst, 423
Bess, Forrest, 282
Better Schools Campaign, 364–65
Betty McLean Galleries, 284
Betty Parson Gallery, 282
Beveridge, Albert J., 224
Bible, D. X., 316
Biddle, George, 275
Big Bend National Park, 391
Big Thicket, 9–10, 31, 391, 393
Big Town, 241
Biggers, John, 282
Billion Dollar Brain, 260
Bino, 241
Bino's Blues, 241
Biracial Committee, 374 (See
    Houston, segregation)
Bird, Sarah, 224
Bishop College, 229
Bishop's Committee for the Spanish
    Speaking, 139
Bissinger, H. G., 381
Black blizzards, 400 (See
    Environment, dust storms)
Black Panthers, 96, 382

Blanc, Flora, 279
Blanton, Annie Webb, 117, 365–67
Blanton, Carlos K., 3, 366
Blessed McGill, 234
Blessings the Body Gave, 237
Blood Meridian, 233
blood quantum (See Tigua Indians)
Blood Simple, 263
"blowouts" (See Mexican Americans)
Blue-Ribbon Commission, 380
    (See Select Committee on Public
    Education)
Bomar, Bill, 279
Bonner, Mary, 270
Bonnie and Clyde, 258
Book of Golden Deeds, 342
Boom Town, 258
Bordersnakes, 242
Boshier, Derek, 288
Boudreaux, Denise, 201
Bowie, Jim, 252, 262
Boyd, Richard Henry, 152
Boynton, Jack, 282
Bozzi, Julie, 288
bracero program, 49–51, 64, 178
Brackenridge Hall, 328
Brackenridge Park, 180, 350
Brackenridge, George, 328–30,
    347
Bradley, Jerry, 237
Brammer, Billy Lee, 234
Branding Cattle, 245
Brandon, Jay, 241
Brickell, Edie, 201
Bridges, Calvin, 432
Briggs, Waverly, 333
Brin, Leonard M., 178
Brisac, Edith, 279
Briscoe, Dolph, 60
British Open, 319
Brokeback Mountain, 231
Brooks, Van Wyck, 273
Brown and Root, 344
Brown Foundation, 344

*Brown v. Board of Education of Topeka,
    Kansas* (1954), 93, 372–74
Brown, Herman, 344
Brownfield, Tx., 275 (See also African
    Americans)
Brubaker, Harley, 282
Bryan, John Neely, 353n.
Bryant, Bear, 307, 309
Bryant, Keith L., 3
Bryce, James, 352n
Buchanan, James, 274
Buddhists, 142–43
Buffalo Bill's Wild West Show, 247
Bugbee, Harold Dow, 275
Bullock, Sandra, 263
Bureau of Chemistry and Soils of
    the United States Department of
    Agriculture (USDA), 434
Bureau of Indian Affairs (BIA), 19,
    20, 23, 27, 30
Burke, James Lee, 234
Burleson, Albert Sidney, 166–67
Burmah Agate, 399
Burns, Tommy, 320
Burns, Walter T., 167
Busey, Gary, 261
Bush, George H. W., 359, 429
Bush, George W., 7, 30, 156, 212,
    230, 358, 429
Bushland, Raymond, 436
But Not for Love, 234
Butt, Mary Elizabeth, 345
Buu Mon Buddhist Temple (Port
    Arthur), 143–44
Byrd, James, 97
Bywaters, Jerry, 272, 274, 278, 289

Cabato Sentora: Poems, 237
Caddo, Tx., 393
Caddo Lake, 397
Cadena, Carlos, 54, 56
Cadillac Ranch, 267, 287
Caldwell County, 344

Caliban in Blue and other Poems, 237

California v. Cabazon Band of Mission Indians (1987), 28

Callaway, Isadore Miner (Pauline Periwinkle), 115

Calvert, Robert A., 2

Campaign for Human Development (CHD), 140

Campbell, Earl, 309

Campbell, Randolph, 1

Canadian Open, 319

Canales, Laura, 200

Cancer Hospital Bill, 423

cantineras, 203

Canyon, Tx., 221, 268–69, 273, 275–76, 397, 444

Carnegie, Andrew, 324, 326, 328

Carr, Vicki, 200

Carroll, Southlake, 312

Carter, Nenetta, 342

Casablanca, 180

Cashdollar, Cindy, 201

Cashion, Ty, 2

Castaneda, Carlos E., 178

Castillo, Victoria, 201

Cates, Molly, 240

Catholic Church, 5, 135
    ascendancy of, 136–38
    and Mexican Americans, 136, 138–41, 152
    diocesan and archdiocesan expansion, 137–38
    priests and nuns, decline of, 138
    social justice, pursuit of, 139–40
    internal ethnic divisions, 140–41, 238–39

Catholic Church Extension Society, 139

Catlin, George, 289

Cattle Fording Stream, 245

cattle industry, 132n, 319, 391–92

Cattle Leaving the Corral, 245

Caucasian Race Resolution (1943), 50

Cavazos, President Dr. Lauro, 359

Central Flyways Council, 407

Ch<vez, CJsar, 58

Chafer, Lewis S., 156

Chaffee, Roger, 426

Challenger Park, 235

Chaparral Rangers, 247

charity, 324–25, 328, 337, 341, 421–22

Charles, Ray, 201

Charlton, Gene, 281

Chenier, Clifton, 97

Cherry, Blair, 307

Cherry, Mrs. E. Richardson, 281

Chicago, 20, 73, 85, 139, 237, 255, 268, 271, 277–78, 303, 304

Chicanos (See Mexican Americans)

Chicken Ranch, 240

Child Guidance Center, 338, 340

child labor, 114, 326

Children's Health Insurance Program (CHIP), 351

Children's Mental Health Service, 340

Chinese Tea Garden, 180

Christ Church (Plano), 158

Christian Advocate, 174

Christian Life Commission (CLC), 149, 153

Christoval High School, 309

Cisneros, Henry, 61

Cisneros, Sandra, 224, 237

Cities of the Plain, 233

civic stewardship, 325

civil rights,
    Mexican Americans, 41, 46, 48, 57–58, 212, 371–72
    civil rights movement, 53–54, 93, 96–99, 117, 127–29, 153, 285, 359, 371, 374, 378
    court-ordered integration, 54–56, 92–96, 371–75
    African Americans, 75–76, 87–90, 145, 153

violence, 76, 96–99
education, 90–92, 372–75, 382
women, 117, 126–30, 197–98
Civil Rights Act (1964), 58, 96
Civil War, 17, 19, 81, 106, 268, 300, 328, 343–44, 418, 446
Civilian Conservation Corps, 47
Clarendon, Tx., 273, 275, 286
Clark, Dr. R. Lee, 424
Clarke, J. J., 302
Clayton Foundation for Research, 356n
Clean Air Act, 398
Clean Water Act, 398
Clear Channel Communications, 348
Clements, Gov. William Jr., 144
Clift, Montgomery, 255
Clinton, Bill, 61, 156, 429
Clomenero, Damasio, 15, 16
Coastal Zone Management Act, 398
Coburn, D. L., 239
Coen brothers, 262, 264
Cohen, Henry, 146
Cold War, 4, 185, 281, 371, 379, 408
College Station, 101, 142, 336, 435–36, 443
Colorado Springs, 268
Colored Teachers State Association, 91
Columbus, Christopher, 352n.
Colvin, Shawn, 200
Colyer, Vincent, 289
Comal County, 345
Committee for Sound American Education (CSAE), 185
Committee to Study Integration, 374 (See Houston, segregation)
Communities Organized for Public Service, 140
Community Chest, 332, 334, 338
Compean, Mario, 59, 61
Conference for Education in Texas, 362

Conference for Education in the South, 362
Conference of Southwest Foundations, 346
Confessions of a White Racist, 240
Congress of Industrial Organizations (CIO), 48.
Congress of Racial Equality, 96
Congressional Budget Office, 429
Connally, John, 58
Conradt, Jody, 314
Conservation
wartime, 165–66, 169–70, 173
wildlife, 390–91, 406–07
natural resources, 396, 401–07
(See also environment)
Contemporary Arts Association (CAA), 280
Convicts, 239
Coolidge, Pres. Calvin, 14
Cooper Foundation, 344
Cooper, Samuel Branson, 13
Cooper, J. California, 224
Cooper, Madison A. Jr., 344
Copeland, Kenneth, 155
Coplin, Nancy, 201
Coppini Academy of Fine Arts, 271, 280
Coppini, Pompeo, 271
Cornell, Joseph, 289
Coronado Corporation, 430
Coronado's Children, 226
Corpron, Carlotta, 279
Corpus Christi, 46–47, 52, 59, 60, 61, 62, 65, 187, 350
desegregation, 94
religion, 137, 142
Mexican Americans, 138, 139, 152
corridos (See music)
Cortez, Gregorio, 45
Cortina, Juan, 45
Cosell, Howard, 312
Cotton Bowl, 307–08, 312
Cotton Jammers' Association, 77

Cottrell, Debbie, 365–66
Cotulla, Tx., 375–76
Counting Survivors, 237
Country Life Commission, 364
Country Life Movement, 364
Cousins, Robert Bartow, 363
Cowboy Artists of America, 286
Cox Committee, 356n
Crazy, 209
Crider, Bill, 240
Criswell, W. A., 149–50
Critic Club, 332–33
Crockett, David (Davy), 250, 262
Crosby, Bing, 180
Crow, John David, 309
Crozier Tech of Dallas, 314
Crumley, James, 242
Crystal City, Tx., 59, 60, 375
Cuban, Mark, 315
Cullen Foundation, 356n
culture wars, 154, 158
Culwell, Ben L., 282
Cuney, Norris Wright, 72
Cunningham, Minnie Fisher, 116, 118–19
Curley, Stephen, 2
Cushman Gallery, 284

Dallas, 3, 11, 15, 17, 98, 172, 174, 177, 229, 234, 327, 331, 332, 375, 378
    American Indians, 20–21, 25, 31–32
    African Americans, 70, 73, 74, 79, 85–87, 372
    the KKK, 83
    the NAACP, 88, 90–92
    civil rights, protests for, 95–96
    Mexican Americans, 136
    religion, 137, 142–49
    WW I, 173
    communism, fear of, 185
    the military, base closures, 187

music, women in, 198, 199
art and entertainment, 238–39, 241
    the movies, 245, 258, 260, 263
    painting, 269–70, 272–74, 275, 277–84, 287–89
    sports, 301, 203–05, 311, 313–19, 321–22
    Dallas Cowboys, 308, 311
    Cowboy Cheerleaders, 313
    philanthropy, 332–33, 344, 348, 350
    water resources, 405
    medical facilities, 422
Dallas Art Association, 269
Dallas Artists League, 274
Dallas Citizens Council, 332
Dallas Community Trust, 354
Dallas Foundation, 332–33, 350
Dallas Inter-Tribal Center, 25
Dallas Morning News, 23, 115, 260, 332
Dallas Museum for Contemporary Arts (DMCA), 280
Dallas Museum of Art, 269, 444
Dallas Museum of Fine Arts, 280
Dallas Museum of Fine Arts School, 277
Dallas Theater Center, 238
Dallas Theological Seminary, 156
Dallas-Fort Worth, 11, 20, 25, 31–32, 143, 304, 378, 406
Dancer, Texas, Population 81, 263
Daniel, Price, 94
Darby, John Nelson, 156
Daves, Delmer, 259
David Crockett's Last Stand (The Fall of the Alamo), 270
Davidson, McNeill Ola, 281
Davis, Buddy, 316
Davis, Edgar B., 271, 344
Davis, Gussie Nell, 313
Davis, Mollie E. Moore, 225
Davis, W. L., 73

Dawn at the Alamo, 270
de Menil, Dominique, 281
de Menil, John, 281
de Vlaminck, Maurice, 282
Dealey, George B., 354
Dealey, Sam, 164
Dean, Dizzy, 302
Dean, James, 256
DeAnda, James, 54
"death penalty," (See sports)
Deep Ellum, 85
Defender, 73
Del Mar Junior College, 94–95
DeLeon, Arnoldo, 2
Delgado, Minerva, 371
Dell Computers, 348
Dell, Michael, 348
Delleney, Marie, 279
Delta Kappa Gamma, 367
Demaret, Jimmy, 318
Democratic Party, 81, 118
Dempsey, Jack, 320
Denn, Val, 201
Denton, Tx., 95, 241, 273, 278–79,
    280, 282, 361
Denton, Lois, 273
Department of Energy, 408, 428,
    437
Department of Health, 396
Derain, Andre, 283
DeShields, James T., 270
Desprez, Frank, 248
Destiny's Child, 98
Detroit, 96, 277, 308
Devin, Robin, 201
Dewey, John, 273
Diamond, Tom, 23–24, 28
Dickson, Robin, 201
Didrikson, Mildred Ella "Babe," 181,
    317
Die Gelbe Rose von Texas (German
    version), 206
Different Ways to Pray, 236
Digital Light Processing, 431–32

Digital Signal Processing, 431–32
*Dime, Mal Hombre (Tell Me, Evil
    Man)*, 198
DiNardo, Daniel, 138
Dingell-Johnson Act, 406
Directory of Texas Foundations,
    347–48
Dix, Richard, 259
Dixie Chicks (See music)
Dixiecrats, 57
DNA, 437
Dobie, J. Frank, 7, 225, 227, 236,
    249, 250, 252, 276, 443
Dodge, Todd, 312
Dolejska, Frank, 282
Douglas, Aaron, 86
Douglass, John, 274
Downs, Fane, 2, 125
Dozier, Otis, 274
Dr T and the Women, 263
Dr. Strangelove, 260
Driscoll Children's Hospital, 350
Duane's Depressed, 231
DuBois, W.E.B., 69, 73
Dunson, Tom, 254
Dust Bowl, 399, 401
Duvall, Robert, 239, 261
Dyer, Dallas, 185

Eagle Lunar Module, 426
Eagle Pass, Tx., 9, 18, 27, 375
East Texas State College, 314
Ebenezer Baptist Church (Austin),
    153
Ebey, George W., 185
Eby, Frederick, 359
Edgar, J. W., 373
Edgewood High School, 377
Edgewood ISD v. Kirby, 377
Edison, Thomas, 245
Education, 91–93, 117, 168, 183,
    185, 329–30, 336, 340, 351
    higher education, 74, 80, 87,

91–92, 113, 172, 182, 348,
    365, 367, 417, 419, 434
women's education, 113, 337,
    365–67
school prayer, 158
rural schools, 313, 360–64
kindergartens, 326, 378
home schooling, 359
themes, 359, 381
reforms, 360–62, 366, 369–70,
    376–78, 380–81
mandatory school attendance, 361
normal schools, 361
teachers associations, 361–63
one room schools, 362
permanent school fund, 362
state superintendent, 364
surveys, 367
school disasters, 368
World War II, impact of, 368–70,
    378, 382
academic freedom, 370
segregation, 371–75
dropout rates, 371, 379
urban schools, 378–79
Edwards Plateau, 406
Edwards, Cash, 201
Eighteenth Amendment (See
    Prohibition), 169
Eisenhower, Dwight D., 358, 373–74
Eisenlohr, Edward G., 270
El Bautista Mexicano, 150
El Camino Del Rio, 241
El Paso, 221, 236, 250, 252, 261,
    350
    Tigua Indians, 9, 10, 12, 15, 21,
        23–25, 31
    Raza Unida Party, 60
    racial tensions, 93, 179
    African Americans, 86
    NAACP, 88–89
    Texas Equal Suffrage Asso.,
        116–17
    religion, 137, 142–43

great influenza epidemic, 174
WW II, impact of, 175
art, 274, 275
sports, 313, 314–15
Elementary and Second Education
    Act of 1965, 375
Ellington, Duke, 86
Elliot Medal, 433
Ellis, Caswell A., 340
Emergency Immigration Act (1921),
    45
Ennis, Michael, 289
Enstam, Elizabeth, 2
Environment, 2, 4, 8, 114, 267, 327,
    387–88, 391, 407–08, 412, 418,
    426, 434
    pollution, 387, 389, 394–99
    fencing, 392
    timber, 392–93
    oil, 393–99
    drought, 399–402, 404
    dust storms, 400–02
    water, 404–06
    nuclear power plants, 408
    waste dumps, 408–09
    (See also conservation)
Episcopal Church, 135, 153
    "culture wars," 158–59
Equal Rights Amendment, 127
Erdman, Loula Grace, 230
Erwin, J. B., 287
Espionage Act (1917), 166
European Organization for Nuclear
    Research's Large Hadron Collider,
    429
Evans, Cecil, 359
Evans, Dale, 200–01
Evolution, 4, 147, 158, 289, 360
Ewing, J. R., 260
Exchange Club, 342
Executive Action, 260
Express (Dallas), 73, 83 (See African
    American, newspapers)
Express Publishing Company, 328

Extreme Prejudice, 261
Exxon Valdez oil spill, 397

Fabens, Tx., 321
Fade the Heat, 241
Fain, Clem Jr., 14
Fairchild Semiconductor, 431
Falk, Bibb, 305
Falwell, Jerry, 154
Fandango, 263
Farmer, James, 96
Farmers' and Laborers' Protective
    Association, 167
Faubus, Orval, 373
Faulkner, William, 230
Feagin, James C., 13
Federal Economy Act (1932), 120
Federal Employment Practices
    Commission, 178
Federal Food Administration (FDA),
    166
Ferguson, James E.,117–18
Ferguson, Miriam, 118
Fermi National Accelerator
    Laboratory, 429
Fever in the Earth, 231
films/movies
    early films, 245–46
    cattle-drive films, 246–47, 249–52,
        255
    westerns/cowboys, 246–52
    westerns, sources of:
        Buffalo Bill's Wild West shows,
            247
        dime novels, 247–48
        stage plays, 248
        pulp novels, 248
    the Alamo, 252–54, 262
    oil, early portrayals, 253, 255,
        258, 260
    the cattle kingdom, 254
    the "Big Four":
        Red River, 254–55, 257

        Giant, 255–56
        Hud, 257
        The Last Picture Show, 257–58
    the "westernization" of east Texas,
        259–60
    John Kennedy assassination,
        impact of, 260
    recent efforts, uneven quality of,
        260–64
First Baptist Church (Dallas), 149
Fish and Oyster Commission, 390
Fish, Game, and Oyster Commission,
    406
Fisher, Vernon. 289
Fisk, Frances Battaile, 268, 297
Fitzgerald, Barnaby, 287
Fitzsimmons, Bob, 320
Flashpoint, 261
Flemmons, Jerry, 241
Flesh and Bone, 263
Flores, Father Patricio, 140
Flowing Gold, 253, 258
Fly, Nancy, 201
Flynn, Robert, 232
Foote, Horton, 239
Footprints, 237
Ford Foundation, 349
Ford, Frank, 409
Foreman, George, 320
Forestry Service, 401
Formosa, 271
Fort Worth, 11, 20, 25, 31–32, 75,
    94, 136–37, 142–43, 148–49,
    153, 158, 165, 177, 341–44, 350,
    373–74, 378, 406
    art, 269, 273–75, 278–80, 282
    sports, 301–02, 304, 319, 321
    philanthropy, 341–43
Fort Worth Art Association, 274
Fort Worth Art Center, 280
Fort Worth School of Fine Arts, 274
Fort Worth Star-Telegram, 341
Fortune, 432
Foster, Ruthie, 201

Foundation Center, 356n.
Fourteenth Amendment, 78
Foyt, A. J., 321
Franklin, Ione Ruth, 280
Frazier, "Smokin' Joe," 321
Free Will Baptists, 148
Frezzell, Lefty, 209
Friday Night Lights, 381
Fridge, Roy, 283
Friedman, Kinky, 209, 240
Friends (Quakers), 147
From a Limestone Ledge, 234
Frontier, 4, 8, 224–25, 231, 242,
    245, 253, 257, 268, 277, 300,
    301, 320, 324, 388, 396, 404,
    412
Frost, Robert, 236
Fugate, Francis, 402

G. I. Bill, (Servicemen's
    Readjustment Act), 183, 279, 368
Gagarin, Yuri, 426
Gaines County, 342
Gains, Matthew, 72
Gallardo, Gloria, 140
Galveston, 70, 87, 234, 277, 289,
    330, 350, 389, 395, 399
    hurricane of 1900, 6, 76–77, 246
    African Americans, 71, 76–77, 79,
        320
    religion, 137–38, 140–41, 146,
        154
    sports, 172, 301, 305, 320
    base closures, 187
    philanthropy, 343–44
Gaming Regulatory Act, 1988, 28
Garcia, Gus C., 54, 56
Garcia, Hector P., 53
Garcia, Macario, 52
Garner, James, 260
Garner, John Nance, 334
Garrido, Augie, 305
Garvey, Marcus, 87

Gee, I Wisht I was a Single Girl Again,
    198
General American Oil Company, 344
General Baptist State Convention,
    152
General Education Board, 363
General Federation of Women's
    Clubs, 114
Geophysical Service, Inc., 430
George Peabody Educational Fund,
    363
George W. Brackenridge Foundation,
    328–29
George Washington Gomez, 235
Gere, Richard, 263
German Americans, 297, 366
Germany, 311, 444
Gerrymandering, 373
*Get Your Biscuits in the Oven and
    Your Buns in the Bed*, 209
Geto Boys, 98
Giant, 7
Gibbs Memorial Library, 336
Gifford, Frank, 312
Gilb, Dagoberto, 224, 236
Gilded Age, 326, 328, 348
Gilkyson, Eliza, 198, 201
Gilmer-Aikin laws, 369–70, 372, 376
Gipson, Fred, 230, 259
Girls Industrial College, 365
Gish, Lillian, 229, 253
Glasco, Joseph, 282
Glory Road, 315
Goetzmann, William H., 267, 285
Goff, Lloyd, 274
Going My Way, 180
Golden Shadows Old West Museum,
    240
Gonzales, Boyer, Jr., 278
Gonzales, Father Antonio, 140
Gonzales, Rodolfo ("Corky"), 60
Gonzales, Xavier, 278
Gonzalez, Jovita, 229
Good Hearted Woman, 209

Good Neighbor Commission (GNC), 50
Goodbye to a River, 221, 233–34
Goodbye, Earl, 199
Goodfellow Air Force Base, 184
Goodnight Cattle Trail, 276
Goodwyn, Larry, 223
Governor's Committee on Public School Education, 386
Goyen, William, 230
Graham, Bette Nesmith, 128–29
Graham, Billy, 154
Granite City, Oklahoma, 401
Graves, Curtis, 98
Graves, John, 220, 233
Gray, A. W., 241
Great Depression, 175, 177, 367, 418, 421
    Mexican Americans, impact on, 47–48, 114, 139
    women, 114, 119, 122, 130
    art, 274
    philanthropy, 333, 335
    education, 419–20
Great Plains, 1, 226, 400–01, 403–04
Great Plains Conservation Program, 403
Great Society, 58
Greater St. Stephen First Baptist Church (Ft. Worth), 153
Greater Texas and Pan American Exposition, 289
Greed, 238
Green, George, 285
Greenberg, Hank, 302
Gregory, Thomas Watts, 166
Grey, Zane, 248
Griffith, D. W., 83
Griggs, Sutton E., 229
Grissom, Virgil "Gus," 426
Grovey, Richard, 90
Guion, David, 206
Guldahl, Ralph,, 318
Gulf Oil Foundation, 366n.

Gunfighter National: The Myth of the Frontier in Twentieth-Century America, 224
Gustafson, Cliff, 305
Gutiérrez, JosJ Angel, 59–60
Gwynn, R. S., 237

H. E. Butt Foundation, 345
Hagar, Conger "Connie," 407
Hagee, John, 155
Haggard, Merle, 209
Hall of Negro Life, 86
Hall, Carol, 240
Hall, Kenneth, 307, 309
Hall, Tom T., 198
Hampton Institute, 279
Hancock, John Lee, 262
Hands on a Hard Body, 263
Hanson, Debora, 201
Hanson, Susan, 234
Happy, Texas, 263
Hard Country, 260
Hard Scrabble, 234
Harding, Warren G., 174
Harlem Renaissance, 85–86
Harnden, Art, 316
Harper Valley, P.T.A., 198
Harrigan, Stephen, 234
Harris and Eliza Kempner Fund, 344
Harrison, Dena, 157–58
Hart, William S., 249
Harvey, Laurence, 259
Haskins, Don, 314
Hastie, William, 90
Hawkins, Art, 407
Hayden, Fry, 310
Hayes, Elvin, 315
Haynes, Abner, 311
Heifner, Jack, 239
Helfensteller, Veronica, 279
Hendricks, Emma, 273
Hendrix, Terri, 201
Henley, Don, 209

Henry, Vida, 171
Hermann Park, 424
Hernandez, Pete, 56
Herrera, John J., 54
Hickel, Walter, 398
Hickey, Dave, 284
Hickey, Tom, 167
Hightower, Nikki van, 128
Hill, Jonathan, 437
Hindus, 142, 143–45
Hinojosa, Rolando, 224, 236, 241
Hinojosa, Tish, 201
Hispanic Baptist Theological
   Seminary (Mexican Bible
   Institute), 150
Hispanics, 61, 113–14, 129, 136,
   138, 141, 150–51, 153–54, 229,
   270, 290, 337
   diversity of, 61, 63–65
   negative image of, 64
   (See also Mexican Americans)
*Historic Sketches of the Cattle Trade of
   the West and Southwest*, 252
Hitler, Adolf, 146
Hobby, Oveta Culp, 123, 358
Hobby, William P., 117,168–69, 364
Hoblitzelle Foundation, 356n
Hogan, William Ransom, 1
Hogg Auditorium, 350
Hogg Foundation for Mental Health,
   338, 340
Hogg, Ima, 338, 340–41
Hogg, James S., 338
Hogg, Mike, 354n
Hogg, Will, 338
Hogue, Alexandre, 274, 278
Hold Autumn in Your Hand, 230,
   259
Holly, Buddy, 209
Holmes, Josephine E., 75
Holt, Jack, 248
Holub, E. J., 308, 311
Home from the Hill, 231
Hondo Army Airfield, 184

Honeysuckle Rose, 261
Hood, Dorothy, 282
Hoover, Herbert, 166
Hope Center for Youth, 340
Hope Floats, 263
Hope, Bob, 180
Hopis, 20
Hopkins, Lightnin', 86
Hopwood v. Texas (1995) (See Mexican
   Americans)
Hornsby, Rogers, 303
Horsehead Crossing, 276
Horsemen, Pass By, 221, 231
House Bill 72 ("No Pass, No Play"),
   381
House of Corrections, 241
Houston, 3, 4, 18, 87, 98, 123, 125,
   128, 156, 199, 207, 234, 241,
   252, 272, 275, 327, 334, 406
   NASA, 4, 418, 425–28
   American Indians, 25–26, 31–32
   African Americans, 70–73, 75, 83
   segregation, 78–80, 374
   the KKK, 83–84
   African-American newspapers,
      83–87
   the NAACP, 88–89, 125–26
   education, 91–93, 99, 358, 361,
      372
   Texas Southern University, 94–97
   music, 97–98
   women, 128
   Mexican Americans, 135, 137,
      151, 372
   religion, 135, 138, 140, 143–47,
      154, 158
   military bases, 165, 170
   WWI, racial tensions, 170–71
   movies, 173
   Great Influenza epidemic, 174
   communism, fear of, 185
   artistic center, 277–90, 298n
   sports, 300–06, 309–11, 313,
      315, 318–19, 321–22

Astrodome, 304
philanthropy, 335–37, 338–39,
    345, 350
pollution, 394
refineries, 395
medical/scientific complex,
    421–25
Houston Child Guidance Center, 338
Houston Endowment, 335–36
Houston Independent School
    District, 79, 99, 358, 374
Houston Independent School
    District's College for Negroes, 373
Houston Symphony, 338, 350
Houston, Sam, 250, 262, 271, 305,
    336, 361, 363, 375
Houston Zen Center, 143
Howard Association, 324
Hubbard, Bess Bigham, 280
Hubbell, Carl, 302
Hud, 7, 257
Huddle, William Henry, 270
Hudson, Rock, 255
Huerta, Benito, 290
Huerta, Dolores, 58
Hugging the Juke Box, 236
Hughes, Langston, 86
Hughes, Sarah T., 127
Huie, Janice Riggle, 154, 157
Human Genome Project, 432, 434,
    437
Humphrey, William, 230
Hunt, Lamar, 311
Hunter, Russell Vernon, 273
Hurricane Rita, 351
Hutchinson, Kay Bailey, 128
Huxley, Aldous, 432
Huxley, Julian, 432
Huxley, Thomas Henry, 432

I Labor So Far From Home (lyrics),
    208
Idar, Ed, 54

If I had Wheels or Love, 236
Iker, Jack Leo, 158
Immigration and Nationality Act
    (1965), 141
Imperium in Imperio, 229
In a Narrow Grave, 222, 224, 231
Independent Voters League, 88
Indian Gaming Regulatory Act
    (1988), 28
Indian Reorganization Act (1934),
    (See Alabama-Coushatta,
    government recognition of)
Indians (See Native Americans)
influenza epidemic (1918), 174
Informer, 73, 83, 87
Interfaith Ministries of Greater
    Houston (Church Welfare Bureau,
    Protestant Charities,
    Houston Metropolitan Ministries),
    147–48
International Space Station, 420, 428
Interscholastic League, 173, 181,
    226, 306, 310, 361
Intertribal Council of Houston, 25
Irvin, Michael, 312
Islamic Circle of North America, 142
Islamic Society of North America,
    142
Isleta Pueblo Indians, 24
Ixtoc I, 398

Jackson, Oliver, 316
Jains, 142, 145
Jakes, T. D., 155, 156
Jalonick, Mary M., 350
Jameson, Betty, 318
Japanese, 176, 181, 238, 248, 397,
    425
Japanese Texans, 179–80
Jaworski, Leon, 376
Jefferson, Blind Lemon, 86
Jehovah's Witnesses, 152
Jenkins, Ferguson, 305

Jenkins, Jerry, 156
Jenkins, Lew, 321
Jennings, Waylon, 209
Jews, 145–47
Jimenez, Luis, 285
Johnson, Avery, 315
Johnson, Jack, 320
Johnson, Jimmy, 312
Johnson, Lyndon Baines, 24, 53,
    57–58, 127, 185, 286, 359,
    375–76, 425–26
Johnson-Reed Act (1924), 45
Jones, George, 201
Jones, Jerry, 312
Jones, Jesse H., 334–37, 347
Jones, Johnny "Lam," 317
Jones, Mary Gibbs, 335–37
Jones, Nancy Baker, 2
Jones, Norah, 201
Jones, Preston, 238–39, 443
Jones, Tommy Lee, 264
Joplin, Janis, 198, 200
Joplin, Scott, 86
Jordan, Barbara, 98, 127
Judd, Donald, 267
Julie Rogers Theater for the
    Performing Arts, 350
Junction Boys, 309
Justice, William Wayne, 376

Kahn, Robert I., 147
Karankaway County, 227
Karr, Mary, 224, 234
Keasbey, Lindley Miller, 168, 189,
    190n.
Keller, William Henry, 374
Kelton, Elmer, 232
Kemp, J. A., 404
Kempner, Eliza, 344
Kempner, Harris, 344
Kennedy Center, 239
Kennedy, John F., 57, 127, 185, 187,
    257, 375, 425

Kennedy, Tom, 53
Kent State University, 186
Kentucky Wildcats, 315
Khuon-Viet Buddhist Monastery of
    America in Grand Prairie, 143
Kickapoo Indians, 5, 9, 10–11, 27
    Traditional Tribe, 9, 10, 27
    settlement in Nacimiento, 18
    relations with state and federal
        authorities, 26–27
    Eagle Pass International Bridge,
        27
    state recognition of, 27
    casino gambling, 28, 30–31
Kidd-Key College, 277
Kilby, Jack, 430
Kilday, Owen, 48
Killing Floor, 238
Kimbrough, "Jarrin' Jawn," 308, 309
King Ranch, 230, 359, 402
King, Larry L., 240
King, Martin Luther, Jr., 96
King, W. E., 73
Kiowa, 249
Klail City and its Environs, 236
Kleberg, Dick, 402
Knell from the Stone, 236
Knipling, Edward, 436
Knipling-Bushland Southwest Animal
    Research Foundation, 436
Knowles, Beyoncé, 98, 200
Kommodore, Bill, 287
Kopriva, Sharon, 289–90
Korean War, 185–87, 257
Kraft, Otto "Big Boy," 302
Kronkosky, Albert and Bessie Mae,
    345
Krueger, Walter, 180
Ku Klux Klan, 44, 83–84, 118, 145

L'Amour, Louis, 232
la marcha, 58, 140 (See Mexican
    Americans)

La Mordida, 241
La Prensa, 44
La Raza Unida, 212
Ladies Professional Golf Association
    (LPGA), 318
Ladino, Robyn Duff, 373
LaHaye, Tim, 156
laissez-faire economics, 326, 328
Lakewood Church, Houston (See
    Osteen, Joel)
Lamar State College of Technology
    (Lamar University), 95
Landmark Baptists, 148
Landry, Tom, 311
Las Hermanas, 140
"Lasca: The Story of a Texas
    Cowboy," 248–49
LaSelle, Toni, 279
Lassoing Steer, 245
Last of the Duanes, 248
Laundry and Bourbon, 239
Lawrence, Jacob, 282
Layne, Bobby, 308
Layover, 241
Lea, Tom, 230, 274
Leadbelly (Ledbetter, Hubbie), 86
League of United Latin American
    Citizens (LULAC) (See Mexican
    Americans)
League of United Mexican American
    Citizens, 371
League of Women Voters, 118
Leaving Cheyenne, 221, 231
Lee, Harper, 239
Leeper, Paul, 435
Lee, Robert E., 301
Left Behind (See Jenkins, Jerry and
    Tim LaHaye), 156
Legal Defense Fund (See NAACP)
Leland Scarbrough Foundation, 346
Leland, Mickey, 144
Lemmon, Thetis, 279
Leopold, Aldo, 227, 403, 407
Lester, William, 274, 278

Levers, Robert, 287
Levias, Jerry, 310
Lewis, William Luther, 342
Lieber, Jerry, 198
Lilly, Bob, 308, 311
Lindsey, David, 240
Lindsey, Hal, 156
Linebarger, Libby, 130
Lines & Mounds, 237
literary themes/expressions
    sexism, 127, 224, 228, 239, 242
    journeying, 220–21
    frontier mythology, 221–23
    primitivism, 223–24, 242
    Texas mythology, duality and
        elements of, 223–24
    racism, 224
    landscape diversity, 224, 242
    violence, 224, 242
Little League, 321
Littlefield, Clyde, 315
Livingston, Tx., 10, 12, 17, 275
Lockridge, Joseph E., 98
Loeb, Lisa, 201
Logan, Alice Dunn, 72
Lone Star, 444
Lonesome Dove, 222, 226, 231–32,
    258
Long Island, 288
Longhorn League, 304
Longoria, Arturo, 234
Longoria, Beatriz, 52–53
Longoria, Felix, 6, 52–53, 183
Longview, Tx., 82, 88, 263, 303
Loose Woman, 237
Lopez, Jennifer, 63, 261
Lopez, Jose Dolores, 288
Los Angeles, 20, 49, 261, 263, 317
Lotus Garden Tour (Port Arthur),
    143
Love, Charles N., 73, 87
Love, Jim, 283
Lovell, James Jr., 427
Lowenfield, Viktor, 279

Lozano, Ignacio E., 44
Lu Ann Hampton Laverty Oberlander, 238
Lucero, Vickie, 201
Lucey, Archbishop Robert E., 139
Lucky Eagle Casino (See Kickapoo Indians, casino gambling)
Luling, Tx., 271, 344
Luling Foundation, 344
Lund, E. J., 434
Lynching (See African American, racial violence)

M. D. Anderson Award for Scientific Creativity and Teaching, 433
M. D. Anderson Cancer Research Center, 420
M. D. Anderson Foundation, 356n, 421, 423
MacAgy, Douglas, 238
MacAgy, Jermayne, 281, 283
Magritte, Rene, 283
Mahayana Buddhism, 143
Maher, Peter, 320
Maines, Natalie, 212
Majer, Carlyn, 201
Mal Hombre (Evil Man), 198
Mamie McFaddin Ward Heritage Foundation, 345
Mandrell, Barbara, 200
Manhattan Project, 428
Manned Spacecraft Center, 425 (See Science/space exploration)
Mansfield, Tx., (See Shivers, Allan)
Marcus, Rabbi Jacob Rader, 145
Maria's Poems, 237
Marine Corps Women's Reserves, 123
Marsh, Stanley, 267
Marshall, Tx., 86, 314, 320
Marshall, Thurgood, 90–91, 93, 372
Martin, Barbara, 201
Martin, Mary, 200
Martin, Slater, 313

Martinez, Bob, 61
Martinez, Max, 241
Martyrs of the Alamo, 253
Mary Hardin-Baylor, 277
Mary Kay Ash Charitable Foundation, 350
Masterson, Peter, 240
Maston, T. B., 149–50, 153
Matson, Randy, 316
Maverick, Brander, 248
Mayer, Sigmund, 333
Mayfield, Earle, 83
McArdle, H. A., 270
McCann, Charles, 274
McCarthy, Cormac, 233, 264
McCarthy, Joseph, 185
McCloskey, John "Honest," 301
McCombs Foundation, 348
McCombs, Billy Joe "Red," 348
McCoy, Joseph, 252, 255
McDonald Observatory, 427
McDonald, Archie P., 2
McDonald, Walt, 236
McFaddin-Ward House, 345
McFee, Henry Lee, 278
McGonagill, Clay, 320
McGuire, Dorothy, 230
McKnight, Reginald, 224
McLuhan, Marshall, 225
McLure, James, 239
McManaway, David, 283
McMurtry, Larry, 222, 224, 231, 257–58, 291, 443
McNamara, Robert S., 187
McNay, Koogler, 277
McVeigh, Blanche, 274
Mead, Ben Carlton, 273, 275
Meadows Foundation, 344
Meadows, Algur and Virginia, 344
Medellin, Octavio, 280
Memory Fever: A Journey El Paso Del Norte, 237
Men of Art Guild, 280
Mendez vs. Westminister (1946), 371

Mendoza, Lydia, 198, 200
Mennonites, 147
mental health
   hygiene, 339
   illness, 339–40
   care, 339–41
Meredith, D.R. (Doris), 242
Meredith, Don, 311
Metzinger, Barbara, 157
Mexia, Tx., 336, 393
Mexican American Cultural Center, 350
Mexican American Legal Defense and Education Fund (MALDEF), 61, 62, 140
Mexican Americans, 41
   historical periods, 41–42
   as Tejanos, 42–43, 44, 47, 51–52, 62–63, 65, 66–67n, 171, 207, 210, 212
   as Chicanos, 42, 43, 56, 58–61, 66, 237, 241, 375
   growth of, 43
   and Texas Rangers, 44, 59–60
   WW I, impact of, 45–46
   LULAC, 46–47, 49, 51, 53–54, 56, 58, 126
   mutualistas, 46–47, 324, 337
   Great Depression, impact of, 47–48
   women, 48, 109, 111, 114, 120–21, 139
   WWII, impact of, 49, 51–52, 61
   bracero program, 49–51
   and education, 53–56, 62
   and poll taxes, 56–57
   Mexican American Youth Organization (MAYO), 59–61
   "blowouts," 59
   Raza Unida Party, 59–61
   as Hispanics, 61–62
   Hopwood v. Texas, (1995), 63
   Minutemen, 63–64
Mexican Baptist Convention, 150–51

Mexican Revolution, 43, 44–45, 64, 136–37, 327
Mexico City, 289, 316
Michael and Susan Dell Foundation, 348
Mantle, Mickey, 304
Milam, Marsha, 201
Miller, Char, 2
Miller, Marvin, 435
Miller, Melissa, 288
Miller, Mitch, 206
Miller, Vassar, 236
Million Dollar Appropriation for Rural Schools, 364
Milstead, Charles, 308
Mims, Jack, 285
Minimum Foundation Program, 379
Minute Women, 124, 185
Minuteman II, 430
Minutemen (See Mexican Americans)
Missionary Baptist Association, 148
Missionary Catechists of Divine Providence, 139
Mississippi Flood Relief, 342
Missyplicity Project, 437
Mistaken Identity, 145
Mix, Tom, 249, 250
Model Game Law, 390
Monday Night Football, 312
Monet, Claude, 267
Money Tree Mama Blues (lyrics), 208
Montejano, David, 45
Montgomery, J. K., 53
Moody Foundation, 344
Moody, Dan, 84
Moody, William L., 343
Moody, William L. Jr., 343
Moore, Mrs. M. E. Y., 75
Moorer, Michel, 321
Morales, Dan, 62
Moreno, Sara, 53
Morgan, Col. James, 204
Morgan, Hunt Thomas, 432
Morgan, Joe, 304

Mormons, 152
Morris, Sheriff W. T., 235
Morrow, Bobby, 317
Morrow, Marie Betzeer, 434
Motion Picture News, 250
Moyers, Bill, 236
Mr. Potter of Texas, 253
Mrs. Miniver, 180
Mucho Mojo, 241
Muleshoe Wildlife Refuge, 391
Mulford, Clarence E., 248
Mulkey-Roberts, Kim, 314
Muller, Hermann, 432–33
MuZiz, Ramsey, 60, 61
Munoz, Celia Alvarez, 290
Murchison, Clint, 311
Murder by Reference, 242
Murder Past Due, 242
Murphey, Mimi, 280
Murphy, Audie, 164, 257
Museum of Modern Art, 280, 283
Museum of Natural History, 350
music
    Dixie Chicks, 5, 7, 196, 199,
        200–01, 212–14
    femininity/masculinity, 197,
        203–04, 207–08
    frustrations, expressions of,
        197–99
    church, 199
    courtship and marriage, 200
    cantineras, 202–03
    non-whites, stereotypes of, 206–07
    women, images of "good" and
        "bad," 209
    corridos, 210, 212, 234
Muslim Arab Youth Association, 142
Muslims, 142
Muslin Students Association, 142
mutualistas (See Mexican Americans)
My Blood's Country, 222
My Dear Rafe, 236
Myself and Strangers, 234

Nadine, 263
NAFTA (North American Free Trade
    Agreement), 348
National Academy of Sciences, 433
National Aeronautics and Space
    Administration (NASA), 4, 418,
    425–28
National Aeronautics and Space
    Council, 425
National Afro-American Council, 73
National American Woman Suffrage
    Association, 116
National Association for the
    Advancement of Colored People
    (NAACP), 73, 89
    growth of, in Texas, 87–88
    civil rights efforts, 89–90
    spearheads desegregation, 91–96
National Association of Colored
    Women, 75
National Association of Colored
    Women's Clubs, 114
National Association of Intercollegiate
    Athletes (NAIA), 310
National Baptist Convention, 152
National Baptist Convention of
    America, 152
National Baptist Convention of the
    United States of America (NBC,
    USA), 152
National Baptist Publishing Board,
    152
National Basketball Association
    (NBA), 315
National Catholic War Council, 174
National Catholic Welfare Council,
    139
National Clonal Germplasm
    Repository for Pecans, Hickories,
    and Chestnuts, 435
National Collegiate Athletic
    Association (NCAA), 305
National Commission on Excellence
    in Education, 379

National Council of Defense, 165
National Endowment of the Arts, 286
National Environmental Policy Act, 397
National Farm Workers Association, 285
National Football League (NFL), 308
National Hockey League (NHL), 321
National Housing Authority, 176
National Human Genome Research Institute, 457
National Immigration Act (1917), 171
National Invitation Tournament (NIT), 171
National Junior College Athletic Association (NJCAA), 305, 310, 314
National League, 301, 303–04
National Medal of Science, 430
National Negro Business League, 86
National Park Service, 397
National Rodeo Hall of Fame, 320
National Women's Conference for International Women's Year, 127
National Women's Political Caucus, 128
National Youth Administration (NYA), 419, 425
Native American Graves Protection Act (1990), 32
Native Americans, 5, 9–40, 273, 319, 392
Navajos (Dallas-Ft. Worth), 20
Navy (U.S.), 430
Nazarenes, 147
Nelson, Byron, 181, 318
Nelson, Willie, 209, 261
Network of Anglican Communion Dioceses and Parishes, 159
New Deal, 119, 121–22 (See Art)
New Orleans, 87, 137, 301
New World, 387, 429, 352n
New York Times, 235, 226

Newman, Barnett, 282
Ney, Elisabet, 268, 271
Nichiren Shoshu of America, 143
Nichols, Perry, 274
Nicholson, Jack, 261
Nimitz, Chester 164, 180
Nixon v. Herndon (1927), 89
Nixon, Dr. Lawrence, 89–90
Nixon, Richard, M. 57, 103n, 187
No Country for Old Men, 233, 264
No Word of Farewell: Poems 1970–2000, 237
noblesse oblige, 325, 338
Nonpartisan League, 167
Norris, J. Frank, 148–49, 158
North of 36, 252
North to Yesterday, 221, 233
Not Ready to Make Nice, 214
Noyce, Robert, 431
Nunn, Ancel, 287
Nye, Naomi Shihab, 224, 236

O'Brien, Davey, 308
O'Daniel , W. Lee, 182
O'Keefe, Kathleen, 202
O'Keeffe, Georgia, 273
Oberholser, Harry, 406
Odd Fellows, 74
Odessa, Tx., 32, 276
Odessa High School, 381
Oh, Pretty Woman, 209
Oil, 1, 7, 123, 164–65, 172–76, 184, 220, 231, 234, 324, 326–27, 335, 338, 342, 347, 349, 363, 387–88, 393–99, 404, 408, 419, 411
oil industry, 174, 335, 395, 397, 418
oilfields, 257, 259, 368, 342, 430–31,
Olan, Levi, 146
Old Yeller, 230
Oldenburg, Claes, 283
Old-Time Gospel Hour, 154

Oliphant, Dave, 237
Oliver, Kermit, 287
Olmos, Edward James, 261
Olmsted, Frederick Law, 221
Olympics, 316–18
  1936, 318
  1948, 316
  1956, 317
  1968, 316
  1976, 317
Omohundro, Texas Jack, 247
On Valentine's Day, 239
Onderdonk, Eleanor, 270
Onderdonk, Julian, 286
Onderdonk, Robert Jenkins, 268,
  270
One Dead Dean, 240
Operation Desert Storm, 187, 399
Orange, Tx., 175, 235, 350
Orbison, Roy, 201, 209
Order of Sons of America, 46
Organic Trade Association, 410
Ortego, Gregoria, 140
Osborn, Carolyn, 224
Osteen, Joel, 155
Our Lady of Guadalupe, 141
Ousley, Clarence N., 363
Owens, William A., 362

Padres Asociados para Derechos
  Religiosos, Educativos y Sociales,
  140
Paige, Roderick, 99, 358
Painter, Theophilus S., 432
Palmer, Louann Bierlein, 359
Palo Duro Canyon, 268
Panhandle-Plains Historical Museum,
  269, 275–76, 400
Panorama of East Galveston, 246
Panorama of Orphans Home,
  Galveston, 246
Panoramic View, 246
Pantex, 408

Parades, Américo, 235, 261
Pardee, Jack, 308
Parent-Teacher Associations (PTA),
  360
Parker, Fess, 230
Partners in Crime, 241
Parton, Dolly, 240, 261
Pate, Joe, 303
Patl<n, Juan, 59
Patman, Wright, 346–47, 356n
Patterson Laboratories Building, 433
Patterson, John T., 432
Payne, Lawrence, 421
PeZa, Federico, 61
Pearl Harbor, 49, 179, 181, 397, 425
Peckinpah, Sam, 258
Peden, E. A., 166
Penn, Arthur, 258
Pennington-Russell, Julie, 157
Pentecostals, 152
People's Party II, 96
Peoples Community Clinic, 350
Perez, Ignacio, 59
Perez, Selena Quintanilla, 62
Perez, Severo, 235
Perkins, Pete, 264
Permanent University Fund, 419, 426
Perot Commission, 380 (See Select
  Committee on Public Education)
Perot Foundation, 348
Perot, Ross H., 348, 380
Perry, George Sessions, 230, 260
Peterson, Henry, 185
Philanthropy, 324–28, 331–32,
  334–38, 341–50, 352n, 363, 421
  general purpose foundation, 325
  private foundations, 325–28, 336,
    338, 346–48, 350
  retail philanthropy, 325
  wholesale philanthropy, 325–26,
    335
  organized philanthropy, 325–28,
    331, 338, 342, 345, 352n
  gifts, 330–33, 336–37, 342

community foundations, 331–33
endowments, 331, 337
cultural philanthropy, 343
religious philanthropy, 421
Pickens, T. Boone, 406
Pickett, Bill, 247, 319
Pierce, Johnnie, 307
Pike, Leonard, 435
Pilkington, Tom, 222, 226
Pitre, Merline, 2
Pittman-Robertson Act (1937), 391
Places in the Heart, 263
Plessy v. Ferguson, 1896, 78
Pohl, Hugo, 277
Pollock, Jackson, 282
Port Arthur, 82, 143–44, 165, 181,
    198, 234–35, 312, 395
Porter, Katherine Anne, 224, 227–28
Porter, William Sydney (O. Henry),
    225
Post, C. W., 405
Powell, Boone Sr., 421
Prairie View A&M College, 79, 91
Prairie View Interscholastic League
    (PVIL), 310
Prairie View Normal School, 330
Presbyterian Church, USA, 135,
    152–54, 157–58
Preschool Instructional Classes for
    Non-English Speaking Children
    program, 371
Presley, Elvis, 198, 201
Pretty Boy Floyd, 231
Preusser, Robert, 281
Price, Homer E., 434
Primitive Baptists, 148
Privett, Samuel "Booger Red," 320
Procter, Ben, 2
Progressive National Baptist
    Convention, 152
Prohibition, 116–17, 169, 365
Project Head Start, 372
Proulx, Annie, 231
Psychology, 155, 340, 445

Pueblo Indians, 10, 24
Pvt. Wars, 239

Race/Racism, 2, 3, 6, 41, 47
    Mexican Americans, 48, 50,
        252–54, 256
    Caucasian Race Resolution, 50
    African-Americans, 70, 76–77,
        372–73
    Mansfield incident, 373–74
Racial violence, 69, 76, 78, 81, 96–97
    lynching, 81, 84, 347
    Jesse Washington, 81–82
    black troops, 82–83
    riots, 82–83
    KKK, 83–84
    King, M. L. Jr., assassination of, 96
    Byrd, James, killing of, 97
Rafting the Brazos, 221, 237
Rage, 241
Raggedy Man, 263
Rainey, Homer, 370
Raleigh, Eve, 229
Ramos, Basilio, 44
Ranch Romances, 286
Randolph Air Field, 181
Ransom, Harry, 229
rationing (Korean War), 176–77, 184
Raynor, John B., 72
Raza Unida Party (RUP) (See
    Mexican Americans)
Reagan, Ronald, 26, 359, 429
Reaugh, Charles Franklin "Frank,"
    268, 277
Reconstruction Finance Commission,
    334
Red Cross, 167, 169–70, 174, 334
Red Deviltry As It Is, 248
Red McCombs Automotive Group,
    348
Red River, 70, 187, 255, 399
Red Scare, 185, 374
Reece Committee, 356n

Reeder, Dickson, 279
Reid, Vernon S., 172
religion, 2, 46, 111, 135–36, 146,
    154
    emerging pluralism, 3, 135, 141,
        147–48, 159
    African Americans, 74, 136,
        152–53
    immigration, impact of, 136, 141
    Asians, 141–45
    apocalyptic literature, 156
    women ministers, 157–58
    school prayer, 158
    "culture wars," 158–59
    megachurches, 151, 155–56
Remington, Frederic, 246, 343
Renoir, Jean, 230
*Report of the Results of Texas Statewide
    School Adequacy Survey* (Works
    Progress
    Administration), 367
Republic of Texas, 1, 19, 254, 268,
    324, 349, 419
reredos, 289
Reyes, Albert, 151
Reyes, Gus, 151
Reynolds, Burt, 240, 261
Reynolds, Clay, 241
Rhea, Sophia Jane, 228
Rice University (Rice Institute), 146,
    278, 432
Rice, Ben, 54, 371
Richards, Ann, 128
Richardson, Clifford F., 83, 87, 90
Richardson, Sid W., 344
Richardson, Tony, 261
Rickard, George "Tex," 320
Riders of the Purple Sage, 248
Riley, Jeannie C., 198
Riley, Pat, 315
Riley, Polly, 318
Rimes, LeAnn, 200
Rio Grande, 10, 18, 24, 26, 32,
    45–46, 58, 105, 111, 136, 139,

140, 150, 175, 221–22, 236, 261,
    303, 328, 366
Riordan, Rick, 241
Ritter, Tex, 249
Rivera, Tomás, 235
Road Kill, 240
Robert A. Welch Foundation, 356n
Roberts, Annie Lee, 348
Roberts, O. M., 360
Roberts, Oral, 154
Roberts, Summerfield G., 349
Robertson, Pat, 154
Robin Hood Plan, 377
Robinson, Brooks, 302
Robinson, Frank, 302
Robinson, Isabel, 273
Robison, James, 155
Roche, Jim, 285
Rockefeller Foundation, 363, 433
Rockefeller, John D. Sr., 326
Rodriguez v. San Antonio (1968),
    377
Rodriguez, Johnny, 209
Roe v. Wade (1973), 127
Rogers, Roy, 249
Rogers, Will, 248
Roosevelt, Eleanor, 15, 401
Roosevelt, Franklin D., 15, 49–50,
    177, 334, 423
Roosevelt, Theodore, 82, 364
Roseberry, David H, 158
Rosenberg Library, 350
Rosene, Hilda Florence, 434
Rosinger, Samuel, 146
Rosser, Dr. Charles, 421
Rote, Kyle, 308
Rote, Kyle Jr., 321
Royal, Darrell, 309
Ruby, George T., 72
Ruby, Jack, 234
Rumble Tumble, 241
Rupp, Adolph, 315
Russell, Charles, 343
Ruth, Babe, 317

Ryan, Nolan, 303–05
Rylander, Carole Keeton, 128

Safe Delivery, 241
Sage, Margaret Olivia, 326
Saldivar, Yolanda, 62
Salinas, Porfirio, 271, 286
Salvatierra v. Del Rio, 371
Salvation Army, 334, 348
Samaroff, Olga, 200
San Antonio, 3, 32, 53, 59, 61–62,
     70, 75, 142, 150–51, 168, 174,
     180, 201, 327–29, 345, 350, 375,
     406, 436
    immigration to, 43–44
    pecan shellers, 48, 121
    KKK, 83
    desegregation, 95
    Mexican Americans, 136–37,
         139–41
    military camps, 165
    entertainment, 173
    anti-communism in, 185
    base closures, 187
    arts, 236–37, 241, 268, 270–72,
         274–81, 284, 286
    film, 253
    sports, 301–02, 308, 313, 315
    philanthropy, 328–31, 350
    court cases, 377
San Antonio (arts), 277
San Antonio Area Foundation, 350
San Antonio Competitive Exhibitions,
     271, 274
San Antonio Loan and Trust, 328
San Antonio National Bank, 328
San Antonio Spurs, 315
San Antonio Water Works Company,
     328
San Jacinto Day, 301
San Jacinto Monument, 335
Sanchez, Tony, 62
Sanctuary Movement, 140

Sanders, Heywood T., 2, 3
Sanderson, Jim, 241
Santa Anna, Antonio López de, 7,
     204
Santayana, George, 273
Sayles, John, 254
Scarborough, Dorothy, 229, 253
Scarbrough, Margaret, 346
Scene from the Movie GIANT, 237
Schachtel, Hyman Judah, 146–47
Schiwetz, E. M., 287
Schlesinger, Arthur M. Sr., 352n.
school disasters
    New London (1937), 368
    Texas City (1947), 368
Schorre, Charles, 282
Schramm, Tex, 311–12
science/agriculture, 435
    onions (Super Sweets), 435–36
    pest control, 436
    Agriculture Research Service, 436
science/biology, 436
    biological therapy, 424
    gene therapies, 424
    fruit fly genetics, 432–34
    Human Genome Project, 432,
         434, 437
    cloning 432, 436–37
    Missyplicity Project, 437
    DNA, 437
science/medicine, 256, 330, 419, 422
    mental illness, 339–40
    medical schools, 417, 420–23
    cancer research/treatments,
         422–24
    cardiac research/treatments, 422
science/physics
    electronics, advancements in, 418
    integrated circuit, 418, 420,
         430–31
    Superconducting Super Collider,
         428–29
    14- and 40-TeV proton collisions,
         429

Big Bang, 429
reflection seismography, 430
science/space exploration
    Sputnik I, 378, 425
    NASA, 4, 418, 425–28
    Manned Spacecraft Center
        Projects:
        Mercury, 425–26
        Gemini, 425–26
        Appolo, 419, 425–27
        Eagle Lunar Module, 426
    Skylab, 428
    Challenger explosion, 428
    Columbia disintegration, 428
    International Space Station, 428
Scofield Reference Bible, 156
Scofield, Cyrus I., 156
Scott, Emmett J., 72
Sea of Tranquility, 426
Seastrom, Victor, 253
Secondhand Lions, 263
Sedition Act (1918), 166
Seewald, Margaret, 273
segregation
    African Americans, 69, 72–73, 75,
        78–80, 83, 86–87, 89–96, 99,
        113, 125, 179, 183, 315, 337,
        347, 361, 372–75
    Mexican Americans, 6, 50, 54,
        126, 179, 183, 371–72,
        374–75
    challenges to, (See civil rights,
        court-ordered integration)
Seitsinger, Mayor Ralph, 23
Select Committee on Public
    Education, 380
Selective Service Act, 182
Selena (See Perez, Selena
    Quintanilla)
Sellors, Evaline, 274, 280
Senate's Special Committee on Space
    and Astronautics, 425
Senior Citizens Services of Wichita
    Falls, 350

Servicemen's Readjustment Act
    (1944), (See G. I. Bill)
Shadow of an Eagle, 230
Shafer, Whitey, 209
Shepard, Alan Jr., 426
Sheppard, Morris, 168
Shivers, Allan, 19, 93–94
Shivers, Robin, 201
Shocked, Michelle, 198
Shoemaker, Willie, 321
Shrake, Edwin "Bud", 234
Shrine of Our Lady of San Juan del
    Valle, 139
Shults, Ginger, 201
Sibley, Marilyn, 329
Sikhs, 142, 145
Silva, Chelo, 200
Simmons, Al, 302
Simple Versions of Disaster, 237
Sims, Billy, 309–10
Sin, 238
Singa Sabha Gurdwara (Austin), 145
Single Hand, the Comanche Attila,
    247
Singleton, H. E., 364
Size, 241
Skelton, Red, 180
Sketches of the Valley and other Works,
    236
Slotkin, Richard, 224
Smith v. Allwright (1944), 90, 92
Smith, Antonio Maceo, 88
Smith, Bessie, 86
Smith, David, 284
Smith, Dr. Lonnie, 90
Smith, Emmitt, 312
Smith, Henry Nash, 225, 273
Smith, Lee, 287
Smith, Robert L., 81, 98
Smithson, Robert, 267
Snider, Duke, 302
Social Darwinism, 325, 328
Socialist Party, 167
Sociedad Benito Juárez, 47

Society of Western Artists, 269
Soler, Urbici, 273
Soto, Ishmael, 280
South Plains Wildlife Rehabilitation
    Center, 350
Southern Association of Colleges and
    Universities, 182
Southern Baptist Convention, 142,
    149, 155, 157
Southern Baptists of Texas (SBT),
    148, 150
Southern Methodist University
    (SMU) 186, 239, 277, 288, 297,
    306, 308, 310–312, 314,
    321, 444
Southwest Conference (SWC), 95,
    172, 181, 307–10, 312, 316
Southwest Intercollegiate Athletic
    Conference (Southwest
    Conference), 172
Southwest Review, 272–73
Southwest Texas League, 303
Southwest Texas Normal School,
    277
Southwest Texas State Normal
    College (Southwest Texas State
    Normal School), 361, 375
Southwest Texas University, 314
Southwest Voter Registration and
    Education Project (SWVREP), 61
Southwestern Baptist Theological
    Seminary (Ft. Worth), 149
Southwestern University, 305
Soviet Institute of Genetics, 433
Speaker, Tris, 302
Spellman, Coreen Mary, 279
Spindletop, 1, 326–27, 393, 395,
    397, 419
Spiral, 241
Spivey, Victoria, 200
Sports, 8, 172, 181, 304–05, 318,
    320–22, 348, 381, 445
    football, 8, 172–73, 181, 300,
        305–13, 315–17, 322, 381
    basketball, 13, 181, 306, 310–11,
        313–17, 322
    baseball, 95, 172, 181, 300–03,
        305–06, 310, 317, 322, 445
    track and field, 181, 306, 315–17
    golf, 181, 318–19
    tennis, 181, 318, 322
    rodeo, 232, 247, 319–20
    Hall-of-Fame, 302–03, 305,
        307–08, 312, 318, 320
    scandals, 310–11
    and African Americans, 310,
        314–15, 319–21
    cheerleading, 313
    and women, 317–18
    swimming, 318, 322
    prize fighting, 320
    racing, 321
    horse racing, 321
    hockey, 321
    soccer, 321–22
    softball, 322
Spruce, Everett, 274, 278, 288
Sputnik, 378, 425
Sri Meenakshi Temple, 144
St. Cecilia Catholic Church
    (Houston), 141
Staley, Earl, 287
Stankiewicz, Richard, 284
Stark Museum, 350
State Board of Education, 367, 369,
    380
State Commissioner of Education,
    369, 373
State Department of Education, 382
State Fair of Texas, 269–70
State Game Preserve, 390
Staubach, Roger, 312
Stephen F. Austin University, 392
Sterling, Ross, 172
Stevenson, Coke
Stewart, James, 303
Stoller, Mike, 198
Story of Texas Schools, 359

Stout, Richard, 282
Strange Peaches, 234
Stratton, Monty, 303
Student Nonviolent Coordinating
    Committee (SNCC), 96
Study Out the Land, 222
Sturtevant, Alfred, 432
Sul Ross State Teachers College, 278
Summerlee Foundation, 348–49
Sundown, 252
Sunken Gardens, 180
Surls, James, 288
Surrender of Santa Anna, 270
Sutherland, Dr. Robert, 345–46
Sutton, William Seneca, 363
Swaggart, Jimmy, 154
Swanson, Doug, 241
Sweatt v. Painter (1950), 92
Sweatt, Heman, 92, 372
Sweeney, James Johnson, 283
Switzer, Barry, 312

Taco Bell, 65
Taking the Long Way Home, 214
Taoists, 142, 145
Taqueria Acapulco, 65
Tarrant County, 271, 342
Tauch, Waldine, 271
Tax Act, 1935, 333
Tax Reform Act of 1969, 347, 349,
    356–57n
Taylor, "Buck," 247
Taylor, Elizabeth, 255
Taylor, Rolla, 270
Teachers State Association of Texas,
    361
Teel, Lewis Woods, 273
Teich, Frank, 271
Tejanos (See Mexican Americans)
Temple Beth Israel (Houston),
    146–47
Temple Emanu-El (Dallas), 146
Tenayuca, Emma, 48, 120–21

Tender Mercies, 239, 261
Terms of Endearment, 231, 258
Terrell Election Laws, 1903, 80–81
Terry, Bill, 302
Texarkana, 95, 154, 187, 302, 346
Texas A & M at Kingsville, 310
Texas A&M University, 101, 410,
    417, 418, 419, 431
    WWI, impact of, 172
    sports, 182, 305, 307–11, 313,
        316
    cloning research, 347
    rapid growth of, 420
    agricultural research, 435–36
Texas Agricultural Extension Service,
    435
Texas and Texan, 260
Texas Association of Colored
    Women's Clubs, 114
Texas Baptist Memorial Sanitarium,
    421
Texas Cambodian Buddhist Society
    (Houston), 143
Texas Centennial Exposition, 15, 86,
    272, 391
Texas Children's Hospital, 424
Texas Christian University (TCU),
    181, 277, 305, 342
Texas City, 368, 395
Texas Commission for Democracy in
    Education, 91
Texas Commission on Environmental
    Quality, 396
Texas Commission on Indian Affairs,
    26
Texas Congress of Colored Parents
    and Teachers, 361
Texas Congress of Mothers (Parent-
    Teacher Association), 114, 361
Texas Constitution, 1876, 71, 78
Texas Education Agency (TEA), 25,
    382
Texas Educational Survey
    Commission, 367

Texas Educational Survey Report, 367

Texas Farmers' Congress, 364

Texas Federation of Colored Women's Clubs, 75, 114

Texas Federation of Women's Clubs, 14, 114

Texas Fine Arts Association, 271

Texas Folklore Society, 229

Texas Food Administration, 166

Texas Freeman, 73, 87

Texas Grano 1015Y (Texas Early Grano) See science/agriculture

Texas High School Coaches Association, 307

Texas Indian Bar Association, 32

Texas Indian Commission, 25, 27

Texas Industrial Commission (TIC), 48

Texas Instruments Incorporated, 4, 419, 430–32

Texas Intercollegiate Athletic Association (TIAA), 314

Texas Interscholastic Athletic Association (Interscholastic League), 173

Texas Interscholastic League of Colored Schools (TILCS), 310

Texas League, 117, 172, 181, 301–303

Texas League of Women Voters, 117

Texas Medical Center in Houston, 422

Texas Natural Resources Conservation Commission, 396

Texas Railroad Commission, 394

Texas Rangers, 44, 59, 94, 179, 211, 220, 226, 248, 250, 252, 303–304, 373

Texas Southern University, 92, 95–96, 99, 282, 372, 446

Texas Sports Hall of Fame, 318, 320

Texas State Cancer Hospital and Division of Cancer Research, 422

Texas State College for Negroes, 79, 282

Texas State College for Women (TSCW), 279

Texas State Historical Survey Committee (TSHSC), 23

Texas State Teachers Association (TSTA), 117, 361, 364, 382

Texas State University for Negroes (Houston), 92, 372

Texas Teacher Career Ladder, 380

Texas Tech University (Texas Tech), 186, 236, 306–07, 311, 314–15, 359, 420, 445

Texas University at Georgetown, 277

Texas Water Pollution Advisory Council, 396

Texas Water Pollution Control Board, 396

Texas Wildflower Competitive Exhibition, 271

Texas Woman Suffrage Association (Texas Equal Suffrage Association, TESA), 116

Texas Woman's University, 279, 365

Texas Women's Amateur Championships, 318

Texas Women's Political Caucus, 128

Texasville, 231

That'll Be the Day, 209

That's Way Love Goes, 209

The Alamo (1960), 253

The Alamo (2004), 262

The Ballad of Gregorio Cortez, 210

The Battle of San Jacinto, 205, 270

The Best Little Whorehouse in Texas, 240, 248, 261

The Birth of a Nation, 83

The Birth of Texas, 253

The Border, 261

The Borderland, 234

The Brave Bulls, 230

The Challenge and the Chance, 376, 378

The Corrido of Kiansis, 212

The Crisis, 73

The Crossing, 233

The Day the Cowboys Quit, 232

The Development of Education in Texas, 359

The Drive-In, 237

The Eagle's Wings, 173

The Fatal Environment: The Myth of the Frontier in the Age of Industrialization, 1800–1890, 224

The Final Country, 242

The Gates of the Alamo, 235

The Gay Place, 234

The Ghost of John Wayne, and Other Stories, 237

The Gin Game, 239

The Good Girl, 263

The Good Old Boys, 232

The Great Plains, 226

The Great Train Robbery, 246

The Hammon and the Beans and Other Stories, 235

The Hawk, 319

The Heart of Texas Ryan, 249

The Heat of Arrivals: Poems, 237

The Home Place, 259

The House of Breath, 231

The Immortal Alamo, 253

The Kid From Texas, 257

The Killdeer Crying, 236

The Kingfish, 240

The Last Known Residence of Mickey Acuña, 236

The Last meeting of the Knights of the White Magnolia, 238

The Last Picture Show, 231, 254, 257, 264

The Late Great Planet Earth, 156

The Liar's Club, 235

The Log of a Cowboy, 225

The Magic of Blood, 236

The Man from Texas, 249

The Man Who Rode Midnight, 232

The Mexican Tree Duck, 242

The Mustangs, 226

The Narcissiad, 237

The New Handbook of Texas, 349

The Night Hank Williams Died, 240

The Oldest Living Graduate, 238

The Potter's House (Dallas) (See Jakes, T. D.)

The Prairie Chicken Kill: A Truman Smith Mystery, 241

The Prairie Queen, 247

The Quadroon Spy, 247

The Ranger and His Horse, 248

The Ranger's Bride, 247

The Rebel, 167

The Red Scream, 240

The Return of the Texan, 259

The Road, 233

The Sand Hill Chronicles, 241

The Scouts of the Prairie, 248

The Sense of Smell, 227

The Sheriff and the Branding Iron Murders, 242

The Slacker, 173

The Souls of Black Folk, 69 (See also W.E.B. Dubois)

The Southerner, 230, 259

The Super-Americans, 254

The Texan, 250

The Texas Rangers, 226, 250, 304

The Three Burials of Melquiades Estrada, 264

The Time it Never Rained, 232

The Useless Servants, 236

The Valley, 236

The Virginian, 225

The Wheeler Dealers, 260

The Wild Bunch, 258

The Wind, 229, 253

The Wire-Cutters, 225

The Woman the Germans Shot, 174

The Wonderful Country, 230

The Yellow Rose of Texas (See Music)

The Young Man from Atlanta, 239

Theravada Buddhism, 143
This Stubborn Soil, 362
Thomas, Albert, 425
Thomas, Seymour, 270
Thomason, John W., 164
Thompson, Richard, 287
Thornton, Billy Bob, 262
Thornton, Willie Mae "Big Mama,"
 198
Three Rivers News, 53
Thurston, Fern and Eugene, 274
Tibbits, Randolph, 281
Tibetan Buddhism, 144
Tie Fast Country, 232
Tigua Indians, 5, 9, 10–13
 tribal sovereignty, 10, 15, 21,
  23–25, 33
 Roman Catholicism, 12
 declining numbers, 21
 "blood quantum," 27, 30, 35n
 relations with state and federal
  authorities, 27
 casino gambling, 28–30
Tijerina, Reies Lopez, 59
Tijernia, Felix, 372
Tinguely, Jean, 283
To Hell With the Kaiser, 173
To Kill a Mockingbird, 239
Tocqueville, Alexis de, 352n.
Tolbert, Frank X., 23
Tolson, Melvin B., 86
Tom Western, The Texas Ranger, 247
Tom, Dr. Charles, 434
Tomkins, Jane, 255
Torrey Canyon, 397
Tour de France, 321
Tracy, Michael, 289
Travis, Olin and Kathryne Hail, 277
Travis, William B., 293
Trevino, Lee, 319
Tribal Enterprise Tourist Project, 22
Truett Memorial Hospital, 421
Trull, Don, 311
Tucker, Tanya, 200

Turner, Frederick Jackson, 222,
 225
Turning Muslim in Texas, 142
Turtle Pictures, 237
Twenty-fourth Amendment, 57
Two-Seed in the Spirit Baptists, 148
Tyson, Paul, 306–07

U. S. Navy, 430
U. S. News and World Report, 422
U. S. Supreme Court, important
 decisions of, 56, 90, 93, 371–72,
 381
U. S. v. Shurbet et ux, 404
U.S. House Committee on Indian
 Affairs, 24
U.S. Indian Claims Commission, 24
Umlauf, Charles, 280
Unfettered, 4, 229
United Cannery, Agricultural, Packing
 and Allied Workers of America
 (UCA PAWA), 48
United Farm Workers of America
 (United Farm Workers), 58
United Methodists, 135, 152,
 153–54
 on women ministers, 157–58
United States Bureau of Biological
 Survey, 407
United States Department of Energy,
 408
United States Hockey League
 (USHL), 321
United States Livestock Insects
 Laboratory, 436
United States v. Texas, Civil Order
 5281 (1970), 376
Universal Negro Improvement
 Association, 87
University Interscholastic League
 (UIL), 226, 306, 361
University of Houston, 146, 186,
 311, 315, 319, 445

University of North Texas (North Texas State College), 141, 186, 279, 314, 364, 375, 420
University of Texas (UT), 95, 126, 168, 172–73, 182–83, 186, 229, 235, 278, 328–30, 338–40, 360–61, 363, 418–20, 427, 434–35, 443
  law school, integration of, 63, 89, 92, 372
  sports, 172–73, 181, 305–06, 308, 311, 313–16, 319
  Board of Regents, 182, 364–65, 370, 433
  Medical Branch, Galveston, 330
  Health Science Center, 420, 424, 432
  dental branch, 424
Univision, 65
Urban Cowboy, 252, 260
urban Indians, 5, 9, 11, 25
  growth of, 31–32
  intertribal efforts, 32–33
Ursuline Sisters, 139
USS Arizona, 397
Utter, Bror, 279

Vaca, Cabeza de, 220
Valásquez, William ("Willie"), 59, 61
Vallabh Priti Seva Samaj (Houston), 144
Valley Baptist Academy, 150
Valley House Gallery, 284
Van Dyke Art Club, 270
Van Dyke, John, 227
Van Gogh, Vincent, 282
Vanities, 239
Vargas, Kathy, 290
Veblen, Thorstein, 234
Vegetable and Fruit Improvement Center, 436
Velásquez, William, 59–61
Vice, 238

Vietnam War, 186–87, 195n
Vietnamese Buddhist Pagoda Phat-Quang (Houston), 143
Villanuevo, Tino, 237
Virgin Land, 225
Vogel, Donald, 278–79
Voting Rights Act (1965), 58, 93
Vytlacil, Vaclav, 279

Wachtel, Paul, 302
Waco, 5, 70, 81–83, 89, 165, 170, 301, 306–07, 326, 344
Wade, Bob, 285
Wade, Charles, 153
Walker, Cindy, 201
Walker, Doak, 308
Walker, Eddie, 426
Walker, Mary Willis, 240
Walker, T-Bone, 86
Walker, Texas Ranger, 226
Wallace, Beulah "Sippe," 199
Walsh Commission, 356n
Walter Benjamin at the Dairy Queen, 231
Walter Camp Trophy, 308
Waltz Across Texas, 259
Wanderer Springs, 232
Waxahachie, Tx., 318, 429
Ware, Andre, 310
Washington, Booker T., 69, 86
Washington, Jesse, 6, 81
Wasson Pool, 342
Wayland Baptist College, 314
Wayne, John, 254, 257, 399
Webb, Walter Prescott, 7, 226–27, 233
Weddington, Sarah, 127
Wesley, Carter, 87
West Dallas Multipurpose Center, 350
West of Everything: The Inner Life of Westerns, 255
West, Emily D. (Emily Morgan), 204–07

Western Star, 73
Western Stories, 286
Westhusin, Mark, 437
Weyhe Gallery, 273, 279
Whipple, T. K., 222
Whisenhunt, Donald, 2
White Leg, 241
white primary laws, 89
White, Hattie Mae, 93
White, Lavelle, 200
White, Lulu, 88, 125–26
White, Mark, 380
Whitmire, Kathy, 128
Whitney Gallery, 280
Wichita Falls, Tx., 181, 185, 231,
    268, 350, 404
Wiggins, Bernice Love, 86
Wiley College, 86
Wiley, William T., 288
Willard, Jess, 320
Willet, Donald, 2
Williams, Charles, 280
Williams, Clarence R. "Reggie," 350
Williams, Lacey Kirk, 74
Williams, Ricky, 313
Wills, Bob, 201
Willis, Kelly, 200
Wilson, Woodrow, 308, 336
Winter, Roger, 287
Winthrop, John, 352n.
Wister, Owen, 246
Witte Museum, 270
Woeltz, Julius, 276
Womack, Lee Ann, 200
*Woman Hollering Creek and Other
    Stories*, 237
women, 6
    clubs importance of, 75, 114–17
    suffrage, 75, 115–17, 364
    everyday life, rural areas, 106–09
    family economy, contribution to,
        109
    cattle ranches, 110
    as agricultural laborers, 111–12
    and urban life, 112–14
    WW II, 112, 122–25
    political involvement of, 114
    Great Depression, 114, 119–22,
        130
    gender ideology, 115
    WW I, 117
    suburban growth, impact of,
        124–25
    post-WW II job opportunities,
        125, 128–29
    changing legal rights, 126–28
    growth of minorities, 129
    organized womanhood, 337
Women Accepted for Voluntary
    Emergency Service (WAVES), 123
Women and Oxen, 230
Women Army Auxiliary Corps
    (WAAC), 123
Women's Christian Temperance
    Union (WCTU), 115
Women's Reserve of the Coast Guard,
    123
Wood, Gordon, 307
Wood, Robert, 272
Woodcuts of Women, 236
Woods, Littleton A., 370
Works, George A., 367
World Columbian Exposition, 271
Wray, Dick, 282
Wreckage along Shore, Galveston, 246
Written on the Wind, 358
WW I, 164, 327, 419–22
    Alabama-Coushattas, 17
    Mexican Americans, 45–46, 171,
        366
    African Americans, 73, 83, 170–71
    racial conflict, 83, 170–71
    women, 117, 169
    economic impact of, 165–66
    military camps/fields
        Bowie (Fort Worth), 165, 168
        Kelly (San Antonio), 165
        Brooks (San Antonio), 165

Travis (San Antonio), 165
MacArthur (Waco), 165, 170
Ellington (Houston), 165, 184
Logan (Houston), 170
Funston (Central Tex.), 172
Bliss (El Paso), 179, 184
Hood (Killeen), 184
opponents, treatment of, 166–68
higher education, impact on, 168,
    172–73
and organized labor, 171–72
sports, impact on, 172–73
entertainment, impact on, 173–74
religion, 174
great influenza epidemic, 174
English only law, 366
WW II, 5, 33, 47, 61, 248, 277, 279,
    281, 316, 327, 360, 367, 368,
    370, 378, 395, 402, 422, 435
urban Indians, 11
Alabama-Coushattas, 17–18,
    22–23
Navajos, 20
Mexican Americans, 43, 49,
    52–53, 56, 178–79, 212
African Americans, 178–79
racial conflict, 179
Japanese Texans, 179–80
German Texans, 180
radio, 180

movies, 180
sports, 181–82
education, impact on, 182,
    381–82
controversy, University of Texas,
    182–83

. . . y no se lo tragó latierra (And the
    Earth did not Part), 235
Yarborough, Ralph, 24
Yelvington, Ramsey, 230
(You Ain't Nothing But A) Hound
    Dog, 198
Young Men's Christian Association
    (YMCA), 174, 342
Young Women's Christian Association
    (YWCA), 114
Young, Vince, 313
Ysleta Indians (see Tigua Indians)

Zaharias, Mildred "Babe" Didrickson,
    181, 317–18
Zanuck, Daryl F., 259–60
Zen Buddhism, 143
Zionism (See Jews)
Zorach, William, 280
Zoroastrians, 142, 145
Zydeco, 97